The Role and Meaning of Religion for Korean Society

The Role and Meaning of Religion for Korean Society

Special Issue Editor

Song-Chong Lee

MDPI • Basel • Beijing • Wuhan • Barcelona • Belgrade

Special Issue Editor
Song-Chong Lee
The University of Findlay
USA

Editorial Office
MDPI
St. Alban-Anlage 66
4052 Basel, Switzerland

This is a reprint of articles from the Special Issue published online in the open access journal *Religions* (ISSN 2077-1444) from 2018 to 2019 (available at: https://www.mdpi.com/journal/religions/special_issues/Korean).

For citation purposes, cite each article independently as indicated on the article page online and as indicated below:

LastName, A.A.; LastName, B.B.; LastName, C.C. Article Title. *Journal Name* **Year**, *Article Number, Page Range.*

ISBN 978-3-03897-888-6 (Pbk)
ISBN 978-3-03897-889-3 (PDF)

Cover image courtesy of Kristine J. Park.

Contents

About the Special Issue Editor

Song-Chong Lee, Professor, is an associate professor and the chair of the Religious Studies and Philosophy Department at the University of Findlay. He earned his Ph.D. degree from Temple University. His scholarly and teaching interests include religious education, religion and society, Neo-Confucianism, and Korean Christianity. Lee currently serves as the chair of the Asian Religion section of the Mid-Atlantic Region of the American Academy of Religion.

Preface to "The Role and Meaning of Religion for Korean Society"

The idea for this Special Issue on Korean religion began with a conversation with Managing Editor, Bingjin He, last January. We felt a need for a focused conversation on Korean religion to expand the geographical coverage of *Religions'* published themes. Considering the growing contribution of Korean scholars to various fields of religious studies, including theological studies, I thought that offering a new publication venue for scholars of Korean religion would be an excellent idea, and it would be even better if the venue were the MDPI platform, which is known to be extremely efficient and transparent in both the peer-review process and editorial procedure. Of the many discussed themes, the role of religion in Korean society came first to my mind.

Religion is one of the most effective human reactions to cope with various challenges of life. Similar to other major institutions, such as family and government, religion plays a powerful role in swinging the pendulum of our destinies between hope and despair, between liberation and enslavement, and between forgiveness and vengeance. There would be arguably no better place than Korea for finding exemplary cases, memories, and narratives. We can see, in the emergence of Buddhism during the Three Kingdom Period, a pendulum's swing—a political transformation from *parochialism* to *central government*. We can see a paradigm shift with respect to the purpose of politics from superficial utility for power to inner cultivation through the enhanced axiology and metaphysics of Neo-Confucianism. We can see a pendulum's swing with respect to our perception of religion from the priestly role to the prophetic role in leading and reshaping a society through the *Donghak Movement* and *Minjung Theology*. The pendulum's swing can be witnessed in many other domains, including socio-cultural phenomena, textual understanding, and political movements. Examples would further include new, creative interpretations and utilizations of Confucian texts, engaged and patriotic Buddhism, explosive church growth, nationalist and democratization movements, and revolutionary roles of religious figures.

In this Special Issue, each of our contributors present their convincing cases to show the powerful role of religion and the creative adoption and utilization of religion to deal with various challenges of Korean society. The role has never been monolithic. It is moral, political, and psychological. It is sometimes of poetry, narrative, and paradigm. The contributed papers focus specifically on four major characteristics of the role: *Creativity*, *Greater Responsiveness*, *Adaptability*, and *Prophethood*. With respect to *creativity*, Hyun Choo, a Buddhologist at Stony Brook University, shows how the practice of the *Satipatthana* (mindfulness), which she believes was attenuated in the Chan tradition, has been preserved and revived in the form of *Ganhwanseon hwadu* by prominent Korean Seon Buddhists, including the 14th century Seon Master Naong Hye-geun. Choo argues that the spirit of *Satipatthana* has been reinterpreted and its notion has been expanded with the practice of counter-illumination and mindfulness of breathing. She asserts that the spirit of *Satipatthana* eventually crystalized into the mindful *hwadu Sisimma*, 'Sati-Sisimma'. Bongrae Seok, an expert in Confucian philosophy and moral psychology at Alvernia University, presents a collective effort of 16th century Korean Neo-Confucian scholars to make sense of the *li-qi* dynamic for the grounding of moral feelings. Toegye and Kobong found the logical dilemma of the Cheng-Zhu Neo-Confucian understanding and tried to come up with their own alternatives to better explain the embryology of moral emotions and virtues. These Korean Neo-Confucians' intellectual exploration of the cosmic principle of the physical world and morality set the tone for many other later religious, philosophical, and spiritual efforts to save the country from moral corruption and political chaos. Seok calls attention to the theistic turn of the 19th century Neo-Confucian scholars and religious leaders, such as Jeong Yakyong (pen name Dasan 茶山, 1762–1836) and Choi Je-wu (崔濟愚, 1824–1863). They both found the original source of our moral feelings in something independent of the *li-qi* metaphysics, which is *Sangje* (上帝, the Emperor on High), *Hanulnim* (한 울 님, Heavenly Being), or *Cheonju* (天主, Heavenly Lord). Along the same lines, Sung Uk Im, a biblical scholar at Yeonsei University, presents a variety of creative ways that Korean Christians have utilized to make the most of Biblical narratives for their unique context. He shows how brilliantly biblical narratives have been internalized and recreated by Korean Christians for new inspiration. His case is supported by *pansori*, *bibliodrama*, and *TongDok*, which are great examples of the Korean church's performative use of the Bible.

With respect to *greater responsiveness*, So-Yi Chung, a Confucian scholar and Korean philosopher at Sogang University, presents one of the best examples of this theme, showing Korean intellectuals' active engagement in investigating, interpreting, and reshaping a foreign system of thought and spirituality. She highlights the three different approaches developed by 18th century Neo-Confucian scholars regarding Christian ideas, particularly the immortality of the soul, after-life, and resurrection. Woncheol Yun and Beom Seok Park, director of the Center for Religious Studies and a Ph.D. student at Seoul National University, respectively, discuss the challenges that Korean Buddhism has experienced. Their tone is obviously anxious; however, it also captures the perseverance and resilience of Korean Buddhism. Although Korean Buddhism has gone through numerous incidents of identity crisis due to chaotic political situations, such as Japanese colonialism and military dictatorship in the 20th century, it has always found a way to persist. National crises and the invasion of secularism could not stop Korean Buddhism from finding its role, creating a positive direction and change. It has persistently responded to such crises with various efforts, including the salvific effort represented by *Hoguk Bulgyo* (호국불교) and *Minjok Bulgyo* (민족불교), doctrinal modification, and *Hoetong Bulgyo*. Kim Sung Moon, director of the Center for East Asian and Comparative Philosophy at City University of Hong Kong, found the Confucian ethos, which seeks moral ideals in the political leadership, in the Candlelight Revolution. Korean Confucianism, which exists as a cultural DNA, does not always respond to social challenges and political crises as an elitist ideology. Nor does it compromise with liberal pluralist values. It has constructed and enhanced the empathetic dimension of political leadership, which the liberal constitutional understanding cannot cover. Our emotional attachment to and moral expectation for the government and leaders often plays a positive role in solving various problems that the political community, based solely on law and meritocracy, would suffer. A discussion of the apologetic writing of *minung* theology by Andrew Eungi Kim, a professor of international studies at Korea University, presents a similar case. For Koreans, Christian messages are heard not just in the sanctuary but on the street and sometimes in prison. Korean *minjung* theologians, pastors, writers, and artists fought against the oppressor and the collective sin. For Kim, their contribution to Korean democracy and their care for the underprivileged are counterevidence to the secularization theory.

With respect to *adaptability*, Jaesang Jung, a professor of oriental science at Wonkwang Digital University, makes an interesting case, which shows how intentional Korean religious thinkers are in finding effective ways to make their religious rituals adaptable to highly complex social norms, expectation, and rules. He explores how the 17th century Korean Neo-Confucian culture ritualized two different feelings: *affection* for the family and *respect* for the honorable. His discussion of royal mourning demonstrates the process by which human emotions are translated into religious rituals, aligning with the social, political, and familial hierarchy. For Korean Confucians, rituals were not just coded patterns of behavior but organic systems through which various social interests, concerns, norms, and expectations find a point of contact to properly express one's intended virtues. Similarly, Hyo-Dong Lee, a professor of comparative theology at Drew University, shows the adaptability of Korean Confucian philosophy, which is the *li-qi* metaphysics. He presents a convincing case that Confucian metaphysics does not just serve the elitist political regime. Some Korean intellectuals, such as Hwadam Seo Gyeong-Deok (花潭 徐敬德 1489–1546) and Nongmun Im Seongju (鹿門 任 聖周 1711–1788), developed significant philosophical insights into Confucian metaphysics to adapt to a new pluralistic political environment. Overcoming the limitations of Cheng-Zu Neo-Confucian metaphysics, Hwadam's *Great Void* (太虛 *taeheo*) and Nongmun's *one transparently all-encompassing and overflowingly large thing-event* (一箇虛圓盛大底物事 *ilgae heowon seongdae jeo mulsa*) embraced the seemingly conflicting and contrasting *li* and *qi* in the understanding of a divine cosmic process, positing the former as the principle and the latter as manifestations.

Finally, with respect to *prophethood*, Yohan Yoo and Minah Kim, a professor of comparative religion and a Ph.D. student at Seoul National University respectively, revisited the Korea National Prayer Breakfast (*Gukgajochangidohoe*, 국가조찬기도회, KNBP hereafter) and reevaluated its historic meaning with an unconventional perspective, which is contentious particularly in the academic study of religion. Recognizing the partial validity of the criticism of the progressive camp, including progressive theologians and church historians, their paper rather sheds light on the insider's view of the KNBP. Investigating the common theological stance of the first organizers, Yoo and Kim highlight their genuine spiritual vision, which they characterize as "prophetic consciousness." According their analysis, the founders' embrace of military dictators and corrupt politicians in their prayer meeting was not intended to fuel political ambitions and calculations but rather to deliver prophetic messages to move Korea in a better direction. Their whole discussion ultimately leads to a point that the conventional evaluation of KNBP has missed. It is the parallel between the organizers' rhetoric and sermons and the prophetic narratives of the Hebrew Bible, which seems very intentional and coherent. Last, but not least, two papers remind us of the fundamental functions of religion for the well-being and progress of our society. While most of the other papers demonstrate the positive functions of Korean religion, these two papers reveal some chronic problems and seek a solution. Chae Young Kim, a professor of psychology of religion at Sogang University deals with the misguided and misinformed public perception of religious education particularly in the domain of primary and secondary schools. According to Kim, the public confusion between the confessional study of religion and the academic study of religion has caused policymakers fail to provide religious education appropriate to the particular religious orientation, affiliation, and educational demand of the students and the schools in question. Kyungrae Kim, Eunyoung Kim, Wangmo Seo, and Cheoghwan Park, professors of Buddhist Studies at Dongguk University, deal with the recruiting and attrition problem in the Jogye Order, which is the major Buddhist denomination in Korea. They scrutinize the most recent periodic report on the educational system of the Jogye Order. They point out some important errors in selecting data sets, interpreting data, and coming up with solutions. Both articles promote the critical examination of religious education and anticipate the positive role of religion in Korean Society. Although these papers present different cases from different time periods, they all remind us of the vital, creative, and resilient character of Korean religion.

Song-Chong Lee
Special Issue Editor

Article

Tracing the *Satipaṭṭhāna* in the Korean Ganhwa Seon Tradition: Its Periscope Visibility in the Mindful *hwadu Sisimma*, '*Sati-Sisimma*'

B. Hyun Choo

Department of Asian and Asian American Studies, Stony Brook University, 1046 Humanities Building, Stony Brook, NY 11794, USA; bhyun.choo@stonybrook.edu

Received: 25 September 2018; Accepted: 30 October 2018; Published: 3 November 2018

Abstract: The Buddha is said to have awakened to the true nature of existence and attained final liberation from suffering through the practice of *Satipaṭṭhāna*. This practice begins by addressing sensations from the processes of body and mind, as characterized by 'bare attention' and 'clear comprehension' through non-judgmental observation, ultimately effecting a transformation into a unique religious experience. During its transmission to East Asian countries, particularly in the Chan tradition, the essence of *Satipaṭṭhāna-sutta* has become transformed, while maintaining the theme of intense concentration, perhaps in the form of 'counter-illumination'—an extended equivalent of 'bare attention'. Not much has been written on which aspects of the Indian contemplative tradition were passed on to the Chan/Seon schools. In the Korean Ganhwa Seon practice, however, there are some indications that the spirit of *Satipaṭṭhāna*, resonating as a role of sustained attention with mindfulness, has been partially manifested, having crystallized into the mindful *hwadu* called *Sisimma*, or '*Sati-Sisimma*'. To substantiate this, this paper investigates how the two seemingly different practices can be seen to link together in the Korean Seon tradition, and proposes *pari passu* meditative parallels, *Satipaṭṭhāna* and *Sati-Sisimma*, recommending for an 'attentive' mode and a 'non-attentive' mode respectively, in modern meditative practices.

Keywords: *Satipaṭṭhāna*; mindful *hwadu Sisimma*; *Sati-Sisimma*; bare attention; counter-illumination; Chan/Seon/Zen; Korean Ganhwa Seon

---

1. Introduction

Sati (S; *smṛti*) means "to remember," "to recollect," "to bear in mind," as in the Vedic tradition. *Satipaṭṭhāna* is a compound term that has been translated in two ways, namely *Satipaṭṭhāna and Satiupaṭṭhāna*: *Satipaṭṭhāna* is translated as "foundation of mindfulness" underscoring the object used to gain mindfulness, and *Satiupaṭṭhāna* as "presence, establishment or arousing of mindfulness" underscoring the mental qualities co-existent with or antecedent to mindfulness (Anālayo 2003, pp. 29–30; Bodhi 2000, p. 1504). The early Buddhist practice of *Satipaṭṭhāna* exemplifies its empirical nature by focusing concentration on all incoming sensory data or experiences, enabling one to lead toward the ultimate religious experience. This process begins with the conscious registering of the sensations experienced through the six sense faculties, characterized by detaching from the processes of body and mind in non-judgmental observation and awareness. Being 'non-judgmental' refers to an undistracted watchfulness, which calmly observes each emerging sensory or mental object to systematically notice certain ubiquitous characteristics of experience such as arising and passing away, whereas being 'judgmental' has the tendency to promote ensuing emotional turbulence. The practice of *Satipaṭṭhāna* is said to provide a "direct path" for the development of liberating insight in which the practitioner faces whatever happens with awareness. This requires an effort in order to ensure that mindfulness is established with continuity and in combination with the presence of clear understanding

(Anālayo 2013, p. 19). Bodhi states that mindfulness does not occur automatically but is a quality to be cultivated. It also has an ethical function in that it distinguishes wholesome qualities from unwholesome ones, good deeds from bad deeds, and beneficial states of mind from harmful states (Bodhi 2011, p. 26). It is said that *Satipaṭṭhāna* operates on the principle that tranquility (P. *samatha*) is initially cultivated which finally leads to insight (P. *vipassanā*). Both *samatha* and *vipassanā* are aspects of liberating direct knowledge. The practice thus requires the continuous observation of reality, in which the practitioner microscopically analyzes the very process of perception.

During its transmission from India to East Asian countries, namely China, Korea and Japan, this practice may have subsequently infused its message into the Mahāyāna/Chan traditions. However, there is relatively scant evidence of research on this issue. One may wonder if its teaching has been sustained in the Mahāyāna tradition, especially the Chan tradition. If it has ever been preserved, what aspects of the *Satipaṭṭhāna* formula are visible in the later traditions and in what particular form?

This paper emerged from the endeavor to detect any evidence of the *Satipaṭṭhāna* or any of its special features within the Chan/Seon/Zen tradition, particularly in the form of *huatou* 話頭 (K. *hwadu*, J. *watō*, the topic of inquiry). Specifically, the spirit of *Satipaṭṭhāna*, if it has ever been recognizable, will be explored to determine to what extent it appeared in the Korean Ganhwa Seon practice. However, this does not mean that Korean Buddhism, the Chogye Order in particular, would view itself as a unique heir to *Satipaṭṭhāna* in its contemplative practice, nor should it hold an exclusive monopoly on this practice.

To support this proposal, *Satipaṭṭhāna* with its emphasis on the functions of the human mind will be reexamined in order to explore the ways in which these seemingly different traditions may become amalgamated and reconciled in the Korean Buddhist tradition, which is uniquely identifiable as a distilled meeting point, the mindful *hwadu Sisimma*, '*Sati-Sisimma*'. During the Indian-Sino-Korean encounter with the *Sisimma*, a bridging mechanism will be identified through the input of "counter-illumination" (McRae 1986, p. 114) or "tracing back the radiance" (廻光返照 C. *huiguang fanzhao*/K. *hoe-gwang ban-jo*) (Buswell 1992, pp. 103–4) utilizing a number of early Mahāyāna and Chinese scriptures.

2. *Satipaṭṭhāna*, the Foundation of Mindfulness

Buddhist scholars generally agree that the *Satipaṭṭhāna-sutta*[1] is one of the most widely commented upon texts in the Pāli canon and continues to hold a central place in the modern *Vipassanā* movement. In the text, the Buddha is reported to have set forth the discourse under a fourfold rubric called the "four foundations of mindfulness" (P. *Satipaṭṭhāna*; C. *nianchu*; K. *nyeomcheo* 念處), which are comprised of 'contemplation of the body'; 'contemplation of sensations', that is, physical sensations that are pleasurable, painful, or neutral; 'contemplation of mind', in which one observes the broader state of mind or units in the ephemeral mind-stream of momentary duration; and 'contemplation of mental objects' or factors of consciousness making up the respective states of mind, which involves the mindfulness of several key doctrinal categories, such as the five aggregates, the Four Noble Truths, and so forth.

The central theme of *Satipaṭṭhāna* practice is insight into the true nature of the body, feelings, mind-states and reality-patterns (phenomena, mind-objects, or *dhamma*): this enables the practitioner to achieve a transformation through awareness by means of a rigorous detachment. Specifically, the practice supports a sustained analysis resulting in the arising of wisdom into the true nature of reality, namely the 'three marks' of all conditioned phenomena in *saṃsāra*: impermanence (P. *anicca*, S. *anitya*); suffering (P. *dukkha*, S. *duḥkha*), and non-Self (P. *anattā*, S. *anātman*).

---

[1] *Satipaṭṭhāna Sutta* (Discourse on the Foundations of Mindfulness) appears in two versions in the Pāli canon: (1) A long account known as the *Mahāsatipaṭṭhāna Sutta* in the *Dīgha Nikāya* (Walshe [1987] 1995, chp. 22, pp. 335–50); (2) A slightly shorter text called the *Satipaṭṭhāna Sutta* in the *Majjhima Nikāya* (Ñāṇamoli and Bodhi 1995, chp. 10, pp. 145–55).

In the *Satipaṭṭhāna-sutta*, being mindful of the body in the body is explained in the following six ways: mindfulness of breathing (*ānāpāna-sati*), the four postures (walking, standing, sitting, lying), clear awareness of all activities of the body, reflection on the repulsive parts of the body, analysis of the four bodily elements (earth, water, fire, and air), and the nine charnel ground contemplation (Ñāṇamoli and Bodhi 1995, pp. 145–55). While one abides contemplating in the body, supreme insight is developed through being mindful of its arising and vanishing factors to the extent necessary for bare knowledge and awareness. In mindfulness of feeling, one recognizes three kinds of feelings: pleasant, unpleasant, or indifferent, and sees clearly their transitory quality. Supreme insight is developed similar to the contemplation of the body. In contemplation of mind, one remains mindful of every state of consciousness, whether the mind is possessed or not of the impulses of greed, hatred, or delusion. Supreme insight is developed similar to the contemplation of the body and feeling. How does a practitioner abide by the contemplation of mental objects? This is to be practiced in five areas with reference to the Five Hindrances,[2] the Five Aggregates of Clinging,[3] the Six Internal and External Sense-bases,[4] the Seven Factors of Enlightenment,[5] and the Four Noble Truths (Nyanaponika [1965] 1988, pp. 123–35). Likewise, supreme insight is to be developed similarly. The methodical practice of *Satipaṭṭhāna* operates on the principle that tranquility (P. *samatha*) is initially developed which finally leads to insight (P. *vipassanā*). Here, the mental phenomena are analyzed and viewed in the light of the three characteristics of all conditioned phenomena as stated above. Properly practiced, the technique developed in the *Satipaṭṭhāna-sutta* is said to lead to the realization of *Nibbāna* (S. *Nirvāṇa*) through the attainment of *jhāna* states, or states of absorption.

In psychological terms, *Satipaṭṭhāna* appears to impart a type of *de facto* melting mechanism of ego formation, namely the dissolution of ego through cultivating penetrating insight. As the Dalai Lama states that the nature of non-Self is not a matter of something that existed in the past becoming nonexistent, the 'Self' is to be understood as being never-existent right from the start (His Holiness Tenzin Gyatso 1984, p. 40). Further details can be extracted from available publications.[6]

3. 'Bare Attention' as Shared with the *hwadu Sisimma* Practice in the Form of 'Counter-Illumination' as Its Extended Equivalent

In the *Majjhima Nikāya*, a collection of writings representing some of the teachings of the Buddha, the repetition of the phrases "contemplating the body as body, feelings as feelings" and so forth, is meant to impress upon the meditator the importance of remaining aware, utilizing sustained attention directed on a chosen object (Ñāṇamoli and Bodhi 1995, p. 145). The writings state that the Buddha is reported to have taught the systematic cultivation of Right Mindfulness (*sammā sati*) as the simplest and most direct method for training and developing the mind. The object of Right Mindfulness comprises the entire human being as well as one's entire field of experience.

Similarly, Chan practice is distinguished by intense concentration, or *samādhi*, but not through seeking for an analytic, rational answer; thus it is different from a cognitive understanding of the mind, or *vipassanā*. Having said this, out of all known *hwadus* in Chan practice, the *hwadu Sisimma* is unique, in that a student is advised to sustain the questioning: 'What is seeing?' 'What is hearing?' 'What is smelling?' 'What is moving the body?' and so on, in essence asking 'What is one's true nature?' Unlike other *kung-ans* or *hwadus*, there are several parallels in the *hwadu Sisimma* to *Satipaṭṭhāna* practice, specifically the idea of being mindful of the body, feelings, mind, and mental objects. As such, the

---

2   S. *pañcâvaraṇa*; Five obstructions of wisdom: desire, wrath, sloth & torpor, agitation, and doubt.
3   Material form, feeling, perception, mental formation, and consciousness.
4   The six loci of perception or sensation; they are six organs of sense, which constitute the fifth of twelve links of dependent origination. The term is also used for the six sense fields and the six objects.
5   Mindfulness, investigation of reality, energy, rapture, tranquility, concentration, and equanimity.
6   (Ñāṇamoli and Bodhi 1995, p. 155). Also see (Anālayo 2003, pp. 117–249).

utilization of bare attention provides the key to the distinctive method of intense concentration in both the *Satipaṭṭhāna* and likely the *hwadu Sisimma* practice as its modified equivalent.

In the discourse of *Satipaṭṭhāna* mindfulness (*sati*) and clear comprehension (*sampajañña*) are essential for the actual practice of meditation, in which *sampajañña* becomes insight into impermanence, that is, direct knowledge of the arising and passing of phenomenon. The word *sati* may best be characterized as mindfulness, in the sense of a lucid awareness of the present, and is commonly described as 'bare attention,' a term first rendered by Nyanaponika Thera (Bodhi 2011, p. 28). However, Bodhi asserts that Nyanaponika did not regard 'bare attention' as non-conceptual or non-verbal. He argues that the expression 'bare attention' can be pragmatically useful to guide a beginning practitioner in the method of setting up mindfulness; this is presumably what Nyanaponika had in mind when he used the expression 'bare attention' (Bodhi 2011, p. 30). Interestingly, while the role of 'bare attention' is emphasized, *sampajañña* is not only discouraged but also positively prohibited in Chan practice.

How does this 'bare attention' influence the proper practice of *samatha*? Nyanaponika Thera sums up the general principle underlying the practice of bare attention in the *Satipaṭṭhāna*: "Bare Attention is the clear and single-minded awareness of what actually happens in us . . . kept to a bare registering of the facts observed, without reacting to them... Any such comments arising in one's mind are neither repudiated nor pursued, but are dismissed, after a brief mental note has been made of them" (Nyanaponika [1965] 1988, p. 30).

However, the word *dismissed* may not be appropriate in describing the method of bare attention because it connotes implicitly an active sense of rejecting or refusing. The practitioner is not supposed to actively dismiss the facts of perception, but to just gently 'let go' of them. It is similar to the idea of not chasing a fly away, but rather just letting it buzz off by itself. The term *letting go* is used in the sense of relinquishing or renouncing. Why is it important to clarify the meaning of letting go? The phrase encompasses a considerable scope of meaning in early Buddhism; it is a central theme that underlies the path to liberation from its outset to its final completion of letting go of any clinging whatsoever (Anālayo 2012, p. 266). What has to be let go of in a deeper sense is *control*. Anālayo aptly states that the desire to control is simply a manifestation of clinging to the sense of 'I'. A correlate to clinging to an 'I' notion is the sense of ownership towards goods and possessions. To gradually undermine this sense of ownership, 'letting go' is repeatedly recommended in the early discourses (Anālayo 2012, p. 267). Anālayo elaborates that the benefit of such letting go is the attainment of the concentrative depth of the mind, following which the sense of 'I' goes into abeyance, allowing for a subjective experience of the merger between the observing subject and the observed meditative object (Anālayo 2012, pp. 267–68). Here it is interesting to note that the *hwadu Sisimma* practice stresses sustaining questions by addressing various sensations, which arise from the processes of body and mind, in the form of 'counter-illumination'. This serves as an extended equivalent of 'bare attention', ultimately effecting a transformation into a unique religious experience, that of 'Oneness', or the Buddha-nature. The *hwadu Sisimma* will be further delineated in Chapter 8.

Practically speaking, one may wonder how to incorporate 'letting-go' in one's daily life. Here is a hypothetical illustration of how bare attention may be practiced while meditating on *Satipaṭṭhāna*: Imagine a practitioner jogging while being mindful of breathing (*kāya*); then s/he happens to fall into a thorny rose bush and pricks her/his face on a thorn, becoming mindful of feeling a sharp pain (*vedanā*) from a swollen, dirty, and bleeding wound. S/he may then become aware of various thoughts of rising anger, name-calling, regretfulness, and so forth (*citta*). Through mindfulness of mental objects, one recognizes clearly their ephemeral quality, devoid of everlasting substance, thus being mindful of their arising, abiding and vanishing factors. While thus engaged, one's mind is settled, calm and detached, and not clinging to the bodily sensations. As such, the supreme wisdom of dependent origination, that is, the interdependent nature of all phenomena may be developed accompanied by insight into the two aspects of non-Self: lack of ego and absence of substance.

In short, when feelings arise upon sense contact with one's surroundings, the practice of mindfulness meditation, monitored at a default setting using a heuristic method, can assist one in transforming her/his natural faculty of ordinary perception into the status of enlightenment. As Ayya Khema states, "Instinctively we are a constant reactor, but deliberately we become an actor" (Khema 2010, p. 16).

4. *Satipaṭṭhāna* in the Mahāyāna Tradition

Although most of the Mahāyāna writings affirm the harmony between *samatha* (calmness) and *vipassanā* (insight), it is noted here that the latter aspect is not emphasized to a similar extent in the *Satipaṭṭhāna* of Indian Buddhism. As Sujato has indicated, the emphasis on non-Self is more prevalent in the later Mahāyāna scriptures, and less so in the Indian context of *Satipaṭṭhāna*. The early *suttas* have a more balanced approach, embracing both the attractive [breath, pleasant feelings, purified mind, and so forth] and unattractive [charnel ground, painful feelings, defiled mind, and so forth] aspects of experience within *Satipaṭṭhāna* (Sujato 2012, p. 356). In the later Mahāyāna and particularly the Chan tradition, the typical Indian description of the *Satipaṭṭhāna* practice begins to be described in a slightly altered and condensed form: the body, feeling, mind, and mental objects are recognized as essentially empty (*śūnya*), and there is less emphasis on the heuristic methodology through the six sense faculties and the consequent transformation into an ultimate religious experience. It seems apparent among extant commentaries that the Chan adepts attempted to skim the essence of *Satipaṭṭhāna*, making light of its paramount centrality while also bypassing its elaborate, empirical, and practical instruction. Although the vital message of the *Satipaṭṭhāna-sutta* formula had been transmitted in the earlier Mahāyāna literature, especially in the later Chan tradition, the heart of the teaching was often eviscerated and categorized merely as one of the so-called "Hīnayāna" practices.[7] What motivated such an implicit (and later explicit) neglect of this practice in the Chan tradition? This issue is to be examined by addressing a subtle but significant difference in the ultimate concerns of the Buddha and Chan, respectively.

It is a matter of great significance to compare the primary object of the Buddha's search for truth, as stated in early Buddhism, to that of Chan practice. It is apparent from the Buddha's discourses as described in the *Nikāya*, that the Buddha's primary concern was complete liberation from suffering, not merely the transient alleviation of physical or emotional pain. However, during the Sinification of Buddhist doctrine and meditation, what transpired regarding the Indian meditative concepts, especially as they were passed on to the Chan/Seon tradition?

Although this is a vast area which lies beyond the scope of this article, a brief explanation may suffice here. In sum, the primary concern regarding practice in the Chan tradition is to attain ultimate enlightenment, with the understanding that all sentient beings at their core are inherently preloaded with True Suchness/Self Nature (*tathatā/svabhāva*),[8] this issue closely parallels the debate regarding the sudden (頓悟頓修 K. *dono donsu* C. *dunwu dunxiu*) vs. gradual (頓悟漸修 K. *dono jeomsu* C. *dunwu jianxiu*) approach to enlightenment and cultivation, which has been extensively discussed elsewhere.[9]

The Chan tradition's precedence for such an ultimate enlightenment itself is based on the implicit premise that enlightenment, once attained, resolves all suffering *instantaneously* and *simultaneously*. This appears to differ significantly from the Buddha's primary concern of suffering and its remediation. Seongcheol, the late Supreme Patriarch of the Korean Buddhists Jogye Order, stated, "When the clouds get cleared away, simultaneously the sun does shine. It is one instantaneous step, not two steps" (Park 2009, p. 42). In this context, Seongcheol pronounced in his monumental writing, *Seonmun Jeongro*, that in the Chan school, "Seeing one's own originally enlightened mind is fundamental. Seeing

---

7 Hīnayāna (C. *xiaosheng*, Lesser Vehicle, 小乘) a pejorative term coined by the Mahāyāna (Greater Vehicle) tradition of Buddhism. *Hīna* has the negative connotations of lesser, defective, and vile.
8 *Tathatā* (如, True Suchness, Thusness, which is the ultimate reality beyond)/*Svabhāva* (自性, inherent self-nature).
9 See the following: (Buswell 1987, pp. 321–80; McRae 1987, pp. 227–78).

one's original nature means a penetrating understanding of *tathatā/svabhāva*."[10] This may be one reason why the lack of sufficient emphasis on moral practice has been acquiescently permissible among practitioners of Chan. Buswell asserts that Chan eventually not only discarded but also condemned both *samādhi* (concentration) and *prajñā* (wisdom) as having only provisional value for dullards who were as yet unprepared spiritually for the more sophisticated techniques of Chan (Buswell 1987, pp. 324–25, 328, 330). It could then be claimed that the dual nature of *samādhi* and *prajñā* in the Indian teaching collapsed into the nondual nature in Chan's single inseparable system which espoused that enlightenment is operative at all levels of meditative practice.

Here, it may be logical to question whether the terms 'enlightenment', referred to as *Nibbanā*, or final liberation from suffering in early Buddhism, and 'True Suchness/Self-Nature' in Chan, are even addressing the same issue. Given its apparently differing approach, does the Chan tradition preserve the spirit of the *Satipaṭṭhāna* as taught in early Buddhism? A plausible explanation has been presented briefly in Chapter 6, which discusses counter-illumination, although a comprehensive critical comparison between the two traditions remains to be explored.

5. Traces of Early Buddhist Meditation in the Chinese Buddhist Tradition

The Chan school in the Sinitic system can hardly be said to have any equivalents with the Indian Buddhist tradition. Despite its adoption of the word 'Chan 禪' (meditation), its theory and practice predominantly emphasize wisdom (*prajñā*), unlike the classical Indian meditative absorption (*dhyana*) as taught in the *Satipaṭṭhāna*. While the investigation of various traditions of meditation in Chinese Buddhism requires much detailed discussion, this paper shall focus by and large on the mindfulness of breathing (P. *ānāpānasati*; C. *annabanna-nian*; K. *annabanna-nyeom* 安那般那念)[11] and "counter-illumination"[12] as they relate to the *Satipaṭṭhāna*.

Sometime during the 1st–4th centuries, a group of early Buddhist meditation texts, which are preserved in Chinese translation, known as the *Dhyāna Sūtras* 禪経 (C. *Chanjing*) emerged. Broadly, the *Dhyāna Sūtras* are said to have laid the foundation for the development of Sinitic Buddhist meditation practices, especially the later writings of Tiantai Zhiyi 天台智顗 (538–597). One of his texts, the *Six Gates to the Sublime Dharma* (六妙法門, 575~585), is particularly worthy of note. It discusses the six-fold practice of inhalation and exhalation, that is, counting (數), following (隨), fixing (止), contemplation (觀), shifting [turning] (還 or 反轉), and purification (淨). The 'shifting' aspect is focused on the impermanence of the five aggregates and also reflects the impermanence of inhalation and exhalation, and is called the "shifting contemplation," which eliminates the five obstacles and various defilements (Yamabe and Sueki 2009, pp. 29–30, see also *T* 1917.46.0550a23-24). Particularly, it characterizes the cultivation of "shifting back to the contemplating mind" (反觀觀心) as an essential factor in the elimination of both the objective realm and the faculty of knowing.[13] This is reminiscent of the later concept, so-called 'counter-illumination', the practice of which reflects back on one's original nature, the putative enlightened source of one's clear mind, in which the subject and the object merge to become 'Oneness'. This precisely echoes the praxis of the later Chan school. The process referred to as 'counter-illumination' involves turning the light inwards onto oneself, to reflect on one's original nature, or 'brightly shining mind'.

This paradigm of 'counter-illumination' has a long history, dating from early Buddhism and continued through to Chinese Buddhism. It is to be remembered that in the Indian Buddhist meditative traditions the idea of practicing 'counter-illumination' was seldom addressed explicitly, but a latent form of the technique can be implicitly alluded to via the way of 'bare attention' as employed in the

---

[10] (Toei-ong 1981, p. 2). *Seonmun Jeongro* 禪門正路 (*Right Road to Seon School*).
[11] Focusing the mind by counting inhalations and exhalations as a method of stilling the mind. One of the five meditations and four bases of mindfulness.
[12] See "turning back the brilliance in counter-illumination" as John McRae labels it (McRae 1986, p. 114).
[13] (Dharmamitra 2009, p. 43) the *Six Gates To the Sublime Dharma* (六妙法門), *T* 1917.46.0550a24-25: 觀觀心.

Satipaṭṭhāna-sutta. It is intriguing to note here that the technique of "turning back the attention and contemplating the mind that hears sound" (反觀聞聲) reappears some hundred years later in the *Śūraṃgama Sūtra* (首楞嚴經, *The Sūtra of Heroic Progress*), where it is further elaborated in the theme of the "perfect penetration of the organ of hearing" (耳根圓通) and later 'counter-illumination' (廻光返照). This technique survived and found its way into Kanhua Chan (K. Ganhwa Seon)[14] practice in the 12th century.

6. Early *Sutta* Evidence of 'Counter-Illumination' for a *Bhavaṅga*-Type State: A Key Theme in the *Śūraṅgama Sūtra*

Throughout the Sinitic transformation, one of the elements in Indian Buddhist spiritual practice seems to have survived and been further developed, which is the process referred to as 'tracing back the radiance' (廻光返照 C. *huiguang fanzhao*/K. *hoe-gwang ban-jo*) or 'counter-illumination', as discussed above. The radiant *citta*, or 'luminous mind', is examined briefly here for the light it sheds on the early Buddhist view of human potential. The expression "luminous mind" first appeared in *Aṅguttara Nikāya*, I. 49–52: "Luminous, bhikkhus, is this mind, but it is defiled by adventitious defilement" (Bodhi 2012, p. 97). Bodhi notes that it is identified with the *bhavaṅgacitta*, an Abhidhamma (a collection of the philosophical and psychological teachings of early Buddhism) concept denoting the type of mental event that occurs in the absence of active cognition (Bodhi 2012, p. 1597). Bodhi states that it corresponds roughly to the subconscious or unconscious of modern psychology. The word *bhavaṅga* means "factor of existence," that is, the factor responsible for maintaining continuous personal identity throughout a given life and from one life to the next. However, the *bhavaṅga* is not a persistent state of consciousness or a permanent self, Bodhi adds. It is a series of momentary flow of mind that alternates with active cognitive processes, the *javana*, "sequences of cognition," in which the mind consciously apprehends an object. It is sometimes expressed as "stream of *bhavaṅga*" to highlight the fluid nature of this type of mental process. In regard to *bhavaṅga*, Peter Harvey discusses the "brightly shining mind" as a mysterious form of *citta* often alluded to in the Theravādin tradition, and also serves as the basis for Mahāyāna expositions of the 'Buddha-nature', or 'enlightenment-potential' in all beings (Harvey 1995, p. 166). He asserts that one of the key early *suttas*, *Aṅguttara Nikāya*, indicates the existence of a radiant *citta* which pervades everywhere, whether defiled or translucent. Thus, even a corrupt person possesses a "brightly shining *citta*," although it is covered by the defilements, which obscure it. This expresses a very positive view of human nature and of the nature of all beings (Harvey 1995, p. 167). Later in the Chan tradition, it is reflected in Mazu's statement that the mind is identical with the Buddha, emphasizing that sentient beings are inherently and immanently awakened Buddhas.[15]

Interestingly, a latent form of 'counter-illumination' can be found in the method of 'bare attention' as employed in the *Satipaṭṭhāna-sutta*; when attention is restricted to a bare noting of the object, the activity of mind reverts to the very first phase of the process of perception, where it is in a purely receptive state. The four contemplations of body, feeling, state of mind and mental contents, which are observed mindfully and non-judgmentally in order to reach the insight that 'all things are impermanent', converge in the central conception of the *dhamma*: *anattā*, non-Self. This is the ultimate instruction for the realization of the liberating truth of *anattā*. Thus the meditator is taught simply to observe the arising, abiding and vanishing factors of any mental thought process, devoid of any everlasting 'Self' or substance.

While the principal mental technique of the Kanhua Chan praxis can be described positively as 'counter-illumination', it appears from a psychological perspective to reflect an evolved form or an

---

14 Kanhua Chan (K. Ganhwa Seon 看話禪, phrase-observing meditation). A Seon meditation method that seeks direct attainment of enlightenment through investigation of the 'key phrase'(C. *huatou*; K. *hwadu*), first popularized by the Chinese Linji monk, Dahui Zonggao 大慧宗杲 (1089–1163).

15 是佛 此心即佛 http://tripitaka.cbeta.org/X69n1321.001.

extended equivalent of 'bare attention'. Specifically, single-minded attention to the *hwadu* is believed to create an introspective focus that would eventually lead the practitioner back to the *putative* enlightened source of one's own mind. As Buswell elaborates, once the meditator rediscovers the source of her/his own mind through such counter-illumination, s/he would come to know the enlightened intent of the *kung-an* or *hwadu*, and in turn consummate in her/himself the same state of enlightenment.[16] Through this technique, the sense of subjective 'I' goes into abeyance, allowing for an experience of the merger between the observing subject and the observed meditative object. This, in turn, leads to the transcending of the subject/object duality, a *nonduality*. There then emerges a liberating insight into the emptiness of inherent nature/existence. The *hwadu Sisimma* practice stresses sustaining questions as associated with various sensations, arising from the processes of body and mind, ultimately effecting a transformation into a unique religious experience, 'Oneness', or the Buddha-nature. It can be said that the idea of counter-illumination is critical to induce an experience of 'Oneness', or status of nonduality. However, how did the idea of 'counter-illumination' come to permeate the Chan/Seon tradition?

In the search for a vestige of *Satipaṭṭhāna* practice in the later Chan tradition, it is particularly worth focusing on one of the eighth century Chinese apocryphal scriptures, the *Śūraṃgama Sūtra* 首楞嚴經 (*Sūtra of the Heroic Progress*), in which an emphasis on the mind's discernment of the hearing faculty is presented distinctively as a tool for enlightenment.[17] According to Yong-Heon Jo, the *Śūraṃgama Sūtra*'s author(s) point(s) specifically to the "perfect penetration of the organ of hearing" (耳根圓通, C. *ergen yuantong*, K. *e-geun wontong*) which involves two steps: first focusing on sounds, the sound profound, the seer of sound, the purifier, and the sound of ocean tides;[18] and then "turning one's faculty of hearing inward to hear one's own nature," (反聞聞聲) (Jo 2002, p. 84) as in the practice of 'counter-illumination'. This appears to have become the basis for the setting of one of the most popular *huatou*s, "Who is it that recites the name of the Buddha?" (*Nianfo sh* (念佛是誰), that is, who recites the invocation to Amitābha Buddha without interruption in one's daily devotional practice? (Harvey 2013, p. 366). The *Śūraṃgama Sūtra* claims that mindfulness meditation through turning inward particularly to the organ of hearing is selected by "the Buddha" as the most suitable way of attaining enlightenment for humanity in a degenerate age because the organ of hearing is characterized as containing 'Three Truths' that are complete and perfect: its all-around hearing faculty is able to pierce a screen (通眞實), hear simultaneously from ten directions (圓眞實), and hear with or without the sound (常眞實). Yet despite the issue of questionable authenticity, modern scholars seem to have drawn attention to the importance of the *Śūraṃgama Sūtra* in the development of Chan in China, and its further significant impact on Seon practice in Korea (Jo 2002, pp. 20–42).

The spirit of 'the perfect penetration of the organ of hearing' is believed to have maintained its place in the Chinese Chan tradition by Jeongjung Musang 淨衆無相 (C. Jingzhong Wuxiang, 680–756), who is said to have been a prince of the Silla dynasty (57 BCE–935 CE), a kingdom located in the Korean Peninsula, and later by Linji Yixuan. Jeongjung Musang was a Korean-Chinese Chan master of the Tang dynasty, who became famous for his ascetic practices and meditative prowess, and he taught a practice known as *inseong yeombul* 引聲念佛, a method of reciting the name of the Buddha by extending the length of the intonation (Jo 2002, pp. 59–69). He was said to have taught and influenced several renowned Chan monks, including Mazu Daoyi, whose tradition was evidently practiced by Linji Yixuan, the founder of the Linji School.

---

[16] See more in (Buswell 2011, p. 190).

[17] Due to questionable authenticity and conflicting evidence regarding its provenance, the later Tang version (714–723), is widely acknowledged by modern scholars to be one of the Chinese apocryphal scriptures. See (Mochizuki 1946, pp. 493–509; Jo 2002, pp. 20–42).

[18] *T* 0945.19.0130c23: 妙音觀世音 梵音海潮音.

7. The Emergence of Kanhua Chan in the Evolution of the Chan School

A brief explanation may suffice here to present some of the major influential Chan adepts in order to indicate how the Sinitic transformation of molding and accentuation has progressed to the appearance of Kanhua Chan in the 12th century Song dynasty, and also to examine to what extent the Indian Buddhist meditative culture has survived.

In terms of contemplative praxis in the Chan school, as Robert Buswell states, one of the most striking transformations in the Sinicization of Buddhism is characterized by the imposition of the idea of *doubt* (C. *yi*; K. *ui* 疑), which is viewed as the motive force that impels this type of meditation (Buswell 2011, p. 190). Buswell asserts that doubt plays no constructive role in Indian Buddhist spiritual culture but is instead an obstacle that must be overcome if progress is to proceed. Some may argue that the approach to handling doubt in two traditions may be different, but it is to be remembered that the five hindrances, one of which is doubt, are included as among the mind-object contemplations (Ñāṇamolí and Bodhi 1995, pp. 151–55). In these practices, the meditator is taught to contemplate the arising and vanishing factors of doubt as well as the other four hindrances of the mind. Although doubt is consistently associated with unwholesome states as an obstacle and thus viewed negatively in Indian scripture, there was a Chan adept of the Southern Song who ironically capitalized on doubt as a most crucial dimension of Kanhua Chan. It means literally "Chan of observing the key phrase" (or "phrase-observing meditation") practice, which is strikingly different from the Indian Buddhist spiritual traditions. This was Dahui Zonggao 大慧宗杲 (1089–1163) who transformed doubt, normally seen as a debilitating mental concomitant, into the principal force driving one toward enlightenment (Buswell 2011, p. 192). Dahui Zonggao inherited the Linji lineage as the seventeenth generation successor of the Linji school, championing exclusively Kanhua Chan which employs the investigation of the topics of inquiry (*huatou*). Thus he revitalized the teachings of the Chan master Linji Yixuan 臨濟義玄 (d. 866–7), the putative founder of the eponymous Linji Zong 臨濟宗 in the tradition of the dharma-grandfather Mazu Daoyi 馬祖道一 (709–788). The latter was one of the most influential Chan masters of the Tang dynasty and retrospective patriarch of the Hongzhou zong, the broadest Chan tradition in China.

The principal tool of Kanhua Chan involves focusing intensely on the crucial phrase (*huatou*) of the *kung-an*.[19] The term *huatou* 話頭 (K. *hwadu*), the "head of speech," can be interpreted figuratively as the apex of speech or the point beyond which speech exhausts itself (Buswell 1992, p. 104). It is a short *holophrase*, functioning as a phrase or sentence, which is often extracted as a part of *kung-an*. It represents the concise summary of an entire "encounter dialogue" model (機緣問答; C. *jiyuan wenda*), which is the spontaneous and unstructured repartee between Chan masters and interlocutors as passed down from an earlier *kung-an* and is conducive to enlightenment.[20] The purpose of focusing on the *huatou* is to bring the practitioner beyond the point of rationalization and conceptualization, thus enabling a great enlightenment to occur. While this phrase is closely connected with the gist of the entire dialogue, it is clearly representative, becoming the subject of meditation and introspection in its own right. The *huatou* can be described as equivalent to a computer shortcut key input, which operates as a means of facilitating a function [the ultimate state of great enlightenment] in the computer [Buddhist practitioner] by pressing [breaking the final barrier of the rationalistic intellectual capacity while focusing single-mindedly] on a combination of keys on the keyboard [a *huatou*].

Kung-an/huatou meditation has been increasingly popular in Asian Buddhist societies. In China, it is well known that the most popular *huatou* is the question "Who is it that recites the name of the Buddha (*Nianfo shìshéi* 念佛是誰)?" (Harvey 2013, p. 366). This particular *huatou* was advocated by Xuyun (1840–1959), the most famous Chan monk of the 19th and 20th centuries in China; he taught

---

[19] Schlütter notes that Dahui himself did not provide the name, Kanhua Chan, but clearly distinguished it (Schlütter 2009, p. 107).
[20] For a definition of "encounter dialogue," see (McRae 2000, pp. 47–48).

this as his favorite form of meditation practice until he passed away at the age of 120 years (Shi 2010, pp. 248, 255). The Chan view of Amitābha Buddha at the intuitive noumenon level is that he represents the True Mind/One Mind or the self-nature of the Buddhas and sentient beings (Choo and Choi 2017, p. 55). In China, there are two other common *huatous*:[21] "What was my original face before my father and mother were born?"[22] and "*Wu*" 無.[23] In the Japanese Zen tradition, especially the Rinzai (C. Linji) school, the two most popular *koans* are "*Mu*" 無 and Hakuin's "What is the sound of one hand?"[24]

The Sinicized Chan tradition, in transforming the Indian Buddhist spiritual tradition, is said to have culminated in the Linji soteriological system, allegedly for the benefit of achieving enlightenment. It seems obvious that early Indian Buddhist principles such as the four *dhyānas*, seven branches of enlightenment, and four bases of mindfulness, and so forth, have been progressively suppressed and even revoked by most Chan masters for almost seven hundred years since the period of Bodhidharma. What has survived in the later Kanhua Chan, then?

8. The Evolution of a *kung-an/huatou*, the *Shishenmo* 是什麼, to *Sisimma* in the Korean Seon Tradition

Although the *Śūraṃgama Sūtra* was initially introduced to Korea in the ninth century,[25] it was formally publicized by Uicheon 義天 (1055–1101), one of the major Korean scholar-monks of the Goryeo dynasty (918–1392), having organized twenty-eight commentaries of the *Sūtra* in his *Sinpyeon jejonggyojangchongrok* 新編 諸宗教藏總錄 (*New Edition General Recording of All Religions*).[26] Approximately one hundred years later, the method of 'tracing back the radiance' was adopted by Bojo Chinul 普照 知訥 (1158–1210) of the Goryeo dynasty in Korea (Buswell 1992, pp. 103–4). Chinul was the first teacher in Korea to advocate the use of the *hwadu* in its formalized sense and established it with his disciple Jingak Hyesim 眞覺 慧諶 (1178–1234). Chinul proposed, as the principal means for catalyzing the initial awakening, the tracing of the radiance emanating from the luminous core of the inner mind back to its source, thus restoring the mind to its natural enlightened state (Buswell 1992, pp. 103–4). Thus, the message of through-the-sensation in the formula of the 'perfect penetration of the organ of hearing' was specifically communicated to Korean Buddhists by Chinul. A century or so later, the key technical formula in the *Satipaṭṭhāna* was further emphasized by Naong Hyegeun 懶翁 惠勤 (1320–1376), who introduced the *hwadu Sisimma* to his followers in Korea while instilling its message with new meaning.

In Korean Seon, unlike the Chinese/Japanese traditions, the *hwadu 'Sisimma'* 是什麼 (C. *Shishenmo*, K. *Sisimma*, J. *Zejinmo*)[27] is one of the most popular *hwadus* among Ganhwa Seon practitioners. This particular *huatou* is arguably one of the most famous *huatous* of the entire Kanhua Chan, which traces its origin to the first encounter of the sixth patriarch Huineng 六祖 慧能 (638–713) and Nanyue Huairang 南嶽 懷讓 (677–744). Specifically, it first appears in the *Platform Sūtra of the Sixth Patriarch Huineng*.[28] Nanyue Huairang was one of Huineng's two disciples who was conferred the dharma transmission of mind-seal, the other being Qingyuan Xingsi 清原 行思 (d. 740); the Chan lineage

---

[21] (Harvey 2013, p. 366).

[22] This *huatou* was originated from an encounter dialogue of the Sixth Patriarch, Huineng (638–713 CE) with his first disciple, Huiming, which is listed as the 23rd case in the *Wumen guan* 無門關, *T* 2005:48.0292a25–0299c25). (Yamada 1979, pp. 118–24), see *T* 2008:48.0347c20.

[23] The *huatou 'wu'* 無 (K. *mu*, J. *mu*, nothing or empty) centers on the response of Zhao Zhou (778–897) when asked if a dog had the Buddha-nature, described in Case 1 of *Mumonkan*, "Zhao Zhou's Dog." (Blyth 1966, pp. 26–27). See also *T* 2005:48.0292c21-24. This is perhaps the most famous *kung-an/huatou* used among Chan practitioners.

[24] See (Hoffmann 1975, pp. 47–54). Hakuin Ekaku 白隱慧鶴 (1685–1769), Japanese Zen Master renowned for revitalizing the *Rinzaishū*, was a strong advocate of questioning meditation (Jap. *Kanna* Zen).

[25] Jeongjin Guksa (878–956) was said to have recited the *sūtra*, which is recorded in the *Stupa Recording of Jeongjin Guksa Won-O* (Jo 2002, p. 19).

[26] (Jo 2002, p. 18).

[27] This is translated as What is it?; also *Imwotgo*, a vernacular translation of *Sisimma* in Korean.

[28] The *Platform Sūtra of the Sixth Patriarch Huineng* (六祖大師法寶壇經), *T* 2008:48.346c06–357b28.

branched out into a number of sublineages thereafter. The first historical anecdote concerning the *kung-an Shishenmo* depicts Nanyue Huairang's first encounter with Huineng as follows:

> The patriarch asked Nanyue Huairang where he came from. He replied, 'From Sung Shan.' The patriarch asked, 'What thing came in this way? (什麼物恁麼來)' 'To say it is a thing is not on the mark [right],' he retorted. 'Is it attainable by training or not?' asked the patriarch. 'It is not impossible to attain it by training but it is quite impossible to pollute it,' he replied. [29]

In the Korean Ganhwa Seon practice, however, in the earlier depiction of this encounter dialogue, *Shishenmo* evolved into the mindful *hwadu Sisimma*, which integrated the classical Sinitic Chan praxis with the *spirit* of *Satipaṭṭhāna* in a format of 'counter-illumination'.

9. The Mindful *hwadu Sisimma*, '*Sati-Sisimma*' of the Korean Seon Tradition

In the Korean Seon tradition, the practice of *Satipaṭṭhāna* has further evolved into a new version, the mindful *hwadu Sisimma*, '*Sati-Sisimma*', which is reminiscent of the *Satipaṭṭhāna* formula, never having been presented as such elsewhere. Both *Satipaṭṭhāna* and *Sisimma* require the retaining of concentration when awake and alert, the difference being that the former requires the systematic cultivation of Right Mindfulness, one of the Buddha's Eightfold Noble Path, while the latter demands an incessant questioning. In Korean Buddhist history, Naong Hyegeun 懶翁 惠勤 (1320–1376) was known as the first Seon Master who emphasized the importance of *Sisimma* (Kim 1997, p. 258). He was a famous Seon master in the late Koryeo period (918–1392) and one of the great authorities on the restoration of the present Korean Buddhists Jogye Order. Ganhwa Seon is generally acknowledged as the most authentic way of practice as indicated in *Ganhwa Seon, Path to the Jogye Sect Practice*.[30] This publication indicates that Ganhwa Seon retains the core of the Patriarchal Seon and inherits the same view of the enlightenment experience as emphasized by the Chan patriarchs in the past (Choo 2014, vol. 22, pp. 92–93).

Ever since Naong introduced *Sisimma*, its usage as one of the most famous *hwadus* has prevailed widely, often practiced as *Imwotgo*,[31] among most Korean Buddhist Seon practitioners up until the present day. Since its introduction, some of the most influential Seon masters who extensively employed the *hwadu Sisimma* in their period include Gyeong-heo Seong-u 鏡虛 惺牛 (1849–1912), Man-gong Wolmyeon 滿空月面 (1871–1946), Gusan Su-ryeon 九山 秀蓮 (1909–1983), Toei-ong Seongcheol 退翁 性徹 (1912–1993), Seungsahn Haeng-won 崇山 行願 (1927–2004), and Songdam Jeong-eun 松潭 正隱 (1929–). Seungsahn used the metaphor of *Ahn Su Jeong Deung* 岸樹井藤 (A Tree Vine off the Cliff hanging into the Well) as a *gong-an/hwadu* and urged the student not to attempt to solve it using stereotyped knowledge, but rather to proceed only with the question "What is it?" (是甚麼) Then he said, "One day you will surely hear the sound of a *Stony Rooster*"(Choo 2014, vol. 22, pp. 98–100).

Notably, Gusan was one of the renowned Korean Seon masters who provided a wealth of practical teaching, particularly with regard to the Korean practice of *hwadu Sisimma*. He was the first Seon teacher to have accepted and trained Western students in a Korean monastery. He emphasized that the key factor is to maintain a constant state of questioning, 'a doubt mass', and not just recite a simple repetition of the words. Having taken hold of the *Sisimma*, a student is advised to sustain the questioning: "What is seeing?" "What is hearing?" "What is smelling?" "What is moving the body?" and so on (Batchelor 2009, pp. 59–63). Whenever the *hwadu Sisimma* arises in the meditator's mind, s/he is to trace the radiance back to its source, restoring the mind to its natural enlightened state and to thus effect an integration, creating a wholeness. This is reminiscent of the inductive empiristic practice of *Satipaṭṭhāna*. The process of questioning should continue uninterruptedly, with each new question

---

[29] *T* 2008.48.0345c06–07: 六祖大師法寶壇經 古筠比丘異撰, *T* 2008.48.0357b19–28: . . . 什麼物恁麼來.
[30] (Hyeguk and Hwarang 2005, pp. 33–34).
[31] A Korean dialect of What Is It?

adding to the previous one, as if it were overlapping it. When the mass of questioning becomes enlarged to a critical degree, it is said to suddenly burst and the entire universe is shattered. Finally, one's 'original nature' is said to appear; this is considered the beginning of so-called enlightenment, or an awakened state (Batchelor 2009, pp. 59–63). Recently, Ryan Joo chose to focus on three contemporary Korean Seon masters: Songdam, Seongcheol and Subul (1953–), and concluded that their practice did impart a considerable weight to the critical role of sustaining the 'sensation of doubt'[32] (疑情, K. *uijeong*) during pre-enlightenment (Joo 2010, pp. 236–37). Among the three Seon masters, Songdam teaches his students how to practice the meditation of counting the breath (K. *susikgwan*, C. *shuxiguan*數息觀) before the actual *hwadu* practice of "What is it?" Specifically, he has presented a technique, that is, how to couple the *hwadu Imwotgo* [*Sisimma*] with the breath. While inhaling slowly, one should recall *Sisimma*, hold the breath for a few seconds, and while exhaling, recall another *Sisimma* shortly afterwards. As one becomes accustomed to *Sisimma*, one can recall it every second or third breath. Later, when one becomes more familiar with holding the *Sisimma*, one can recall it only once a day, when opening the eyes in the morning, and then holding it for the entire day. In this way, one can move one step closer to experiencing a great sudden burst of enlightenment (Songdam 1988, No. 445, 455).

It is particularly worth mentioning that mindfulness of breathing refers to a very close observation of one of the fundamental sensations of the body. It holds the highest place among the various techniques of Buddhist meditation since the Buddha recommended and praised its value, as described in the *Majjhima Nikāya*. This is what Korean Seon practitioners place great emphasis in their teaching, seeing it as a basic requirement to any Buddhist meditation. Specifically, when one attempts to be mindful of each breath attentively, the *hwadu Sisimma* can be an especially helpful reminder for sustaining awareness of the mind. The question "What is it?" is to be held onto firmly at every moment of moving, abiding, sitting, lying, speaking, being silent, and being tranquil. It creates an ambience for the undivided attention or mindfulness so that the mind of the practitioner is fully employed at each and every moment of breathing during all biological functions. With the help of the *Sati-Sisimma*, one can learn to divert one's discursive attention, reverting it back to awareness of one's original nature. This can be an invaluable tool in alleviating the ubiquitous issue: the inattentive tendency to constantly switch the focus of attention in a complex daily environment, which results in a state of disharmony and thus unwholesomeness.

10. Korean Influence on the East Asian Buddhist Traditions: A Case of "Countercurrent" Influence on Chinese Buddhism and Even to Early Buddhism

Bernard Senécal critically reflected on the Chogye Order's campaign for the worldwide propagation of Ganhwa Seon, raising three questions with regard to the uniqueness, the homogeneity and the continuity of the Korean Ganwha Seon tradition (Senécal 2011, pp. 75–105). He concluded that the powerful and fascinating narrative presenting it as the hallmark of Korean Buddhist tradition is far from fully convincing (Senécal 2011, p. 87). Be that as it may, however, despite some evident historical facts, the overall understanding of Korean Buddhism seems remiss in identifying some of its unique aspects.

Admittedly, the dominant current of the eastward dissemination of Chinese Buddhism creates important eddies, or countercurrents, of influence from various "peripheral regions" of East Asia. Buswell asserts that among these peripheral regions, Korea, in particular, has clearly participated in the evolution of the broader Sinitic tradition of Buddhism (Buswell 2005, pp. 1–2). He further states that there is definitive evidence that such an influence occurred with the writings of Korean Buddhist exegetes. Korea was a vibrant cultural tradition in its own right, and its Buddhist monks were intimately involved in contemporary activities occurring in neighboring traditions. Korean

---

[32] *Euijeong* 疑情 (C. yiqing); This refers to a constant state of intense questioning of the 'doubt mass'. Most Buddhist scholars often translate this literally as 'sensation of doubt', but an 'emotionalized and sustained doubt' may be rendered better than a 'sensation of doubt' as a doubt itself is not sensible.

Buddhism, exercising a syncretic harmonization of various doctrines and meditations, is commonly characterized as *tongbulgyo* 通佛教, or "ecumenical Buddhism" (Buswell 1989, p. 116) or "Buddhism of total interpenetration" (Park 1983, p. 37). Korean scholars generally agree that Wonhyo (617–686), one of the most distinctive Korean Buddhist monk scholars of the United Silla period (668–935), attempted to explicate the Buddhist teachings as being fundamentally congruous and pioneered a hermeneutical technique which he called "reconciling doctrinal controversies" (*hwajaeng*). Wonhyo's *hwajaeng* thought seeks to demonstrate that various Buddhist doctrines, despite their apparent differences and inconsistencies, can be integrated into a single coherent whole. His basic principle is explained chiefly in his *Simmunhwajaeng non* 十門和諍論 ("Ten Approaches to the Reconciliation of Doctrinal Controversy"), *Daeseung gisillon so*大乘起信論疏 ("Commentary to the Awakening of Faith According to the Mahayana"), and *Geumgang Sammaegyong non*金剛三昧經論疏 ("Exposition of the *Vajrasamādhi-Sūtra*") (Buswell and Lopez 2014, p. 998).[33] Buswell states that Wonhyo's exegesis, *hwajaeng*, so inspired the Silla intellectual community that "syncretism" became the watchword of Korean Buddhism from Wonhyo's time onward. Since at least the twelfth century, Wonhyo's *hwajaeng* exegesis has come to be portrayed as characteristic of a distinctive Korean approach to Buddhist thought (Buswell 1989, p. 116).

For this reason, it seems reasonable to behold the birth of *Sati-Sisimma* as "no surprise" since the development of *Sati-Sisimma* in the Korean Seon tradition may have been enabled by the ideological basis of syncretic harmonization, which was widely prevalent in Korean Buddhism. Considering the idea of "ecumenical Buddhism," the emergence of *Sati-Sisimma* has not been the result of a simple grafting of two different traditions, but rather the outcome of an insightful application of fervent aspiration concerning the ideology of early Buddhism beyond the orthodoxy and the orthopraxis of Dahui Zonggao's teachings in Chan tradition. This latter radically transformed the Indian Buddhist spiritual tradition and thoroughly suppressed early Indian Buddhist principles such as the four *dhyāna*s, seven branches of enlightenment, four bases of mindfulness, and so forth.

Further, the *Sati-Sisimma* may offer a useful applicability for the practice of *pari passu* meditative parallels in modern meditative practices: *Satipaṭṭhāna* as suitable for 'attentive' modes such as driving, working, and so forth; *Sati-Sisimma* for 'non-attentive' modes such as waiting in line, walking in the park, and so forth. This will greatly assist the practitioner to sustain an uninterrupted continuity of meditation practice. If one keeps this understanding in mind, it can be said that *Sati-Sisimma* provides a practical dialogue between scholars and practitioners, in which scholarship can inform Seon practice and Seon practice can vivify scholarship.

11. Conclusions

The Buddha is said to have awakened to the true nature of existence and attained the ultimate religious experience of enlightenment, *Nibbanā*, through the practice of the *Satipaṭṭhāna*. The practice itself begins with registering sensations stemming from the processes of body and mind, characterized by utilizing non-judgmental observation and awareness. During its transmission to East Asian countries, it evolved into alternative ways of teaching, particularly in the Chan tradition. The author contends that the Mahāyāna tradition maintained some essence of *Satipaṭṭhāna*, but that the Chan tradition, in particular, placed significantly less emphasis on it than did the Buddha, as can be evidenced by early Buddhist writings. The practice appears to have rather faded and become truncated, transformed or even excluded altogether, especially by the Tang to later Song dynasty Chan practitioners. In the Korean Seon tradition, however, some elements of *Satipaṭṭhāna* appeared to have been introduced into one of the famous Ganhwa Seon *hwadus*, identified as *Sisimma*, by the 14th century Seon Master Naong Hye-geun as well as numerous influential Seon practitioners following him.

---

33 Wŏnhyo's *Kishillonso*, "Commentary on Awakening Mahayana Faith," also called the *Haedongso* (Park 1983, p. 37).

To date, there has been little study concerning which aspects of the Indian contemplative traditions were passed on to the Chan/Seon schools. In the Korean Seon tradition, there are indications that the spirit of *Satipaṭṭhāna*, particularly in the form of 'counter-illumination' and 'mindfulness of breathing' has been manifested, at least in part, and further expanded and crystallized into one of the popular *hwadu*s of the Ganhwa Seon, the mindful *hwadu Sisimma*, '*Sati-Sisimma*'. Of all the known *gong-an*s/*hwadu*s, the *Sati-Sisimma* resonates as a reminder of the value of sustaining mindfulness, effectively linking the significantly different emphasis of practices. With all due respect to other traditions, it can be concluded that Korean Buddhist practitioners have made a meaningful contribution to the *Satipaṭṭhāna* teaching by imbuing the element of religious experience with the practice of *Sati-Sisimma* as a distilled denominator.

Further, while *Satipaṭṭhāna* practitioners may find that the *gong-an*/*hwadu* practice may not prove to be as concrete or clear-cut as mindfulness practice, conversely Chan practitioners may feel that mindfulness practice may not induce a state of deep concentration as easily or extensively as *gong-an*/*hwadu* practice. In view of this understanding, it is possible that a balance of the weaknesses and strengths of each tradition may be reached between the two practices. This may offer a potential basis for the useful practicality of optional meditative parallels in modern meditative practices: *Satipaṭṭhāna* as suitable for 'attentive' modes and *Sati-Sisimma* for 'non-attentive' modes.

Funding: This research received no external funding.

Conflicts of Interest: The author declares no conflicts of interest.

References

Anālayo, Bhikkhu. 2003. *Satipaṭṭhāna, The Direct Path to Realization*. Cambridge: Windhorse Publications.

Anālayo, Bhikkhu. 2012. *Excursions into the Thought-World of the Pāli Discourses*. Onalaska: Patiyatti Publishing.

Anālayo, Bhikkhu. 2013. *Perspectives on Satipaṭṭhāna*. Cambridge: Windhorse Publications.

Batchelor, Martine. 2009. *The Way of Korean Zen by Kusan Sunim*. Boston and London: Weatherhill.

Blyth, Reginald H. 1966. *Mumonkan—The Zen Masterpiece*. Tokyo: The Hokuseido Press.

Bodhi, Bhikkhu. 2000. *The Connected Discourses of the Buddha: A Translation of the Saṃyutta Nikāya*. Somerville: Wisdom Publications.

Bodhi, Bhikkhu. 2011. What Does Mindfulness Really Mean? A Canonical Perspective. *Contemporary Buddhism* 12: 19–39. [CrossRef]

Bodhi, Bhikkhu. 2012. *The Numerical Discourses of the Buddha, A Translation of the Aṅguttara Nikāya*. Boston: Wisdom Publications.

Buswell, Robert E., Jr. 1987. The 'Short-cut' Approach of K'an-hua Meditation. In *Sudden and Gradual: Approaches to Enlightenment in Chinese Thought*. Edited by Peter N. Gregory. Honolulu: University of Hawai'i Press.

Buswell, Robert E., Jr. 1989. *The Formation of Ch'an Ideology in China and Korea: The Vajrasamā dhi-Sūtra, a Buddhist Apocryphon*. Princeton: Princeton University Press.

Buswell, Robert E., Jr. 1992. *Tracing Back the Radiance: Chinul's Korean Way of Zen*. Honolulu: University of Hawai'i Press.

Buswell, Robert E., Jr. 2005. *Currents and Countercurrents: Korean Influences on the East Asian Buddhist Traditions*. Honolulu: University of Hawaii Press.

Buswell, Robert E., Jr. 2011. The Transformation of Doubt (Ŭijŏng 疑情) in Kanhwa Sŏn: The Testimony of Gaofeng Yuanmiao. Paper presented at the 2nd International Conference on Ganhwa Seon, GSIW's Proceedings, Dongguk University, Seoul, Korea, August 20–21, pp. 187–202.

Buswell, Robert E., Jr., and Donald S. Lopez. 2014. *The Princeton Dictionary of Buddhism*. Princeton: Princeton University Press.

Choo, B. Hyun. 2014. Can Seon Master Ven. Seungsahn's Four Suchness (四 如) Measure the Buddhist Enlightenment? *International Journal of Buddhist Thought & Culture* 22: 87–114.

Choo, B. Hyun, and Jay J. Choi. 2017. Amitābha Buddha Revisited: Into the Twenty-first Century Modern Science. *International Journal of Theology, Philosophy and Science* 1: 54–70. [CrossRef]

Dharmamitra, Bhikshu. 2009. *The Six Dharma Gates to the Sublime* (六妙法門): *A Classic Meditation Manual on Traditional Indian Buddhist Meditation by the Great Tianti Meditation Master & Exegete Sramama Zhiyi (Chih-i)*. Seattle: Kalavinka Press.

Harvey, Peter. 1995. *The Selfless Mind: Personality, Consciousness and Nirvna in Early Buddhism*. Richmond Surrey: Curzon Press.

Harvey, Peter. 2013. *An Introduction to Buddhism: Teaching, History and Practices*, 2nd ed. Cambridge: Cambridge University Press.

His Holiness Tenzin Gyatso. 1984. *Kindness, Clarity, and Insight by Dalai Lama XIV*. Ithaca: Snow Lion Publications.

Translated by Yoel Hoffmann. 1975, *The Sound of the One Hand, 281 Zen Koans with Answers*. New York: Basic Books, Inc.

Hyeguk and Hwarang. 2005. *Ganhwa Seon* 看話禪, *Path to the Jogye Sect Practice*. Seoul: Buddhist Study Research Center.

Jo, Yong-Heon. 2002. *Neug-yeom Gyeong Suhaengbeob eui Hangukjeok Suyong, Surangama-Sūtra's Meditation Method in Korea*. Korea: Wonkwang University.

Joo, Ryan Bongseok. 2010. Gradual Experiences of Sudden Enlightenment: The Varieties of Ganhwa Seon Teachings in Contemporary Korea. Paper presented at the International Conference on Ganhwa Seon, GSIW's Proceedings, Dongguk University, Seoul, Korea, August 12–13, pp. 219–40.

Khema, Sister Ayya. 2010. Here and Now: Ten Dhamma Talks. Access to Insight, III. Awake and Aware. Available online: https://www.accesstoinsight.org/lib/authors/khema/herenow.html (accessed on 1 May 2017).

Kim, Hyungwoo. 1997. Naong Hwasang 懶翁 和尙. In *Hangukbulgyo Inmul sasangsa, (Thought History of Korean Buddhist Figures)*. Edited by Bulgyo Sinmun Sa. Seoul: Minjoksa.

McRae, John R. 1986. *The Northern School and the Formation of Early Ch'an Buddhism*. Honolulu: University of Hawaii Press.

McRae, John R. 1987. Shen-hui and the Teaching of Sudden Enlightenment in Early Ch'an Buddhism. In *Sudden and Gradual: Approaches to Enlightenment in Chinese Thought*. Edited by Peter N. Gregory. Honolulu: University of Hawaii Press.

McRae, John R. 2000. The Antecedents of Encounter Dialogue in Chinese Ch'an Buddhism. In *The Kōan: Texts and Contexts in Zen Buddhism*. Edited by Steven Heine and Dale S. Wright. New York: Oxford University Press.

Mochizuki, Shinko 望月信亨. 1946. *Bukkyō kyōten seiritsu shiron* 佛教經典成立史論. Kyoto: Hozokan.

Ñāṇamolī, Bhikkhu, and Bhíkkhu Bodhi. 1995. *The Middle Length Discourses of the Buddha, A New Translation of the Majjhima Nikāya*. Translated by Bhíkkhu Ñāṇamolī. Edited by Bhíkkhu Bodhi. Boston: Wisdom Publications.

Nyanaponika, Thera. 1988. *The Heart of Buddhist Meditation*. York Beach: Samuel Weiser, Inc. First published 1965.

Park, Sung Bae. 1983. *Buddhist Faith and Sudden Enlightenment*. Albany: SUNY Press.

Park, Sung Bae. 2009. *One Korean's Approach to Buddhism: The Mom/Momjit Paradigm*. Albany: SUNY Press.

Schlütter, Morten. 2009. *How Zen Became Zen*. Honolulu: University of Hawai'i Press.

Senécal, Bernard. 2011. A Critical Reflection on the Chogye Order's Campaign for the Worldwide Propagation of Kanhwa Sŏn 看話禪. *Journal of Korean Religions* 2: 75–105. [CrossRef]

Shi, Zhiru. 2010. Who is Recollecting the Buddha? Xuyun and Investigating Huatou in Modern Chinese Buddhism. Paper presented at the International Conference on Ganhwa Seon, GSIW's Proceedings, Dongguk University, Seoul, Korea, August 12–13; pp. 239–63.

Songdam. 1988. Hwalgu Chamseon Beop, Alive Phrase Meditation Method. Bulil Hoebo: 445 & 455. Available online: http://emokko.tistory.com/61 (accessed on 31 October 2018).

Sujato, Bhikkhu. 2012. *A History of Mindfulness: How Insight Worsted Tranquility in the Satipaṭṭhāna Sutta*. Kerikeri: Santipada.

Toei-ong, Seongcheol. 退翁 性徹. 1981. *Seonmunjeongno* 禪門正路 *(The Right Road to the Seon School)*. Habcheon: Haeinchonglim.

Walshe, Maurice, Trans. 1995. *The Long Discourses of the Buddha: A Translation of the Dīgha Nīkāya*. Boston: Wisdom Publications. First published 1987.

Yamabe, Nobuyoshi, and Fumihiko Sueki. 2009. *The Sutra on the Concentration of Sitting Meditation*. (BDK English Tripitaka Series). Berkeley: Numata Center for Buddhist Translation and Research.

Yamada, Kōun. 1979. *Gateless Gate*. Los Angeles: Center Publications.

Article

The Four–Seven Debate of Korean Neo-Confucianism and the Moral Psychological and Theistic Turn in Korean Philosophy

Bongrae Seok[⦿]

Department of Humanities, Alvernia University, Reading, PA 19607, USA; bongrae.seok@alvernia.edu

Received: 21 September 2018; Accepted: 15 November 2018; Published: 19 November 2018

Abstract: This paper discusses how Korean Neo-Confucian philosophers in the Joseon dynasty (1392–1910) explained the moral nature of the mind and its emotions. Among the philosophical debates of Korean Neo-Confucianism, the author of the paper focuses on the Four–Seven Debate (a philosophical debate about the moral psychological nature of the four moral emotions and the seven morally indiscrete emotions) to analyze its *li–qi* metaphysics (a philosophical explanation of the universe through the intricate and interactive relation between the two cosmic processes, *li* and *qi*) and its conflicting viewpoints on the moral psychological nature of emotion. Because of the ambiguities and inconsistencies in the Neo-Confucian explanation, specifically those of the Cheng–Zhu schools of Neo-Confucianism on the nature and functions of the mind, Korean Neo-Confucians struggled to bring Neo-Confucian *li–qi* metaphysics to the moral and practical issues of the human mind and moral cultivation. Later in the Joseon dynasty, some Korean Neo-Confucians discussed the fundamental limitations of *li–qi* metaphysics and developed their explanations for the goodness of the moral mind and the world from an alternative (i.e., theistic) viewpoint.

Keywords: Korean Neo-Confucianism; the Four–Seven Debate; *li* and *qi*; moral metaphysics; moral psychology; theistic turn

---

1. Introduction: Korean Neo-Confucianism and the Moral Goodness of the Mind

Korean Neo-Confucian philosophers in the Joseon dynasty (1392–1910) discussed the moral goodness of the mind and the nature of human beings through the ultimate order of the universe. Specifically, they raised and discussed deep and challenging questions of moral metaphysics and moral psychology: How do the world and the mind interact and follow the same principles of the Neo-Confucian universe? How are the good and evil nature of the mind and its emotions explained? How are Confucian virtues and their foundations in the naturally given abilities of the mind explained? Over the period of the Joseon dynasty, Korean Neo-Confucians explored and developed their answers to these questions with careful explanations and rigorous analyses. They also elaborated their views and sharpened their arguments by actively engaging in philosophical debates. Although most of the debates were run by Neo-Confucian scholar-officials who were often politically active and socially engaged, the philosophical significance of the debates should not be overshadowed by their political interest and party affiliations. These debates were seriously philosophical and highly intellectual disputes that cast doubts on some of the fundamental principles of Neo-Confucianism. In this paper, I will explore, discuss, and explain the unique philosophical tradition of Korean Neo-Confucianism in the Joseon dynasty by focusing on how it explained the moral goodness of the mind and the world.

There are different ways to interpret and understand Korean intellectual tradition in the Joseon dynasty. The most popular interpretation of Korean philosophy in the Joseon dynasty is to characterize it as the study of nature (*xing*, 性) and the cosmic order (*li*, 理) in accordance with Cheng Yi (程頤, 1033–1107) and Zhu Xi's (朱熹, 1130–1200) Neo-Confucian philosophy. Although Wang

Yangming's (王陽明, 1472–1529) Neo-Confucianism was studied by a few Korean Neo-Confucians such as Nam Un-Gyung (南經, 1529–1994), Jang Yu (張維, 1588–1638), and Jeong Che-Du (鄭齊斗, 1649–1736), the mainstream of Neo-Confucianism in the Joseon dynasty was *Sunglihak/Xinglixue* (性理學, the study of nature and the order of the universe) or *Jujahak/Zhuxixue* (朱子學, the study of Zhu Xi's teaching).[1] In this paper, however, I will interpret Korean Neo-Confucianism in the Joseon dynasty from the perspective of the moral psychological orientation developed in the 16th and 17th centuries and the theistic turn developed in the 18th and 19th centuries. I will discuss how Korean philosophers in the Joseon dynasty, specifically in the Four–Seven Debate and the following debates, explained the moral goodness of the mind and how their explanations inspired a critical and analytic approach to the Neo-Confucian discourse of *li* and *qi* and influenced the theistic orientations of the later centuries of Korean philosophy. More specifically, from the perspective of Korean Neo-Confucians' effort to explain, analyze, and emphasize the philosophical significance of the moral mind and emotions, I will argue that the Four–Seven Debate, despite its original intention to make a consistent and comprehensive philosophy of morality and moral psychology, showed the fundamental limitations of Neo-Confucianism. As revealed in the process of the Four–Seven Debate, the version of Neo-Confucianism founded and developed by Cheng Yi and Zhu Xi did not clearly and consistently explain the moral goodness of the mind. Since the Cheng–Zhu Neo-Confucianism integrated the cosmology of *li* (理) and *qi* (氣) (a metaphysical explanation of how the universe comes to exist and change with its underlying principles and processes such as *li* and *qi*) and its normative order (the moral order of goodness and virtue in the world), it often provided ambiguous and inconsistent explanations of how the mind and its emotions receive innately good moral nature and how they cultivate moral virtues.

In what follows, I will take three steps in discussing the uniqueness of Korean Neo-Confucianism in its explanation of the moral goodness of the inner mind and the normative order of the outer world. First, I will discuss how Song Neo-Confucianism, specifically that of Cheng Yi and Zhu Xi, explained the nature of moral goodness. This general overview will help us to understand the historical and philosophical background of Korean Neo-Confucianism, which is often indiscriminately and generically characterized as a philosophical follower or an intellectual heir to the Cheng–Zhu Neo-Confucianism (Cheng Yi and Zhu Xi's Neo-Confucianism, which emphasizes the penetrating cosmic unity and dynamic forces in the world). Second, I will discuss the Four–Seven Debate, a major philosophical debate in Korean Neo-Confucianism, and analyze its philosophical messages and implications. Particularly, I will explain how the participants of the debate attempted to disambiguate and overcome the inconsistencies of Cheng Yi and Zhu Xi's Neo-Confucianism in its explanation of moral emotions, and I will analyze how they developed their own theories of moral goodness of the mind. Although the Korean Neo-Confucians who participated in the Four–Seven Debates were not the followers of the Lu–Wang School of Neo-Confucianism, they focused on the mind and its functions in the cultivation of moral virtues.[2] Third, I will discuss the theistic orientation of Korean philosophy in the 18th and 19th centuries from the viewpoint of Korean philosophers' efforts to resolve the inconsistencies of Neo-Confucianism and the philosophical tension raised by the early debates such as the Four–Seven Debate.

---

[1] In addition to the two well-recognized schools, there is another school of Neo-Confucianism discussed by several scholars. It is called the Hu–Liu school, named after Hu Hong (胡宏, 1106–1161) and Liu Zongzhou (劉宗周 1578–1645). According to some scholars, the lineage of the school goes back to early Neo-Confucians such as Zhou Dunyi, Zhang Zai, and Cheng Hao. Jeong (Jeong 2016, p. 67) explained that Yulgok Yi I's (a leading Korean Neo-Confucian in the Joseon dynasty) philosophy was closer to Zhang Zai and Hu Hong's Neo-Confucianism than to the Cheng–Zhu's Neo-Confucianism.

[2] The Lu–Wang (陸王) school was a Neo-Confucian school founded by Lu Jiuyuan (陸九淵, 1139–1192) and Wang Yangming (王陽明, 1472–1529), often called the school of *xin* (i.e., the school of the Confucian heart–mind).

2. Neo-Confucianism, Its Cosmology, and Moral Metaphysics

As a philosophical successor of classical Confucianism (i.e., the Confucianism of Confucius, Mencius, Xunzi, and other Confucian philosophers in the pre-Qin era), Neo-Confucianism is a renovated version of Confucianism of the Song and later dynasties of China. Neo-Confucianism expanded its moral horizon by developing comprehensive philosophical theories of moral virtues and a good life from the perspective of the governing order of the universe and the moral metaphysics of the mind.[3] For example, Cheng Yi and Zhu Xi introduced and discussed a set of metaphysical principles and explained the penetrating and universal order that integrates the outer universe and the inner moral mind. Specifically, they believed that the universe and its metaphysical and moral nature can be explained by the two foundational processes *li* and *qi*. *Li* (理) is the inherent pattern and the governing order of the universe. It is the foundation of the true and original nature of things and what they should ideally become. *Qi* (氣), on the other hand, is the foundation of the concrete, local, dynamic, and physical properties of the universe. It is the force and energy behind the physical processes and diverging tendencies of individual objects. It takes tangible forms, serves particular physical functions, and stimulates dynamic changes in the universe. With *li* (generative, penetrating, coherent order, and unity), *qi* (interactive, localized, physically diversifying energy), and their intricate interplay, Cheng Yi and Zhu Xi explained the nature of the mind, morality, and the generative processes of the universe.

As a theory of cosmology or moral metaphysics, the Cheng–Zhu Neo-Confucianism provided or at least attempted to provide a systematic explanation of the reality and goodness of the universe. According to them, everything comes to exist and change in accordance with universal principles that are not arbitrary or random. However, it is debatable whether the Cheng–Zhu approach provided a sufficient and successful explanation of moral properties, specifically moral properties of the mind. From the perspective of moral metaphysics, if everything is an intricate combination of *li* and *qi*, moral properties are no exception: They are explained by the interactivity of *li* and *qi*. From the perspective of moral agency and moral cultivation, however, the Cheng–Zhu approach can be inconsistent or incomplete. If everything comes out of the same principles and processes such as *li* and *qi*, why are some intentions and emotions good, but others are evil? As the underlying foundations of the cosmic processes, *li* and *qi* are responsible for both the moral and immoral properties of the world. Because of this morally indiscrete nature of *li* and *qi*, the unique and distinctive nature of moral properties such as moral goodness, normativity, and virtue are not fully explained by Neo-Confucian *li–qi* metaphysics. Since *li* and *qi* are involved in both the existence and the morality of the world, the clear and full distinction between ontology and morality is not made in Neo-Confucian philosophy. Additionally, explaining the moral nature of the mind is another challenge to the Cheng–Zhu Neo-Confucianism. Since the mind consists of the constant nature (*xing*, 性) that reflects the goodness of the universe and, at the same time, varying emotions (*qing*, 情) that can be evil, it is not easy to explain the intrinsically moral but spontaneously aroused emotional states of the mind that Mencius (2A6, 6A6) characterized as the foundation of Confucian virtues.

Usually, theories of metaphysics or cosmology explain what and how things happen in the world through their intrinsic nature (ontology) and origination (cosmology). They explain the function, process, and existence of reality through the ultimate causes or elements of the universe. From this general viewpoint, they provide answers to questions such as, "What is x and how does it come to exist?" However, they do not necessarily explain "what x ought to do" or "what x should become". As many philosophers (Hume 1739/1975; Moore 1903/2004) have pointed out, moral properties, unlike metaphysical or ontological properties, are related to the prescriptive, evaluative, or normative

---

[3] Broadly, Neo-Confucianism is defined as "a category employed to describe a set of 'family resemblances' discerned across clusters of philosophical ideas, technical terms, arguments, and writings . . . in other words, concepts, ideas, and discourse rather than schools" (Makeham 2010, p. xii). See (Angle and Tiwald 2017) for a general explanation of Neo-Confucianism.

(i.e., non-descriptive) aspects of the world. They relate to what one ought to do and what should ideally happen in the world, not to what is happening in the world.[4] For this reason, *li* and *qi*, as metaphysical elements or principles, do not discretely or exclusively explain the moral nature of the mind independently of its metaphysical origination and constitution.[5] The difference, or conflict, between metaphysical cosmology and moral psychology, therefore, is a formidable philosophical challenge to those Neo-Confucians who wished to develop a consistent explanation of moral goodness in the minds of virtuous individuals. This is exactly the conflict or tension one could observe in the philosophical debates of Korean Neo-Confucianism in the Joseon dynasty.

One can find excellent introductions and in-depth discussions of Neo-Confucianism in recent publications (Angle 2009; Angle and Tiwald 2017; Bol 2008; Ching 2000; Huang 2014; Makeham 2010). According to them, Neo-Confucianism was not just a philosophy of personal virtues and ethics, but also a comprehensive theory of cosmology, metaphysics, and social-political philosophy. Perhaps, the intellectual endeavor to build a consistent and comprehensive system of philosophy was one of the important strengths of Neo-Confucianism. Currently, however, most Neo-Confucian scholarship focuses on the ethical and political dimensions more than the cosmological or metaphysical dimensions of Neo-Confucianism, not simply because the metaphysical or mythological theories of Neo-Confucianism were not continuous or compatible with modern science, but also because their hidden ontological biases or parochialism favor the Heavenly Principle (*tianli* 天理) and the ruling elites over foreign barbarians, commoners, females, and people with personal desires (人欲) and subjective feelings (Ching 2000). The major concern here is that the unitary and monistic metaphysical schemes of Neo-Confucianism or Confucianism in general may not serve as the aspirational and guiding moral foundation for pluralistic, egalitarian, and democratic society (Angle 2012; Chan 2014; Kim 2014; Tan 2004). For this reason, metaphysical Confucianism is often discussed independently of or in total separation from Confucianism as a public culture or as a political philosophy (Kim 2014). In this paper, however, I will focus more on the logical gap or conceptual incommensurability between moral metaphysics and moral psychology within the Cheng–Zhu school from the perspective of the philosophical debates in the Joseon dynasty. In their philosophical analyses, some Korean philosophers in the Joseon dynasty realized that even within the unitary and generative Neo-Confucian system of *li* and *qi*, moral mind and emotions were not fully and properly explained.

3. Korean Neo-Confucianism in the Joseon Dynasty

As a philosophical tradition that integrated the ultimate order of the universe and the virtue of human beings, Neo-Confucianism (specifically the Cheng–Zhu Neo-Confucianism) explained Confucian ideals of *ren*, *yi*, *li*, and *zhi* (仁 義 禮 智, compassion, righteousness, ritual propriety, and wisdom) through the dialectic interfusion between *li* and *qi*. The interaction between *li* and *qi*, however, is not necessarily smooth, consistent, and mutually complementary, as the Chinese Neo-Confucians in the Song dynasty would have thought. The gap or inconsistency between moral metaphysics (how *li* and *qi* generate a myriad of things in the universe) and moral psychology (how the mind functions to generate moral emotions) was a major philosophical challenge to Korean Neo-Confucians of the Joseon dynasty. The two major philosophical debates of Korean Neo-Confucianism, the Four–Seven Debate (*Sachil Nonjaeng*, 四七論爭, 1559–1572, a philosophical debate about the moral psychological nature of the four innately moral emotions and the seven ordinary emotions) and the Horak Debate (*Horak Nonjaeng*, 湖洛論爭, 1712–1724, a philosophical debate about the nature of the unaroused and pure state of the mind) started when Korean Neo-Confucians realized that the nature of the mind and its emotions were not fully and naturally explained by the complementary interactivity between the

---

4   (Hume 1739/1975) pointed out that a statement of moral ought is not justified by a statement of fact. In a similar context, (Moore 1903/2004) argued that moral properties cannot be explained by natural properties.
5   The mind can represent and understand how and why things happen, but it can also represent and intend how things should (ideally) happen in its understanding of moral values and virtues.

li and *qi* of Neo-Confucian metaphysics. Some Neo-Confucians argued that the mind is intrinsically good since the mind inherits the ordered pattern (*li*) of the universe. Others argued that the mind is not necessarily good because its specific states and functions come to exist by the energy of *qi* that is not necessarily consistent or regularized (i.e., unbalanced or uneven). The main concern of Korean Neo-Confucians, therefore, was to find a conceptually consistent and practically effective way to integrate the cosmic principles of *li* (理), *qi* (氣), *xing* (性, nature), and *xin* (心, mind), and to explain the nature of the mind and its emotions that are partially good and partially evil, partially *li* and partially *qi*.

Regardless of their philosophical differences, Korean Neo-Confucians accepted the overarching philosophical framework of Confucianism and defended their philosophical legitimacy by citing the alleged philosophical authority of the Cheng–Zhu Neo-Confucianism. Generally speaking, they all agreed and accepted the same philosophical discourse of Neo-Confucianism (i.e., the philosophical discussion and explanation of the universe and the nature of moral virtue through *xing* (性, the inherent nature of things), *li* (理, the governing order of the universe), *qi* (氣, the dynamic force of the universe), and *xin* (心, the Confucian heart–mind)). Unfortunately, the inconsistent and ambiguous details of *li–qi* metaphysics (a philosophical explanation of the universe through the intricate and interactive relation between the two cosmic processes *li* and *qi*) of the Cheng–Zhu Neo-Confucianism raised a formidable difficulty to Korean Neo-Confucians, as the Four–Seven Debate and the Horak Debate demonstrated.

Some scholars believe that the irresolvable philosophical conflicts in Neo-Confucian debates in the Joseon dynasty were exacerbated by the underlying political conflicts that most Korean Neo-Confucians participated in.[6] Korean Neo-Confucians in the Joseon dynasty were mostly scholar-officials with specific party affiliations, and they often fought for political hegemony along with philosophical or ideological dominance: Bloody political purges and struggles were not infrequent throughout the history of the Joseon dynasty. However, independently of political issues, debates of Korean Neo-Confucianism had deep philosophical significance. In many debates, Korean Neo-Confucians engaged in rigorous philosophical argumentations and analyses. They disambiguated and analyzed abstract and metaphysical theories of Neo-Confucianism to explain the moral psychological nature of the Confucian heart–mind. Additionally, when they realized the philosophical challenge inherent in Neo-Confucian *li–qi* metaphysics, they did their best to resolve its conflicting details by developing new interpretations of the mind and its moral nature. In fact, Korean Neo-Confucianism is a great philosophical tradition of moral psychology that focused on the mind and its emotional energy at the foundation of moral virtues.[7] The Four–Seven Debate delivered these intellectually stimulating characteristics of Korean philosophy.

4. The Four–Seven Debate

The Four–Seven Debate was a philosophical debate over the moral psychological nature of the two distinct groups of emotions. In this debate, Korean Neo-Confucians discussed whether the four moral emotions (i.e., the four innate and morally specific emotions discussed in the *Mencius* (孟子), such as the emotions of pity and compassion (惻隱), shame and dislike (羞惡), compliance and deference (辭讓), and right and wrong (是非) are fundamentally different from the seven feelings (i.e., the seven

---

6   Takahashi's (Takahashi 1929/2001) discussion of Korean Neo-Confucianism was close to this type of interpretation. He explained Toegye's and Yulgok's (the two major philosophers of Korean Neo-Confucianism) philosophical views along the lines of party politics. According to him, Toegye was the founder of the *li* school (主理派), and Yulgok was the founder of the *qi* school (主氣派). From the perspective of politics, the two groups were in direct conflict (*li* against *qi* and the Eastern party (東人) against the Western party (西人)). However, from the viewpoint of philosophy, they were not necessarily conflicting or contradicting with each other. For example, it is wrong to say that Yulgok was the founder of the *qi* school (主氣派). He did not believe in the ontological dominance of *qi*: He believed that everything is a particular combination of *li* and *qi*. He even said that "it is a mistake to conclude that filthy things do not have principle [*li*]" (Yulgok's letter to Ugye's second letter) (Kalton 1994, p. 119).

7   See (Choe 2009) for the mentalizing tendency of Korean Neo-Confucianism.

ordinary, morally neutral emotions listed in the *Book of Rites* (禮記), such as joy, anger, grief, fear, love, hate, and desire (喜 怒 愛 懼 哀 惡 欲).[8] The two major discussants of the debate, Toegye (退溪, Yi Hwang 李滉 1501–1570) and Kobong (高, Ki Daesung 奇大升 1527–1572), explored and discussed the moral psychological nature of the Four and the Seven through Neo-Confucian *li–qi* metaphysics.[9] The debate started when the Korean Neo-Confucians realized that a linear and contrastive explanation of the Four and the Seven through *li* and *qi* did not work.[10] That is, the explanation that the Four were always good because of *li* but the Seven could be evil because of *qi* was not consistent with some of the fundamental doctrines of Neo-Confucian metaphysics: *Li* and *qi* are different but not separated from each other (不相雜 不相離) and everything is under their mutual interaction. Then, how could the difference between the Four and the Seven be explained by *li* and *qi*?

Toegye argued that the Four and the Seven are different emotions because the morally specific (i.e., morally dedicated, pure, and normative) nature of the Four is explained by *li*'s exclusive generation (*libal* 理發, generation or issuance by *li*) of the Four but not of the Seven. Kobong, however, argued that the Four and the Seven are not essentially different emotions because they are all aroused states of the mind caused by *qi*'s activity.[11] Additionally, all emotions, even morally neutral emotions like the Seven, can become good through one's careful self-cultivation and balanced regulation of the aroused emotions. Kobong also pointed out that Toegye's *libal* is not compatible with Zhu Xi's general distinction between *li* and *qi*: *Li* does not have any physical form and, therefore, does not assume any active physical function.[12] Therefore, *li* does not have any causal efficacy even though it may provide the underlying nature or governing order of the Four.[13]

After Toegye and Kobong's initial rounds of discussion, the debate continued with Yulgok's and Ugye's exchange. Yulgok followed Kobong's view. Yulgok (栗谷, Yi I 李珥 1537–1584) argued for *li* and *qi*'s combined and unified causation of emotions whether they are morally specific or not and argued against Toegye's distinction between the Four and the Seven on the basis of his (Yulgok's) rejection of *li*'s exclusive contribution to or generation of the Four. Ugye (牛溪, Seong Hon 成渾 1535–1598) followed Toegye's view on *libal* (理發) as the unique moral signature that distinguishes the Four from the Seven. He argued that, without *li*'s critical contribution to the Four, the distinction between the Four and the Seven could not be maintained.

In this debate, Toegye focused on *li*'s critical role in the intrinsic moral nature of the Four. He believed that *li* contributes to the intrinsic goodness of the Four, which is different from the Seven's "accidental" or "circumstantial" moral nature. The Four are always good. The Seven can become good but they are not always good. To Kobong and Yulgok, however, Toegye's view implied that

---

[8] For a full explanation of the historical and philosophical background of the Four-Seven Debate, see (Ahn 2009a, 2009b). For a book-length discussion of the Four–Seven Debate, see (Chung 1996). In what follows, the Four refers to Mencius's four morally specific emotions and the Seven refers to the ordinary, morally neutral emotions listed in the *Book of Rites*.

[9] In this paper, I use the pen names of Korean Neo-Confucian philosophers following the general convention.

[10] In his letter to Kobong, Toegye wrote, "Some years ago, when Mr. Chong [Jeong Ji-Un] made his diagram, it included the thesis that the Four Beginnings issue from principle and the Seven Feelings issue from material force. My opinion was that the dichotomy was too stark and would lead to controversy" (Toegye's response to Kobong's first letter) (Kalton 1994, p. 8).

[11] Toegye and Kobong disagreed on the contributions of *li* and *qi* to morally specific and morally neutral emotions. Toegye stated that " ... The issuance of the Four Beginnings [the Four] is purely a matter of principle and therefore involves nothing but good; the issuance of the Seven Feelings includes material force and therefore involves both good and evil" (Toegye's first replay to Kobong) (Kalton 1994, p. 11). Against Toegye's view, Kobong argued that, "Man's feelings are but one, and what they are as feelings definitely combines principles [*li*] and material forces [*qi*] and has both good and evil" (Kobong's second response to Toegye) (Kalton 1994, p. 21).

[12] Basically, *li* does not have physical form (無形) and active function (無). Kobong stated that, "The two [*li* and *qi*] are certainly distinct, but when it comes to their presence in actual things, they are certainly mixed together and cannot be separated. It's just that principle is weak while material force is strong; principle has no concrete sign, but material force is physically in evidence" (Kobong's first letter to Toegye) (Kalton 1994, p. 6). See Yulgok's reply to Ugye's sixth letter (Kalton 1994, p. 175).

[13] Zhu Xi (Zhu 1997, *Zhuxiji* 朱熹集 45) stated that one can talk about the movement of *li* or *taiji* (太極, the ultimate supreme, the ultimate foundation of all beings) figuratively but, in its original sense, *li* or *taiji* cannot move or affect other things because if they do, they violate the distinction between the two states (i.e., having physical form and not having physical form (形而上下者不可分). *Li* and *taiji* are beyond physical forms. They do not have physical forms. Therefore, they do not physically affect other things.

li has the power to originate the Four. If *li* is understood as the holistic governance or coherence above the physical form (形而上), it does not have the power to generate the affective arousals that are conditioned by local and physical properties of mental processes. That is, the causal power to generate emotional arousals belongs to the physical energy of *qi*'s local activity, not to *li*'s universal governance. It seems that Toegye successfully explained the unique moral nature of the Four through *li*'s governing order, but his view on *li*'s involvement in the arousal of the Four conflicted with the well-received Neo-Confucian view on *li*'s formal, not causal, nature: *Li* does not have physical form (無形) and active function (無 爲). Although Kobong seriously considered Toegye's view on *li*'s and *qi*'s differential contributions to moral emotions, the debate ended with no consensus. Toegye and Kobong could not fully agree on the role *li* plays on the generation of the Four.

5. Analysis of the Four–Seven Debate

Imagine, in a very simplistic manner, that the difference between the four morally specific and the seven morally unspecific emotions could be explained by *li* as the cause of good and *qi* as the cause of evil as illustrated below.[14]

Li   (governing order, above the form)   → the Four (good)
Qi   (dynamic force, below the form)   → the Seven (evil)

One may hypothesize that moral goodness comes out of the coherent and intrinsic nature of *li*, but evilness comes out of the uneven and diverging nature of *qi*, and believe that the correlation between "*li*-good-Four" and "*qi*-evil-Seven" is less confusing but more consistent and understandable. However, the moral distinction between good and evil does not smoothly and consistently correlate with *li* and *qi*, because both *li* and *qi* are involved in good and evil. It is possible that good things derive from the interactive combination of *li* and *qi* and the Seven, even under the influence of *qi*, can become good. That is, both *li* and *qi* are involved in moral, immoral, and amoral actions and intentions: Everything is under some interaction between *li* and *qi*. In other words, good and evil are not directly or consistently correlated with *li* and *qi*, respectively. In fact, good and evil are conceptually incommensurable (not sharing any consistent commonalities) with *li* and *qi*. One of the reasons why Toegye started the Four–Seven Debate was his awareness of this incommensurability, that good and evil are not clearly and systematically correlated with *li* and *qi* in their contributions to the Four and the Seven.[15] At the beginning of the Four–Seven Debate, Toegye pointed out the incommensurability when he commented on Jeong Jiun's (鄭之雲, 1509–1561) interpretation of the Four arising from *li* and the Seven arising from *qi* (四端發於理 七情發於氣).[16] Toegye did not believe that the Four and the Seven are caused directly by *li* and *qi*, respectively. Nor did he believe that good and evil are generated directly by *li* and *qi*, either. Since *li* and *qi* are the cosmic principle and force, they both are involved in any processes

---

[14] Generally, this view (*qi* is the cause of evil) was received widely among Neo-Confucians. For example, by quoting the following passage from the *Neo-Confucian Anthology* (*Jinsilu* 傳習錄), Wong (Wong 2009, p. 149) states that "according to the Cheng Brothers the sources of moral badness lie in the native endowment of *qi*, the body, and the inherent desires of human beings." Someone asked Cheng Yi, "Man's nature is originally good. Why is it that some people cannot change?" [Cheng Yi replied], "In terms of their nature, all men are good. In terms of their 'native endowments' (*cai*, 才), there are the most stupid who do not change. The most stupid are of two kinds, those who do violence to their own nature and those who throw themselves away."

[15] See note 10 above (Toegye's response to Kobong's first letter, Kalton 1994, p. 8).

[16] Toegye commented on Jeong Jiun's view expressed in Jeong's the *Diagram of the Mandate of Heaven* (天命圖). Jeong stated that the Four arise from *li* and the Seven arise from *qi* (四端發於理 七情發於氣). On the basis of his understanding of Zhu Xi's statement (四端是理之發 七情是氣之發, Zhu 1986, *Zhuzi Yulei* 53:20a), Toegye corrected Jeong's statement to "the Four originate from *li* and the Seven originate from *qi*"(四端理之發 七情氣之發). Jeong focused on the causal generation of the Four and the Seven, but Toegye stressed their different originations (i.e., different natures or founding sources). Later Toegye changed his own view in the process of the Four-Seven debate.

or properties whether they are good or evil.[17] That is, the Four–*li*–good and the Seven-*qi*-evil are not lined up correlatively as illustrated below.

Li–Qi   → the Four (good)

Li–Qi   → the Seven (good, evil)

Toegye felt the need to discuss whether Neo-Confucian metaphysics could explain the distinction between the Four and the Seven through *li* and *qi*. He wrote a letter to Kobong asking Kobong's view on this matter, and the Four–Seven Debate started.

The incommensurability in the Four–Seven Debate can be explained as follows: A set of two contrastive categories were not correlative with another set of two contrastive categories. In other words, the moral distinction (good, evil) did not correlate with the metaphysical distinction (*li*, *qi*) in a discrete one-on-one fashion. This incommensurability (i.e., lacking common or comparable conceptual elements) posed a formidable challenge to any philosophical attempt to translate good and evil into the language of *li* and *qi*, specifically in the context of distinguishing the intrinsically moral emotions and the morally neutral emotions. Korean Neo-Confucians, through their careful analyses and debates, tried to solve or resolve this philosophical challenge by developing their own moral psychological approach within the framework of Neo-Confucian metaphysics of *li* and *qi*, but they did not successfully accomplish their goals because the incommensurable gap between the metaphysical distinction (*li* and *qi*) and the moral distinction (good and evil) in human emotions cannot be completely bridged.[18]

As a way to solve the problem, Korean Neo-Confucians, specifically Toegye, used the notions of the original nature (本然之性, the intrinsic and innate human nature) and the *qi*-affected nature (氣質之性, the nature affected by *qi*'s activity in a given environment).[19] Often goodness was explained by the original nature of the human being because *li*'s ordered and balanced tendencies are reflected in the original nature. Evil was explained by the *qi*-affected nature because of *qi*'s deviant activities or diverging tendencies. For example, in many philosophical debates in Korean Neo-Confucianism, moral goodness was explained by *benranzhixing* / *bonyeonjiseong* (本然之性, the original, intrinsic nature), but evil was explained by the uneven, unregulated activities of *qi* in *qizhizhixing* / *gijiljiseong* (氣質之性, the *qi*-affected nature).[20] However, the suggested solution did not work completely. *Qi* does not necessarily stimulate or facilitate evil. Even with *qizhizhixing* (*qi*-affected nature), one can become good and the *qi*-driven emotions such as the Seven can be developed, through the process of harmony and balance, to support and cultivate moral goodness. Additionally, since both the original nature and the *qi*-affected nature derive from the same nature (*xing*, 性), they are not fundamentally different: They are only different modes of the same foundational nature. Once again, the Four-good and the Seven-evil are not lined up with the two types of natures (i.e., 本然之性 氣質之性).[21]

---

[17]   Kobong noted that "if one regards the Four Beginnings as being issued by principle and [hence] as nothing but good, and the Seven Feelings as issued by material force and so involving both good and evil, then this splits up principle and material force and makes them two [distinct] things. It would mean that the Seven Feelings do not emerge from the nature and the Four Beginnings do not mount on material force [to issue]. What such wording conveys cannot but be considered problematic and the later students of the matter will certainly have doubts about it" (Kobong's Letter to Toegye) (Kalton 1994, pp. 4–5).

[18]   I will explain the nature of this unbridgeable gap in the following section.

[19]   "Nature" (*xing*, 性) here means very generally a deeply engrained disposition or trait. It does not necessarily refer to the permanent and essential property of a given species or individual in a Platonic or Aristotelian sense.

[20]   For example, Toegye once thought that the distinction between the Four and the Seven is similar to the distinction between the original nature and *qi*-affected nature: He stated that, "Once I thought confusingly that the distinction between the Four and the Seven is similar to the distinction between the original nature and *qi*-affected nature" (故愚嘗忘以情之有 四端七情 之分 猶性之本性氣稟之異也) (Yi 1997, vol. 2, pp. 411–12).

[21]   Later Yi Ik (李瀷 1681–1763, pen name Seong Ho 星湖) argue against the distinction between the original nature and the *qi*-affected nature. He does not believe that human beings have two entirely different forms of nature. The two forms of nature are just two different modes of the same underlying nature founded on *li*'s activity. He simply states that "the original nature and the *qi* affected nature are not two natures. ... The nature is one" (本然之性與氣稟之性 非二性也 ... 性 一也) (Yi 1999; Jeong 2013, p. 46 n16).

本然之性 (Original, *li*-governed nature)   → the Four (good)
氣質之性 (*Qi*-affected nature)   → the Seven (good, evil)

Another suggested solution to this incommensurability was to introduce a new element (i.e., the balance and articulation 中節) to Neo-Confucian moral metaphysics.[22] Good and evil are not directly lined up with *li* and *qi* but derive from the balanced and harmonious articulation (中節) of *li* or *qi*. If *li* and *qi* are not balanced and harmoniously articulated (不中節), evil comes out. That is, good and evil are not the matter of *li* and *qi* but the matter of their balance and harmonious articulation.[23] In fact, Zhu Xi stated that moral emotions, whether they are the Four or the Seven, derive from the specific conditions of the balance and articulation.[24] In other words, good and evil are not directly explained by the presence or absence of *li* and *qi* but by their particular conditions of the balance and articulation in relation to emotions, intentions, and other psychological or situational contexts.

中節   (balance-articulation in *li qi*)   → the Four (good)
中節/不中節   (balance-articulation or its absence in *li qi*)   → the Seven (good, evil)

This explanation, however, is not successful because the standard of the balance and articulation needs to be provided independently of or in addition to the activity or interactivity of *li* and *qi*. Why are certain (i.e., balanced or articulated) activities or processes of *li* and *qi* good while others are not good? It seems that the answer to this question should be found somewhere other than *li* and *qi*, since good and evil are not determined by *li* and *qi* alone but by their specific patterns of activity. That is, in order to explain good and evil, the Cheng–Zhu Neo-Confucianism had to offer a formal principle regarding the optimally balanced pattern of *li* and *qi* outside of *li* and *qi*. If one takes this solution, however, one has to give up the completeness of Neo-Confucian *li–qi* metaphysics because one has to find the foundation of good and evil outside of *li–qi* metaphysics or make it circular or redundant if one, in order to maintain the completeness of *li-qi* metaphysics, uses *li* and *qi* to explain the balance between *li* and *qi*. It seems that Neo-Confucian *li-qi* metaphysics failed to provide a full and satisfactory explanation of good and evil through the process of the balance and articulation.

As these conflicting viewpoints and the failed consensus show, the Four–Seven Debate revealed the fundamental limitation of the Cheng–Zhu Neo-Confucianism in its explanation of the mind and morality: *Li* and *qi* are morally indiscrete, but the mind can be morally specific with some of its spontaneous emotions. It became quite clear at the end of the debate that Neo-Confucian *li–qi* metaphysics provided only limited explanations on the goodness of the mind and its emotions. Both Toegye and Kobong, in their heated debates on moral emotions, knew the incompleteness and inconsistency of Neo-Confucianism and did their best to provide their own explanations for how the cosmic principles and processes of *li* and *qi* give rise to moral emotions and virtues. Yet, as I discussed in this section, the incommensurability of metaphysical terms (such as *li* and *qi*) and moral terms (such as good and evil) cannot be easily resolved unless Neo-Confucian *li–qi* metaphysics is fully revised or even abandoned. The revision, or in some cases gradual abandonment, of Cheng–Zhu's

---

[22] In the *Doctrine of the Mean* (*Zhongyong* 中庸), there is a passage where the balance and articulation (中節) are mentioned: "The state before the arousal of pleasure, anger, sorrow, or joy is called balance (中). When they are aroused with balance and articulation, they are called harmony (和)" (喜怒哀樂之未發謂之中 發而皆中節謂之和).

[23] When emotions reach their due measure, they achieve heavenly harmony and goodness. For example, Kobong stated that, "Although the Seven can be categorized as *qi*, *li* is already included in it. When they issue and reach their due measure, they are called heavenly endowed nature and the original substance. In that case, how can they be regarded as issuing from *qi* and be different from the Four?" (Yi 1997, 1:440b, 441a). However, Kobong also believed that even the Four can be unbalanced or unharmonized in actual experience of the Four (Hong 2014, p. 274). That is, to Kobong, harmony and disharmony were a more important distinction than intrinsic and accidental goodness of the Four and the Seven in the moral psychology of emotion.

[24] Zhu Xi (*Zhu Xi Yulei*, 53) states that "regarding the moral emotions of pity/compassion and shame/dislike, there are balance/harmony and imbalance/disharmony. It is as if there are appropriate and inappropriate pity/compassion and appropriate and inappropriate shame/dislike depending on their balance and harmony" (惻隱羞惡也 有中節不中節 若不當 惻隱而惻隱 不當羞惡而羞惡 便是不中節).

Neo-Confucian *li–qi* metaphysics is exactly what one can witness in the later development of Korean philosophy in the 18th and 19th centuries.

6. The Theistic Turn in Korean Philosophy

In the Cheng–Zhu Neo-Confucianism, moral properties such as good and evil were explained by the cosmic or metaphysical properties and interactivities of *li* and *qi*. However, the two types of categories (metaphysical and moral categories), as I analyzed above, do not correlate consistently and coherently, and the relations between the mind (*xin*), nature (*xing*), and moral goodness are not fully explained by the metaphysical framework of *li* and *qi*. In the 18th and 19th centuries, through the Practical Learning school (sirhak 實學) of Jeong Yakyong (pen name Dasan 茶山, 1762–1836) and the school of Donghak (東學, the Eastern [i.e., Korean] Learning, a philosophical school and a religious social movement founded by Choi Je-wu [崔濟愚, 1824–1863]), some Korean philosophers finally settled on a solution or a resolution to the challenging philosophical issues of Neo-Confucianism.[25] They discussed an independent foundation of morality (i.e., a different type of moral authority outside of the original nature [本然之性] or the *li*-driven nature of the Four) and a new philosophical viewpoint that can replace the Cheng–Zhu Neo-Confucianism.[26]

Inspired and influenced by the theology and philosophy of Roman Catholicism imported from China, Dasan found the moral authority (i.e., the normative and practical standard) in *Sangje* (上帝, the Lord or the Emperor on High).[27] He stated that *"li* cannot stand on its own. Therefore, it does not have the power [the Way] to generate physical difference."[28] More specifically, he argued that *"li* is intrinsically devoid of responsiveness and active authority. If that is the case, is there anything one should be seriously cautious and fearful of?"[29] Additionally, Dasan criticized the relevance of *li–qi* metaphysics in the moral discourse. He stated that,

> People today respect, praise and honor *xing* [性] as if it is as great as Heaven when they integrate it with the theory of *taiji* [太極, the ultimate supreme, the ultimate foundation of all beings] *yin yang* [陰陽, negativity and positivity, the two alternating forces or movements in the universe] and combine it with the original and the *qi*-affected natures [本然氣質] in a confused, deceptive, illusive, and exaggerated manner. They think they analyzed minute distinctions in the secretive details of Heaven and human beings but they fail to use them to promote the practical values of ordinary life. It is impossible not to notice the confusion.[30]

In addition to Dasan's philosophy, the collapse of Neo-Confucian moral metaphysics can be observed in Donghak. Donghak found a non-Neo-Confucian foundation in *Hanulnim* (Heavenly Being) or *Cheonju* (天主, Heavenly Lord). *Hanulnim* is a divine and personal, but not completely

---

[25] For example, (Kim 2015, p. 563) stated that to explain practical effectiveness and moral efficacy, direct moral authority is necessary in Neo-Confucian thought. That is, beyond *li* and *qi*, Korean Neo-Confucians felt a need to develop a separate foundation for morality. "Tasan [Dasan] put the Lord on High in the place of *li* for the very practical reason that people had ceased to acknowledge the authority of *li*. He took this stance of putting practical effectiveness above logical consistency, but it was not just because he was a scholar of the Practical Learning School (*Sirhak*) in the late Choson [Joseon] Dynasty. This viewpoint is also found in the discussions by Neo-Confucian scholars in the early Choson [Joseon] Dynasty, such as the debates on the Four Beginnings and the Seven Emotions. In that sense, the effectiveness for realizing Confucian ideals is often more decisive than theoretical consistency in the formation of theories or arguments in Confucianism or Neo-Confucianism, even though it cannot be denied that logical consistency or theoretical preciseness are important for the validity of Confucian theories, given that the goal of theoretical debates in Confucianism is the actualization of moral life and realization of an ethical society."

[26] (Takahashi 1929/2001), a Japanese Neo-Confucian scholar in the early 20th century, believed that Dasan was faithful to the spirit of Toegye's philosophy that emphasized the primacy of moral philosophy over and beyond the *li–qi* cosmology of Zhu Xi's Neo-Confucianism. See (Kim 2010) for further discussion.

[27] For the broad historical background of Dasan's philosophy, see (Baek 2012).

[28] "理非自植者 故無先發之道也" 與猶堂全書 中庸講義補 (Jeong 2002; Jeong 2013, p. 59 n59).

[29] "理本無知 亦無威能 何所戒而之 何所恐而懼之乎" (Jeong 2002, p. 282, 49a).

[30] "今人推尊性字, 奉之天樣大物, 混之以太極陰陽之説, 雜之以本然氣質之論, 眇芒幽遠, 恍忽夸誕. 自以毫分縷析, 窮天人不發之秘, 而卒之無補於日用常行之則, 亦何益之有矣. 斯不可以不辨" (Jeong 2002; Jeong 2013, p. 61 n63).

transcendental, being. It is an ultimate and immanent moral authority in the mind and the world outside.[31] Choi was very intentional on the fundamental connection or penetration between the mind and *Hanulnim* (the divine moral authority) in his philosophy of Donghak.[32] Considering the heavily stratified social structure of the Joseon dynasty, Donghak's vision of universal equality and the fundamental unity between the mind, the world, and the divine being was simply revolutionary (Kim 2002; Park 2015). Specifically, its egalitarian and humanistic tendency was not only expressed in its philosophy but also reflected in its religious rituals and codes of conduct. According to (Kim 2015), the leaders of Donghak (i.e., Choi Je-Wu and Choi Sihyeong (崔時亨1827–1898)) developed and implemented rules of equality and respectful behavior to fellow humans in Donghak rituals and the common conduct of Donghak followers. All followers of Donghak, regardless of their social statuses, gender, wealth, and education, could participate in Donghak rituals and could serve the leadership positions (Kim 2015). Choi Je-wu called his disciples friends, and Choi Sihyeong appointed a person from the lowest class to one of the major Donghak leadership positions.

Although both Dasan's Sirhak and Choi's Donghak were influenced by the Confucian philosophy of self-cultivation and moral excellence of virtue, they focused on the practical (not just the metaphysical) order of the universe and the independent and universal authority of morality. That is, their philosophical viewpoints significantly deviated from the two major Neo-Confucian convictions, the governing order of *li* throughout the universe and the *li*-driven nature of moral authority. Specifically, in both schools of Korean philosophy, moral properties were not regarded as properties derived from *li* and *qi* but as one of the original properties of the world that derive from their own foundation and justification independent of *li* and *qi*.[33] Instead of explaining what is good or what one should do from the perspective of what is out there at the foundation of universe, these later schools of Korean philosophy and religion explained good and evil directly from the perspective of the ultimate and independent moral authority that we can refer to and respectfully emulate in our actions and decisions independently of Neo-Confucian metaphysics.

As the theistic orientation of the Practical Learning and the Eastern Learning demonstrate, many Korean philosophers attempted to explain the intrinsic and nonderivative nature of morality and secured the foundation of the practical moral mind through the independent standard of practically effective and universal normativity. Reliance on the authority of a divine figure such as *Sangje* (上帝, the Emperor on High), *Hanulnim*(한 울 님, Heavenly Being), or *Cheonju* (天主, Heavenly Lord), therefore, can be understood in this philosophical context of the theistic turn (i.e., a theistic way to solve philosophical problems regarding the nature of the universe, the mind, and morality).[34]

On the one hand, this theistic tendency seems to be an anachronistic or irrational solution to the problems of moral issues and distinctions. Divine authority such as Heaven (天) was not entirely foreign to Chinese and Korean traditions, but the theistic solution to moral issues seemed unprecedented or even unacceptable. Classical Confucian philosophers such as Mencius talked about Heaven (天 *tian*) as the ultimate justification of moral goodness (*Mencius*, 7A1), but Heaven is not a moral agent or a personal god,[35] nor does it refer to a realm of divinity. Neo-Confucian philosophers such as Zhou Dunyi (周敦頤, 1017–1073) developed a universal and systematic explanation of the

---

31 *Hanul* (한 울) means heaven, oneness, and unity. The two major teachings of Donghak (東學, the Eastern Learning) are (a) serving and respecting the Heavenly Lord (侍天主) and (b) recognizing the oneness of human being and Heaven (人乃天).

32 See Lee's (Lee 2017) discussion of Choi Je-wu's Donghak philosophy and its practical moral orientation.

33 In his discussion of the practical learning (Sirhak) school, Choe Namseon (崔南善) (Choe 1930) identified two subsections of the Sirhak school, introspective practical philosophy and political economical philosophy. Both Seongho's (Yi Ik's) and Dasan's (Jeong Yakyong's) discussions of moral psychology and cultivation belonged to the former subsection of Sirhak.

34 This type of theistic orientation can be found in Nakae Toju's (中江藤樹, 1608–1648) philosophy from the perspective of Yangming Neo-Confucianism. See (Bodart-Bailey 1997, p. 670). Although there are some comparable philosophical orientations, Dasan and Choi Je-wu were not Yangming Neo-Confucians.

35 Mencius stated (7A1) that, "To preserve one's mental constitution, and nourish one's nature, is the way to serve Heaven" (存其心 養其性 所以事天也).

universe through *taiji*, *li*, and *qi*, but they are not theistic divine figures.[36] A well-known Korean Neo-Confucian's (Shin Hudam [慎後聃, pen name Habin 河賓, 1702–1762]) criticism of Catholicism (the Western Learning, 西學) clearly articulated this type of philosophical concern. Habin argued that cultivation of goodness and discussion of right and wrong on the basis of a theistic religion (Catholicism) and its divine authority are not recommendable because our moral effort and cultivation of virtue, under the theistic framework, derive from the selfish and instrumental interest of *insim* (人 心, the human mind with personal interests and desires). If people cultivate their virtues in order to be rewarded by God or gods in the afterlife, their moral intention is compromised by their pursuit of personal profit (利), which is a major Confucian evil. Habin believed that the Western Learning (i.e., Catholicism) promotes this type of selfish interest, which goes against the ideal moral vision of Confucianism (i.e., a sense of duty and compassion embedded in the Confucian heart–mind).[37] He also argued that the notion of *Shangdi* or *Sangje* (上帝, the Emperor on High) as a governor god existed in classical Confucianism but it is not a creator god. The notion of a creator god, specifically with the ability to create the universe out of nothing (*creatio ex nihilo*), was completely foreign to Confucianism.[38]

On the other hand, this theistic orientation in Korean philosophy in the 18th and 19th centuries can be understood broadly as a philosophical pursuit of a universal, rational, and practical ground of morality in a world full of practical concerns and moral challenges. Dasan found the judge and the enforcer of moral goodness in the personal God of Christianity.[39] God provides the standard of right and wrong (i.e., the standard of normativity), and promotes moral goodness (practical efficacy), which, as I explained above, many Korean Neo-Confucians attempted to explain and articulate over several hundred years of philosophical debates. If the intrinsic nature of morality could not be explained by *li* and *qi* in the nature (*xing* 性), the mind (*xin* 心), and the emotions (*qing* 情), it should be found somewhere else. The notion of divine authority, perhaps, provides a viable solution to many philosophical and moral confusions and challenges that Korean Confucians had to face in the Joseon Korea.

Perhaps, from a broad philosophical viewpoint, the theistic turn in Korean philosophy (i.e., finding a non-derivative divine moral authority to overcome the philosophical limitations of the *li–qi* metaphysics of Neo-Confucianism) can be understood from the perspective of rationalized religion, a philosophy of religion developed by Kant (1793/1998) in his *Religion within the Boundaries of Mere Reason*. Kant argued that a religion, specifically Christianity, could be rationally accepted and practiced through the clear articulation and unification of morality and the ultimate goals of life. He stated that morality "inevitably leads to religion, and through religion it extends itself to the idea of a mighty moral lawgiver outside the human being in whose will the ultimate end (of the creation of the world) is what can and at the same ought to be the ultimate human end" (Kant 1793/1998, p. 35–36, 6:6). Against the background of the Kantian ideal of rationalized religion, the unique theistic orientation of Korean philosophy can be understood as a philosophical solution to many limitations and ambiguities of Neo-Confucianism on the identification and distinction of moral properties from other properties of the world. If the normative standard of good and evil cannot be consistently or fully explained by *li*, *qi*, and their interaction, a different foundation of moral value and authority should be considered and pursued. Some Korean Neo-Confucians (such as Dasan and other Neo-Confucians in the school of Practical Learning) in the 18th and 19th centuries did just that. As the name suggests, the school of Practical Learning (Sirhak 實學) emphasized the empirical and pragmatic understanding of the world over metaphysical or cosmological speculation. When it comes to the foundation of morality, Practical Learning challenged Neo-Confucian *li–qi* metaphysics through its emphasis on the direct moral efficacy

---

[36] See (Adler 1999) and (Wang 2005) for full details of Zhou Dunyi's Neo-Confucian philosophy and cosmology.
[37] See (Choi 1988, p. 204–5).
[38] See (Choi 1988, p. 240).
[39] See (Baker 2004, 2013) for further details of Dasan's philosophy and its interaction with Catholicism.

of the mind and its normative standard derived from divine authority.[40] That is, instead of finding the root of morality in transcendental metaphysics or formal principles, some Korean philosophers, specifically those of the Practical Learning (Sirhak) school, pursued an independent and intrinsic foundation of goodness in theistic moral authority.

7. Conclusions

In this paper, I discussed how Korean Neo-Confucians in the Joseon dynasty understood the moral concepts and moral emotions in their debates, specifically in the Four–Seven Debate. According to many Korean Neo-Confucians in the Joseon dynasty, the cosmology and metaphysics of Neo-Confucianism, because of its preoccupation with the cosmic process that encompasses the mind, morality, and the intrinsic goodness of the universe, could not successfully explain the moral and immoral tendencies of the mind and its emotions. If the whole universe is generated and governed by the same ultimate foundations such as *taiji*, *yin-yang*, *wuxing* (五行, the five cosmic elements), and *li–qi*, why are some emotions inherently good but others are only accidentally good? Why and how do morally deviant intentions and emotions exist? The Four–Seven Debate is a perfect example where these serious philosophical questions were discussed in the context of the moral goodness of the mind and its emotions. Since emotion is an aroused state of the mind, *qi* should be critically involved. Then, how can one explain the goodness of the innately given moral emotions (if *qi* has a deviant tendency but its active energy is needed for their arousal)? This conflict between Neo-Confucian *li–qi* metaphysics and moral psychology of the innately good emotions is the main debating point of the Four–Seven Debate. As I discussed in the previous sections, the conflict was not fully resolved, and the gap between moral metaphysics and moral psychology was not completely bridged because of the inherent logical gap or the incommensurability between Neo-Confucian *li–qi* metaphysics and the moral psychology of the Confucian heart–mind.

The philosophical effort of the Korean Neo-Confucians to explain the moral goodness of the mind and its emotions, however, is not necessarily a meaningless or useless dream. They sharpened the conflict between the moral metaphysics and the moral psychology of Neo-Confucianism, developed different interpretations of the moral emotions, and gradually revealed the philosophical limitations of Neo-Confucian *li–qi* metaphysics. They found two general ways to overcome this philosophical challenge. First, they chose and studied moral psychology of emotion and pursued the practical foundation of morality instead of exploring and finding solutions from the viewpoint of *li–qi* metaphysics. For example, philosophical debates following the Four–Seven Debates, such as the Horak Debate, provided rigorous philosophical analyses of moral psychology. Second, some Korean Neo-Confucians also searched for a direct and independent moral authority outside of the Neo-Confucian universe (i.e., the universe of *taiji*, *yin yang*, *wuxing*, and *li–qi*). The standard of right and wrong, for these philosophers, did not derive from *li* and *qi* but from an independent divine source (such as the Emperor on High (上帝), or *Hanulnim*). Korean Neo-Confucianism in the Joseon dynasty, therefore, can be understood from the perspective of Korean philosophers' efforts to bring the moral goodness of the mind to the foreground of ethics and to establish a practical and universal moral authority for everyone. From this viewpoint, the Four–Seven Debate was an inspiring starting point of the moral psychological and theistic turn of Korean philosophy in the Joseon dynasty.

Funding: This research received no external funding.

Conflicts of Interest: The author declares no conflicts of interest.

---

[40] For example, in the same philosophical school, Dasan's senior Yi Ik (pen name Seongho, 1681–1763), emphasized the moral will and intention of an agent and gave up the strict distinction between the Four and the Seven on the basis of *li*'s and *qi*'s differential contributions to human emotion. See (Jeong 2013, pp. 49–50).

References

Adler, Joseph A. 1999. Zhou Dunyi: The Metaphysics and Practice of Sagehood. In *Sources of Chinese Tradition*, 2nd ed. Edited by Wm. Theodore de Bary and Irene Bloom. New York: Columbia University Press, vol. 1, pp. 669–78.

Ahn, Young-sang. 2009a. A Study on the Joseon Neo-Confucian's Four-Seven Debate, Comparing it with the Yangminng School's Debate about Equilibrium in the Meditation and Harmony in the Practice. *Korean Classics Studies* 51: 615–53. (In Korean)

Ahn, Young-sang. 2009b. An Exploration on Zhu Xi's the Theory of Mind's Consolidating Nature and the Emotions for Understanding Four-Seven Debate. *Study of Philosophy and Culture* 32: 281–308. (In Korean)

Angle, Stephen. 2009. *Sagehood: The Contemporary Significance of Neo-Confucian Philosophy*. New York: Oxford University Press.

Angle, Stephen. 2012. *Contemporary Confucian Political Philosophy: Toward Progressive Confucianism*. Malden: Polity Press.

Angle, Stephen, and Justin Tiwald. 2017. *Neo-Confucianism: A Philosophical Introduction*. Malden: Polity Press.

Baek, Min Jeong. 2012. Jeong Yakyong's Philosophy and 18th century East Asia. *Horizon of Knowledge* 12: 200–12. (In Korean)

Baker, Don. 2004. Tasan between Catholicism and Confucianism: A Decade under Suspicion, 1791 to 1801. *Tasanhak* 5: 55–86.

Baker, Don. 2013. Finding God in the Classics: The Theistic Confucianism of Dasan Jeong Yagyong. *Dao. A Journal of Comparative Philosophy* 12: 41–55. [CrossRef]

Bodart-Bailey, Beatrice. 1997. Confucianism in Japan. In *Companion Encyclopedia of Asian Philosophy*. Edited by Brian Carr and Indira Mahalingam. New York: Routledge, pp. 660–74.

Bol, Peter K. 2008. *Neo-Confucianism in History*. Cambridge: Harvard University Asia Center.

Chan, Joseph. 2014. *Confucian Perfectionism: A Political Philosophy for Modern Times*. Princeton: Princeton University Press.

Ching, Julia. 2000. *The Religious Thought of Chu His [Zhu Xi]*. New York: Oxford University Press.

Choe, Namseon. 1930. Sirhak. *Dong-A Daily News*, 3406, Section 4. February 8. (In Korean)

Choe, Young Jin. 2009. A Study of the Mentalizing (*xinxue* 心學) Tendencies of Korean Neo-Confucianism in the 18th to 19th Century. *Korean Folk Culture* 33: 339–68. (In Korean)

Choi, Dong-Hee. 1988. *Korean Sirhak's Response to the Western Learning*. Seoul: Folk Culture Institute, Korean University. (In Korean)

Chung, Edward. 1996. *The Korean Neo-Confucianism of Yi Toegye and Yi Yulgok: A Reappraisal of the "Four-Seven Thesis" and Its Practical Implications for Self-Cultivation*. New York: State of New York Press.

Hong, Seongmin. 2014. On Appropriateness of Moral Emotion in Gi Daeseung's [Kobong's] Philosophy. *Korea Study* 48: 267–93. (In Korean)

Huang, Yong. 2014. *Why Be Moral? Learning from the Neo-Confucian Cheng Brothers*. Albany: The State University of New York Press.

Hume, David. 1739/1975. *A Treatise of Human Nature*, 2nd ed. Edited by L. A. Selby-Bigge. Revised by P. H. Nidditch. Oxford: Clarendon Press.

Jeong, So-yi. 2013. A Study of the Continuity and Discontinuity of Toegye Yi Hwang's, Seongho Yi Ik's and Dasan Jeong Yakyong's Theories of Mind. *Human, Environment, and Future* 10: 37–70. (In Korean)

Jeong, Weon-jae. 2016. Does the Neo-Confucianism of the Chosŏn Dynasty belong to the Cheng-Zhu School? Rethinking the Intellectual History of Chosŏn through the Philosophical Tradition of Yi I (1538–1584). *Journal of Korean Religions* 7–1: 67–92. [CrossRef]

Jeong, Yakyong. 2002. *Yoyudang Jeonseo* (與猶堂 全書 *Complete Works of Jeong Yagyong*). Seoul: Korean Classics Research Institute.

Kalton, Michael. 1994. *The Four-Seven Debate, an Annotated Translation of the Most Famous Controversy in Korean Neo-Confucian Thought*. Albany: SUNY Press.

Kant, Immanuel. 1793/1998. *Religion within the Boundaries of Mere Reason*. Translated and edited by Allen Wood and George Di Giovanni. New York: Cambridge University Press.

Kim, Choon Sung. 2002. Donghak: Towards Life and Spirituality. *Korea Journal* 42: 158–86.

Kim, Hyoungchan. 2015. The *li-ki* [*li-qi*] Structure of the Four Beginnings and the Seven Emotions and the Intention of the Four-Seven Debate: A Critical Reflection on the Methods of Explaining the Theories of the Four Beginnings and the Seven Emotions in Korean Neo-Confucianism. *Acta Koreana* 18: 561–81.

Kim, Jeongin. 2015. Origination and Development of Donghak. In *History toward Democracy: Rediscovery of the 19th Century Korean History*. Seoul: With Books Publishing. (In Korean)

Kim, Sungmoon. 2014. *Confucian Democracy in East Asia: Theory and Practice*. New York: Cambridge University Press.

Kim, Tae Nyun. 2010. From Record of Philosophical Lineage (學案) to History of Philosophy: Viewpoints and Historiography of Korean Neo-Confucianism. *Korean Studies* 23: 41–84. (In Korean)

Lee, Cheol-Seung. 2017. Moral Consciousness Appeared in Donghak Thought. *Inmoonhak Yeongu* 54: 107–30. (In Korean)

Makeham, John, ed. 2010. *Dao Companion to Neo-Confucian Philosophy*. New York: Springer.

Moore, George Edward. 1903/2004. *Principia Ethica*. Mineola: Dover Publications.

Park, Hongsik. 2015. A Meaning of *Donghak* in the History of Korean philosophy. *Journal of East-West Humanities* 4: 1–29. (In Korean)

Takahashi, Dorou. 1929/2001. *The Li School and the Qi School in the History of Korean Neo-Confucianism*. Translated by Hyeong-seong Yi. Seoul: Yemoon Seowon. (In Korean)

Tan, Sor-Hoon. 2004. *Confucian Democracy: A Deweyan Reconstruction*. Albany: State University of New York Press.

Wang, Robin. 2005. Zhou Dunyi's Diagram of the Supreme Ultimate Explained: A Construction of the Confucian Metaphysics. *Journal of the History of Ideas* 66: 307–23. [CrossRef]

Wong, Wai-Ying. 2009. Morally Bad in the Philosophy of the Cheng Brothers. *Journal of Chinese Philosophy* 36: 141–56. [CrossRef]

Yi, Hwang. 1997. *Jeungbo Toegye Jeonseo (Complete Works of Yi Hwang)*. Seoul: Sungkyunkwan University Press, vol. 1–5.

Yi, Ik. 1999. *Sachil Shinpyun* 四七新編 *(A New Edition of The Four Seven Debate)*. Translated by Sangik Yi. Seoul: Daunsam. (In Korean)

Zhu, Xi. 1986. *Zhuzi Yulei* (朱子語類, *Classified Conversations of Master Zhu*). Beijing: Zhonghua Shuju.

Zhu, Xi. 1997. *Zhu Xi Ji* (朱熹集, *Collected Works of Zhu Xi*). Edited by Guo Qi. Cheng Dao: Sichuan Education Press.

Article

Performing the Bible in the Korean Context: Korean Ways of Reading, Singing, and Dramatizing the Scriptures

Sung Uk Lim

College of Theology & United Graduate School of Theology, Yonsei University, Seoul 03722, Korea;
sunguk.lim@yonsei.ac.kr

Received: 7 August 2018; Accepted: 6 September 2018; Published: 10 September 2018

Abstract: The present study explores the performative nature of the Bible as a sacred text in the Korean context. Drawing on the theory of scriptural performance advocated by James W. Watts, I investigate its character as *words* and *contents*. First, I delve into the scriptural performance of thoroughly reading (and listening to) the Bible at the level of words. Second, I scrutinize the scriptural performance of singing and dramatizing the Bible at the level of contents. The specific context of South Korea—whether religious, cultural, or social—alerts us to the performed transformation of the semantic range of the long-standing Christian tradition. Given the cultural differences between Western and Eastern Christianity, I contend that the adaptation of Christianity to Korean soil renders the performative dimension of the scriptures all the more semantic. In other words, the Korean ways of performing the Bible are essentially deeply rooted in those of signifying it. In the long term, Christianity turns out to be such a global religion that it provokes a more complex analysis of its scriptural performance in its widely differing range of semantics.

Keywords: Korean Christianity; Bible; scriptures; performance; semantics; *Tongdok*; *Pansori*; bibliodrama

---

1. The Three Dimensions of the Scriptures in Korea

The present study aims to explore the performative nature of the Bible as a sacred text in the context of Korean Christianity (cf. Smith 1971). Undoubtedly, Christianity in the Korean Peninsula has been shaped by the great influence of Western culture. However, it would be too hasty to consider the history of Korean Christianity as merely western. Rather, a closer look would show that it has been clothed in Korean traditions as it has developed. In the words of Tail Il Wang, Korean churches have been more interested in religious experience rather than doctrinal understanding through the process of performing the scriptures (Wang 2009). With this in mind, I would like to pay special attention to the aspect of Korean Christianity as it pertains to the performance of the Bible in contemporary South Korean society. It is my contention that the performative aspect of the Bible in the Korean context has some bearing on its semantic features.

To this end, I draw on the theory of James W. Watts regarding the three dimensions of scriptures: semantic, performative, and iconic (Watts 2006, pp. 140–43). Let us discuss what is meant by each dimension for the moment. First, in Watts' words, the semantic aspect concerns the process of interpreting the meaning of written text in a religious community (p. 141). For instance, preaching is an attempt to deliver the semantic meaning of the Bible to a congregation; a preacher plays a significant role as an exegete in such a way as to derive meaning from the given text.

Next, the performative aspect deals with the performance of written text (cf. Austin 1975, pp. 141–42). Watts is correct to divide the performative dimension into two ways on the assumption that the scriptures are performed at the level of *words* and *contents*. On the level of words, scriptures can be read, recited, or memorized in private or public settings. On the level of contents, scriptures can be illustrated in the form of arts. To illustrate, scriptural performance as words can be found in the act of reading through the Bible as part of a ritual or otherwise. On the other hand, scriptural performance as contents appears in the form of song, drama or cinema. In the process, the performance of the Bible as words is conventionally under the authority of religious leaders, while the performance of the Bible as contents is contingent on the creativity of the artist (pp. 141–42).

Lastly, the iconic aspect touches on the symbolic representation of scriptures (pp. 142–43). As Watts explains, religious people have a keen desire to make scriptures ostensibly distinguishable from other secular books in concrete terms. Probably the best example of iconic scripture can be found in a well-embellished Bible with regard to its color, size, and/or substance. Specifically, a black, large, or leather-bound Bible symbolically conveys the significance of the Bible as a sacred text. Displaying a large Bible on a podium gives weighty meaning to ritual by emphasizing its unparalleled importance as a sacred text.

In recent years, there arises a new tendency to reexamine the Bible from the vantage point of performance studies. Terry Giles and William Doan adamantly suggest that some of the materials in the Hebrew Bible were vibrantly recited in front of an audience (Giles and Doan 2008, p. 273). Likewise, David Rhoads reconstructs the New Testament writings as records of "performance literature—either as transcriptions of prior oral compositions or as written compositions designed for oral performance" at a communal level (Rhoads 2006, p. 119). It has been further observed in the field of Q studies that the sayings of Jesus were, by nature, oral performance (Horsley 2006). Thus, performance studies within biblical studies make sure that the scriptures, both Jewish and Christian, at the outset were performed in various ways.

Out of the three dimensions, the current study turns its attention to the performative dimension of the Christian scriptures in a Korean milieu. Perhaps the best benefit from Watts's theory is that it enables us to look more closely at scriptural performance at two different levels: the performance of the scriptures as *words* and as *contents*. Prior to analyzing diverse performances of the Bible in the Korean context, it is important to clarify the underlying assumption that Watts's theory can be rendered all the more complicated, given that performing the Bible calls for sensibilities of cultural differences in a society. That is to say, the idiosyncratic nature of Korean Christianity makes the performance of the Bible extraordinary. The reason for this is that the performative dimension goes hand in hand with the semantic dimension. As a corollary, the performance of the Bible in Korea has long been appropriated to Korean societal and cultural values. This indicates that performing the Bible in the *Sitz-im-Leben* of South Korea would and should demonstrate how Koreans understand the Bible in contemporary society. For instance, performing the scriptures is to be understood in the context of Korean religions such as Shamanism, Buddhism, Confucianism (Wang 2009, p. 41). It is my contention in the present study that the performative dimension of the scriptures has flourished alongside their semantic dimension in the context of South Korea.

I will explore scriptural performance in the Korean context in three stages. To begin with, I will delve into the performative dimension of scriptures as words. I find it interesting that thoroughly reading (and listening to) the Bible in a holistic and collective manner has gained popularity. Next, I will investigate the performative dimension of scriptures as contents in song and drama forms, respectively. The Bible's musical and dramatic representations bring the cultural and social imaginations of Korean Christianity to light. Finally, I will re-examine the implications of the performance of the Bible at the semantic level. Henceforth, it is suggested that performing the scriptures in the Korean context calls for a semantic analysis as well.

2. Performing the Scriptures as *Words*: The Korean Way of Thoroughly Reading (and Listening to) the Bible

In this section, I will probe the ways in which Korean Christians read (and listen to) the Bible in its entirety, which is called *TongDok* (통독) in Korean. *TongDok* can be simply defined as a Christian way of reading through the Bible from cover to cover. As mentioned above, the Jewish and Christian scriptures were originally recited before audiences. *TongDok* may well be seen as a continuation of the Jewish and Christian liturgical readings of the scriptures. However, it should be remembered that Western missionaries rarely, if ever, introduced such a Jewish and Christian oral performance to Korean Christians. When seen in this way, *TongDok* is undoubtedly a unique tradition in the history of Korean Christianity.

Let us take a brief look at the *TongDok* tradition in the history of Korean Christianity in a narrow and broad context. In a narrow context, Yohan Yoo adeptly introduces the public reading of the Bible in critical engagement with the history of early Korean Protestantism (Yoo 2006, pp. 230–32). Yoo traces the origin of *TongDok* to the revival meetings in the early 20th century. Studying the Bible in a collective mode was central to the revival meetings in early Korean churches. It is significant to remember that the Pyongyang Great Revival of 1907, an epoch-making event in the history of Korean Christianity, initially took the shape of a Bible study meeting (Min 2007, pp. 287–308). The Great Revival meetings took both reading aloud and listening to the Bible very seriously, encouraging Christians to feel the pangs of conscience at their sins in the act of reading and listening (Yoo 2006, p. 230). Fundamental to the revival meetings was a religious performance of vociferously reading and listening to the Bible. In a broad context, Yoo also argues that the Christian ritual of reading the Bible in a public setting is closely interlocked with other Korean religions (Yoo 2006, p. 231). Korean Buddhism and Confucianism alike have traditionally deemed it pivotal to blatantly recite the scriptures in public. To illustrate, reciting the *Maha Prajna Paramita Hrdaya Sutra* (반야심경) or the *Vajracchedika Prajna Paramita Sutra* (금강경) has been considered as a popular devotional practice in the Buddhist tradition. Likewise, reading the *Thousand Character Classic* (천자문) or the textbook of the *Early Learning* (소학) aloud has been an important pedagogical practice in the Confucian tradition. Thus, a brief survey of the historical origin and religious background of the performance of loudly reading through the Bible in a public environment helps us scrutinize the newly emerging religious practice of *TongDok*.

In recent years, Byungho Zoh has been arguably the most well-known advocate for *TongDok* in South Korea. Outside liturgical settings, Zoh elaborates on *TongDok* as an endeavor to read the Bible thoroughly (with as little interruption as possible), primarily for the sake of holistic comprehension (Zoh 2012, p. 137). He deliberately makes a marked contrast between an expository method of preaching the Word of God and a comprehensive method of reading it. He adamantly asserts that Korean Christianity has recently shifted its focus from expositional preaching to thorough reading (pp. 132–33). When it comes to the way of understanding the Bible, he labels the former a Western and analytical approach, and the latter an Eastern and synthetic approach (p. 137). To put it otherwise, he understands *TongDok* as an Eastern method based on integration of knowledge, in stark contrast with the expository sermon as a Western method for the dissection of knowledge. To illustrate this further, he takes as an example the case of a Korean pastor currently eager to broadcast *TongDok* at the ecclesial level, who used to read aloud the Confucian scriptures in *Seodang*—a traditional Korean Confucian school in a smaller village—in his youth (p. 134). Wang notes: "The tradition of reading 'Four Books and Three Classics of Confucianism' (四書五經) was newly changed into a custom of reading and memorizing the words of the Bible" (Wang 2009, p. 45). As noted above, it is important to remember that the public reading of scriptures in Korea has traditionally been regarded as a religious convention in the approach to sacred texts.

In Zoh's estimation, thorough listening is as equally important as thorough reading on the assumption that the first is supplemental to the second for the purpose of a holistic understanding of the Bible. If such is the case, thorough listening has good reason to take the place of thorough reading on the part of modern Christians who are extremely busy with work but enthusiastic about understanding the Bible in an audible manner, at the very least. Nowadays, it is not hard to find a special conference in which those Christians devoted to the comprehension of the Bible get together to finish listening to the entirety of the scriptures within a few days. In today's highly technologically advanced society, it comes as no surprise that applications are available through the Google Play and Apple Store services. All in all, thorough listening, on a par with thorough reading, stays at the cutting edge of a comprehensive understanding of the Bible in Korean context, albeit in an individualistic mode.

So far, we have succinctly reviewed the performative dimension of the Bible as words through the example of *TongDok* as a Korean Christian way of reading and listening to the Bible as a whole. It is intriguing to observe that the performative dimension has shifted from its Christian ritual as a form of Bible study to a modus operandi of understanding the Bible outside ritual settings. In the beginning, the public reading of the scriptures was performed in the middle of revival meetings as part of the Christian ritual. The underlying implication is that the communal performance of reading the scriptures constitutes the most significant part of Bible study. Apart from a liturgical setting, *TongDok* has recently been recognized as a holistic way to comprehend the Bible by dint of an either visible or audible sense, especially on an individual, rather than collective, level. Overall, an important point to bear in mind is that the performative dimension of *TongDok* has a closer connection to the long-standing traditions of Korean religions that stress the practice of vociferously reading scriptures in a public space.

3. Performing the Scriptures as *Contents*: the Korean Way of Singing the Bible

In addition to performing the scriptures as words, Korean Christianity concentrates on performing the scriptures as contents in artistic ways. Above all, the present study concerns the Korean Christian way of singing the scriptures. I draw specific attention to *pansori* (판소리)—a Korean traditional way of singing—through which we run into the distinct features of Korean musical performance of the Bible. The words *pan* (판) and *sori* (소리) signify a public space and sound, respectively. Taken together, *pansori* means to sing in an open area such as a public square or market. *Pansori* consists of a combined performance of both a vocalist and drummer. The performance of a singer involves *chang* (창 singing), *aniri* (아니리 narration) or *sasol* (사설 narration), and *ballim* (발림 gestures). In correspondence, that of a drummer is made up of the beating of a traditional Korean drum and shouting words in interactions with the singer. *Pansori* is *ipso facto* a type of dramatic music, namely, a melodic unfolding of a story, in a vibrant mode (Kim 2008, p. 45).

As Kyung-hee Kim points out, it is interesting that *pansori* retains the musical elements of Korean Shamanism in the Southern area (p. 45). A shaman would dedicate a song to divine beings in the midst of ritual with the result that it could entertain the audience simultaneously. In other words, *pansori* derives its origin from a shaman's performance (Yang 2013, pp. 48–49). Surprisingly, *pansori*, the Korean traditional musical performance, has recently had occasion to transfer to the other religion than Shamanism: that is, Christianity, as it has rapidly grown in Korean culture.

Perhaps the best example is the *pansori* entitled *Jesus' Story* (예수전), which was originally performed by Dong Jin Park (1916–2003). The *pansori* of *Jesus' Story* is a ground-breaking work in the history of Korean traditional music. Remember that there had been only five extant works around the time when the *pansori* of *Jesus' Story* came into being—namely, *Chunhyangga* (춘향가 a love story between a noble man and the daughter of a courtesan), *Simcheongga* (심청전 a filial story about the daughter of a blind man), *Heungbuga* (흥부가 a moral story about a wealthy wicked older brother and a poor kind younger brother), *Sugungga* (수궁가 a humorous story about a sharp-witted rabbit and a deceitful turtle), and *Jeokbyeokga* (절벽가 a military story about Chinese heroes). When Park started performing the *pansori* of *Jesus' Story* in 1969, many (though not all) critics spoke poorly of this innovative enterprise to embody Christianity in a Korean way (Yi 2009, pp. 311–17). Specifically, the Christian *pansori* was initially quite provocative to both *pansori* experts and conservative Christians. *Pansori* specialists did not believe that the *pansori* of *Jesus' Story* conveyed a set of traditional Korean emotions such as *han* (한 the Korean description of abysmal pain), *jeong* (정 the Korean description of mutual love), and *heung* (흥 the Korean description of indefatigable exhilaration) through the platform of western religion (cf. Park 1993, p. 15; Joh 2004, pp. 152–53). Meanwhile, stubborn believers were suspicious of the indigenized expression of Christianity as represented by the so-called Christian *pansori* for fear that it might distort the alleged essence of Christianity. In spite of all this, there has been a recent tendency to look positively at the rendezvous between Korean traditional culture and western religion in the sense that it has generated a third space in which both can flourish, expanding the regime of one into that of the other.

Keeping this in mind, I turn my attention to the narrative structure of the *pansori* of Jesus' Story. Reportedly, the version of the *pansori* tale of Jesus was originally written by Tae Ik Joo, a dramatist, and composed and, presumably, slightly re-written by Park. This can be confirmed by my personal interview with Yang Sook Kim as the director of the Dong Jin Park *Pansori* Training Center. The work is divided into two parts: the first is concerned with the story of Jesus' birth and the second is with the story of his passion, death, and resurrection. Apparently, the first is based on stories drawn from the Gospels of Matthew and Luke and the second on the four canonical gospels of the New Testament. As the title *Jesus' Story* literally indicates, the *pansori* has an increased focus on his life itself for the sake of brevity.

As suggested above, the *pansori* of Jesus's Story remains loyal to the storylines of the New Testament gospels in general terms. Still, a closer examination reveals that the work encompasses the *Sitz-im-Leben* of Korean Christians such that it becomes recognizable as a by-product of Korean contextual theology (Yang 2013). At the very beginning, the *pansori* of *Jesus' Story* undertakes to situate the narratives of Jesus' birth in a broader Asian context by creating a stark contrast between ancient kings in Asia and Jesus in Palestine. Ancient Asian kings' births are described as noble ones, with the emergence of colorful rainbows, blue and brown dragons, and pairs of phoenixes, all of which represent the magnificence of heroes in Asian traditions and culture. By comparison, Jesus' birth is depicted as the humble birth of the savior descending from heaven to earth. However, it is noteworthy to mention that the emphasis for the current study is not that the *pansori* of *Jesus' Story* makes a distinction between ancient Asian kings and Jesus in terms of their birth narratives, but that it attempts to reinterpret Jesus' birth against the ancient Asian cultural background.

Furthermore, the *pansori* of *Jesus' Story* paints his birth and passion with sorrow in such a way that it can evoke sympathy among the audience for his wretched life. On the one hand, a greatly expanded elaboration of Joseph and Mary's journey to a place of delivery accentuates their miserable life. It is remarkable that *jinyangjo* (진양조), the slowest rhythm of *pansori*, is employed to express the dejection of Jesus' mother (Kim 2008, p. 34). In a similar fashion, the soliloquy from Jesus' father indicates his despair over the impoverished birth of Jesus in the form of *aniri* or storytelling: "How regrettable and mortifying it is that the Messiah was born among livestock in a foreign land". Strikingly, even a donkey in the manger addresses the irony that the greatest savior is about to be born in such a shabby place. On the other hand, the *pansori* of *Jesus' Story* describes Jesus' carrying of the cross up to Golgotha more scrupulously than the four gospels, especially in *jinyangjo*, to stress his suffering in an elongated manner. In my assessment, the portrait of Jesus' birth and passion as sorrowful, both consciously and unconsciously, transmits the emotion of *han*, or appalling grief, to the Korean audience.

What is interesting is that the *pansori* of *Jesus' Story* understands the abandonment of Jesus' followers immediately after the crucifixion from the perspective of *jeong*, or mutual affection. Park regretfully comments that all the crowd and Jesus' disciples turn their backs on the crucified Jesus, which reflects the sheer lack of *jeong*. In the scene that immediately ensues, Park's praise of the dauntless action of Joseph of Arimathea and Nicodemus to bury Jesus insinuates that their intrepidity conveys a type of emotion translatable as an abundance of *jeong* in the semantics of Korean culture. For the most part, the *pansori* of *Jesus' Story* signals Korean emotions such as *han* and *jeong* in a static mode.

However, it would be too rash to understand Korean emotions at a static level alone. By way of illustration, the use of Korean words of encouragement such as *eolssiguna* (얼씨구나) and *jeolssiguna* (절씨구나) demonstrates a way of expressing passionate emotion called *heung*, or the Korean ingrained emotion of jubilation, in a dynamic mode. For instance, the shepherds exclaim with great joy as soon as they find the infant Jesus in a manger, saying *eolssiguna* (얼씨구나) and *jeolssiguna* (절씨구나). In a similar vein, the women in the empty tomb utter the greatest happiness of finding the resurrected Jesus, using the same Korean words. In this way, such interjections as *eolssiguna* (얼씨구나) and *jeolssiguna* (절씨구나)—comparable to הנה (behold) in Hebrew, ἰδού (behold) in Greek or ἀμήν ἀμήν (verily, verily) in Greek—bespeak a kind of unshakable exuberance in the Korean semantics of emotion.

It is also worth noting that the rhythm of *jungjungmori* (중중모리) is deliberately designed for a delightful mood, such that both shepherds in the birth scene and women in the resurrection scene are motivated to jubilantly dance, ironically in adverse circumstances (Kim 2008, p. 37). As can be seen above, the *pansori* of *Jesus' Story* discloses a wide range of Korean emotions in both static and dynamic manners.

Apart from the Korean cultural background and emotion, the *pansori* of *Jesus' Story* runs parallel to the social and political context of Korea under the long shadow of the Japanese colonial empire (1910–1945). There is a sufficient reason for assuming that Park is well aware of the colonial situation of the New Testament in that he mentioned the presence of empire in the birth and passion narratives and described the Jews as "colonial subjects" in the passion narrative. More often than not, the work under consideration substantially concerns the desires of the so-called *Minjung*—equivalent to the Greek term ὄχλος—which denotes those who are socially, culturally, or economically alienated from the dominant society, in the Korean context (Ahn 1993, pp. 167–70). When viewed from a *Minjung* theological perspective, the *pansori* of *Jesus' Story* betokens the situation of *Minjung* in the form of *aniri*. As an example, let us consider the conversation between anonymous characters in the beginning. A *Minjung* despondently remarks that s/he had better die than live under imperialist oppression. In correspondence, another *Minjung* proclaims hope for a bright future yet to be created by the long-awaited Messiah. In this conversation, the Messiah is presented as the one who emancipates the *Minjung* from the bondage of suppression, both politically and economically. Similarly, a lengthy conversation between shepherds in the birth narrative underscores their perennial expectations for the savior from oppressions under the domination of a series of empires (Yang 2013, p. 116). This emphasis on harsh repression and hope for the future brings to the fore the liberating message of the *pansori* of *Jesus' Story*.

All things considered, Park has established Christian identity by performing the story of Jesus through the Korean traditional musical medium of *pansori*. Regarding identity formation, performance may be mistakenly taken to mean that it reiterates the same identity across a range of temporal and spatial scales. This position assumes that Park's dramatic and musical performance repetitiously reaffirms what was believed to be Christian identity in the first century Mediterranean world. This being the case, the performance of *pansori* may well be supposed to repeat the very Christian identity that was originally embedded within the Christian scriptures. However, I would rather posit a quite different notion that performance in a specific context makes a difference in the construction of identity. To elaborate on this point further, Christian identity is, to some extent, contingent on scriptural performance (Lieu 2004, p. 21). Overall, Christian identity can be considered as either shaping or being shaped by the scriptures, depending on whether one takes a static or dynamic perspective. Likewise, Christian identity in Korean context molds and is molded by Christian *pansori* in a static and dynamic mode, respectively. Even though both perspectives may be equally possible, I emphasize the latter over the former to concentrate on the construction of Korean Christianity by the performance of the *pansori* of *Jesus' Story*. Taking a dynamic perspective, I am convinced that Christian *pansori* creates Christian identity in the context of Korea rather than copying its original identity. Needless to say, Park's performance of the *pansori* of *Jesus' Story* is an attempt to contextualize Christian identity within both the range of Korean emotions and the *Umwelt* of Korea through the history of colonialism and imperialism (cf. Gifford 2008). Along these lines, I believe that Park will also have performed a Korean version of Christian identity in ongoing interactions with his anonymous audiences, who were concerned about their life context. I go further by arguing that the performative dimension collaborates with the semantic dimension, particularly when Christianity migrates from West to East.

4. Performing the Scripture as *Contents*: the Korean Way of Dramatizing the Bible

Up until now, I have investigated an artistic way of performing the Bible at the individual level through the *pansori* of *Jesus's Story*. In the current section, I will explore a Korean way of performing the Bible at the communal level by investigating bibliodrama, or an improvised play created by imaginative engagement with biblical stories (Pitzele 1998, p. 11). Let us elucidate the meaning of bibliodrama for the moment. Through his publication *Sachbuch Bibliodrama: Praxis und Theorie*, Gerhard M. Martin opens the new possibility of turning a biblical narrative into an extemporaneous drama through a process of voluntary interactions between participants (Martin 2001). For the sake of clarity, it is helpful to make a clear-cut distinction between sacred drama and bibliodrama. Distinct from sacred drama, as a rehearsed play based on a script, bibliodrama is an improvised play built on the interpretation of every participant in a biblical narrative (Koh 2016, pp. 8–9). Bibliodrama invites real readers to engage in the narrative world of the Bible through their creative performance.

Having said that, it is important to clarify the interpretive framework operative in of bibliodrama. In the words of Peter A. Pitzele, it is commensurate with midrashic interpretation, in which it is intended to read between the lines in pursuit of meaning (pp. 11–12). Like midrashic interpretation, the interpretation of bibliodrama engages ceaselessly with both the context of the text and that of real readers. In marked contrast to the traditional and mainstream biblical interpretation focused on the text and its context in search of the authorial intent, bibliodrama places more emphasis on real readers and their context in quest of the lived meaning of the Bible in today's society. Bibliodrama makes the best use of gaps between the text and readers, in which a scintillating conversation takes place between them. The final result is that bibliodrama performs the surplus of meaning enacted by readers' keenly imaginative engagement with the Bible. In this regard, bibliodrama is, by nature, performative.

Some Korean theologians in the fields of practical theology, in general and pastoral counseling in particular, have introduced bibliodrama to those interested in the lived meanings of the scriptures in ecclesial settings in a way that incorporates the skills of psychodrama into the concerns of pastoral counseling (Koh 2016, pp. 1–2; cf. Kim and Hwang 2018). Se Jun Kim and Hun Young Hwang are right to impute the unforeseen emergence of bibliodrama to difficult situations in life in South Korea, which call on Christians to have a dynamic encounter with the Bible as a source of meaning (p. 11). To illustrate, many—though not all—Christians have trouble finding answers to the problems in their lives by depending solely on the authority of pastors (Sohn 2010, pp. 431–34). Rather, Christians themselves desire to more contextually and critically take part in the communal process of biblical interpretation in their unfavorable conditions, being vulnerable to life crises such as job loss, divorce, illness, death, and the like. The key point here is that bibliodrama in Korea performs the Bible as it pertains to healing through the power of scriptures. Bibliodrama serves to debunk the suffering in today's life in ingenious engagement with that in biblical narrative. By way of comparison, a sheer confrontation of real suffering can assist Christians in finding a solution in biblical story. In other words, while embodying the characters of biblical narrative, the performers interpret the event of the Bible with the purpose of discovering its meaning, which is eventually projected to their real life. In the process, bibliodrama leads to a potential for a message of restoration through communal interactions; sometimes suffering together, other times comforting together. This means that bibliodrama aims to empower the recovery of the Christian community from the agonies of life at the collective level.

In other words, bibliodrama offers an imaginary space in which participants can discover their problems in the past and understand them anew by assuming a role in dramatic settings (Kim and Hwang 2018, pp. 13–15). For instance, a bibliodrama based on the story of the prodigal son (Luke 15:11–32) would enable participants to recognize their traumatic experiences of life in the scene of eating pods for pigs. Alternately, an unscripted role-play as the father of the prodigal son would empower a participant struggling with his/her own father in real life to comprehend him in a drastically different way. In this manner, an impromptu performance can facilitate a transformed understanding of the problems in life.

In addition, bibliodrama can extend itself to social issues beyond the problems of individuals that are primarily relevant to a family setting. A striking example can be drawn from a special bibliodrama that was devised for the citizens grieving over the *Sewol* ferry disaster. Over the past few years, South Korean society has observed its most socially traumatic calamity, which resulted in the loss of 304 innocent lives, including passengers and crew members, on 16 April 2014. The sinking of the *Sewol* ferry has so far inspired Korean society to cast aspersions on the captain and crew who abandoned the ship and the drowning passengers, the Korean government, which took no immediate action to rescue passengers from drowning, and the mass media, which attempted to downplay the social and political consequences of this tragic event. Along these lines, a momentous bibliodrama entitled *Survivors* was invented to heal some of the citizens who had suffered severely from this societal traumatic experience, three months after the *Sewol* ferry disaster.[1] Terry and Done remark: "Theorists of social drama use the language and concepts of performance and drama as a way of examining social conflict, social crises, and the ways performance impacts social unity and conflict resolution" (Giles and Doan 2008, p. 275). As is the case with *Survivors*, the performance of the Bible could and should have social and cultural repercussions upon both Korean churches and society.

In summary, I have accounted for the performative nature of bibliodrama in the following way. First, the dramatic performance of the Bible, though a local, rather than national, phenomenon in Korean churches, transforms Korean Christians from passive readers to active participants in the biblical narrative.[2] Bibliodrama galvanizes Christians into the creative process of making meaning out of the Bible as a sacred text. Second, bibliodrama as an improvised play encourages Korean Christians to utilize the power of their imagination so that the Bible can address them as a living text and vice versa. This imaginary performativity of the Bible gives rise to a surplus of meaning that cannot be expected from traditional biblical interpretation. Third, bibliodrama seeks to respond to the conditions of Korean Christians susceptible to unexpected life risks. Performing the Bible in a modern context can prompt Christians to find a message about recovery from wounds by identifying themselves with certain characters in a biblical narrative. Fourth, bibliodrama hints at the possibility that the Bible constitutes a social cure to an injustice-stricken society. The spontaneous nature of bibliodrama helps catalyze the sensibility that one is disposed to interpret the Bible in a manner that assumes greater accountability for societal problems. Finally and most importantly, we should not forget that bibliodrama is a collective performance in the creation of meaning from the scriptures. With the help of bibliodrama, biblical interpretation is no longer dominated by the religious elite, but rather is equally performed by the common people who possess their own as-yet-undeciphered life stories.

5. Concluding Remarks

According to the categories suggested by Watts, we have thus far explored scriptural performance in South Korea in two ways: one at the level of *words* and the other at the level of *contents*. It is observable in the Korean context that the performance of the Bible at the level of contents gives greater freedom than at the level of words. Regarding the current project, the most important point to stress is that Watts' theory on scriptural performance asks for its modification in a way that allows us to reconsider the cultural differences between Western and Eastern Christianity. The specificity of the *Sitz-im-Leben* of Korean Christianity requires us to be more cognizant of how its religious, cultural, and social values operate in scriptural performance. It is the contention here that the adaptation of Christianity to Korean soil renders the performative dimension all the more semantic.

---

[1]	The *Survivors*—as an attempt for Christian to be involved in social issues—was held in the 100th Anniversary Memorial Church on 3 June 2014. Available online: http://kimdt.net/html/reference/reference02.php?id=754&code=board9&cate=&gfile=view.

[2]	For this, see the sources available from the Bibliodrama & Dramatherapy Institute. Available online: http://kimdt.net/html/main/main.php.

At first, we have seen the performative dimension of the scriptures as words through the example of reading the Bible completely in a collective mode. This Korean method of reading the scriptures has its origin in public reading in the earliest Korean Christian revival meetings. In recent years, the performance of thoroughly reading the Bible has evolved into thoroughly listening to it. It is important to remember that the Korean religious traditions of publicly reading the scriptures, as is the case with Confucianism and Buddhism, have a mediate or immediate impact on the performance of thoroughly reading, and consequently listening to, the Bible in the context of Korean Christianity.

Next, we have probed the performative dimension of the scriptures as contents at the individual level by closely examining the *pansori* of *Jesus' Story*. Park's performance of the Bible in the form of *pansori* reveals that a group of Korean conventional emotions—such as *han* (a feeling of appalling agony), *jeong* (a feeling of reciprocal affection), and *heung* (a feeling of unflagging excitement)—have a Korean version of the gospel under their command. Culturally, the performance of singing the Bible in South Korea therefore implies that Christian *pansori* simultaneously creates and is created by Christian identity.

Finally, we have scrutinized the performative dimension of the scriptures as contents at the collective level, as can be seen from bibliodrama. Dramatizing the Bible indicates that the performance of the Bible can be rendered more participatory, inventive, contextual, social, and collective in consideration of its extemporaneous nature. Lucidly, bibliodrama functions as a medium through which to reinterpret the social issues of South Korea as Christians wrestle with their life problems. In this context, bibliodrama is a communal performance that makes shared meaning of the Bible in a rapidly changing society.

Overall, we have had time to evaluate the performative dimension of the Christian scriptures in conjunction with their semantic dimension. We have observed that the Korean ways of performing the Bible at the level of words and contents are essentially deeply rooted in the Korean means of signifying it. The specific context of South Korea—whether religious, cultural, or social—alerts us to the performed transformation of the semantic range of the long-standing Christian tradition. In the long term, Christianity is such a global religion that it provokes a more complex analysis of its scriptural performance in its widely differing range of semantics. As Paul Gifford suggests, a survey of the performative dimension in the Korean context nudges scholars of theology and religion in the direction of intercultural and/or postcolonial studies (Gifford 2008, pp. 204–5). More specifically, the differences in age, status, gender, etc. would and should significantly affect how the Bible can be performed as a sacred text both in Korean Christianity and beyond (Morris 1996, pp. 380–82).

Funding: This research was supported (in party) by the Yonsei University Future-Leading Research Initiative of 2018.

Conflicts of Interest: The author declares no conflicts of interest.

References

Ahn, Byung Mu. 1993. Jesus and People (Minjung). In *Asian Faces of Jesus*. Edited by Rusiah S. Sugirtharajah. Maryknoll: Orbis Books, pp. 163–72.

Austin, John Langshaw. 1975. *How to Do Things with Words*. Cambridge: Harvard University Press.

Gifford, Paul. 2008. The Bible in Africa: A Novel Usage in Africa's New Churches. *Bulletin of the School of Oriental and African Studies* 71: 203–19. [CrossRef]

Giles, Terry, and William Doan. 2008. Performance Criticism of the Hebrew Bible. *Religion Compass* 2/3: 273–86. [CrossRef]

Horsley, Richard, ed. 2006. *Oral Performance, Popular Tradition, and Hidden Transcript in Q*. Leiden and Boston: Brill.

Joh, Wonhee Anne. 2004. The Transgressive Power of Jeong: A Postcolonial Hybridization of Christology. In *Postcolonial Theologies: Divinity and Empire*. Edited by Catherin Keller, Michael Nausner and Mayra Rivera. St. Louis: Chalice Press, pp. 149–63.

Kim, Kyung-hee. 2008. Theory of Pansori. In *Pansori*. Edited by Yong-shik Lee. Seoul: The National Center for Korean Traditional Performing Arts, pp. 30–69. (In Korean)

Kim, Se Jun, and Hun Young Hwang. 2018. *Bible-Reviving Bibliodrama*. Seoul: Institute of Contemporary Drama and Healing. (In Korean)

Koh, Won Seok. 2016. Bibliodrama as New Approach to Christian Education. *Christian Education & Information Technology* 48: 1–31. (In Korean)

Lieu, Judith. 2004. *Christian Identity in the Jewish and Graeco-Roman World*. Oxford: Oxford University Press.

Martin, Gerhard M. 2001. *Sachbuch Bibliodrama: Praxis und Theorie*. Stuttgart: Kohlhammer.

Min, Kyungbae. 2007. *Korean Christian Church History*. Seoul: Yonsei University Press. (In Korean)

Morris, Leslie A. 1996. Reading the Bible in a Javanese Village. *Journal of Southeast Asian Studies* 27: 374–86. [CrossRef]

Park, Andrew Sung. 1993. *The Wounded Heart of God: The Asian Concept of Han and the Christian Doctrine of Sin*. Nashville: Abingdon Press.

Pitzele, Peter A. 1998. *Scripture Windows: Towards a Practice of Bibliodrama*. Los Angeles: Torah Aura Productions.

Rhoads, David M. 2006. Performance Criticism: An Emerging Methodology in Second Testament Studies. *Biblical Theology Bulletin* 36: 118–33. [CrossRef]

Smith, Wilfred Cantwell. 1971. The Study of Religion and the Study of the Bible. *Journal of the American Academy of Religion* 39: 131–40, Reprinted 1989 in *Rethinking Scripture: Essays from a Comparative Perspective*. Edited by M. Levering. Albany: SUNY Press, pp. 18–28. [CrossRef]

Sohn, Sung-Hyun. 2010. The Educational Possibilities of Bibliodrama. *Christian Education & Information Technology* 27: 429–56. (In Korean)

Wang, Tai Il. 2009. Performing the Scripture: Understanding the Bible from Korean Biblical Hermeneutics. In *Mapping and Engaging the Bible in Asian Cultures: Congress of the Society of Asian Biblical Studies 2008 Seoul Conference*. Edited by Yeong Mee Lee and Yoon-jong Yoo. Seoul: The Christian Literature Society of Korea.

Watts, James W. 2006. The Three Dimensions of Scriptures. *Postscripts: The Journal of Sacred Texts and Contemporary Worlds* 2: 135–59, Reprinted in 2013 *Iconic Books and Texts*. Edited by James W. Watts. London: Equinox, pp. 9–32. [CrossRef]

Yang, Jayhoon. 2013. *A Theological Landscape of Pansori*. Seoul: The Christian Literature Society of Korea. (In Korean)

Yi, Yu Jin. 2009. A Survey of the *Pansori* Jesus Story. *Journal of Pansori* 27: 311–55. (In Korean)

Yoo, Yohan. 2006. Public Scripture Reading Rituals in Early Korean Protestantism: A Comparative Perspective. *Postscripts: The Journal of Sacred Texts and Contemporary Worlds* 2: 226–40. [CrossRef]

Zoh, Byoungho. 2012. Korean Church and the History of *TongDok* Bible. *Monthly Ministry* 427: 132–37. (In Korean)

Article

Minjung Theology in Contemporary Korea: Liberation Theology and a Reconsideration of Secularization Theory

Andrew Eungi Kim

Division of International Studies, Korea University, Sungbuk-gu Anam-dong 5-ga 1, Seoul 136-701, Korea; aekim@korea.ac.kr

Received: 7 November 2018; Accepted: 12 December 2018; Published: 14 December 2018

Abstract: The Sewol Ferry tragedy in April 2014 has drawn a renewed attention to the role of religion in South Korea. Theologians and religiously-motivated NGOs in Korea at the time and thereafter have called for the need for religion, and religious organizations, to become more actively involved with societal needs, especially after disasters, to help alleviate their pain by providing relief aid and counselling. Such calls for the greater involvement of religion in relief efforts have coincided with Pope Francis' repeated calls for the Catholic Church's greater involvement in social affairs on behalf of the poor and the underprivileged. This paper contends that these developments in and outside of Korea provide an opportune time to renew discussion on oft-misunderstood liberation theology. This is because the latter's advocacy of an interpretation of the teachings of Jesus Christ from the perspective of the poor and the marginalized for the purpose of alleviating unjust economic, social, or political conditions is as compelling today as it was some 60 years ago when it first arose. The paper offers a reassessment of the role of religion in light of liberation theology, arguing that religion can make itself more relevant to people's lives today by engaging more actively with social issues. The paper will pay special attention to liberation theology in the Korean context, namely *minjungshinhak* or "people's theology." The paper also discusses the implications of liberation theology for secularization theory, arguing, among others, that the former refutes the "decline of religion" thesis of the latter, since liberation theology manifests a different role of religion in contemporary society rather than its diminishing significance.

Keywords: liberation theology; *minjung* theology; *minjungshinhak*; *minjung*; han; integral mission; secularization; secularization theory; critical theory; metaphysical pathos; ecclesiastical social responsibility

---

1. Introduction

> *... with human suffering you can't be neutral*

> Pope Francis

The sinking of the Sewol Ferry on 16 April 2014, which resulted in the deaths of more than 300 people, most of whom were high school students, has prompted the country as a whole to reflect on what went wrong and what should be done to change for the better (see Suh and Kim 2017; Woo et al. 2015). The ferry tragedy impacted many spheres of Korean society and the religious sector was no exception. In response to the tragedy, some churches and religiously-motivated NGOs did provide medical assistance and daily meals as well as relief aid to the victims' family members staying at the memorial altar set up at the nearest port from where the ferry sank. These groups also provided similar volunteer services at the "tent village," a row of tents set up by the victims' family members on a street in central Seoul near the Blue House, the executive office and official residence of the President.

Also, various religiously-motivated NGOs have been actively participating in a coalition of NGOs which called on the government to pass a special bill to empower a special fact-finding commission that will investigate and indict those responsible for the ferry tragedy. More importantly perhaps, Korean theologians and religiously-motivated NGOs have called for churches to get more actively involved in responding to societal affairs, including disasters. Such a call for churches' greater involvement in societal affairs in Korea is noteworthy, as church's active involvement in socio-political issues was once a hallmark of Korean Christianity from the early 1960s to the late 1980s, during which the church had been, along with labour unions and student unions, the strongest force for the democratization movement. This means that the call for a greater engagement of religion with societal affairs has been renewed in Korea in earnest for the first time in nearly 30 years.

It was during this post-traumatic period that Pope Francis visited the country in August 2014. For the whole duration of his stay in Korea, the pontiff, who has been an outspoken advocate on behalf of the poor and the underprivileged since becoming the leader of the 1.2 billion-member Catholic community in 2013, wore a yellow-ribbon pin, a commemorative pin for more than 300 people who drowned. On his return flight to Rome, the pope reflected on the incident: "I took [the pin] out of solidarity with them, and after a day, somebody came up to me and said, 'You should take it off; you need to be neutral." I answered this way: "Listen, *with human suffering you can't be neutral.*" His comments and actions in Korea and elsewhere at the time and thereafter have been interpreted by some as amounting to an advocacy of liberation theology. The affinity between Pope Francis and the theology of liberation has been proposed, as he, more than any other of his predecessors, has developed a reputation for showing deep concern for the plight of the poor, for criticizing the economic system that is worsening economic inequality, and for calling on major organizations of society, particularly the Church and the government, to do more to help the poor (Catholic News Service 2013).

Liberation theology, which is a theological movement that began in the 1950s and 1960s in Latin America, advocates an interpretation of the Gospel from the standpoint of the poor and the oppressed, and emphasizes the role of religion in the fight against poverty, injustice, and oppression. Despite criticisms from mainstream theologians for its overly "political interpretation" of the Bible, liberation theology has inspired the rise of other forms of liberation theology, including those fighting for feminist, black, African, and Asian causes, as well as those with specific ethnic focuses. *Minjungshinhak*, literally meaning "people's theology," was developed by Korean theologians in the 1970s, and its emergence was prompted by awareness of the historical and contemporary suffering of the masses (Ahn 1993; Lee 1988a; Suh 1991; Suh 1983b). Historically, Koreans' collective memory, real or imagined, of continual foreign invasions and occupations, particularly the atrocities committed by the Japanese during the Japanese colonial rule (1910–1945), have instilled a strong sense of suffering in the minds of Koreans. More importantly perhaps, the rise of *minjung* theology is owed to the suffering of the masses during the country's industrialization drive from the early 1960s. During this period of rapid industrialization, Korean workers were subjected to artificially low wages and long hours of work, with many laborers working upwards of 70 h a week, under poor working conditions. Any attempt to fight against workers' exploitation was met with harsh punishment, including imprisonment. *Minjung* theology first arose under these circumstances. In the 1980s, *minjung* theology shifted its focus to political issues, lending support to the democratic movement against a succession of authoritarian regimes. In the 1990s and 2000s, theological interests in *minjung* theology relatively waned as the country became more industrialized and democratic. In the face of the changing socio-political reality, *minjung* theology has turned its attention to more contemporary issues, such as socioeconomic polarization and the human rights of foreign migrant workers and marriage migrants (Yoo 2009). It is worth noting that *minjung* theology has inspired many religiously-motivated NGOs, Christian or Buddhist, to collectively serve as a major force in the fight for various causes in Korea (Ro and Park 2010).

Minjung theology and other forms of liberation theology entail, among others, a significant change in Christianity, as religious ideas and knowledge are now being interpreted on behalf of the underprivileged in the realm of the non-sacred. Parallel interpretations found in other world religions, including Buddhism, Hinduism, and Islam, further manifest a new meaning and role of religion in the contemporary world (De la Torre 2008). Liberation theology thus has important implications for secularization theory, particularly the decline of religion thesis of the latter. Liberation theology has rarely been examined in relation to secularization theory, but the ideas extant in liberation theology, for example the use of religious messages in the fight for justice, rejects the decline of religion thesis of secularization theory. By lending religious support to various socio-political causes, liberation theology demonstrates a greater involvement of religion in this-worldly matters on the side of the underprivileged. Such development, of course, does not in any way indicate diminishing significance of religion, but rather the changing role of religion that is more socially concerned and involved.

In view of these observations, this paper first examines the nature of liberation theology, followed by a discussion of Korean liberation theology or *minjungshinhak* (*minjung* theology), both of which warrant a renewed discussion on the role of religion in contemporary settings. The paper also reflects on the implications of liberation theology for secularization theory. The paper closes by examining the implications of liberation theology, particularly its potential role in enhancing the relevance of religion in the contemporary world marked by, despite the overall improvement in living standards, the continuity of poverty, inequality, injustice, and violation of human rights.

2. Rethinking Liberation Theology: A Reassessment of the Role of Religion in Contemporary Settings

Liberation theology is a theological movement that began in the 1950s and 1960s among priests and theologians in Latin America in reaction to abject poverty and social injustice in the region (Gutierrez 1973; Nunez 1985; Segundo 1976; Cone 1975). The theology advocates "an interpretation of Christian faith through the poor's suffering, their struggle and hope, and a critique of society and the Catholic faith and Christianity through the eyes of the poor" (Berryman 1987, p. 4). Liberation theology challenges the passive stance of Christian theology in relation to such issues as poverty, social injustice, and violation of human rights, arguing that Jesus Christ's mission in this world was to fight against injustice and against oppression. Accordingly, liberation theology has criticized economic and social structures which bring about conditions that engender poverty and cause human suffering and indignity. It further argues that religion can be a force for attaining liberation from unjust economic, social, or political conditions, and that salvation should be realized not only in the next world but also in this world as well, so that people are free from suffering.

Liberation theology, as a term that covers various theological movements which interpret the Christian gospel in terms of current needs for promoting justice and human emancipation, thus represents a new system of religion that is conspicuously concerned with political and social problems. In particular, four areas of oppression are especially considered paramount: poverty or economic exploitation of the poor, violation of human rights, racism, and sexual prejudice against women. All liberation theologies—Latin American, feminist, black, African, Asian—represent struggles, the struggles which seek to justify their movements with the revelation of biblical messages. Latin American liberation theology, for example, manifests an understanding of Christian gospel from the experience of the poor (Gutierrez 1973; Nunez 1985; Segundo 1976). It is a critique of economic structures and ideologies that perpetuate conspicuous inequality in Latin America. Feminist theology, including that of "Third World" women, looks for biblical themes that support gender equality, arguing that churches have ignored women's needs and aspirations, taking up on issues such as the "maleness" of deity, the rights of women over their bodies, the role of women in church governance and ministry, and the place of the feminine in worship (Fiorenza 1996; Welch 1985; Isherwood 2004). Black theology in the United States uses the basic biblical theme of liberation to better understand the history of slavery and to protest against the institutionalization and systematization of racism and its cultural impact (Cone 1970, 1975; Hopkins 1989). They rely upon the central message of Exodus and the figure of Jesus in raising "black-consciousness" and its integrative power. African theology is concerned with the interpretation of Christian faith from the perspective of African people and their culture

(See Martey 1993; Bujo 1992; Hood 1990). Similarly, Asian theologians incorporate into Christianity various aspects of their traditions that reflect Asian concerns as well as Asian worldview and way of life (See Sugirtharajah 1994; Pieris 1988; Fabella 1988). Also, there are liberation theologies which have a specific ethnic focus, such as Chicano (Guerrero 1986), Jewish (Ellis 1987), Palestinian (Ateek 2017), Caribbean (Erskine 1981), Hispanic (Elizondo 1983), and Korean, which will be discussed in more detail below.

Scholarly attention to liberation theology relatively waned in the 1990s following the end of the Cold War, as many theologians and scholars assumed that the theology was no longer necessary. It is also true that liberation theology has had its share of criticism. Critics argue that liberation theology "over-politicizes" liberation, making the spiritual or evangelical aspect secondary to socio-political causes (Congregation for the Doctrine of the Faith 1990). Liberation theology is also criticized for making use of various ideas in social sciences without critical caution (Congregation for the Doctrine of the Faith 1990). A related problem is that liberation theology relies too heavily on atheistic Marxist analysis, leading to an unnecessary anti-capitalistic view and an overt emphasis on class struggle. These negative views can be said to have limited the theological and social influence of the theology in many parts of the world. Irrespective of these criticisms, and as many recent works on liberation theology demonstrate, the very conditions that gave rise to liberation theology have persisted in the twenty-first century under democratic capitalism and under the neoliberal economic system (Cooper 2013; Floyd-Thomas and Pinn 2010; Sung 2007). These studies also show the enduring relevance of liberation theology in the struggle against oppression and injustice, be it economic inequality, gender inequality, racial inequality, or sexual inequality, which continues largely unabated in many parts of the world.

It is interesting to note that there is a movement in Protestantism called "integral mission" or "holistic mission", which is similar to liberation theology but is much less known. Integral mission began among Evangelicals in the mid-1960s, and like liberation theology, it rejects conceptions of Christian mission based on dualistic views on evangelism and social involvement (Padilla 2002, 2010; Kirkpatrick 2016).

> God is both the Creator and the Judge of all men. We therefore should share his concern for justice and reconciliation throughout human society and for the liberation of men from every kind of oppression . . . .we express penitence both for our neglect and for having sometimes regarded evangelism and social concerns as mutually exclusive. (Stott 1996, p. 24)

Integral mission understands Christian mission as embracing both evangelism and social responsibility, arguing that they are "inseparable" (Nicholls 1986, p. 81). Like liberation theology, integral mission is committed to improving the life of those living in poverty and to pursuing justice. In achieving these objectives, integral mission calls for greater social involvement on the part of the Church. Since the First International Congress on World Evangelization in 1974 (aka the Lausanne Congress or Lausanne '74), integral mission has been embraced by a large number of evangelicals all across the globe (Kirkpatrick 2016).

What both liberation theology and integral mission represent is, therefore, a "new" interpretation of Christianity that calls for the latter's greater involvement with social issues on behalf of the poor and the oppressed. Another common element is their sensitivity to flagrant social problems and their commitment to active engagement in social reform. The ends may be diverse, for example economic justice or protection of human rights, however, the uniform aim is to rectify secular societal problems through sacred justification and means.

3. Korean Liberation Theology: *Minjungshinhak* ("People's Theology")

As noted above, liberation theology inspired the development of similar theological movements outside the continent. Korean theologians developed their own theology of liberation called *minjungshinhak* or *minjung* theology, literally meaning "people's theology" in the 1970s (Ahn 1993;

Lee 1988a; Suh 1991; Suh 1983b; NCC shinhakyeonguwiwonhoe 1982; Commission on Theological Concerns of the Christian Conference of Asia 1981). Like its counterparts elsewhere, the Korean liberation theology emerged in awareness of the suffering of the masses and in reflection of the role of the church and Christians in alleviating their pains (Kim 1987, pp. 211–21; Suh 1983b, p. 29). As Suh (1991, p. 17) puts it, *minjungshinhak* represents not only "a development of the political hermeneutics of the Gospel in terms of the Korean reality", but also a demand for justice and a more compassionate society.

> What is happening here and now is recognized as 'God's intervention into human history, the work of the Holy Spirit, similar to the event of the Exodus, and we participate in God's work in history and theologize it. This is the work and role of doing *Minjung* theology. (Suh 1983a, p. 3; cited from Kwon and Küster 2018, p. 21)

Central to *minjung* theology are the concepts of *minjung* and *han*. While the term *minjung* can be literally translated as "people," it refers to "those who are oppressed politically, exploited economically, alienated socially, and kept uneducated in cultural and intellectual matters" (Moon 1985, p. 1). As Suh (1983b, pp. 188–89) argues, the "historical Jesus" was also *minjung*, who identified himself as a poor and oppressed person who underwent great ordeals, much like Korean *minjung*. While there is no English equivalent, *han* is often translated as sadness, sorrow, resentment, bitterness, grief, or regret. The term expresses both personal sorrow, such as hunger, poverty, discrimination, or serious illness, and "shared suffering" felt collectively as Koreans throughout history, for example from continual foreign invasions and occupations, including the exceptionally atrocious Japanese occupation (1910–1945) (Kim 2017). Indeed, "the history of the Korean people is a history of oppression, of sadness and frustration, which has given rise to a unique mind-set called *han*", which is a pent-up resentment and despair about the unfairness and injustice of life (Clark 1986, p. 44). And it is the shared suffering of the Korean people to which *minjung* theology pays more attention, especially the *han* felt by Koreans from the early 1960s to the late 1980s, the period during which Koreans were subjected to the harsh reality of rapid industrialization and urbanization, as well as a succession of authoritarian regimes. *Minjung* theology, which was developed during this period, is thus "the theology of *han*, the inner dynamics of the oppressed Korean *minjung*" (Moon 1982, p. 13). The theology represents an ideology and act of protest against *han*, as it has served to legitimize political struggle and social action as a "biblical act." As Suh (1983b, p. 243) argues, until now, Christian theology has been preoccupied with the problem of sin; however, the task of *minjung* theology is to "resolve the *han* of the people," because it is "more meaningful than being forgiven for committing sins." The leading *minjung* theologians, often considered the first generation, or "fathers" of *minjung* theology, including Nam-dong Suh, Byungmu Ahn,[1] David Kwangsun Suh, Yong-bock Kim, and Young-Hak Han, all shared these views on the concepts of *minjung* and *han*.[2]

It can be said that there are three periods of development for *minjung* theology: (1) the developmental period in the 1970s during which theological reflections on current issues were made, with a particular attention focused on the economic suffering of the masses (workers); (2) the 1980s, during which *minjung* theology shifted its focus to the democratization movement; and (3) the 1990s, when *minjung* theology formed an "alliance" with the JPIC Movement after the latter's world convention was held in Seoul, Korea, in March 1990[3] (Lee 2001, p. 44). Byungmu Ahn

---

[1]   Ahn is particularly known for having tried to advance *minjung* theology as not only uniquely Korean (and Asian) but also as a genuine alternative to Western theology.

[2]   These theologians, who laid the foundation for the rise of *minjung* theology in Korea, all studied abroad, especially the United States or Germany, being exposed to liberal and progressive theologies. They rejected, and were markedly different from, the overwhelmingly conservative faith and theology that marked mainstream Korean Christianity at the time, and to a large degree, still does.

[3]   JPIC stands for Justice, Peace, and Integrity of Creation and is a "movement" adopted by the World Council of Churches (WCC) at its Vancouver assembly in 1983. The movement began with the understanding that humanity was faced with a

(Ahn et al. 1993, pp. 9–19) further argues that *minjung* theology comprises of three starting points. The first starting point is *minjung* theology's resistance against the fundamentalism of Korean Christianity, particularly Protestantism; the second is a resistance against dictatorship; and the third is an attempt to "bring together" both Korean and Christian traditions, facilitating a "cultural indigenization" or "Koreanization" of Christianity, as Nam-dong Suh advocated (see Kim 2013).

As noted above, the period during which *minjung* theology first arose in the 1970s was when Korea was undergoing rapid industrialization. The Korean government imposed artificially low wages on workers to attract foreign investment and to maintain price competitiveness in the international market. That meant subjecting workers to long hours of work under poor, grueling working conditions. It was not uncommon for workers to work upwards of 70 hours a week, typically with no or very little overtime pay. What made the lives of the workers even more difficult was the fact that most of them were uprooted from the comfort of the close-knit rural way of life and were new to the impersonal and harsh lifestyle of urban settings. Economic inequality between those who were reaping the early success of the country's industrialization and the working poor was also widespread. Additionally, any type of labour or student activism which attempted to intervene on behalf of the workers was banned and harshly punished. Under these circumstances, *minjung* theology arose as a new form of theology committed to the promotion of justice and to the stoppage of the exploitation and oppression of workers. For example, *minjung* theology in the 1970s provided a theological foundation for the expansion of urban industrial mission (UIM), which began in earnest in the late 1960s (Lee 2001, p. 41). Appalled by both the poor working conditions and violation of human rights taking place at workplaces, those involved in the UIM were progressive pastors and preachers who actually worked at factories among the workers. They were inspired by the theology of "solidarity in suffering," as they shared, and reflected on, the "suffering experience" of those oppressed. *Minjung* theology in the 1970s thus served as a rallying force against the economic exploitation of Korean workers. No wonder then that *minjung* theology became closely associated with both the labor movement and the democratization movement of the 1970s and 1980s. The new theology at the time redefined the role of Christianity in Korea by articulating and sympathizing with the economic and social sufferings of the underprivileged and by championing their rights for better treatment (see Suh 1991; Küster 2010).

Minjung theology in the 1980s shifted its focus to political issues, as the country was, as noted above, under a succession of authoritarian regimes, highlighted by indirect presidential elections in which an electoral college elected presidents (this system was implemented since the 1972 enforcement of the Yushin Constitution by then president Park Chung-hee and continued until 1987, when a direct presidential election was reintroduced). The 1980s was a particularly difficult time politically for the country, as after nearly two decades of authoritarian rule, Park was assassinated in October 1979. But the then army general Chun Doo-hwan carried out a coup d'état in December the same year, prompting more intense pro-democracy rallies in Seoul and other cities. The country's democratic movement culminated in the May 18 Gwangju Democratization Movement in 1980 which, following a military intervention, resulted in a large number of casualties. Chun's presidency was not much different from that of Park Chung-hee, as political opposition was ruthlessly crushed and media censorship continued unabated. It was in this political milieu that a second generation of *minjung* theologians, including Park (1990, 1995), put more effort into finding ways to facilitate the practicality and applicability of *minjung* theology to rapidly changing Korean society. They took issues with not only democratic movements, but also the feminist movement and anti-Americanism, trying to offer theological explanations and, to a certain extent, justifications for these movements. In addition, in spite of the oppressive political milieu, proponents of *minjung* theology, along with "progressive" South

---

crisis and that the church's involvement in worldly affairs was a concern of Christian ethics. The movement called for its member churches to coordinate efforts for justice (taking issues with economic inequality, racism, sexism, and violation of human rights), peace, and integrity of creation (being concerned with environmental protections) (Beyer 1994, pp. 214–16). The movement later expanded to include churches which are not members of the WCC.

Korean theologians, focused on the issue of reunification with North Korea, in the belief that ordinary North Koreans were also suffering from oppression (Kim and Kim 2014, pp. 263–89; Lee 1988b; Han and Kim 2006; Chung 2003). Their engagement with the reunification issue was partly prompted by the realization that the Korean government's monopoly of the issue of reunification had been a major drawback in bringing about peace on the peninsula, and that the whole Korean people, not just the government, are responsible for achieving reunification (Yeon 2000). Inspired by liberation theology, Korean Christianity played an important role in opening the way for non-governmental sectors to provide input to the reunification discussion, which until then had been monopolized by the government.

In the 1990s, as the country's living standard markedly improved and political stability was secured through democracy, it can be said that scholarly and theological interests in *minjung* theology relatively waned. More importantly, the theology experienced a turning point. As Koreans began to enjoy greater material abundance and political freedom, the meanings inherent in the concept of *minjung* became less cogent or relevant, as the Korean people as a whole were now less poor, less exploited, and less oppressed. Faced with this changing socio-political reality, *minjung* theology turned its attention to issues championed by various civic movements, including the human rights of foreign migrant workers and marriage migrants (Yoo 2009). Also, *minjung* theologians realized that in spite of the rapid economic development of the country, there was still a considerable number of Koreans who were economically disadvantaged, many of whom had been victims of the negative impacts of globalization and neoliberalism. In particular, neoliberal economic policies which became prevalent in the wake of the financial crisis in Korea in 1998 led to labor flexibility, producing a large number of irregular workers. This new reality spawned, and still continues to engender, a great economic inequality between regular and irregular workers. And it is this socioeconomic polarization and an intense sense of relative deprivation, which has worsened over the years, to which twenty-first century *minjung* theology has turned its attention (Lee 2018; Kim 2011; Kwon and Küster 2018). The leading research organizations concerned with these issues have been the Korean Minjung Theology Association, the Christian Institute for the 3rd Era, and the Institute of Minjung Theology. The latter two institutes even published scholarly journals solely devoted to the study of *minjung* theology, namely *Sidaewa Minjungshinhak* (Epoch and Minjung Theology) and *Minjunggwashinhak* (Minjung and Theology), which were published between 1994–2009 and 2000–2005, respectively. It is also noteworthy that *minjung* theology in recent years has expanded its focus to issues such as the environment, gender inequality, and inter-religious tensions (Moon 2000; Kang et al. 2010; Kim 2011). Moreover, over the years, *minjung* theology has inspired the rise of not only *minjungbulgyo*, literally meaning people's Buddhism (Han 1986; Beop 1989), but also many religiously-motivated NGOs, Christian or Buddhist, to collectively serve as a major force in the fight for various causes in Korea (Ro and Park 2010). The most prominent ones include, just to name a few, the Catholic Human Rights Committee, Catholic Women Groups Alliance, Christian Alliance for Justice and Peace, Korean Christian Environmental Movement Solidarity, Christian Alliance for the Abolition of Capital Punishment, Buddhist Coalition for Economic Justice, Buddhists Alliance for Activism, Buddhist Coalition for Human Rights, and Buddhist Coalition for Environment. As the names of these groups suggest, they are concerned with wide-ranging issues and believe that religion can be, and should be, a force of reform and change in society.

4. Rethinking Secularization Theory: Implications of Liberation Theology

What *minjung* theology and all other liberation theologies entail is what can be called a "sacralization" of various social movements for a more humane and just world, meaning that religious ideas and knowledge are now being interpreted on behalf of the underprivileged in the realm of the non-sacred.[4] Parallel interpretations found in Buddhism (Queen and King 1996; Jones 1989), Zen Buddhism (Habito 2008), Hinduism (Rambachan 2015; Thomas 1988), and even Islam (Dabashi 2008; Engineer 1990), as well as the rise of various religiously-motivated NGOs, further manifest a new meaning and role of religion in the contemporary world (see also De la Torre 2008). Despite many of its compelling arguments, however, liberation theology had failed to make a greater impact when it first arose as it had the misfortune of having arisen at the height of the Cold War and was unjustly branded as Marxist, although the former's analysis of economic and social conditions shares many commonalities with that of the latter. It can be said that liberation theology was simply ahead of its time. However, liberation theology is perhaps even more pertinent today, as hundreds of millions of people all over the world are still suffering from various forms of social ills, including starvation, malnutrition, and lack of safe drinking water, just to name the most basic human needs. Other problems, such as discrimination against women and violation of human rights, still persist in many parts of the world today. The ideas found in liberation theology can be used today to legitimize religion's greater involvement with these issues, thereby allowing religion to make greater contributions to the making of a more humane, more caring, and more hopeful society.

Such socio-political articulations of liberation theology necessitate, as the paper argues, a reflection on secularization theory. There have been many important studies done on secularization theory, including the works by Wilson (1966, 1976), Martin (1969, 2005), Fenn (1978), Dobbelaere (1981), Casanova (1994, 2006, 2009), Stark (1999), Bruce (2002, 2011), Asad (2003), Norris and Inglehart (2004), Hurd (2004), Taylor (2007), and Warner (2010). As Dobbelaere (1981) argues, the concept of secularization is multidimensional, entailing many different meanings (Shiner 1967). Also, as Glasner (1977) notes, how we define secularization and how we define religion largely determine how we conceptualize the process of secularization. A more recent attempt at clarifying the concept of secularization led to the so-called "neo-secularization theory," which narrows the focus of secularization to only the declining authority of religion (Chaves 1994; Yamane 1997). For example, Yamane (1997, p. 116) describes secularization as occurring when "religious authority structures decline in their ability to control societal level institutions, meso-level organizations, and individual level beliefs and behaviors." Chaves (1994, p. 757) writes:

> Secularization at the societal level may be defined as the declining capacity of religious elites to exercise control over the other institutional spheres. Secularization at the organizational level may be understood as religious authority's declining control over organizational resources within the religious sphere. And secularization at the individual level may be understood as the decrease in the extent to which individual actions are subject to religious control.

Of all the different meanings of secularization, five points are most representative: decline of religion; social change; institutional differentiation; rationalization; and privatization (see Shiner 1967; Dobbelaere 1981; Sommerville 1998).[5] The most familiar notion of secularization is the decline of religion. Also expressed as "disengagement of society from religion," "desacralization of the world," or people's declining religious involvement. The decline of religion means that previously accepted religious doctrines, symbols, and institutions lose their prestige and influence, of which the culminating effect would be an irreligious society. As Bruce (2002, p. 3) puts it, secularization refers to:

> (a) the declining importance of religion for the operation of non-religious roles and institutions such as those of the state and the economy; (b) decline in the social standing of

---

4   It is not argued here that religion was never a force of liberation in the past. Although the protest element of religion was evident, the underprivileged used it primarily as a means of escape from reality rather than as a challenge to the existing social order. For a full explication of this issue, see Cohn (1970) and Lanternari (1963).

5   Using the phrase "secularization paradigm," Tschannen (1991) argues that secularization also refer to "worldliness," "autonomization," "generalization," "pluralization," and "scientization," and "socioligization," among others.

religious roles and institutions; and (c) a decline in the extent to which people engage in religious practices, display beliefs of a religious kind, and conduct other aspects of their lives in a manner informed by such beliefs.

Secularization as a process of social change refers to a shift from "sacred" to "secular" society. It is an inevitable process where the change in social structure, i.e., from *Gemeinschaft* to *Gesellschaft*, results in less religiosity. In this sense, secularization is seen as the decline of community and as the shift in social control from moral or religious to bureaucratic or technical control. Similarly, the perspective of differentiation views secularization as a part of general social change in which religious ideas, organizations, and activities are separated from other social institutions (i.e., cultural, legal, economic, and political institutions of society become increasingly specialized and grow more distinct from one another). A fourth meaning of secularization can be described as a process of rationalization. Science as a secular force undermines the impact of the theological outlook on the world and modifies the philosophical one. These changes completely reorient other social institutions, including education, politics, and law, and allow morals to become private matters. Rationalization also refers to a process in which the religious group or the religiously oriented society becomes more absorbed in this world. All of these different meanings of secularization culminate in the fifth meaning—the privatization of religion—which refers to the process of regarding religion as a personal phenomenon that is not shared with others (Luckmann 1967). Secularization, according to Luckmann, is the process in which church-oriented religion or public spheres of religion diminish in importance and in which religion increasingly becomes "privatised" and "invisible." The private sphere is consumer-oriented, and an individual can choose his or her own subjective preferences from the variety of ultimate meanings, the same way one chooses hobbies, services, goods, and friends (Luckmann 1967, p. 99). Thus the individual selects certain religious themes from the available menu of ultimate meanings and builds them into a private system of ultimate significance.

Inherent in these meanings of secularization, of course, are many problematic assumptions. First, is the assumption that there was once a golden age of faith. Martin (1969, p. 30) calls it "Catholic utopianism"—the most common view of secularization lies in a Utopian conception of feudal Christianity. Glasner (1977, p. 8) agrees that the concept of secularization involves "idealization" of the past periods where empirical data are scarce. Similarly, in refuting a religious-secular or sacred-profane polarity, Douglas (1970, p. 36) rejects the idea that primitive people were deeply religious by nature, for all varieties of spiritual scepticism were also found in tribal societies. As Greeley (1973, p. 7) argues: "The sacred and the secular, the religious and the profane, are not opposite poles of an evolutionary model, but alternative dimensions of reality, which interrelate to one another, and interpenetrate each other in complex periodicity." A related problem is the assumption of a linear religion-in-decline theorem. According to Martin (1969), for example, the process of secularization is not invariable and is subject to various cultural influences. He argues that the seemingly universal process of secularization operates in a variety of ways, according to the nature of a particular socio-cultural complex. Subject to historical and cultural variations, these processes result in different patterns of religious changes. Similarly, Fenn (1978, p. 39) five-step theory of secularization demonstrates that the process of secularization involves overlapping stages that are reversible. Another problem with the concept of secularization is its preoccupation with the institutionalized aspects of religiosity. The decline in religious affiliation does not necessarily imply that individual consciousness also has become irreligious. A further problem of secularization theory is the tendency to confuse the analytic and the evaluative, that is, they fail to distinguish between secularization (description of a process) and secularism (rejection of religion) (Cox 1965).[6]

---

6   Other problems with traditional secularization theory include "(1) far too much abstraction; (2) a lack of human agency; (3) a sense of over-deterministic inevitability; (4) an orientation (primarily among historians) of idealist intellectual history; (5) an

As for an explanation for the primacy of secularization theory, despite its many problematic assumptions, an insightful explanation is offered by Smith (2003), who argues that the reason for dominance of secularization theory is that those championing the ideology of the decline of religion had something to gain from it. In repudiating secularization as an inevitable by-product of "modernization" in the American context, Smith (2003, p. 1) argues that the secularization of American institutions was "much more like a contested revolutionary struggle than a natural evolutionary progression." In what Smith calls a "secular revolution," she contends that secularization of American public life did not happen by accident but was the result of "the political accomplishment" of American scientific and cultural elites who deliberately sought to displace a Protestant establishment that "stood in the path of upwardly mobile academic and literary intellectuals, blocking their bids for increased group status, autonomy, authority, and income" (Smith 2003, p. 39). Smith's explanation is consistent with Collins (2000, p. 595) suggestion that "secularization is not a zeitgeist but a process of conflict."

As the above discussion amply demonstrates, the main problem with secularization theory is its many unwarranted assumptions, particularly that of relating the concept with the decline of religion. Liberation theology has rarely been mentioned or examined as a phenomenon which may have implications for secularization theory, but the ideas extant in liberation theology are consistent with the view which rejects the decline of religion thesis of secularization theory. By lending theological support to various socio-political causes and by becoming more socially involved in the fight for justice, liberation theology demonstrates a greater involvement of Christianity in this-worldly matters on the side of the underprivileged. Such development, of course, does not indicate diminishing significance of religion. Rather, it is the opposite: liberation theology manifests the changing role of religion that is more socially concerned and involved. Liberation theology shows that religion can actually become more socio-politically meaningful and still be spiritually important for the adherents than it has been in the past.

The meanings of secularization expressed by "disengagement of society from religion" and "desacralization of the world," both of which assume dualistic views on religion and society, also largely miss the implication of liberation theology. That is because the latter reinforces the values of both spiritual and social needs, rejecting the view that religious or spiritual needs and social needs can be neatly separated. Liberation theology views "liberation" as somehow grounded in the human context, thereby allowing human beings themselves to overcome obstacles in the realization of full emancipation. It thus eliminates the dialectic between things of eternity and universality on the one hand, and things of immediacy and historicity on the other. In this sense, salvation on earth becomes no less important than salvation in heaven. The breakdown of the barrier between what is supernatural and what is human allows liberation theology to bridge the gap between the two spheres. In view of the arguments above, it can be cautiously argued that liberation theology necessitates the addition of a new dimension to the concept of secularization: *secularization as referring to the increased use of sacred institution—belief and practice—for secular purposes*. Such understanding of religion, as inspired by liberation theology, directly disputes the decline of religion thesis: as underprivileged groups fight for justice in the name of God or gods, religion can be said to have become actually more important for many people in contemporary society. Additionally, an understanding of theology as being immersed in a historico-cultural situation not only marks a significant departure of liberation theology from the conventional or classical theology, but also reflects significant changes within the religious institution itself.

---

over-romanticization of the religious past; (6) an overemphasis on religious self-destruction; and (7) an under-specification of the causal mechanisms of secularization" (Smith 2003, p. 14; see also Smith 2003, pp. 14–25).

5. Over-Secularized Conception of Society: Implications of Liberation Theology for the Sociology of Religion

The new interpretation of religion in light of liberation theology negates an "over-secularized" conception of the world. That is because the accepted meanings of secularization are more readily relevant to industrialized countries. For a significantly large number of the world's population living in developing countries, religious beliefs are still central to their lives, as their lives and communities, as well as their worldviews and behaviours, continue to be shaped by the religious values they hold. The enduring vibrancy of religion in these countries indicates people's continuing need for religion in this increasingly inhumane, "disenchanted" society. In spite of the centrality of religion in people's lives in many parts of the world, the "over-secularized" conception of society has been established in the mainstream sociology of religion as a consequence of what may be called the "metaphysical pathos" of the theory of secularization. The term, coined by Lovejoy (1948), refers to the notion that every theory generates, or is associated with, a set of feelings and sentiments, which those embracing the theory can only dimly sense. According to Lovejoy (1948, p. 11), the metaphysical pathos of ideas is "exemplified in any description of the nature of things, any characterization of the world to which one belongs, in terms which, like the words of a poem, evoke through their associations and through a sort of empathy which they engender, a congenial mood or tone of feelings." A commitment to a theory, therefore, often occurs because the theory is consistent with the deep-lying sentiments or the mood of its proponents, rather than because it has been found valid. Also, a theory bound in metaphysical pathos comes packaged, meaning that it allows little room for new ideas, and contains an underlying mood of pessimism. Ultimately, a theory induces or reinforces in the adherent a subtle modification in the structure of thoughts through which he or she views the world.

Such is the case with the theory of secularization. Instead of making more intelligible the processes of social change, some of the meanings of secularization are instilled with a metaphysical pathos which portray a gloomy future of religion. Many theories of secularization adopt the framework of decline thesis and uncritically accept it as an incontestable truth. Such blind faith in the decline of religion thesis has led to many generalizations and oversimplifications about various social changes. As a result, human beings are seen as fully rational, having no need for religion, and religion itself is seen as no longer significant for the survival and functioning of society. Instead of explaining how religion in contemporary society can be utilized to ameliorate people's lives, these theories of secularization proclaim the death of God. They emphasize the process of secularization as inevitable and as being hospitable to rationality, instead of offering ideas which may mitigate the harshness of contemporary society. Martin's declaration that "secularization is less a scientific concept than a tool of counter-religious ideologies", and his call for the elimination of the concept have much in common with the above discussion of the metaphysical pathos of the theory of secularization (Martin 1969, p. 9).

Besides its implications for the rethinking secularization theory, liberation theology has important implications for a number of theoretical issues in the study of religion, especially the sociology of religion. One area is the scrutiny of how religion continues to be a powerful legitimating and ideological force. Stimulated by Antonio Gramsci's rethinking (Gramsci 1976) of the functions of ideology, liberation theology holds that religion has long defended the interests of the ruling groups, thereby serving as an instrument of class domination. The notion that religion can be a force of liberation is also pertinent here; liberation theology takes Gramsci's analysis one step further by championing a form of religion that is free from the interest of the dominant classes and by providing a theological justification for reforms aimed at eliminating injustice.

Liberation theology also entails concerns akin to the critical theory of religion, including the use of materialist definition, emancipatory theme, and an emphasis on critical reflection and praxis.[7] They

---

[7] For the present purpose, the critical theory of religion here refers to relevant ideas found in the thought of its central figures, namely Max Horkheimer, Theodor Adorno, and Erich Fromm (see Kim 1996; Siebert 1974, 1985).

both point out that religion is a social product and that Christianity and other world religions have not been critical enough of oppressive societies. They generally view religion as having served as an influential ideology, which legitimizes the unjust state and society, thereby failing to perform its role of promoting justice and goodness. Furthermore, critical theory and liberation theology both have played crucial roles in developing the modern encounters of Marxism and Christianity. In view of this, some political theologians and critical theologians scrutinized the organization, political involvement, and ideological interests of the Church to evaluate their findings in comparison with the emancipatory potential of religion as suggested by liberation theology (See Metz 1973; Moltmann 1970).

By considering the aforementioned issues that are raised by liberation theology, the sociology of religion can enhance our understanding of the dynamics of religious phenomena in contemporary society. Not only does liberation theology contain fresh insights into religious phenomena, but also raises many important sociological questions and theories of religion. We need to consider these new ideas, as they indicate that religion is, and can become, more integral part of life in this world that is increasingly becoming inhumane.

The Future of Religion: Towards an "Ecclesiastical Social Responsibility" (ESR)?

As a way of musing about the implications of liberation theology—and the integral mission and JPIC Movement—for the future of religion, the paper suggests that religious organizations may have something to gain from reflecting on the ideas extant in the concept of corporate social responsibility (CSR). While CSR can be defined in many different ways, the following definition captures the essence of the concept: "actions that appear to further some social good, beyond the interests of the firm and that which is required by the law" (McWilliams and Siegel 2001, p. 117). Also pertinent to the concept is the firm's "pyramid of responsibilities" towards the community in which it operates, including ethical, environmental, and philanthropic responsibilities (Sheehy 2005). When CSR first began as an organizational policy, it was rejected by many firms, citing the fact that it is incongruent with the firm's profit motives. CSR is now established as an important feature that cannot be ignored by firms, as the latter have embraced the view that while profits are important, being socially responsible is also meaningful.

Therefore, would it be too far-fetched to think about something similar for world religions in general and Christianity in particular? For example, can there be what can be termed "ecclesiastical social responsibility" (ESR), which can be defined as something akin to "actions that appear to further some social good, beyond the interests of the church and that which is required by the doctrines"? At this point, it is worth asking questions inspired by a central viewpoint of liberation theology: How can religious organizations remain silent about the state of the world in which so many people of the world population, including children, are still being starved and undernourished and so many people's human rights are being violated? Isn't life in this world that is less afflicted by hunger, poverty, injustice, and oppression just as important as salvation in the next world? In the case of Christianity, isn't that what Jesus Christ would have wanted? Instead of asking "why should religion be involved with social issues?" as most conservative theologians have argued, we should ask "why shouldn't religion be more actively involved with socio-economic and political affairs, so that life on earth is more liveable and hopeful?" After all, religious organizations as a whole are perhaps the most powerful non-governmental organizations in the world, complete with enormous financial resources, strong organizational structure, and a large number of devotees who can easily be swayed for socio-political actions. Religious organizations have the power to change society for the better, but they have not had the will to do so and have willingly supported the existing socio-economic system that has privileged only some, while disadvantaging many. Those people living under unforgiving conditions are not living in countries where there are no churches, temples, or other places of worship. One could name a developing country and there is typically a dominant religion. It is definitely not a problem of too little religion. Rather, it is a problem of indifferent religion. With ESR, religion can have a more real impact on the people, spiritual or material, and can become even more relevant to their lives in contemporary society. After all, if even mundane organizations like corporations are doing it, why not religious organizations?[8]

6. Conclusions

The central theme of this paper has been the need to rethink both the role of religion in contemporary settings and the theory of secularization in light of liberation theology, including *minjung* theology. Like its counterparts elsewhere, *minjung* theology has redefined the role of Christianity in the country by articulating and sympathizing with the economic and social concerns of the underprivileged. It also served as a powerful voice in the country's democratic movement. More recently, *minjung* theology has taken issues with other causes, including reunification, gender equality, and environmental protection, as well as economic polarization between the haves and the have-nots. *Minjung* theology has also inspired Buddhism to follow in its footsteps, as there are now numerous religiously-motivated NGOs which are of Buddhist origin.

Liberation theology thus shows how religious beliefs can be newly interpreted to understand and challenge injustice in today's world. This new understanding of religion can make faith or religion become less distant from reality. Such development within religion does not indicate its diminishing significance, but rather manifests a different role of religion in contemporary society. Because liberation theology represents a new way of understanding human existence, of interpreting the Bible, and of formulating theological reflections, it is a new way of thinking about and "doing" religion. This new conception of theology sees religion as a historical, as well as a social product which should befit various needs of societies in relation to geographical, political, or socio-economic differences. Such contextualization of religion indicates changes that are taking place within religion and in its relation to society. Liberation theology thus rejects both oversimplified conceptualization of secularization and over-secularized conception of society.

The paper has also suggested that liberation theology, by redefining the role of religion, may add a new dimension to the concept of secularization. That is, *secularization as referring to the increased use of sacred institution—belief and practice—for secular purposes.* Liberation theology shows that individuals in the modern world will continue to need religion, particularly as a means of challenging injustice and oppression that persist in today's world. Now, instead of absorbing ourselves with the question of the future of religion, it is time that we ask, "what is the future of secularization?".

Funding: Research for this article was supported by a Korea University Grant.

Conflicts of Interest: The author declares no conflict of interest.

References

Ahn, Byungmu. 1993. *Minjungshinhak 2, minjungshinhakeulmalhanda (Minjung Theology 2: Minjung Theology Explained)*. Seoul: Hangilsa.

Ahn, Byungmu, David Kwangsun Suh, Young-Hak Han, and Suil Chae. 1993. Minjungshinhakui oneulgwa eoje (The Present and the Future of Minjung Theology). *Shinhakgwasasang* 81: 7–39.

Asad, Talal. 2003. *Formations of the Secular: Christianity, Islam, Modernity*. Stanford: Stanford University Press.

Ateek, Naim Stifan. 2017. *A Palestinian Theology of Liberation: The Bible, Justice, and the Palestine-Israel Conflict*. Maryknoll: Orbis Books.

Beop, Seong. 1989. *Minjungbulgyoui tamgu*. (An Inquiry into People's Buddhism). Seoul: Minjoksa.

---

8   The arguments above are not intended in any way to regard religion as an instrument or tool for specific purposes. The paper does argue that ideas like "ecclesiastical social responsibility," if accepted by religious organizations, can make religions become more socially responsible, without being disrespectful or "violating" the religious tradition itself. Being devout to one's faith and being involved with socio-political issues do not need to be mutually exclusive, as in a zero-sum game. For example, those involved in religiously-oriented NGOs for various causes cannot be said to be more socially involved because of their weak faith or lack of faith. In fact, their faith may actually have inspired them to be more socially engaged.

Berryman, Phillip. 1987. *Liberation Theology: Essential Facts about the Revolutionary Movement in Latin America and Beyond*. New York: Pantheon Books.

Beyer, Peter. 1994. *Religion and Globalization*. London: Sage.

Bruce, Steve. 2002. *God is Dead: Secularization in the West*. Oxford: Blackwell Publishing.

Bruce, Steve. 2011. *Secularization: In Defense of an Unfashionable Theory*. New York: Oxford University Press.

Bujo, Benezet. 1992. *African Theology in its Social Context*. Translated by John O'Donohue. Maryknoll: Orbis Books.

Casanova, José. 1994. *Public Religions in the Modern World*. Chicago: University of Chicago Press.

Casanova, José. 2006. Rethinking Secularization: A Global Comparative Perspective. *The Hedgehog Review* 8: 7–22.

Casanova, José. 2009. The Secular and Secularisms. *Social Research* 76: 1049–66.

Catholic News Service. 2013. Under Pope Francis, Liberation Theology Comes of Age. September 13. Available online: http://www.catholicnews.com/services/englishnews/2013/under-pope-francis-liberation-theology-comes-of-age.cfm (accessed on 29 October 2018).

Chaves, Mark. 1994. Secularization as Declining Religious Authority. *Social Forces* 72: 749–74. [CrossRef]

Chung, Sung Han. 2003. *Hanguk gidokkyo tongil undongsa (A History of Unification Movements in Korean Churches)*. Seoul: Grisim.

Clark, Donald N. 1986. *Christianity in Modern Korea*. New York: University Press of America.

Cohn, Norman. 1970. *The Pursuit of the Millennium*. New York: Oxford University Press.

Collins, Randall. 2000. *The Sociology of Philosophies: A Global Theory of Intellectual Change*. Cambridge: Harvard University Press.

Commission on Theological Concerns of the Christian Conference of Asia, ed. 1981. *Minjung Theology: People as the Subjects of History*. Maryknoll: Orbis Books.

Cone, James. 1970. *A Black Theology of Liberation*. Philadelphia: Lippincott.

Cone, James. 1975. *God of the Oppressed*. New York: Seabury.

Congregation for the Doctrine of the Faith. 1990. Instruction on Certain Aspects of the 'Theology of Liberation'. In *Liberation Theology: A Documentary History*. Edited by Alfred T. Hennelly. Maryknoll: Orbis Books, pp. 393–414.

Cooper, Thia, ed. 2013. *The Reemergence of Liberation Theologies: Models for the Twenty-First Century*. New York: Palgrave Macmillan.

Cox, Harvey. 1965. *The Secular City*. New York: Macmillan.

Dabashi, Hamid. 2008. *Islamic Liberation Theology: Resisting the Empire*. New York: Routledge.

De la Torre, Miguel A., ed. 2008. *The Hope of Liberation in World Religions*. Waco: Baylor University Press.

Dobbelaere, Karel. 1981. Secularization: A Multi-Dimensional Concept. *Current Sociology* 29: 3–153. [CrossRef]

Douglas, Mary. 1970. *Natural Symbols*. London: Barrie and Jenkins.

Elizondo, Virgilio. 1983. *Galilean Journey: The Mexican-American Promise*. Maryknoll: Orbis Books.

Ellis, Marc H. 1987. *Toward a Jewish Theology of Liberation*. Maryknoll: Orbis Books.

Engineer, Asghar Ali. 1990. *Islam and Liberation Theology: Essays on Liberative Elements in Islam*. New York: Sterling Publishing Co.

Erskine, Noel. 1981. *Decolonizing Theology: Caribbean Perspective*. Maryknoll: Orbis Books.

Fabella, Virginia. 1988. *Asia's Struggle for a Full Humanity*. Maryknoll: Orbis Books.

Fenn, Richard. 1978. *Toward a Theory of Secularization*. Storrs: Society for the Scientific Study of Religion.

Fiorenza, Elisabeth Schussler, ed. 1996. *The Power of Naming: A Concilium Reader in Feminist Liberation Theology*. Maryknoll: Orbis Books.

Floyd-Thomas, Stacey M., and Anthony B. Pinn, eds. 2010. *Liberation Theologies in the United States: An Introduction*. New York: New York University Press.

Glasner, Peter. 1977. *The Sociology of Secularization*. London: Routledge & Kegan Paul.

Gramsci, Antonio. 1976. *Selections from the Prison Notebooks*. Translated by Quentin Hoare, and Geoffrey Nowell Smith. London: Lawrence and Wishart.

Greeley, Andrew. 1973. The Persistence of Community. In *The Persistence of Religion*. Edited by Andrew Greeley and Gregory Baum. New York: Herder & Herder, pp. 23–35.

Guerrero, Andrew G. 1986. *A Chicano Theology: Guadalupe and La Raza as Keys to Liberation*. Maryknoll: Orbis Books.

Gutierrez, Gustavo. 1973. *A Theology of Liberation: History, Politics, and Salvation*. Maryknoll: Orbis Books.

Habito, Ruben L. F. 2008. Zen Buddhism. In *The Hope of Liberation in World Religions*. Edited by Miguel de la Torre. Waco: Baylor University Press, pp. 155–74.

Han, Jongwoo. 1986. *Hangukgeundaeminjungbulgyoui inyeomgwa jeongae (The Ideology and Development of People's Buddhism in Modern Korea)*. Seoul: Hangilsa.

Han, Gil-Soo, and Andrew Eungi Kim. 2006. The Korean Christian Movement towards Reunification of the Two Koreas: A Review in Retrospect. *International Journal for the Study of the Christian Church* 6: 235–55. [CrossRef]

Hood, Robert. 1990. *Must God Remain Greek: Afro Cultures and God-Talk*. Minneapolis: Fortress Press.

Hopkins, Dwight. 1989. *Black Theology USA and South Africa: Politics, Culture, and Liberation*. Maryknoll: Orbis Books.

Hurd, Elizabeth Shakman. 2004. The Political Authority of Secularism in International Relations. *European Journal of International Relations* 10: 235–62. [CrossRef]

Isherwood, Lisa. 2004. The Embodiment of Feminist Liberation Theology: The Spiralling Inspiration. *Feminist Theology* 12: 140–56. [CrossRef]

Jones, Ken. 1989. *The Social Face of Buddhism: An Approach to Social and Political Activism*. London: Wisdom.

Kang, Wondon, Eungsup Kang, Jingwan Kwon, Youngchul Kim, and Eungyu Kim. 2010. *Dashi minjungshinhakida (It is Minjung Theology Again)*. Seoul: Dongyeonchulpansa.

Kim, Yong-bock. 1987. *Hanguk minjungui sahoejeongi (A Social Turning Point of the Korean People)*. Seoul: Hangilsa.

Kim, Andrew Eungi. 1996. Critical Theory and the Sociology of Religion: A Reassessment. *Social Compass* 43: 267–83. [CrossRef]

Kim, Jungsuk. 2011. 21segi segyehwa sidaeui minjungshinhak (Minjung Theology in 21st Century Era of Globalization). *Shinhakgwasegye* 72: 97–122.

Kim, Huiheon. 2013. *Suhnamdongui cheolhak: Minjungshinhake ireuda (The Philosophy of Nam-dong Suh: Reaching Minjung Theology)*. Seoul: Ehwa Women's University Press.

Kim, Sandra So Hee Chi. 2017. Korean Han and the Postcolonial Afterlives of "The Beauty of Sorrow". *Korean Studies* 41: 253–79. [CrossRef]

Kim, Sebastian C. H., and Kirsteen Kim. 2014. *A History of Korean Christianity*. Cambridge: Cambridge University Press.

Kirkpatrick, David C. 2016. The Widening Christian Mission: C. Rene Padilla and the Intellectual Origins of Integral Mission. In *The End of Theology: Shaping Theology for the Sake of Mission*. Edited by Jason S. Sexton and Paul Weston. Minneapolis: Fortress Press, pp. 193–210.

Küster, Volker. 2010. *A Protestant Theology of Passion: Korean Minjung Theology Revisited*. Leiden: Brill.

Kwon, Jin-kwan, and Volker Küster, eds. 2018. *Minjung Theology Today: Contextual and Intercultural Perspectives*. Leipzig: Evangelische Verlassanstalt.

Lanternari, Vittorio. 1963. *The Religions of the Oppressed*. New York: Alfred Knopf.

Lee, Jung Young. 1988a. *An Emerging Theology in World Perspective: Commentary on Korean Minjung Theology*. New London: Twenty Third Publications.

Lee, Samuel. 1988b. Hanguk gidokgyowa tongil undong (Korean Christianity and Reunification Movement). *Gidokgyosasang* 355: 14–30.

Lee, Seokgyu. 2001. 21segi minjungshinhakeul wihan han jean (A Suggestion for the Minjung Theology of the 21th Century). *Minjung and Theology* 7: 40–59.

Lee, Jeonghee. 2018. *Minjungshinhak, gotongui sidaereul ikda (Minjung Theology: Understanding the Suffering Time)*. Seoul: Bundochulpansa.

Lovejoy, Arthur. 1948. *The Great Chain of Being*. Cambridge: Harvard University Press.

Luckmann, Thomas. 1967. *The Invisible Religion*. New York: Macmillan.

Martey, Emmanuel. 1993. *African Theology: Inculturation and Liberation*. Maryknoll: Orbis Books.

Martin, David. 1969. *The Religious and the Secular*. New York: Schocken.

Martin, David. 2005. *On Secularization: Towards a Revised General Theory*. London: Routledge.

McWilliams, Abagail, and Donald Siegel. 2001. Corporate Social Responsibility: A Theory of the Firm Perspective. *Academy of Management Review* 26: 117–27. [CrossRef]

Metz, Johannes B. 1973. *Theology of the World*. New York: Seabury Press.

Moltmann, Jurgen. 1970. *Political Theology*. Montgomery: Huntington College.

Moon, Donghwan. 1982. Korean *minjung* Theology. In *Korean-American Relations at Crossroads*. Edited by Wonmo Dong. Princeton Junction: Association of Korean Christian Scholars in North America.

Moon, Cyris H. S. 1985. *A Korean Minjung Theology—An Old Testament Perspective*. Maryknoll: Orbis Books.

Moon, Donghwan. 2000. 21segiwa minjungshinhak (Minjung Theology in the 21st Century). *Shinhaksasang* 109: 20–54.

NCC shinhakyeonguwiwonhoe, ed. 1982. *Minjunggwa hangukshinhak*. Seoul: Hangukshinhakyeonguso.

Nicholls, Bruce J., ed. 1986. *In Word and Deed: Evangelism and Social Responsibility*. Grand Rapids: Eerdmans Pub Co.

Norris, Pippa, and Ronald Inglehart. 2004. *Sacred and Secular: Religion and Politics Worldwide*. New York: Cambridge University Press.

Nunez, Emilio A. 1985. *Liberation Theology*. Chicago: Moody Press.

Padilla, C. Rene. 2002. Integral Mission and Its Historical Development. In *Justice, Mercy & Humility: Integral Mission and the Poor*. Edited by Tim Chester. Cumbria: Paternoster Press, pp. 42–58.

Padilla, C. Rene. 2010. *Mission between the Times: Essays on the Kingdom (Revised and Expanded Edition)*. Cumbria: Langham Monographs.

Park, Jae-Soon. 1990. Minjungshinhak, mueoti gwajeinga? (Minjung Theology: What is its Task?). *Gidokgyosasang* 34: 37–47.

Park, Jae-Soon. 1995. *Yeollinsahoeleul wihan minjungshinhak (Minjung Theology for an Open Society)*. Seoul: Hanul.

Pieris, Aloysius. 1988. *An Asian Theology of Liberation*. Maryknoll: Orbis Books.

Queen, Christopher S., and Sallie B. King, eds. 1996. *Engaged Buddhism: Buddhist Liberation Movements in Asia*. Albany: SUNY Press.

Rambachan, Anantanand. 2015. *A Hindu Theology of Liberation: Not-Two is Not One*. Albany: SUNY Press.

Ro, Kil-myung, and Hyung-shin Park. 2010. *Hangukui jonggyowa sahoeundong (Korean Religions and Social Movement)*. Seoul: Ihaksa.

Segundo, Juan Luis. 1976. *The Liberation of Theology*. Maryknoll: Orbis Books.

Sheehy, Benedict. 2005. Defining CSR: Problems and Solutions. *Journal of Business Ethics* 131: 625–48. [CrossRef]

Shiner, Larry. 1967. The Concept of Secularization in Empirical Research. *Journal for the Scientific Study of Religion* 6: 207–20. [CrossRef]

Siebert, Rudolf. 1974. Religion in the Perspective of Critical Sociology. *Concilium*, 56–69.

Siebert, Rudolf. 1985. *The Critical Theory of Religion: The Frankfurt School*. New York: Mouton.

Smith, Christian, ed. 2003. *The Secular Revolution: Power, Interests, and Conflict in the Secularization of American Public Life*. Berkeley: University of California Press.

Sommerville, C. John. 1998. Secular Society Religious Population: Our Tacit Rules for Using the Term Secularization. *Journal for the Scientific Study of Religion* 37: 249–53. [CrossRef]

Stark, Rodney. 1999. Secularization, R.I.P. *Sociology of Religion* 60: 249–73. [CrossRef]

Stott, John. 1996. *Making Christ Known: Historic Mission Documents from the Lausanne Movement, 1974–1989*. Cumbria: Paternoster Press.

Sugirtharajah, Rasiah S. 1994. *Frontiers in Asian Christian Theology: Emerging Trends*. Maryknoll: Orbis Books.

Suh, David Kwang-sun. 1983a. A Biographical Sketch of an Asian Theological Consultation. In *Minjung Theology: People as the Subjects of History*. Edited by Yong Bock Kim. Maryknoll: Orbis Books.

Suh, Nam-dong. 1983b. *Minjungshinhakui tamgu (An Exploration of Minjung Theology)*. Seoul: Hangilsa.

Suh, David Kwang-sun. 1991. *The Korean Minjung in Christ*. Eugene: Wipf and Stock Publishers.

Suh, Jae-Jung, and Mikyoung Kim, eds. 2017. *Challenges of Modernization and Governance in South Korea: The Sinking of the Sewol and Its Causes*. New York: Palgrave Macmillan.

Sung, Jung Mo. 2007. *Reclaiming Liberation Theology: Desire, Market and Religion*. London: SCM Press.

Taylor, Charles. 2007. *A Secular Age*. Cambridge: Harvard University Press.

Thomas, Norman E. 1988. Liberation for Life: A Hindu Liberation Theology. *Missiology: An International Review* 16: 149–62.

Tschannen, Olivier. 1991. The Secularization Paradigm: A Systematization. *Journal for the Scientific Study of Religion* 30: 395–415. [CrossRef]

Warner, Rob. 2010. *Secularization and its Discontents*. New York: Continuum Int'l Pub. Group.

Welch, Sharon D. 1985. *Communities of Resistance and Solidarity: A Feminist Theology of Liberation*. Eugene: Wipf & Stock.

Wilson, Bryan. 1966. *Religion in Secular Society*. London: C. A. Watts.

Wilson, Bryan. 1976. *Contemporary Transformations of Religion*. London: Oxford University Press.

Woo, Hyekyung, Youngtae Choe, Eunyoung Shim, Kihwang Lee, and Gilyoung Song. 2015. Public Trauma after the Sewol Ferry Disaster: The Role of Social Media in Understanding the Public Mood. *International Journal of Environmental Research and Public Health* 12: 10974–83. [CrossRef] [PubMed]

Yamane, David. 1997. Secularization on Trial: In Defense of a Neosecularization Paradigm. *Journal for the Scientific Study of Religion* 36: 109–22. [CrossRef]

Yeon, Gyu-Hong. 2000. Hangukkyohoeui minjoktongil undonggwa pyonghwa munje (Korean Churches' Reunification Movement and the Issue of Peace). *Shinhakyeongu* 41: 425–43.

Yoo, Seungtae. 2009. Gyeolhonijujareul eotteotge bol geotinga? Minjungshinhakui haeseokjeok silcheoneul tonghan 'beomjuron' neomeoseogi (How Should We View Marriage Migrants: Overcoming the 'Category' through a Practical Interpretation of Minjung Theology). *Sidaewa minjungshinhak* 11: 88–110.

Article

Introducing Christian Spirituality to Joseon Korea—Three Responses from Confucian Scholars

So-Yi Chung

Department of Religious Studies, Sogang University, Seoul 04107, Korea; soyichung@sogang.ac.kr

Received: 1 October 2018; Accepted: 23 October 2018; Published: 26 October 2018

Abstract: When the books written by Jesuit missionaries were introduced to Joseon Korea via China during the 18th century, Joseon Confucian scholars were drawn to not only western science and technologies but also to theological ideas centered on Christian spirituality. Among many foreign conceptions, the most alien were the following three: immortality of the soul; eternal life in heaven or in hell after death; and finally, the resurrection of the body. There had been three responses from all levels of society: refutation, recognition, and reconciliation. First, Shin Hudam (1702–1761) wrote a book, *Disputation on Western Learning*, to dispute the above three doctrines as being most unreasonable and contradictory. Meanwhile, Jeong Yag-Jong (1760–1801) found that the doctrines were the true path to the salvation of human suffering and wrote the first catechistic book in vernacular Korean in the way that appealed to common people with Confucian backgrounds. Finally, Jeong Yag-Yong (1762–1836) was extremely careful, neither embracing nor rejecting, yet suggested alternative ways to address the core Christian theological problems without crossing the boundaries of Confucianism. All three were active dedicated responses to Christian spirituality and genuine Christian-Confucian dialogues, which also reflected common concerns and attitudes toward a new religion in Korean society.

Keywords: spirituality; Confucianism; Joseon Korea; Western Learning; Shin Hudam; Jeong Yag-Jong; Tasan Jeong Yag-Yong

1. Introduction

It was around the early 18th century when Jesuit missionaries' first books on Western Learning (kr. *Seohak*) began to spread among Joseon intellectuals. (cf. Cho 2006). Like Chinese intellectuals a century ago, they found western sciences, such as astronomy, geography, Euclidian geometry, and medicine as particularly interesting and practical. Such a good initial impression made their other arguments on so-called 'Western Learning' (kr. *Seohak*), to which the Jesuits referred to as 'Celestial Learning' (*Cheonhak*), sound persuasive and credible. Sungho Yi Ik (1681–1763, Sungho hereafter), for example, claimed that Catholics were different from Buddhists since they were not immersed in quietude and detachment but actively bringing new astronomical and geometrical discoveries to people that would help improve people's lives (S. Kim 2012, pp. 46–47).

Sungho was one of the open-minded scholars who scrutinized their long-held neo-Confucian worldview and at the same time eagerly searched for a new perspective that could replace it. According to his analysis, the main conception of Western Learning can be divided into two: one is the brain that is the foundation of life and memory; the other is the spiritual soul (kr. *yeong-hon*, Lat. *anima rationalis*) that is unique to humans. He found these notions not exactly like the Confucian theory of mind and nature, but confessed that he could not find them entirely wrong (Shin 2014, pp. 41–43). In the traditional neo-Confucian worldview, it is the heart *sim* that plays the central role of controlling other body organs, including feelings and reasons. Humans are different from animals not because they have an individual, immortal soul, or because they have a rational brain, but because only humans are endowed with *sim* comprised with pure and clear material energy *ki* that manages and acts on the inner moral principles given to all humans and animals.

Sungho's active reception of Western Learning and the Catholic idea of human spirituality (c.f. Berthrong 2003) brought about diverse viewpoints among his disciples that led to fierce disputes. Politically, Sungho belonged to the Southern faction that was slowly and steadily declining in power. The search for new ideologies that could effectively transform the established regime was especially intense among Southerners, and Western Learning was at the frontline of the possible 'new' paradigm. As a result, Sungho's disciples debated over human nature and the spiritual soul for decades.

Previous scholars described how Sungho School was divided into two factions: pro-Catholics and anti-Catholics, left and right, young and old (cf. K.-J. Song 2000; Keum 2001) The problem was, there was a third group of scholars who wrote letters and books in the style that had been heavily influenced by Catholic concepts, yet never openly supported Catholicism. They were caught at the middle and unidentified, and later scholars classified them as 'hiddent Catholics with Confucian masks' or 'original Confucians embracing the Western paradigm' (cf. Baker 2002, 2013, 2015; Baek 2007; Cawley 2014, S. Kim 2012).

In this article, I will show that the Sungho School scholars, who were most active and serious among Joseon academics in studying Western Learning and their doctrines on human spirituality, responded in three distinct ways. One was the refutation mainly led by Shin Hudam (1702–1761) who repudiated that Western Learning was fundamentally a heresy *idan* such as Buddhism, which saw humans not as moral beings but selfish, self-interested animals. The other response was the total recognition and respect from Jeong Yag-jong (1762–1801, baptismal name Augustinos, Jeong A. hereafter) and other followers who later converted into Catholic and devoted their lives writing the first catechistic works in vernacular Korean. The last careful response was that of a reconciliation proposed by Jeong Yag-yong (1764–1836, penname Tasan or Sa-am, Tasan hereafter) who weaved the Catholic perspective into the Confucian background, i.e., accepting the Catholic line of reasoning without crossing the boundaries of Confucianism. I shall compare and contrast the three viewpoints by focusing on the main issues of human spirituality: the issue of the immortality of the soul, eternal life in Heaven and Hell, and the resurrection of the body.

2. Refutation of Catholicism

Although the refutation of Catholicism was not limited to the Sungho School scholars, it did begin within the Sungho School, and then spread outward (Keum 2001, pp. 1–25). It is noteworthy to analyze how the first criticism toward Catholic spirituality went on since it provided the blueprint of refutation on Catholicism that what followed generally addressed the same problems and repeated the same criticisms.

As Sungho took an active interest in Western Learning and found it useful and reconcilable with the traditional Confucian values, Shin Hudam, who was a colleague-disciple of Sungho, spent a considerable time studying and scrutinizing the famous books written Jesuits including *Lingyan lishao* (靈言蠡勺; A Humble Attempt to Discuss on the Soul, cf. Sambiasi 1965) and *Tianzhu shiyi* (天主實義, The True Meaning of the Lord of Heaven, cf. Ricci 1985). He came up with the conclusion that they are not only illogical and self-contradictory, but also unethical and deluding people by stimulating their selfish desires.

Shin's first criticism toward the Western Learning was on the special character of the human spirit-soul (靈魂*yeong-hon*). He found absurd the idea that the spiritual souls of humans, unlike sensitive souls of animals or vegetative souls of plants, are self-subsisting and immortal. He wrote:

> In my opinion, this [Westerner] is saying that human souls are independent substances since it is self-subsisting and does not depend on other things. However, when a human is born, a body is formed and then the ethereal force (*ki*) is attached to it. (. . .) When a human dies, the remaining body (*baek*魄) deteriorates and soul (*hon*魂) attached to it also dissipates along it; hence, the soul cannot exist alone. (. . .) Zhu Xi wrote that the "so-called 'soul returns to Heaven' means the ethereal force (*ki*) is dissipating." In conclusion, the soul depends its existence on the bodily form, and as the bodily form degenerates, it also disperses and

returns to nothingness. How can a soul be an independently existing entity! (Shin 2014, pp. 91–92)

Shin's criticism reflects the traditional Confucian viewpoints on life-and-death. *Hon* (soul) and *baek* (remaining body) are a pairing term designating the human mind and body after death. Upon death, *hon* leaves the *baek* like smoke in the air, slowly dissipating into the void. Right after the death, just as the *baek* (remaining body) is still intact and unharmed, the *hon* is also undispersed and can return to the nearby area upon calling. That is why there exists a mourning ritual called *cho-hon* (招魂inviting the soul, calling of the soul to return to earth), but it still entails that the soul can never return to the body and eventually dissipate into the air. Shin argues again:

Westerners speak that only the human soul (*anima*), different from vegetative or sensitive souls, is immortal; however, it is not so. Within one human body, only one soul is attached to it; it grows because of this soul, and it senses because of this soul. (...) The human spiritual soul depends on the human body, just like vegetative and sensitive souls depends on plants and animals. How can a spiritual soul exist alone? How can it be immortal as the vegetative and sensitive souls perish? The western authors try to argue for the immortality of the spiritual soul, but the three souls cannot be divided. As a result, they attempt to argue for the immortality of the *human* soul, and the human soul's vegetative and sensitive *anima* are different from that of plants and animals. These lame justifications just reveal the ambiguities and loopholes. (pp. 95–96)

Shin disputes that the Jesuits' arguments are ambiguous and illogical: they say in one place that the three souls are indivisible, and in another place that one soul remains after two disappear. Apart from the seeming contradictions, there are other reasons why Shin was vehemently opposed to the idea of an immortal soul.

In a neo-Confucian worldview, a human soul is called the *sim* (mind) during one's lifetime: when one is dead, the *sim* departs from the body and becomes *hon*. *Sim* is responsible for all the inner—rational, moral, and aesthetical—reactions toward outside stimulus. Within each mind, there is an innate moral nature *seong* (性), bestowed upon birth by Heaven, which is the origin and the standard of good and proper reactions to the outer world. *Seong* is, in other words, the absolute moral principle embedded within everyone, shared by all living things. To sum, in neo-Confucianism, what is eternal and everlasting is our common nature, not our individual mind; what is transient and temporary is our individual mind and body (cf. S.-Y. Chung 2018). In this schema, we need to control and cultivate our individual and private mind, which is tied to our physical body and its corporeal needs, in order to realize the shared interest of humanity, in particular, and all the living things, in general. If one regarded the 'individual' soul as absolute and immortal, it would mean that the private became more important than the public, and singular interest might come before the common benefit.

Shin further disapproves of the immortality of the individual soul in connection to the Catholic idea of Heaven and Hell.

They say that the vegetative and sensitive souls are no longer in use after death. How can these souls be immortal? If they are no longer use and only the spiritual soul is in use. How is it possible for these three to be one and indivisible while living, and suddenly become two and partly useful after death? If the vegetative and sensitive souls are no longer in use, it would be just the same as no longer existing. Hence, even if there is a heavenly pleasure, the soul cannot recognize it; even if there is a pain in Hell, the soul cannot feel it. Then should a human seek to go to Heaven? (p. 96)

According to Shin's analysis, without bodily sensation, the pleasure and pain of Heaven and Hell described by the Catholics do not hold. Their claims are not merely incongruous; what is the worst about their promise of the afterlife is that the very idea of Heaven and Hell reflects the self-regarding, benefit-seeking way of living, which is far from the Confucian ideal. He claimed:

In my opinion, the entire reason for discussing the nature of *anima* is merely to gain merit after death. The entire theory is based on selfish interest. (pp. 100–101)

The notion of Heaven and Hell was not new to Confucians. For example, Buddhists also claimed that the spirits lasted even after death and that they were sent to various degrees of heaven and hell according to their merits and demerits (p. 89). Shin warns that it is characteristic of all the heresies (*idan*) to lure people by provoking their fundamental desire for life and fear of death (pp. 88–89). Daoism entices people with alchemies and strange practices for longevity; Hindu-Buddhism entices and threatens people with the next life and rebirth. On the contrary, Confucianism focuses on the present world. An ideal Confucian person, *junzi*, does a good action because it is good in itself; it is not because it will bring him or her any further benefits. Confucius urged, "When seeing the benefit, one must think about whether it is righteous: when seeing danger, one must risk one's own life" (*Analects* 14.12) (Confucius 1979). Mencius also ascertained that all humane persons would be alarmed and rush to save a baby about to fall into a well not because of others' praise or condemnation, not because of further benefit, but because it is part of our nature (*The Book of Mencius* 2A.6) (Mencius 1970). Shin regards that if the motivation behind any good action is to go to Heaven after death, then it is not out of one's spontaneous and genuine heart-mind.

Further, if people believed in the eternal life after death and started to see this present life as transient, then they would not put as much effort in everyday familial and social duties in this world.

The way the ideal Confucian person follows does not deviate from everyday actions. Near at hand, the ideal person serves his parents; far out, he serves the Lord. In a large scale, he rules the state and establishes the law and systems; on a smaller scale, he meets, talks, and interacts with people. All of these are everyday actions and the Way does not exist apart from them. What sages taught was only this Way, and what disciples must learn is also this Way. If the western scholars argue that all the worldly actions are futile and only the eternal existence up in the Heaven is worth seeking, then sons would not care to serve their parents and the officials would not tend to serve their lords. (...) People become interested only in the genuine fortune up in the Heaven. It destroys the humane relationships and belittles the Way; it instills the habit of seeking profits only for oneself. How can one not loathe it deeply! (p. 85)

Confucians value this world here and now and it is the only way to bridging this life and the beyond, the limited and the infinite, the temporal, and the eternal. Confucianism holds that humanity can achieve perfection and live up to heavenly principles, by fulfilling their 'mission' in this world—that is, their ethical and moral duties, conscientiously exercised in the form of social and political action (Yao 2000, p. 46).

One may still ask whether there is no notion of retributive justice in Confucianism. In fact, there is a widely quoted passage 'rewarding the good and punishing the wicked' (福善禍淫) in an ancient Confucian text (*The Book of Documents*, Announcement of Tang 3). Shin, however, contends that it bears a completely different meaning:

There is a saying "rewarding the good and punishing the wicked" in our Confucian Classics. However, it only refers to *li*, the universal principle of the world. Humans and the Way of Heaven are on in this principle, and this principle is good in itself. The good people go along with this principle and naturally invoke blessings; the wicked go against this principle and bring misfortunes onto themselves. It is how the principle works. How can the Lord of Heaven judge one by one and mete out fortunes every time? So-called rewards and the punishments are just ways the virtuous and the vicious are treated in this world. How can they be compared with the [Catholic] belief in Heaven and Hell? (pp. 86–87)

This stance of Shin shows the typical Confucianism humanism that seeks sacredness in an ordinary life-principle. It is fundamentally secular, this-worldly in emphasis, yet appealing to transcendent values embodied in the concept of 'heaven' (Rule 1986, p. 31).

After Shin, Confucian scholars of Joseon Korea criticized in the similar vein the notion of the immortal individual soul and that of Heaven and Hell. Ahn Jeong-bok (1712–1791), for example, wrote a script called *A Conversation on Catholicism*, to refute the prevailing theories on the Celestial Learning. He also criticized that Catholic doctrines "focused on a world after this one and tantalized people with promises of Heaven if they did good and threatened people with Hell if they did evil. (...) Jesus encouraged people to focus on what they thought would benefit them in the most personal way" (Baker 2017, p. 127). It was far from the Confucian way of promoting moral behavior, i.e., fostering a common concern for what is best for everyone. People should simply continue to do what is right, and not pay the slightest attention to the possibility of some reward in the next life for what they do in this life (p. 127). In the eye of a Confucian scholar, as a result, the more one emphasized the rewards of the afterlife, Heavenly pleasures, and even the resurrections of the body that Jesus promised, the further one would be away from the moral commitment in this world and a genuine sense of self-cultivation.

3. Recognition of Catholicism

After the novel concepts of Christian spirituality—the immortality of the soul, afterlife in Heaven, and Hell and resurrections of the body—were introduced with quite a resistance, they slowly moved the heart of some Joseon people (cf. Cho 2002; 2006). Not only the commoners and middle-class merchants who were illiterate in Chinese scripts, but also elite scholars who had been deeply engrossed in the Confucian value system. Among the first scholars who opened their mind to this foreign doctrines the family of Jeong Yag-jong Augustinos (Jeong A. hereafter) is worthy of note. The brothers of Jeong A., including Jeong Yag-jeon (1758–1816) and Tasan Jeong Yag-yong, were the first members of a study group to read Jesuit texts that Joseon scholars referred to as Western Learning. Jeong A. was last to join the group but soon completely immersed himself in the Catholic ideas and doctrines. He became the first to write a catechistic work in vernacular Korean called *Jugyo Yoji* (The Essentials of the Lord's Teaching), which made him a patristic theologian of the early Korean Church (cf. S.-J. Song 2002; D.-H. Chung 2003). Even after Jeong A.'s brothers distanced themselves from Catholicism and Western Learning as it came into conflict with the state's regulation of rituals, Jeong A. remained loyal to the faith and suffered martyrdom in a religious trial in 1801 (Y.-J. Jeong 2012, p. 15).[1] In this section, I shall delineate how a Confucian scholar like Jeong A. came to recognize the Christian notion of spirituality and discuss his arguments, with an implicit comparison to Shin's refutation before, which persuaded many people with the traditional Confucian background.

Just as Shin and other Confucians who renounced Catholic doctrines, Jeong A. also encountered the common question on the immortality of the soul. In *Jugyo Yoji*, as Jeong A. preaches that a person receives rewards and punishments after death, a common response goes: "After a person dies once, his body decays and disappears; then how is reward or punishment meted?" (p. 68). Jeong A. answers:

> After death, a person's body decays, but the soul does not die. An animal's soul is formed from its body and it only knows that which takes place in its body, such as hunger, fullness, cold, and warmth. When it dies, the soul attached to the body also disappears. The human soul, however, is not formed from the body. Rather, when the [human] body is birthed, the Lord of Heaven attaches to it a supernatural soul. A human being, therefore, takes pleasure and displeasure even in things that lie outside the body. For instance, when someone praises me, even though this does not fill my stomach, I feel needless pleasure, and when someone insults me, even though this causes no pain to my body, I feel needless displeasure. This mind that takes pleasure and displeasure surely does not originate

---

[1]   His immediate family, including his wife Yu Joy (Cecelia; 1761–1839), first son Jeong Cheol-sang (Carlos; ?–1801), second son Jeong ha-sang (Paul; 1795–1835), and his wife Jeong Jeong-hye (Elizabeth, 1797–1839) were also martyred during the persecutions of 1801 and 1839. Later, they were beatified by Pop Pius XI in 1925, and canonized by Pope John Paul II in 1984 (Y.-J. Jeong 2012, p. 19).

from the body but from the soul. Human beings, therefore, are different from animals in that they have a separate soul, and the soul does not die even if the body dies. Additionally, the divine soul cannot be burned in a fire, cut with a blade, or suffer from a disease, and it has no way to die since it has no physical form. (pp. 68–69)

Jeong A. argues that the human soul is different from that of animals since it is not formed from the body. He brings to the attention that humans, unlike animals, take pleasure or pain even in things that have nothing to do with bodily pleasure and pain: one is pleased with someone's praise, and one is distressed by another's insults. These are the common signs that humans possess a different kind of soul which has nothing to do with one's corporeal body. Since the divine soul is not related to the body, it cannot be injured or harmed, hence, it is eternal in its existence.

If the human soul is not related to the body and its sensations, how would it feel the pleasure and pain after death? Jeong A. again explicates as follows:

All things cannot know pleasure and pain without consciousness, and only after possessing consciousness can they know pleasure and pain. (...) when a person dies and the soul departs, if honey is placed in his mouth he cannot know if it is sweet or bitter, and when his flesh is stabbed with a knife he does not know that it hurts. From this, we see that the soul is truly the source of pleasure and pain. Whether it stays in the body or leaves the body, the consciousness of the soul remains the same. Then how can it not experience pleasure and pain? (pp. 70–71)

Human consciousness or rationality, according to Jeong A., is the true source of pleasure and pain. Here, although he does not explain how the rational soul of humans differentiate itself from the mere vegetative or sensitive souls of plants and animals, he has in mind that the kind of pleasure and pain humans take is not limited to the momentary sensation. As Giulio Aleni puts it, humans possess memories from which they retrieve the old good feelings and painful recollections from the past; moreover, they have questions and imaginations from which they expect in hope and predict in anxiety (Aleni 1873, pp. 50–53). While Shin was adamant that human souls were no different from animal souls in that they are both ethereal force *ki* that would dissipate eventually, Jeong A. focused on the special character of humans that could not be captured in the neo-Confucian *li-ki* framework.

Jeong A. describes the Lord of Heaven as "the father of all fathers, and the lord of all lords" (Y.-J. Jeong 2012, p. 47). Just as a father and a lord would wisely and fairly exercise their authority and power over the members of family and state, the Lord of Heaven would bring final justice to all human beings.

The Lord of Heaven is exceedingly wise, exceedingly powerful, exceedingly good, exceedingly strict, and exceedingly just. Thus, he most certainly rewards the good person and punishes the evil person. As he is exceedingly wise, he will know a person's goodness and wickedness. As he is exceedingly powerful, he will have the authority to reward and to punish according to his will. As he is exceedingly strict, he will hate the wicked person and punish him. As he is exceedingly just, he will certainly set the right reward and the punishment. Therefore, since his arranging of the world, no good person will go without receiving his reward from the Lord of Heaven, and no wicked person will go without receiving punishment from the Lord of Heaven. (p. 66)

Jeong A. further reasons that there must be Heaven and Hell, the symbolic place for reward and punishment after death if there is any justice for individual deeds. He explains that it is impossible to judge goodness or the wickedness during one's lifetime, for various reasons. One may be good in the beginning but later become wicked, and vice versa (p. 66); if the rewards and punishments were meted for every action, then there would be a huge social confusion; if the Lord were to inflict a great punishment and kill a sinner, then he would have no way to repent for his wrongdoing and correct and himself again (p. 66). Moreover, no worldly pleasures or pains can do justice to the number of merits and demerits a person commits during his lifetime. One particularly interesting example of 'worldly riches' Jeong A. describes goes as follows:

> It is impossible to repay the goodness or the wickedness of a person through worldly prosperity or adversity. As a person's goodness and wickedness cannot be determined during his life, he does not receive reward or punishment from the Lord of Heaven. Additionally, worldly riches are limited in number, but there is no fixed amount to the number of good people. For instance, there are three ministers in a country, but if there are ten people who are worthy of becoming ministers, with only three seats, how can all of them be made ministers? (p. 67)

Jeong A. is here appealing to commoners as well as Confucian elites, whose ideal is to become ministers to govern people with humaneness and justice. He wholly understands that, in a Confucian moral society, the appeal to extreme beauty or abundance of food may invite commoner's heart, but certainly put off the interest of the scholar-elites. He is hence portraying the kind of paradise where the righteous Confucians are in top seats, bringing harmony and propriety to the world. In other words, he is suggesting that the riches and wealth in Heaven are not only private satisfactions and corporeal indulgence, but are for the greater, common good.

Jeong A.'s picture assumes that there are no proper rewards in this world, because "there are many good people in this world who are poor, and many wicked people who are rich" (p. 66). During his time, this kind of sentiment was shared not only among pro-Catholics, but also among anti-Catholics like Shin and Ahn, who belonged to the Southern faction declining in power. The only difference was that anti-Catholics held that a true Confucian would still only single-mindedly do what is right, without expecting further consequences (cf. S.-Y. Chung 2011). From the perspective of the common people, however, it was natural for them to doubt the existence of Heaven. Jeong A. saw the urgent need to convince them that there is a just principle, although it may not belong to 'this world':

> In the world, even a wicked person enjoys wealth and fame and lives in pleasure all his life, while even a good person spends his life in pain because he is poor and lowly. Seeing this, people doubt the existence of a master in heaven and earth, or they doubt his justice. (...) On the last day, by raising the person to heaven after death, the Lord of Heaven will make all the people understand clearly how he repays all the good deeds that this person performed throughout his life. (p. 98)

Unlike Shin who explained that the good people abided by the universal principle *li* and thereby naturally bringing upon themselves social recognition and praises, Jeong A. observed that such evaluation from the community could not reflect the true motivation behind a person's action.

> It is impossible to know the state of someone's heart during his life in this world. If a wicked person pretends to be good, those who are ignorant think he is good. If a good person suffers pain, others who are ignorant think he is wicked. Hence, as the goodness or the wickedness of a person does not show clearly, the Lord of Heaven justly carries out his judgment once and for all, fully revealing each person's hidden goodness and wickedness. All people under heaven from every age and place will see each other and know each other, and at this time the Lord of Heaven will make them understand his great justice. (p. 98)

Jeong A. here describes how one's actions are on the day of Last Judgment 'fully revealed' and 'seen and known' by all people under heaven. It implicitly draws on the Confucian value system in which if one continuously does a right thing, the people around him and society at large eventually will recognize his goodness and it becomes his reward for the past good deeds. Jeong A. is painfully aware that the communal and state recognition in the present world does not do justice to one's intentions, decisions, and actions. Although Confucius himself warned that the ideal person *junzi* would not be bitter about others not recognizing him (*Analects* 1.1) (Confucius 1979), Jeong A. still holds onto the hope of social approval and communal respect through the Lord of Heaven.

As Jeong A. translates the wealth and riches of the afterlife into major Confucian values such as governance and social recognition, how does he explain the resurrection of the body? He again brings the interrogator to ask, "A person's soul does not die, and will receive reward and punishment. Yet since the person's body has now died and become dust, how will he live again and receive reward and punishment?" He responds, "the Lord of Heaven created heaven and earth, the angels, human beings, and all things from nothing. How can he not be able to resurrect a person who existed once before?" (p. 100) His reason for the resurrection of the body goes as follows:

> Additionally, only when both the soul and the body become united can a person be complete. Now although a soul may ascend to heaven and enjoy bliss, it will remain only half a person until it unites with its body. Then, in the end, one can say that a person is complete only when the body is resurrected and united with the soul. How then will the Lord of Heaven allow only half a good person to stay in heaven? (...) Moreover, whether a person does a good deed or a wicked deed, the soul does not act alone, but the body assists, and the two act as one. (...) Additionally, at this time, every person assumes his original body and is resurrected. If the soul unites with a different body, his will would be to punish an innocent body and not to reward a body that has done good deeds. How can the exceedingly just law of the Lord of Heaven be thus? (p. 100)

Jeong A. claims that since a person is comprised with a soul and body, one's reward and punishment is only complete when they have united again. One's good and evil actions are decided by mind but assisted by the body; hence, one is rewarded with bodily pleasures and punished by physical pains as one is judged by the Lord of Heaven. The kind of bodily pleasure is described as follows:

> When the bodies of the righteous are resurrected, the Lord of Heaven will bestow a special grace so that there will be no appearance of disease, old age, or even youth, and all will become like Jesus. Their appearance will be kind and good, strong and firm, beautiful and marvelous. (...) This body will ascend to heaven to serve Jesus together with countless angels and countless saints, enjoying boundless blessings. Since blessings and pleasures of the soul are infinitely better than those of the body, how can they be described in words? Having also become a beloved child of the Lord of Heaven, the soul will be a brother and a friend to the angels and the saints. With such infinite happiness, to what can the soul's preciousness and glory be compared? (pp. 100–101)

It is notable here that Jeong A. emphasizes the spiritual blessings and gratifications that are 'infinitely better' than the bodily pleasures. In his descriptions of infinite happiness of the soul, we find some notions adaptable in Confucian terms, such as the 'serving' of Jesus the Lord, 'brotherhood' and 'friendship' with angels and saints.

Jeong A. and his immediate family members were among the first martyrs of the early Korean Catholic Church. They were deeply convinced by the Christian notion of spirituality, with the vision of an afterlife in which the omnipotent and omniscient Lord brings justice to all the individual choices of action. Jeong A. wrote a catechistic book persuasive not only to the commoners but also to scholar-elites like himself, who greatly appreciate the Confucian values such as humane governorship, social recognition, serving parents and lords, brotherhood, and friendship with the neighbors. Such values were subtly weaved into his arguments and descriptions of the human soul, Heaven and Hell, and the resurrection of the body, which helped to mitigate the outlandishness of the foreign thoughts and assimilate them into the Confucian background.

4. Reconciliation of Catholicism and Confucianism

As briefly mentioned before, Jeong A.'s brothers were initially moved by Catholic doctrines and their novel ideas of human spirituality. Tasan and his brother Jeong Yag-jeon so deeply influenced by Jesuit works such as *The True Meaning of the Lord of Heaven*, that while they were scholar-officers at the university *Sungkyunkwan*, their answers were markedly infused in Jesuit ideas. When the Joseon government later identified Catholicism as a heresy and began to oppress the believers, however, they openly renounced Catholicism (cf. (Y.-J. Jeong 2012, (vol. 3), pp. 252–55)).

Despite his open apostasy, Tasan was sent to exile because of his previous interest in Western Learning and family-relation with Catholic martyrs. In the Kangjin province, the place of exile, he built a hut named *Yeoyudang*, meaning 'being wary and cautious as if crossing a half-frozen lake.' He had the academic honesty and sincerity to write what he believed as true, but he needed to be extremely careful to not borrow Catholic terminologies that would plunge him into trouble again. During his 18 years of exile, he wrote and edited five hundred volumes of books, including commentaries on all the major Confucian canons. Looking into Tasan's writings and commentaries on human spirituality, one may find a creative new scheme that neither denounces Catholicism nor implements Catholicism. It distances itself from the rigid neo-Confucian framework on human nature, but it avoids the sensitive issues pertaining to Catholic doctrines (cf. S.-Y. Chung 2016). This section will examine Tasan's reconciliatory perspective on human spirituality by comparing it with earlier stances by Shin and Jeong A.

Regarding the immortality of the human soul (*hon*) or spiritual soul (*yeong-hon*), Shin and other traditional neo-Confucian scholars outright refuted it as impossible, claiming it is tied to one's body. Just as the mind makes one's body its home, it no longer exists as it departs from the body. On the contrary, Jeong A. reasoned that the human mind was built in such a way that it took pleasure and pain beyond its bodily desires. A human's spiritual soul is different from animals and the human mind controls its body, but is not controlled by the body. On this point, Tasan asserts that the human mind and body, spirit and form are neither together nor separate, but "mysteriously united (神形妙合)" in the following sense:

> Human spirit and form are mysteriously united. A body becoming fat or thin is also related [to the spirit]. If one's mind is generous then the body gets large and strong; when one is covetous, then the eyes lose focus. When there is beauty inside, then the face illuminates and the back straightens; when there is guilt inside, then the sweat comes out and the face reddens. These are all clear evidence that the spirit and form are mysteriously united. (Y.-Y. Jeong 2012, (vol. 7), p. 53)

Tasan carefully equates human spirit with the general term *sim*, the heart-mind. He argues that human nature *seong* is not an entity but a common 'quality' shared by all humans. In this way, Tasan is inclined to individuality (mind) rather than commonality (nature). He analyzes:

> Only after spirit and form are mysteriously united, does one become human. Therefore, in ancient Classics, they referred to it as 'body (身)' or 'me (己)'. However, there is no one name particularly designating the empty spiritual conscious faculty. Later scholars who want to call it separately borrowed some names such as mind (心), mysterious (神), spirit (靈), soul (魂), but they are all borrowed names. Mencius called the formless the 'great body,' and the form the 'small body.' Buddha called the formless the 'dharma body,' and the form the 'physical body.' They are all added names. (Y.-Y. Jeong 2012, (vol. 6), p. 195)

Tasan discusses that, in Confucianism, there is no particular name for the 'spirit' or the 'formless' part of ourselves. Neo-Confucian scholars of his time debated over two candidates—*sim* (the heart-mind) and *seong* (the nature)—to name the spirit, and Tasan chooses *sim* over *seong* for the following reason:

> Today, scholars hotly debate over the two words—'heart-mind' and 'nature'. Some speak of the heart-mind as great and the nature as small; some speak of nature as great and the heart-mind as small. (…) Those regarding the heart-mind as great, emphasize the mysterious union of spirit and form, hold that there is only one heart-mind. Those regarding nature as great upholds the word 'nature' as the proper name for the 'great body' or the

'Dharma body (法身).' If one must borrow one word to name the great body, then 'heart-mind' would be closer, while 'nature' would not fit. If we see how the word 'nature' is constructed, then we must read it like it is the appetite of a pheasant, an inclination of a deer, quality of grass, and properties of trees, etc. The term 'nature' refers to dispositions and tendency (嗜好), not something remote and grandiose. (Y.-Y. Jeong 2012, (vol. 6), p. 196)

Tasan holds that human nature is a moral disposition of mind, liking goodness and disliking wickedness. It is quite similar to the Jesuit scholar's description of the human spirit and its appetites for the good (cf. I.-C. Chung 2012), but he found the sources from the ancient Classics like *The Book of Mencius*. The question then is whether Tasan's *sim* is immortal as Jesuits and Jeong A.'s spiritual soul.

As we have seen previously, Shin argued that the word *hon* connoted the dissipation. Jeong A. contended that the human spiritual soul, *yeong-hon*, was special in that it was different from animal souls and immortal by its nature. Within more than five volumes of Tasan work, no single usage of *hon* in the sense of the human spirit can be found; whether it is the *yeong-hon* (spiritual soul), the *shin-hon* (mysterious soul), or the *hon-ryeong* (soul-spirit), the name is heavily burdened with connotation of either dissipation (mortality) or the Catholic doctrine of the immortal soul. Hence Tasan made up special terms for the human heart-mind, such as the '*yeong-myeong* (spiritual brightness, 靈明)', the '*yeong-ji* (spiritual knowing, 靈知)', and the '*yeong-che* (spiritual body, 靈體)'. He only used the word 'spiritual body' once and sparingly used the term 'spiritual knowing'. He did not wish his special terminology to have a Buddhist or Yang-ming undertone. His favorite term was 'spiritual brightness' which designated the faculty of the human mind as rational, balanced, and lucid. It is not to be confused with *ki*, the material energy-force or ethereal, smoke-like entity. The delicate issue of individual immortality is also shrewdly avoided. The term '*myeong* (brightness)' has the connotation of heaven-sent, eternal virtue in the *Great Learning* ('*myeong-deok* the bright virtue'), yet at the same time, it is the 'spiritual' faculty of individual human mind.

In relation to Heaven and Hell, Shin fiercely repudiated that it provokes the selfish interest of people while Jeong A. found it essential for there to be any justice for one's good actions. Tasan again avoided both ends on this issue. Shin asserted that people do get the social recognition if one unfailingly follows the universal principle and does the right thing regardless of the outcome. Jeong A. argued that the final recognition was from the Lord of Heaven. Tasan reconciles both stances in his own way:

If a person does one good thing, then his mind will be filled with pleasure. If he does one bad thing, then his mind will become stained with guilt. Even if he has not done anything good, if others praise him as good, then he will feel good and happy. Even if he has not done anything bad, if others condemn him, then he will feel bad and angry. As such, [the spiritual brightness] naturally knows good acts are praiseworthy and bad deeds are blameworthy. (Y.-Y. Jeong 2012, (vol. 6), p. 195)

Tasan admits that social approval and disapproval is important to guide one's choice of actions. Still, the focus and motivation of one's action should not be to win the good opinion of others, but to be satisfied in himself: even if one can deceive others, one cannot deceive oneself. He illustrates as follows:

Let us speak of a person who accumulates righteous deeds. In the beginning, he does not feel shame confronting others and does not feel guilty confronting themselves. As he accumulates more, his heart-mind opens up and his body grows big, his face brightens and his back straightens. As he accumulates even more, the 'vast, flood-like ki' will flare out, it will be extremely large and strong, as to fulfill all the spaces between heaven and earth. Then no wealth and honor can taint him, poverty and lowliness cannot change him, and threats and weapons cannot defeat him. Thus, he will mysteriously transform himself, as to be one with the heaven and earth in virtue, and be one with the sun and moon in brightness; finally, he becomes a fully virtuous man. (Y.-Y. Jeong 2012, (vol. 6), p. 196)

In the above, Tasan is describing a person going through a complete self-transformation through choosing and carrying out the right action. One becomes strong and marvelous in appearance, not by God's special grace[2] but by his own accumulation of good deeds. Through self-transformation, one goes beyond the social recognition and threat; that is, one is transcending this world without leaving this world.

In the same context, since a person is free to choose one's course of action, one may not abide by the universal principle embedded in one's mind. He vividly pictures that one may deceive people around, but one cannot escape from one's own guilt and fear.

> Suppose another person who does one thing against his own conscience today. Tomorrow, he repeats doing the same thing. He will be dissatisfied and stuffed inside, fearful and guilty. He gives up and tells himself "I am already doomed"; he will be in pieces and tell himself "it is over." Thereby his willpower fades and withers, his *ki* breaks down and crushes him. Then when someone tempts him with small profits, he will yield to it like a dog or pig; when someone threatens him with authority, he will succumb to it like a fox or rabbit. He will grow haggard and flagged, and eventually, die in tears. (Y.-Y. Jeong 2012, (vol. 6), p. 197)

Tasan describes how one is literally being punished by his own actions without appealing to the Lord of Heaven. As a person does one thing against the good conscience, one is making one's own personal hell out of this world. Although there is no state officer or Lord of Heaven who would inflict great pain on oneself, one's spirit becomes as base as that of an animal's, and one's body—appearance and posture—becomes weary and haggard. In summary, human actions are rewarded and punished not by the community nor by the Lord, but by one's own conscience. One is creating one's own personal heaven and hell during one's lifetime. The 'spiritual brightness' of a human is built in such a way that one is bound to feel dignified and proud if one does a right thing and to feel guilty and fearful otherwise (Y.-Y. Jeong 2012, (vol. 4), pp. 163–167).

In this sense, Tasan does not need to address the resurrection of the body after death. The body and spirit are mysteriously combined and the body reflects the state of the spirit. In Confucianism, the 'body' does not need to be one's own physical organism. After death, one's individuality is extended in many forms (cf. Tu 1985). One's organic component is continued by one's children and generations after that; one's spiritual legacy is transmitted by students and disciples. If there is no one to inherit the level of one's scholarship in the present world and time, then one may write and leave books behind, waiting for another generation of young scholars to discover the genuine dimension of one's spiritual brightness. Tasan wrote more than five hundred volumes of books which he compiled meticulously in order (cf. B. R. Kim 2011); he was prepared to be discovered. More importantly, Tasan never called himself 'Tasan'. He always used the penname 'Sa-am (俟菴; waiting-in-hermitage)', waiting for a later generation to find and resurrect him.[3]

---

[2]   However, it is debatable whether, in Tasan's philosophy, there is absolutely no place for the special grace of the Lord. For example, Tasan describes that every person is born neither good nor evil, but one day one 'suddenly' realizes that one good action will transform oneself a little. A hint of God's special grace is implied in such passages. Back (2015) also discusses the special *ming* (mandate) of Heaven in Tasan's philosophy.

[3]   'Tasan (tea-mountain)' is the mountain name in the place of exile. It painfully reminded him of the unnecessarily long period of exile, which prevented him from government service that he had hoped for. I assume that he was widely called, rather humiliatingly, as Tasan after the exile from the scholars from opposing faction. His sons and disciples never addressed him with the penname Tasan. It was officially recorded in his annals compiled by his great-great-grandson, who might not have aware of this fact. The penname Tasan first had was Sa-am (俟菴). I speculate that it was given after his meeting at the Cheonjin-am (天菴) to study Western Learning. It is quite remarkable that almost all the study group members of Cheonjin-am, have their penname ending with 'am (菴): Nok-am (鹿菴) Kwon Chul-sin, Yi-am (移菴) Kwon Il-sin, Son-am (巽菴) Jeong Yag-jeon, Seon-am (選菴) Jeong Yag-jong, Sa-am (俟菴) Jeong Yag-yong, and Bok-am (伏菴) Yi Ki-yang.

5. Conclusions

So far, this paper examined and discussed the three ways of responding to the Christian notion of human spirituality that was new and alien to the Joseon people and scholars deeply entrenched in the Confucian framework. Three scholars from Sungho school and their respective works are chosen to represent the initial reactions to this so-called Western Learning.

The first reaction was that of refutation and repudiation by Shin Hudam, who contested the idea of the immortality of the human spiritual soul. In his neo-Confucian view, the soul belongs to the realm of *ki*, the ethereal force that will dissipate into the air as the dead body deteriorates into dust. They are closely related, they live together during one's lifetime and die together after one's death. In his eyes, the reason why the western scholar-missionaries emphasized the immortality of the individual human soul is to entice them with the promise of Heavenly pleasure and threaten them with pains in Hell by provoking people's selfish interest to pursue what is beneficial only to their physical self. Unlike the Confucian value system in which one does the right thing without ulterior motives, people are motivated to do good only out of hope or fear of reward and punishment in the next life. The notion of Heaven and Hell and the eternity beyond makes this present world temporal and transient. People would not genuinely devote their life and significance in the everyday relational and communal duties if they started to belittle 'this' world as fleeting. There is no need to even mention the resurrection of the body, the very act of appealing to one's bodily pleasure and pain and individual immortality leads people to calculate one's private, selfish interest before their public and communal responsibilities. In a gist, there is no way to find true humanism and friendship from the Christian idea of human spirituality.

The second response is quite the contrary. Early Catholic believers and martyrs like Jeong A. recognized and revered it as the one true way of living. He holds that the humans have a unique place in this world and we can reason out that the human soul is immortal. Humans, unlike animals, take interest in what is beyond their immediate physical sensations and take pleasures and pains in matters that have nothing to do with their bodily comfort. Communal praise and insult are what humans are concerned about and the desire to live forever is unique only to human beings. The spiritual soul, *yeong-hon*, is, therefore, separate from the body and can last after it departs from its form. Moreover, if there was any justice for one's actions, and if there was an absolute ruler of everything under heaven, then there must be a life after death. The merits and demerits of human actions cannot be assessed during one's lifetime and the rewards and punishment cannot be meted out with the limitation in this secular world. The righteous people, according to Jeong A.'s description, will ascend to heaven and become ministers who spread benevolence. They will serve the Lord and become brothers with angels and friends with saints. As the body is resurrected, a person becomes one whole human who enjoys both the bodily pleasures, as well as the spiritual happiness, although the latter is far more powerful and blissful. In other words, the Catholic notion of human spirituality for Jeong A. does not stand against the Confucian ethical values. One is as humane, just, and responsible, if not more, when one adopts the everlasting vision of one's own spiritual soul: one's past deeds are not just buried under one's graves but are to be judged and sentenced to perpetual blessings or condemnations.

Finally, there was a creative attempt to reconcile Christianity with traditional Confucianism. Tasan Jeong Yag-yong was one such innovative thinker who successfully weaved Catholic ideas into the Confucian framework. Although he openly renounced the Catholic faith, it was out of fear of getting into conflict with the government. He criticizes the long-held *li-ki* structure of neo-Confucianism and found the Catholic discussions on human spirituality convincing in certain aspects. He attests that the spirit and form are mysteriously united to become a human being. The human spirit-mind, which he advertently named as the 'spiritual brightness,' is related to, but not bounded by, one's physical body. The human face and body are transformed brilliantly in this world by doing what is right, and it is transformed miserably by doing what is against one's conscience. He portrays humans, together with their innate conscience, as the creator of Heaven and Hell in this present world. Although Tasan does not explicitly mention the eternity of the human spirit and resurrection of the individual body,

Religions **2018**, *9*, 329

he implicitly holds onto the idea of 'living again' by being discovered by later generation of scholars who would study his works and 'resurrect' his individual unique ideas. Such a hope is well-reflected in his real penname Sa-am: waiting-in-hermitage.

Funding: This research received no external funding.

Conflicts of Interest: The author declares no conflict of interest.

References

Aleni, Giulio. 1873. *Xingxuecushu [性學㭊述, Rough Introduction to Study of Nature]*. Shanghai: Shanghai Zimutang Publishers.

Kim, Bo Rum. 2011. On the Formation of the Anthology of Yeoyudang. *Journal of Tasan Studies* 18: 197–236.

Back, Youngsun. 2015. Fate and the Good Life: Zhu Xi and Jeong Yagyong's Discourse on Ming. *Dao: A Journal of Comparative Philosophy* 14: 255–74. [CrossRef]

Baek, Min-jeong. 2007. *Philosophy of Jeong Yagyong*. Seoul: Yihaksa. (In Korean)

Baker, Don. 2002. Thomas Aquinas and Chong Yagyong: Rebels within Tradition. *Journal of Tasan Studies* 3: 32–69.

Baker, Don. 2013. Finding God in the Classics: The Theistic Confucianism of Dasan Jeong Yagyong. *Dao: A Journal of Comparative Philosophy* 12: 41–55. [CrossRef]

Baker, Don. 2015. Pushing the Confucian Envelope: Tasan Chŏng Yagyong as a man of, and not of, his times. *Acta Koreana* 18: 145–62.

Baker, Don. 2017. *Catholics and Anti-Catholicism in Choson Korea*. Honolulu: University of Hawaii Press, ISBN 978-0-8248-6626-6.

Berthrong, John. 2003. New Confucian Spirituality in Interreligious Dialogue. In *Confucian Spirituality*. Edited by Weiming Tu and Mary Evelyn Tucker. New York: The Crossroad Publishing Company, ISBN 978-0824521110.

Cawley, Kevin N. 2014. Dis-assembling Traditions: Deconstructing Tasan via Matteo Ricci. *Journal of the Royal Asiatic Society* 24: 297–313. [CrossRef]

Cho, Kwang. 2002. Jeong Yag-jong and the Early Catholic Church. *Hanguksasangsahak* 18: 3–35. (In Korean)

Cho, Kwang. 2006. On the Vernacular Catholic Books in the 19th Century Korea. *Mijokmunhwayeongu* 44: 199–235. (In Korean)

Confucius. 1979. *Analects*. Translated by Din Cheuk Lau. London: Penguin Books.

Chung, Doo Hee. 2003. The Influence of Jeong Yagjong's *Jugyo Yoji* on the History of Korean Thoughts. *Gyohuisa yeongu* 20: 221–35. (In Korean)

Chung, In-Chai. 2012. The Theory of Anima of Western Learning and the Theory of Mind and Nature in Tasan's philosophy. *Gyohuisa yeongu* 39: 271–326. (In Korean)

Song, Kap Jun. 2000. The Branch and Philosophical issues in Seong-Ho Schools. *The Journal of Human Studies* 13: 147–69. (In Korean)

Keum, Jang Tae. 2001. Shin Hu-tam's (慎後聃) Theoretical Criticism of Western Learning and its Issues. *Journal of Religious Studies* 20: 1–25. (In Korean)

Mencius. 1970. *The Book of Mencius*. Translated by Din Cheuk Lau. 1970. London: Penguin Books.

Ricci, Mateo. 1985. *True Meaning of the Lord of Heaven*. Edited by Edward Malatesta. Translated by Douglas Lancashire, and Guozhen Hu. Taipei: The Ricci Institute, ISBN 978-0912422770.

Rule, Paul A. 1986. *K'ung-Tzu or Confucius—The Jesuit Interpretation of Confucianism*. London: Allen and Unwin, ISBN 978-0868619132.

Song, Seok Jun. 2002. Confucianism with Jeong Yak-jong. *Hanguksasangsahak* 18: 87–123. (In Korean)

Kim, Sun-hee. 2012. *Mateo Ricci, Zhu Xi and Jeong Yagyong*. Seoul: Simsan. (In Korean)

Chung, So-Yi. 2011. Kyonggi Southerners' Notion of Heaven and Its Influence on Tasan's Theory of Human Nature. *Journal of Korean Religions* 2: 111–41. [CrossRef]

Chung, So-Yi. 2016. Tasan's Post Neo-Confucianism. In *Traditional Korean Philosophy: Problems and Debates*. Edited by Youngsun Back and Philip J. Ivanhoe. London: Rowman & Littlefield.

Chung, So-Yi. 2018. Individuality and Immortality in Confucian Spirituality. *Journal of Korean Religions* 9, forthcoming.

Sambiasi, Francesco. 1965. Yeong-eon yejak [靈言蠡勺, Talking about Anima from a Tiny Ladle]. In *Tian-xue chu han* [天學初函 *First Letter on Learning of Heaven*]. Edited by Zhizao Li 李之藻. Taiwan: Taiwan Student Press. (In Chinese)

Shin, Hudam. 2014. *Refutation on Western Learning*. Translated by Sunhee Kim. Seoul: Sungkyunkwan University Press, ISBN 979-11-5550-078-1. (In Korean)

Tu, Weiming. 1985. *Confucian Thought: Selfhood as Creative Transformation*. New York: State University of New York Press, ISBN 978-0887060069.

Jeong, Yag-Yong. 2012. Yeoyudangjeonseo [The Complete Works of Yeoyudang]. Seoul: Tasan Cultural Foundation.

Jeong, Yag-Jong. 2012. *Jugyo Yoji* [主教要旨, *The Essentials of the Lord's Teaching*]. Edited by Jae-hyun Kim. English Translated by Deberniere J. Torrey. Seoul: Kiats.

Yao, Xinzhong. 2000. *An Introduction to Confucianism*. New York: Cambridge University Press, ISBN 978-0-521-64430-3.

Article

Responses of Korean Buddhism to the Ethos of Contemporary Korea: Three Discourses in the Wake of Modernization

Woncheol Yun [1],* and Beom Seok Park [2]

[1] Department of Religious Studies, Seoul National University, Seoul 08826, Korea
[2] Center for Religious Studies, Seoul National University, Seoul 08826, Korea; vine0427@snu.ac.kr
* Correspondence: yunwc@snu.kr; Tel.: +82-10-659-7069

Received: 30 September 2018; Accepted: 21 December 2018; Published: 24 December 2018

Abstract: The revival of Buddhism in Korea began in the 20th century as the nation suffered a downfall from the colonization of the Japanese Imperialists. In this chaotic time of social turmoil, transformation into a modern nation resulted not from a natural flow of events but rather from an articulation through a series of discourses on Korean identity. The modernization process in Korea was precipitated by the Japanese colonialism, thereby adding to the complexity during the time of social transformation. In this paper, we have reviewed the three major discourses of Korean Buddhism in the wake of modernization. The following discourses were attempts to deal with the problems faced by the Buddhist community during modernization: the discourse on secularity and social participation, the discourse on modernity centering on the issue of modifying precepts, and the discourse on identity contemplating the originality of Korean Buddhism. The fact that the old controversies concerning precepts continue even to this day in Korea might be regarded as a proof of the vibrant dynamics of contemporary Korean Buddhism. Accordingly, the next unavoidable discourse regarding Korean Buddhism would be on whether and how it can adapt itself to contemporary society, along with what part it will play in the forthcoming society.

Keywords: Korean Buddhism; modernization and Buddhism; patriotic Buddhism; marriage of monks; all-embracing Buddhism

---

1. Introduction

Ever since Buddhism was first introduced in Korea at the end of the 4th century, the Buddhist sentiment has taken deep roots in the Korean way of thinking and lifestyle. In modern-day Korea, traditional religions and new religions intermingle without much conflict. This balance in religious co-existence could come from a Buddhist influence, which emphasizes tolerance and generosity. Nonetheless, Buddhism has not always been so welcomed throughout Korean history. From the foundation of the Joseon dynasty (조선 朝鮮, 1392–1897) with Confucianism as its national ideology, Buddhism was persecuted for five hundred years. Under such coercion, many Buddhist temples and monks chose to go into hiding, literally and figuratively, for survival.

It is quite ironic that the revival of Buddhism in Korea began in the 20th century during which the nation suffered a downfall from the Japanese Imperialists' invasion. During the colonization, the new influence of Japanese Buddhism advanced. The Buddhist community became more accepted in the society, and there was a significant rise in the social status of Buddhist monks. Such changes brought about a surge of vibrancy in the Buddhist community. During this time, some of the Buddhist community led resistance against Japanese rule, while there were others who appealed to the pro-Buddhist Japanese colonialists to bring about a religious revival. To classify the activities of the era in dichotomy such as pro- versus anti-Japan, or Korean versus Japanese Buddhism would be simplifying and therefore distorting a complex reality. Even though it is true that there was a demand for modernization through provocation of the Japanese invasion, it cannot be denied that there were innumerous controversies surrounding the course of transformation.

We shall contemplate the discourses in Korean Buddhism brought up during the process of modernization by dealing with major controversies of the time. To fully understand the discourses, it would be crucial to comprehend the hardships that the Buddhist community experienced while responding to social changes. It seems that the Buddhist community has taken the best available option during the time of chaos by striving for a breakthrough rather than choosing one between the opposing positions.

In this paper, we shall examine the history of discourses by focusing on major controversies throughout Korean modernity. As some of these discussions are still relevant, this paper will hopefully contribute to a better understanding of Korean Buddhism in today's world.

The first of such topics is the controversy surrounding *Hoguk Bulgyo* (호국불교 護國佛教)—literally 'national defense' or patriotic Buddhism—as a discourse on secularity. The concept is represented by the phenomenon of Korean Buddhist monks taking arms against foreign invaders in times of national crisis. As the significance of the term might be open for discussion, by 'secular', we refer to instances when Buddhism steps out of its seclusion to participate in social and political affairs. Secondly, we will discuss the issue of monks' marriages as a discourse on modernity. As modernization in Korea was precipitated by the Japanese colonization, Japanese influence in Korean modernity caused social confusion. The controversy surrounding the marriage of Buddhist monks is a good example. The third topic is the controversy of *Hoetong Bulgyo* (회통불교 會通佛教)—literally, 'inclusive' or consolidation Buddhism, a name given to emphasize the all-embracing characteristic of Korean Buddhism—as a discourse on identity. This discourse aims to discuss whether there is a trend of Buddhist ideas particular to Korean society, independent from that of China or Japan.

The three discourses touch upon secularity, modernity, and identity, which are the topics the Buddhists in Korea have contemplated over and debated on until recent years. In discussing the controversies, it is essential to understand the socio-political background of modernization in 20th century Korea. During the colonial period, the Japanese government proceeded with the modernization of Korea in order to exploit resources and use Korea as a bridgehead for its advance on the continent. During the national crisis of Japanese occupation, the biggest challenge of Korean Buddhism was to survive. For a way of survival, it had to choose between adapting itself to the new social environment or resisting to changes. On one hand, the three discourses were responses of the Korean Buddhist community to the crises generated by Japanese occupation. On the other hand, they were also the Korean Buddhist community's efforts to deal with the inevitable issues that stemmed from modernization. Such issues show Korean Buddhists' active engagement in resolving issues from the fast-changing secular society, defining and preserving the Buddhist traditional identity, and creating new dynamics. These efforts can be construed as proof of vibrancy in contemporary Korean Buddhism.

2. Background for the Discourses Surrounding Modern Korean Buddhism

At the beginning of the 20th century, Korean Buddhism was not in a state to compete with foreign influences. It was forced to accept the intervening powers of the West and the Japanese Imperialists. Although the Joseon dynasty's ban that kept Buddhist monks/nuns from entering the capital was lifted and there was a slight improvement in the social status of the cleric, the revival of Korean Buddhism was subtle compared to the sudden rise of Christianity. Supported by the powers of the West, Christianity symbolized Westernization. During this era, Westernization meant modernization (Kim 2003, p. 184). For supporters of modernization, all obstacles to modernization—whether stubborn Confucianism, superstitious Shamanism, or the idle Buddhists—were equally subject to eradication (Park 2004, p. 238; Lee 2006, p. 279)

The Protestants proved to be a great threat to Buddhism, as they were aggressive in their proselyting and preached incompatibility with other religious beliefs. At the time, the theory of social evolution was the accepted norm, though it was hardly for the purpose of enlightenment or civilization; it was rather used as a justification for colonialism. Under the theory of evolution, the survival of the fittest can also be applied to human society. From such a perspective, the existence of or exploitation by colonizers can be justified. The Buddhist community attempted to interpret social evolution theory as a method of overcoming outdated notions and moving towards equality, but there wasn't much outcome. Such failure comes from the limits of the theory of evolution itself and its discord with the Buddhist worldview.

In short, as Christianity and social evolution theory were used wrongfully to justify Western colonialism, Japanese Imperialists imitated the West and approached the colonization of Joseon in the name of modernization. Korean Buddhism during the modernization period was caught between the two major forces of Western and Japanese colonialism. It had to deal simultaneously with the growing force of Christianity and the intervention of Japanese Buddhism. During the modernization under colonization, Korean traditions were looked down upon as outdated evils. Likewise, the profound philosophy of Buddhism was degraded as a mere folk religion (You 1985, p. 241).

In addition to such social turmoil, modernity also gave rise to troubles within Buddhism. Traditional Korean Buddhism centers on a firm belief in asceticism and truth seeking. It has put emphasis on them more than any other religion has. Rather than accustoming oneself to the world, one should be willing to go through extreme penance in order to achieve enlightenment on the ultimate significance of life. To leave one's home and become a Buddhist monk/nun means to leave behind all secular pleasures and to embrace such asceticism. Owing to such disconnection from the outside world, the Buddhist community was at times slow to respond to social changes, and its reactions were sometimes inappropriate. In the time of social transition such as the modernization period, there was no clear standard for how the Buddhist community should take part in such changes, resulting in over-intervention or utter insensibility.

Another factor is that Buddhist sentiments have influenced the Korean mind and vice versa for a couple of millennia. It is a common saying that Koreans are innately multi-religious. They are Confucians in family matters, but take Buddhist tendencies when contemplating life, while also taking a Shamanist view of fate. The three religions have blended in a balanced way. Some believe that is why Koreans have so peacefully adjusted to the current multi-religious society. The inclusive, tolerant, and harmonious religious tendencies of the Korean people are often attributed to the influence of the Buddhist worldview of infinite mercy. On the other hand, the fact that Korean Buddhism emphasizes harmony and consolidation compared to other Buddhist cultures seems to have resulted from the Korean tendency of tolerance (Choi 2017, p. 210; Lee 2007, pp. 137–41, 165–66).

It would be impossible to sum up the course of change that Korean Buddhism has gone through in a few discourses. Nonetheless, we shall seek to sympathize with the anguish the Buddhist community experienced during the social transformation by discussing some key words that can encapsulate the major challenges of the modernization process. These key words would lead to three controversies concerning the armament of Buddhists to defend the nation, marriage of Buddhist monks, and the Korean Buddhist tendency of consolidating. Each controversy leads to the discourses of secularity, modernity, and identity.

3. Discourse on Secularity: The Controversy Surrounding *Hoguk Bulgyo*

"*Hoguk Bulgyo*" is a term often used to illustrate Korean Buddhism, but it is a controversial one. *Hoguk,* meaning "defending the nation," emphasizes the role of the Buddhist community to protect the country in times of crisis. Is this a necessary part of being Buddhist in Korea? For the Buddhist community, this term may be accepted as appropriate. Any duty or responsibility to defend the nation arises as an expedient means to protect the dharma or to save living beings, but not as an end. In other words, the term must be understood as a means to realize the Buddhist dharma.

Nevertheless, the term *hoguk* is used in the context of what the nation demands of the Buddhist community. From the nationalist point-of-view, the Buddhist community and believers are the components of the state; they are on the receiving end of government protection and it is natural they be asked to be loyal to the state when the need arises (Kim 2012, pp. 79, 82). In fact, Buddhism has served to consolidate the sovereign power since the Three Kingdoms era and has won a name for taking an active role in fighting back foreign attacks. There is no denying the part, both spiritual and physical, that the Buddhist community has played in resisting aggressors. For example, Buddhists carved the *Tripitaka Koreana*, often called the *Palmandaejangyeong* (팔만대장경 八萬大藏經), in the hope of repelling the Mongolian invasion of the Goryeo dynasty (고려 高麗, 918–1392). Troops of monks fought against the Japanese and the Chinese invasions during the Joseon dynasty.

From the Buddhist community's perspective, national defense was to some point used as a tool for propagation. While it would have been ideal to find a method of evangelism on its own, government support is a momentum that is incomparable with any effort within the Buddhist community. Nonetheless, because of this compromise with political power, the original Buddhist purpose of saving living things has somewhat diminished for the sake of advocating the regime or justifying the ruling class (Kim 2000). Instead of fortifying the ascetic tradition, such social participation might have the effect of satisfying only the interests of the Buddhist ruling class who wish to conspire with political powers.

On the other hand, there are also quite positive evaluations of the Buddhist contribution to the protection of the Korean nation. Since Buddhism was introduced to Korea and officially recognized by royal courts during the Three Kingdom period, the Buddhist community's engagements in social activities have never been ceased. It is especially argued that Buddhist ways of social participation to defend the nation should not be confused with the attempts to advocate certain ideologies or to support particular social classes (Ko 2013, pp. 90, 110-12, and passim). It is also argued that this tendency of social participation led to the independence movement in the Japanese colonial era and to the Buddhist democracy movements in the modern era such as *Minjung* Buddhism (민중불교 民衆佛教), *Seonwu Doryang* (선우도량 善友道場), and *Jeongto-hoe* (정토회 淨土會) (Park 2010b, p. 48; Lee 2010, pp. 49–52).

The Buddhist community, oppressed throughout the Joseon dynasty, strove to find its identity between the two choices of pro-Japan or anti-Japan during the colonization. For this issue, the cause of 'national defense' can be played either way. 'National defense' seems to have been a choice of survival rather than a result of contemplation and discernment over whether one should loyally protect the state. One might guess that there were more pro-Japan priests than the anti-Japan priests because such choice was a matter of survival rather than a 'national defense' issue.

Political participation of priests after the liberation in 1945 seems to have been a choice for safeguarding the possessions and ensuring the safety of the Buddhist community in the post-war chaos. However, it is questionable whether such participation may be considered an aspect of *Hoguk Bulgyo*. Furthermore, the choices the Buddhist community made under the military regime, namely siding with the government authorities rather than fighting in resistance, has caused much shame and regret. Before contemplating whether survival or national safety is at the heart of *Hoguk Bulgyo*, one is forced to ask whether such choices served to "save all living beings."

Even if the fundamental motivation behind *Hoguk Bulgyo* was to save all living beings, it is difficult to escape the criticism that it might be misused or misconstrued to defend certain ideology after all. At times, the term *Hoguk Bulgyo*, like *Minjok Bulgyo* (민족불교 民族佛教 nationalist Buddhism) or *Bangong Bulgyo* (반공불교 反共佛教 anti-Communist Buddhism) might appear to be the result of . Buddhist secularization or political corruption. If *hoguk*, or national defense, is not for the defense of dharma or the defense of all living things, it might become nothing more than support for nationalism. It is simply not permissible that the cause of defending a country becomes the ultimate purpose or a value beyond that of saving all living things. It would be against the spirit of Buddhism to show mercy only towards the ruling class of the state.

Rather than discussing the concept of *Hoguk Bulgyo* itself, it would be more useful to explore its role, that is, the aspects of its development or its functions regarding certain political powers. It would not be ideal to contain Korean Buddhism within the narrow concept of *Hoguk Bulgyo*, or to glorify it by selectively displaying the positive side. A lively discussion of how *Hoguk Bulgyo* differs from the narrow-minded nationalism or the political empowerment of Buddhism is called for.

4. Discourse on Modernity: The Controversy Surrounding Marriage of Monks

In dealing with the discourse on modernity in the early 20th century Korean Buddhism, one cannot leave out the topic of the marriage of monks. It cannot be denied that the Korean Buddhist community was deeply influenced by Japanese Buddhism during the colonization period. The biggest issue in accepting Japanese influence was whether to allow the marriage of Buddhist monks. Traditionally, entering the monkhood means leaving home, renouncing the world, and focusing on ascetic practice. According to traditional views, monks cannot marry while practicing asceticism. For convenience's sake, we shall call those belonging to the order that allows marriage as the 'married monks' and those who do not as *bhikkhus*—the Pāli word for fully ordained celibate Buddhist monks.

The background to the appearance of the married priests in Korean Buddhism is twofold. First is the direct influence of Japanese Buddhism. In Japanese Buddhism, marriage is allowed for the monkhood. Korean Buddhism could not avoid Japanese influences under colonization. In addition, the new generation of Korean monks who had studied abroad in Japan were voluntarily drawn to the trend. In order for the married monks to expand their influence, they had to compete for power and properties with the bhikkhus. Therefore, conflicts between the two groups were inevitable. It was only natural that the Japanese government officials in Joseon favored the pro-Japanese married monks.

Nonetheless, there was a second influence from within the Buddhist community which was making an effort to adapt to modern society. Toward the end of the 19th century, the theory of social evolution had made a huge impact on Korean society. The concept of 'evolution' was applied to all areas of society, and the Buddhist community itself felt the need to change and adapt (Kim 2011, p. 275). For some of the Buddhist reformists, the marriage of monks was justified as the modern 'evolution' of Buddhism.

Young-Un Han (한용운 韓龍雲, 1879–1944), a major reformist monk, gave several reasons why monks' marriage should be allowed (Han 2016). He claimed that as the world is changing, the precepts should be applied flexibly according to the social settings. Moreover, as carnal love between man and woman cannot be relinquished, marriage should be allowed for the sake of the further development of Buddhism. As a 'modern value,' allowing monk's marriage signifies that human carnal desire should be accepted. Such understanding is the direct opposite to the Buddhist ideal of extinguishing such desires in nirvana. To his contemporaries, it must have come across as a ground-shaking idea that allowing priests to marry could modernize the Buddhist institution by affirming human desires.

As is well known, marriage of monks in Japan has a long history. However, since the Meiji government in Japan officially allowed monks to eat meat and marry in 1872, it has become quite natural for Buddhist monks in Japan to have a wife and create a family. It has also become part of the tradition for the offspring of the monks to inherit the temple. An interesting aspect is that in Japan, there was no such controversy and conflict over meat-eating and marrying (Je 2014, p. 249). How the tradition of the marriage of monks settled down so easily in Japan will be a matter that will have to be dealt with elsewhere, but it seems that Japanese culture was more accepting of the idea, as opposed to the fierce debate over allowing the marriage of monks in Korea.

The controversy of the marriage of monks that became prominent during the Japanese colonization seems to be a compound of two issues. The first is whether the marriage of monks conforms to the fundamental precepts of Buddhism, apart from the modernity issue underlined by the controversy. Secondly, monk marriage is a Japanese tradition, therefore many found it unacceptable in Korea. These two were intermingled issues in the minds of many and were used together to criticize the married monks from the bhikkhus' point-of-view. The marriage of monks was condemnable as violating Buddhist precepts while also being pro-Japanese. The married monks, on the other hand, believed that allowing the marriage of monks is a crucial aspect of 'modernizing' Buddhism and making it sustainable in a new era.

When all is said and done, this effort to modernize Buddhism and to override the monopoly of bhikkhus monkhood does not seem to have left a positive effect. The biggest problem was that the married monks, while maintaining the prerogatives of monkhood, could not surrender the comfort of secular life either. The fact that the conflict between the two groups of monkhood appeared nothing more than a dispute over the riches of the temple in the eyes of the public only added to the negative sentiment. Had the demands for priest marriage risen from the purpose of Buddhist modernization eventually leading to fundamental precept reform, then it would not have remained as a mere conflict between the two groups within monkhood. Korean Buddhist leaders failed to win the affirmation of the general Buddhist community because the reform suggested by the modernists was not substantial enough to overcome the criticism that allowing the marriage of monks was simply a pro-Japanese move.

Furthermore, Syngman Rhee, the first president of the Republic of Korea (a.k.a. South Korea), established after liberation from Japanese colonial regime, released a series of presidential instructions that monk marriage was a Japanese legacy and thus should be eliminated to revive the authentic Korean Buddhism. He needed to establish the legitimacy of his government against the communist North Korea, and the most important condition for it was to show an anti-Japanese stance on any given issue. President Rhee's instructions were fatal blows to the reformists' advocacy of monk marriage as a way of 'modernization.'

In today's Korea, the Jogye Order (조계종 曹溪宗) of celibate monks and nuns is the largest, but the Taego Order (태고종 太古宗), which allows the married to be ordained without leaving home, is of similar scale in terms of the number of monks. In recent years, there has been no visible conflict between the two groups of monkhood, as the institutions of both orders have become firmly established. The married and the celibate groups co-exist peacefully. However, the issues concerning the modification of precepts, including monks' meat-eating as well as marriage, remain controversial.

5. Discourse on Identity: The Controversy Surrounding *Hoetong Bulgyo*

In discussing the identity of Korean Buddhism, the controversy concerning *Hoetong Bulgyo* (회통 불교 會通佛敎) is something that never fails to be mentioned. The term *hoetong* means peacemaking among the conflicting opinions of different orders within Buddhism. It can also be applied to external relations with different religions.

It was Nam-Seon Choe (최남선 崔南善, 1890~1957) who explicitly defined Korean Buddhism as *Hoetong Bulgyo* (Choe 1930). According to him, the characteristic of *hoetong* can be found in various aspects throughout the history of Korean Buddhism beginning from Wonhyo (원효 元曉, 617–686) of the Three Kingdoms period. Wonhyo is considered the first philosopher to attempt to consolidate conflicting and controversial Buddhist precepts into a single fundamental purpose (Yun 2009, p. 107; Kim 2007, p. 38). In fact, successors such as Uicheon (의천 義天, 1055–1101) and Jinul (지눌 知訥, 1158–1210) consistently suggested that Seon (선 禪) and Gyo (교 敎) Buddhist orders—with respective emphasis on practice and precept—should be consolidated. Such opinion is relevant to the tendency for *hoetong*.

This *hoetong* point-of-view is again made apparent during the Joseon dynasty when interacting with other religions. In order to survive Joseon's anti-Buddhist policies, the Buddhist community chose to co-exist in peace with other religious beliefs such as Confucianism, Daoism, and Shamanism. Rather than drawing attention to its distinguishable traits and causing conflict, Buddhists supported the *hoetong* point-of-view that all religions fundamentally serve a single purpose.

To this day, with such a historical background, it has long been considered fact that the *Hoetong Bulgyo* sets aside Korean Buddhism from other Buddhist cultures. Under colonization, Koreans going through hard times needed a representation of national pride to distinguish themselves from Chinese or Japanese. *Hoetong Bulgyo* seems to be a product of such necessity (Choi 2013, pp. 103, 105–6 and *passim*). Scholars pondered what would make Korean Buddhism unique from those of Japan or China—as before the Japanese invasion, Korea was under heavy influence from Chinese Buddhism—and came up with this idea.

Nam-Seon Choe's opinion was accepted by some scholars, but it failed to gain popularity at the time. His idea began to be regarded as an authentic characterization of Korean Buddhism after liberation from Japan and during the 1970s and 1980s with the advocacy of nationalist articulation of what Korean identity was. Since then, Nam-Seon Choe's *Hoetong Bulgyo* has been regarded as a central concept for the identity of Korean Buddhism (Shim 1989, pp. 152–54).

It was a series of scholars in the 1980s that started the controversy, criticizing the characterization of Korean Buddhism as *Hoetong* (or *Tong*) *Bulgyo*. According to them, the term *Tong Bulgyo* is not an outcome of meticulous research but rather an ideology that serves nationalistic needs (Shim 2000). To judge by the historical background, the concept was first formed to better emphasize the originality and superiority of Korean Buddhism against the Japanese influence of modernization. Criticism against *Tong Bulgyo* suggests that the scholars accepted this point-of-view without much critical thinking, even though it is difficult to find a consistent point of *hoetong* throughout the history of Korean Buddhism. (Shim 1989, pp. 154–55).

In this context, Eun-su Jo argues that the concept of *hoetong* itself does not refer to a characteristic idea nor point to any specific and distinctive value. To characterize Korean Buddhism as *Hoetong Bulgyo* amounts to regarding Korea Buddhism as a featureless tradition with no identifiable property. In other words, the concept is empty (Jo 2000; Jo 2004, p. 51).

Robert Buswell also criticized that the concept of 'Korean Buddhism' is a product of a nationalist perspective formed during the Japanese colonial period of the 1930s, and that it is wrong to try to find a unique Korean Buddhist tradition. According to him, traditional Korean monks have established their own identities in the universal system of Buddhism, in terms of their positions within sectarian dharma lineages rather than nationalities. Therefore, it is anachronistic and fictional to define the identity of Korean Buddhism as *Hoetong Bulgyo* (Buswell 1998, pp. 103–4).

The major issue of the *Hoetong Bulgyo* debate is whether *hoetong* is a distinctive enough idea to consider it as the identity of Korean Buddhism. Those who criticize *Hoetong Bulgyo* claim that the general disposition of Buddhism is consolidating or peacemaking, so that *hoetong* cannot be considered an idea particular to Korean Buddhism. (Kim 2007, pp. 38–49). The *hoetong* principle is already included in the *Avatamska* (*Hua-yen* 화엄 華嚴) worldview of "neither one nor two" (不一不二) or "one is many, many is one" (一卽多多卽一). Wonhyo's philosophy of *hwajaeng* (화쟁 和諍 harmonizing disputes), often considered the commencing point of *Hoetong Bulgyo*, does not differ greatly from the general Buddhist philosophy of India or China.

It surely is a valid point that defining the traditions of Korean Buddhism in a single term of *Hoetong Bulgyo* is an unjust simplification of innumerous characteristics and dynamic changes that compose the history of Korean Buddhism. Nonetheless, it is undeniable that Korean Buddhism traditionally tends to consolidate the conflicting opinions of different orders rather than to show their distinctive colors, as opposed to Chinese Buddhism, which has the tendency to classify and enumerate the various Buddhist orders. As in the case of Uicheon's *Gyogwan gyeomsu* (교관겸수 教觀兼修) or Jinul's *Jeonghye ssangsu* (정혜쌍수 定慧雙修)—both insist that doctrinal studies and meditation practice should be proceeded together—the tendency for *hoetong* among the major Korean Buddhist thinkers is quite apparent.

Scholars who object to characterizing Korean Buddhism with the term *hoetong* commonly focus on the idea that this concept is a product of nationalism during the Japanese colonial period. Even though it is true that *Hoetong Bulgyo* has been articulated and advocated in response to the particular social demand, there are a large number of thinkers in the history of Korean Buddhism whose dispositions clearly show the legacy of *hoetong*.

It is a natural and universal course for an ideology or culture to go through stages of division and consolidation as time passes. Some traditions show more emphasis on division and others on consolidation. China might be a case for the former, while Korea for the latter. It would be problematic to define the two cultures in a binary way, but if such classification helps to understand the two cultures better, then it is acceptable as one among many methods of illustration. Rather than defining or denying Korean Buddhism as *hoetong*, it would be more productive to discuss how and in what way Korean Buddhism developed such tendencies.

It is not easy to comprehend the identity of even a single individual; how much more difficult would it be to define an identity of an entire culture? It is not that the identity of a group can be granted from outside the group with objective data and basis, nor can it be decided on through discussion and general consent of its members. It requires the passage of time in which such an identity can be naturally accepted from within and without. The fact that there is still controversy concerning the identity of Korean Buddhism signifies that we are still going through a stage of growth and development. Korean Buddhism still seems to be in the midst of active dispute and transformation.

6. Conclusions

In this article, we have discussed the controversies of Korean Buddhism during modernization through three major discourses: the first discourse on secularity, that is, the propriety of social participation; the second on modernity, centering on the issue of modifying precepts; and the third on the identity of Korean Buddhism, especially regarding the uniqueness of Korean Buddhism. The discourses could be considered as attempts to grasp the challenging problems faced by the Buddhist community during the modernization era. The experience of modernization in Korea was forced by Japanese colonialism, causing even more complexity (Park 2010a, p. 2). For Koreans, modernization did not begin from within nor proceed as a natural flow of events. As modernization was advanced by an external force, Korean society underwent a series of challenging controversies and social conflicts during the transformation.

In the three discourses, we can detect Buddhist thinkers' anxiety for breakthroughs in seeking the survival of Buddhism. Longing for growth during the rapid modernization can also be seen. Some wanted Korean Buddhism to revive and remain faithful to the legacies of the past, while others argued for its modern transformation. Conflicts between them could be seen in almost every single debate of each discourse. The former were pro-'*Hoguk Bulgyo* ideology' in the discourse on secularity, while the latter argued for allowing the marriage of monks in the discourse on modernity. The controversy surrounding the *Hoetong Bulgyo* concept was an effort to define the identity of Korean Buddhism on one hand, but may also be understood as a kind of alternative solution to the concerns for traditional legacy and those for modernity.

Compared to the intensity of such controversies during modernity, Buddhism seems to have reacted rather passively to contemporary social issues. During the 1970s and the 1980s, when the whole peninsula was in an uproar of pro-democracy movements, Buddhism sided with the oppressive and authoritarian government rather than with the people. It would be difficult to get over the past when Buddhism stood on the side of the governing ideology, as opposed to Catholic and Protestant leaders who took an active part in the resistance against government oppression. However, the fact that a considerable number of believers and intellectuals of the Buddhist community also took part in the social activism should be noteworthy and considered as a wake-up call for Buddhist leaders.

So, what caused such a decline of Buddhist participation in social issues? One reason may be its principle against secular participation, and another may be found in its loosely knit community. According to a recent religious census in South Korea, even though the Buddhist population has been in decline, its number is still on the level with the major religious groups of Catholics and Protestants. Nonetheless, compared to its Christian counterparts, the network among Buddhist believers is quite weak, making it difficult for the Buddhist community to congregate or reach a consensus.

As seen in other religious groups as well, the growth in the religious population is proportionate to the expansion of social influence. The future prosperity of Buddhism relies on converting the anonymous Buddhists to active Buddhists, as many Koreans who harbor pro-Buddhist sentiments do not identify themselves as believers. The Buddhist community needs to actively participate in current social issues, especially those concerning the minorities and the underprivileged. Suggesting a Buddhist solution in the spirit of 'saving all the living beings' might be a new channel of social participation for the Buddhist community.

Funding: This research received no external funding.

Conflicts of Interest: The authors declare no conflicts of interest.

References

Buswell, Robert E., Jr. 1998. Imagining 'Korean Buddhism': The Invention of a National Religious Tradition. In *Nationalism and the Construction of Korean Identity*. Research Monograph 26. Edited by Hyung Il Pai and Timothy R. Tangherlini. Berkeley: Institute of East Asian Studies, University of California, pp. 73–107.

Choe, Nam-Seon. 1930. *Korean Buddhism: Its Position in Cultural History of the East*. Seoul: Joseon Bulgyo cheongnyeon hoe, Available online: http://rosetta-app.snu.ac.kr:1801/delivery/DeliveryManagerServlet?dps_pid=IE1668681 (accessed on 30 November 2018). (In Korean)

Choi, Byung-Hon. 2013. Systematic Recognition of Korean Buddhist History and Understanding Methodology. In *Introduction to Korean Buddhist History*. Edited by Byung-Hon Choi. Seoul: Jisik-Sanup Publications, vol. 1, pp. 85–106. ISBN 9788942311668. (In Korean)

Choi, Ju Youl. 2017. A Study on Korean Values and Religious Culture in the Multicultural Era. *The Journal of Saramdaum Education* 11/1: 27–42. (In Korean)[CrossRef]

Han, Youngun. 2016. Treatise on the Restoration of Korean Buddhism (Joseon Bulgyo Yusinnon). In *Tracts on the Modern Reformation of Korean Buddhism*. Translation and Introduction by Pori Park. Seoul: Jogye Order of Korean Buddhism, pp. 96–204. ISBN 978897801464994220. First published 1910.

Je, Jum-Suk. 2014. The Colonial Joseon and Buddhism. *Maha Boddhi Thought* 22: 241–78. (In Korean)

Jo, Eunsu. 2000. Recognition of Korean Buddhist History Focused on 'Tong Buddhism' Discourse. *The Buddhist Review*. 21. Available online: http://www.budreview.com/news/articleView.html?idxno=335 (accessed on 13 August 2008). (In Korean)

Jo, Eunsu. 2004. The Uses and Abuses of Wonhyo and the "*T'ong* Pulgyo" Narrative. *Journal of Korean Studies* 9/1: 33–59.

Kim, Jong-Man. 2000. Reflections on the Patriotic Buddhism. *The Buddhist Review*. 3. Available online: http://www.budreview.com/news/articleView.html?idxno=305 (accessed on 20 November 2018). (In Korean)

Kim, Do-Hyung. 2003. The Expansion of Civilization and Enlightenment Theories during the Period of the Great Han Empire. *Korean History Research* 121: 171–204. (In Korean)

Kim, Sang-Hyun. 2007. The Identity of Korean Buddhism within the Context of East Asian Buddhism. *Buddhist Studies* 27: 35–58. (In Korean)

Kim, Sang-Hyun. 2011. Buddhism and the Modern History of Korea. *Journal for the Buddhist Studies* 60: 263–89. (In Korean)

Kim, Sun-Seok. 2012. Reconsideration of the Patriotic Buddhism in the Korea (sic.) Modern History: Historic Example and Theory. *Maha Boddhi Thought* 17: 75–102. (In Korean)

Ko, Young-Seop. 2013. 'Buddha Dharma Protection' in National Buddhism and 'State Protection' in Engaged Buddhism. *Buddhist Studies* 64: 89–116. (In Korean)

Lee, Jae-Hun. 2006. *Recognition of Other Religions in Modern Korean Buddhism. The Development and Character of the Modernization of Buddhism*. Edited by the Institute of Buddhist Studies, Jogye Order of Korean Buddhism. Seoul: Jogye Order Publishing, ISBN 8986821540. (In Korean)

Lee, Won-Gue. 2007. On the Characteristics of the Religious Culture of Korea. *Theology and the World* 60: 129–71. (In Korean)

Lee, Byung-Wook. 2010. The Change of Modern Korean Buddhist Social Participation Thought. *The Asian Journal of Religion and Society* 1/1: 37–65. (In Korean)

Park, No-Ja. 2004. The National Discourse of the Time of Enlightenment and the "Others" in It. In *The Shaping of Korean Modernity: The Introduction of Modern Concepts during the Korean Enlightenment Period (1895–1910)*. Edited by the Research Institute of Korean Culture, Ewha Womans University. Seoul: Somyung Books, pp. 223–56. ISBN 895626096693810. (In Korean)

Park, Jin Y. 2010a. Introduction: Buddhism and Modernity in Korea. In *Makers of Modern Korean Buddhism*. Edited by Jin Y. Park. Albany: SUNY Press, pp. 1–15.

Park, Pori. 2010b. A Korean Buddhist Response to Mdernity: Manhae Han Yongun's Doctrinal Reinterpretation for His Reformist Thought. In *Makers of Modern Korean Buddhism*. Edited by Jin Y. Park. Albany: SUNY Press, pp. 41–59.

Shim, Jae-Ryoung. 1989. On the General Characteristics of Korean Buddhism: Is Korean Buddhism Syncretic? *Seoul Journal of Korean Studies* 2: 147–57.

Shim, Jae-Ryoung. 2000. Is Korean Buddhism a United Buddhism? *The Buddhist Review*. 3. Available online: http://www.budreview.com/news/articleView.html?idxno=304 (accessed on 13 August 2018). (In Korean)

You, Young-Yul. 1985. *A Study on Chi-ho Yun during the Time of Enlightenment*. Seoul: Hangilsa Books. (In Korean)

Yun, Jong-Gab. 2009. One Mind Harmonization Thought of Wonhyo and Dialogues of TongBulgyo Dialogues (sic.). *Korean Association of National Thought* 3/2: 87–123. (In Korean)

Article

Candlelight for Our Country's Right Name: A Confucian Interpretation of South Korea's Candlelight Revolution

Sungmoon Kim

Department of Public Policy, City University of Hong Kong, 83 Tat Chee Avenue, Kowloon, Hong Kong; sungmkim@cityu.edu.hk; Tel.: +(852)-3442-8274

Received: 10 September 2018; Accepted: 26 October 2018; Published: 28 October 2018

Abstract: The candlelight protest that took place in South Korea from October 2016 to March 2017 was a landmark political event, not least because it ultimately led to the impeachment of President Park Geun-hye. Arguably, its more historically important meaning lies in the fact that it marks the first nation-wide political struggle since the June Uprising of 1987, where civil society won an unequivocal victory over a regime that was found to be corrupt, unjust, and undemocratic, making it the most orderly, civil, and peaceful political revolution in modern Korean history. Despite a plethora of literature investigating the cause of what is now called "the Candlelight Revolution" and its implications for Korean democracy, less attention has been paid to the cultural motivation and moral discourse that galvanized Korean civil society. This paper captures the Korean civil society which resulted in the Candlelight Revolution in terms of *Confucian democratic civil society*, distinct from both liberal pluralist civil society and Confucian meritocratic civil society, and argues that Confucian democratic civil society can provide a useful conceptual tool by which to not only philosophically construct a vision of civil society that is culturally relevant and politically practicable but also to critically evaluate the politics of civil society in the East Asian context.

Keywords: Candlelight Revolution; civil society; Confucianism; impeachment; South Korea

---

The candlelight protest that took place in South Korea (hereafter Korea) from October 2016 to March 2017 was a landmark political event, not least because it ultimately led to the impeachment of President Park Geun-hye, the daughter of Park Chung-hee, former military dictator and icon of Korean conservatism. Its more historically important meaning is perhaps that it marks the first nation-wide political struggle since the June Uprising of 1987, where civil society representing the national alliance of citizens won an unequivocal victory over a regime that was found to be corrupt, unjust, and undemocratic. While the 1987 June Uprising was a victory for citizens over an authoritarian regime, thereby bringing about Korea's democratization, the 2016–2017 candlelight protest signified a victory for the citizens over Korea's political past characterized by "accumulated evils" (*chŏkp'ye* 적폐) that had been preventing Korea from advancing into a truly democratic and just society. For Koreans, Park's abuse of power in extorting millions of dollars from big corporations (also known as *chaebol*) to fund foundations created by Choi Soon-sil, her private confidante, Choi's improper and illegal meddling in governmental affairs, and Choi's daughter's shady admission into one of the most prestigious universities in Korea using the connection to the president all signaled the culmination of the accumulated evils, which ought to have been overcome in order for Korea to live up to its normative ideal or its true name as a democratic republic—hence the slogan "*ige naranya* 이게 나라냐? (Is this a country?)" throughout the protest.

Park was removed from office on 9 March 2017 when the Korean Constitutional Court (KCC) upheld the motion to impeach her. Since then a number of studies have been and are still being produced that aim to evaluate the social and political significance of what is now called "the Candlelight

Revolution"[1] as well as to understand the reason for its success, and they have identified several factors as being directly conducive to the victory of civil society: Remarkable order and civility shown by the protesters, the protest's festival-like outlook and operation, and the educational effect of the protest in producing bold, persistent, and yet non-violent citizen activism which built staggering pressure for the political parties to join civil society and eventually to pass the motion of impeachment in the National Assembly.[2]

Less attention, however, has been paid to what galvanized millions of ordinary Koreans to take to the streets in the first place, who are otherwise radically polarized politically, seriously divided by generational differences, and increasingly pluralized as Korean society becomes more liberal and multicultural. One possible explanation could be that Koreans' deep commitment to liberal constitutionalism propelled them to the streets when they found out that the president had critically violated citizens' constitutional rights to private property and more importantly to life (especially, the victims of the "Sewol incident" as will be discussed later). Indeed, this turned out to be one of the key factors that the KCC took seriously in adjudicating Park's impeachment as it saw its core task as preserving Korea's "liberal and democratic constitutional order." But it is difficult to believe that violation of liberal-constitutional rights as such was the major driving force of the nation-wide mass protest, encompassing citizens of all generations, given that similar, even more serious, violations had been committed on several occasions by Park's administration.

If protection of liberal rights was not the most salient motivation of the 2016–2017 Candlelight Revolution, perhaps the protection of democracy? In fact, many scholars agree that the Candlelight Revolution can be better understood as a revolution for democracy, that is, as the citizens' protest against the president's forfeiture of democratic legitimacy upon her violations of the law, including the illegal entrustment of important governmental decisions to her personal friend, who had no experience in public affairs, let alone the democratic mandate to act on behalf of the president. But if it is not (necessarily) liberal rights per se that constitute the essence of Korean democracy, what was at stake in the winter of 2016–2017? What kind of democracy did Korean citizens have in mind when their rancorous voices uniformly chanted "*ige naranya*"? In order to understand the nature of the public frustration that developed into a civil uproar as well as the collective motivation that animated long-sustained civic activism ultimately resulting in the impeachment of the president, therefore, it is imperative to investigate how democratic legitimacy is understood by Koreans, what counts as its critical violations, and how rectification of such violations have been pursued in both traditional and contemporary Korea. Though there may be multiple discourses available to this effect, this paper pays attention to the Confucian moral discourse, which explains the viability of Korean civil society and democratic politics more generally from the perspective of Confucian ethics and values.

There are two reasons for my attention to Confucianism regarding this event. First, despite the conventional view of Confucianism as the single greatest obstacle to Korea's evolution into a modern state and society, many observers have repeatedly pointed out that Koreans are still deeply saturated with Confucian values and moral sentiments, creating an interesting tension between liberal democratic institutions, rights, and values, on the one hand, to which the Korean polity is formally and directly committed, and Confucian societal culture on the other, which continues to inform, often unwittingly, Koreans' habits of the heart, their increasing diversity notwithstanding. From this viewpoint, what appears to be culturally blind or neutral moral arguments that aim to constrain the political leaders

---

[1] Most notably, see Son (2017). Ongoing controversy notwithstanding, I call the candlelight movement that took place in 2016–2017 the Candlelight Revolution not least because it was the only politically successful candlelight movement, but more importantly, this success was achieved within the constitutional structure, bringing the social and political aspirations expressed in the previous mass candlelight movements to their institutional culmination. In this regard, I agree with Nan Kim, when she says, "the Candlelight protesters achieved something far more durable and politically stabilizing by bringing public pressure to bear upon the working of democratic institutions to ensure that the checks instituted by their Constitution would successfully guard against a tyrannical president and one otherwise unfit for office" (Kim 2017, p. 15).

[2] See generally Kim and Lee (2017) and Kim (2018).

and hold them accountable to the public can turn out to be meaningfully Confucian, representing Koreans' shared normative ideals rooted in their traditional conception of the good government. The second reason is more straightforward, that scholars in Korea and beyond are increasingly persuaded of the important role played by Confucianism during Korea's democratization and in the development of Korean civil society. Rather than dismissing this emerging literature as simply idiosyncratic or misinformed, which has largely been the case in Korean social sciences and Korean studies, this paper extends its core findings and arguments to a new interpretation of the Candlelight Revolution and illuminates the underappreciated connection between traditional Confucian moral discourse and contemporary Korean politics.

In investigating public motivation behind the Candlelight Revolution from a Confucian perspective, this paper has an additional aim in relation to theory-building. By understanding the Candlelight Revolution as a political and constitutional achievement of Korean civil society, it also aims to examine its nature in reference to Confucian moral discourse and present a normative model of Korean civil society that is democratic, progressive, and deeply ethical in terms of *Confucian democratic civil society*, distinct from both Confucian meritocratic civil society, marked by moral elitism and epistemic optimism, and liberal pluralist civil society, centered on protection and expression of interests and/or values.

1. Culture and "Confucianism": A Methodological Note

Before embarking upon the Confucian interpretation of the Candlelight Revolution, an explanation seems to be necessary for how I intend to achieve this paper's dual goals—to understand the Candlelight Revolution from a cultural standpoint, on the one hand, and build a normative theory of Confucian civil society by which to justify and evaluate a non-liberal feature of Korean democratic civil society, on the other.

The first question that I would like to address has to do with the term "Confucianism". In normative Confucian political theory Confucianism is commonly understood as a philosophical system (more or less) clearly distinct from other "comprehensive doctrines" such as liberalism. In critical cultural studies, however, culture is viewed not so much as a static and reified system of values that constitute the essence of the national character or determine the cognitive, conative, and attitudinal dimensions of individual agency, but rather as semiotic practice (Swidler 2000) or relational effects, or what Lisa Wedeen (2002) calls "intelligibility".[3] According to critical studies scholars, it is a grave mistake to capture Confucianism (or any traditional religious or ethical tradition for that matter) in terms of comprehensive doctrine because no culture can be "comprehensive" in its make-up and empirical manifestation.

It is beyond the scope of this paper to discuss how these two markedly different approaches to Confucianism might be reconciled in a philosophically robust fashion. Committed to both empirical evaluation and normative theorization, all that this paper proposes is to understand Confucianism as a *partial comprehensive doctrine* that is porous to and actively interacts with other cultures, religions, and moral and philosophical doctrines.[4] What renders partial Confucianism thus understood as still meaningfully (but not fully comprehensively) "Confucian" is its *intelligibility* as a loose constellation of moral discourse, social practice, and ethical aspiration that situates East Asians (Koreans in particular) in their "societal culture", a culture which "provides its members with meaningful ways of life across the full range of human activities, including social, educational, religious, recreational, and economic life, encompassing both public and private spheres," as Will Kymlicka (1995, p. 76) puts it.[5] In this way, we have a less essentialist but more malleable concept of Confucianism that can be attributed to

---

3   Wedeen approaches culture as a complex set of practices of "meaning-making" through which social actors attempt to make their worlds coherent. She calls such thin coherence "intelligibility".
4   On the distinction between partial and full comprehensive doctrines, see Rawls (1993, p. 13).
5   For a more detail discussion of the so-called "intelligibility condition" of Confucian political theory, see Kim (2016, pp. 15–16).

the societal culture of modern Koreans who are increasingly pluralist and multicultural, a concept that I hope critical studies scholars can embrace for methodological purposes, unless they completely deny the place of Confucianism in contemporary Korea.[6]

The second question that I want to clarify from the beginning is that it is far from my intention to fit the Candlelight Revolution into a Confucian framework.[7] The danger of doing so is obvious. As many scholars observe, the Candlelight Revolution can hardly signify one single event following one simple line of social contention, such as between Park and its opponents. Its historical meaning may never be fully clear to us given our lack of God's eye, but certainly, its complex nature as a historic event can be disclosed if various contingent social relations, narratives, and contentions that coalesced into what we now call the Candlelight Revolution are taken seriously and given their due place in our account.[8] The moderate aim of this paper, insomuch as it is considered a cultural study, is to bring to our attention one such narrative by casting a light on the dimension of the Candlelight Revolution that has been near-completely ignored in the existing literature, namely the connection between Confucian moral discourse and Korean democratic civil society. Yet, this aim should be evaluated against the backdrop of this paper's bigger aim of constructing a normative model of Confucian democratic civil society.

2. Confucianism and Korean Civil Society

In its narrowest and formal-institutional sense, "civil society" is defined as "the realm of organizations, groups, and associations that are formally established, legally protected, autonomously run, and voluntarily joined by ordinary citizens" (Howard 2003, pp. 34–35). By contrasting civil society to the primordial collectivity called *Gemeinschaft* by Tönnies, however, Edward Shils pays more attention to its fundamentally ethical nature. He understands civil society in terms of "a collective self-consciousness in which the important referent is the civil quality of its participants, i.e., their being members of a society under a common authority, common laws and living in a common, more or less bounded territory" (Shils 1997, p. 71). Combining the former's formal-institutional and the latter's ethical dimensions of civil society, and with special attention to the revolutionary and emancipatory social movements that were critically instrumental to the democratization of Eastern Europe during the late 1980s, Cohen and Arato provide a more comprehensive definition of civil society that I believe is most relevant to our Korean case, when they reconceive its classical Hegelian notion mainly around "a notion of self-limiting democratizing movements seeking to expand and protect spaces for both negative liberty and positive freedom and to recreate egalitarian forms of solidarity without impairing economic self-regulation" (Cohen and Arato 1994, pp. 17–18). Rather than viewing social movements "as antithetical to either the democratic political system or to a properly organized social sphere," Cohen and Arato consider them to be "a key feature of vital, modern, civil society and an important form of citizen participation in public life" (Cohen and Arato 1994, p. 19). As such, this third conception of civil society best captures civil society's essentially dynamic, strongly participatory, deeply pluralistic, and fundamentally egalitarian characteristics that combine to work toward the protection of public space and public freedom uncoerced by both the state and the market. What undergirds civil society of this understanding is neither economic interest[9] nor liberal pluralism, concentrated on negative liberty and the right to freedom of association (Galston 2002; Rosenblum 1998), but passion for democratic self-government.

---

[6] Notice that even those who are critical of Confucianism acknowledge the substantive influence of Confucianism in shaping Korean liberalism. See Lee (2015).

[7] I am grateful to an anonymous reviewer for drawing my attention to this danger.

[8] For attempts to understand the political meaning of the Candlelight Revolution by placing it in its multifaceted historical context, see Kim (2017) and Doucette (2017).

[9] For the notion of civil society focused on economic interest, see Diamond (1999).

Scholars disagree as to the origin of Korean civil society[10] but it is commonly agreed that the April Revolution of 1960 marks the first nation-wide and student-led democratic movement after the creation of the Republic of Korea, bringing down Syngman Rhee's authoritarian regime. The event also provided a prototype of Korean civil society for the political activists of the 1970s and 1980s when confrontational and militaristic democratic movements against the repressive state would become an integral part of Korea's everyday politics. During this democratizing period, it is frequently heard, Korean civil society grew discontent with authoritarian rule and created a *counterpublic* space, autonomous from the all-penetrating authoritarian state, in which left-minded intellectuals and university students (called "undongkwŏn"), otherwise weak and ephemeral as private individuals, could develop themselves into an organized political force confronting and ultimately dismantling the ruling regime.[11] Sunhyuk Kim's following statement presents the nature of Korean civil society during the democratizing period in quite an illuminating way from a comparative perspective.

> South Korea's democratic transition differed from certain cases in southern Europe and Latin America because conflicts, negotiations, and pacts among political elites were not the primary determinants of democratization. Rather . . . it was civil society groups that initiated and directed the process of democratization by forming a prodemocracy alliance within civil society, creating a grand coalition with the opposition political party, and eventually pressuring the authoritarian regime to yield to the "popular upsurge" from below. *An oppositional, resistant, and rebellious civil society* was one of the most significant reasons behind the most prominent political change in South Korea's postwar history, namely, democratization (Kim 2004, p. 139, emphasis added; also see Choi 2009, pp. 77–78).

The question is, what was the ideational engine of the "oppositional, resistant, and rebellious civil society" in Korea? As noted, there is no denying that the intellectuals and university students who were the main agents of Korea's democratizing civil society were propelled by various sorts of left political ideology and political theory, including *minjung sasang* or *minjung* ideology where *minjung*, literally "common people" as opposed to (educated, cultural, or political) elites and leaders, signifies "those who are oppressed in the sociopolitical system but who are capable of rising up against it" (Lee 2007, p. 5).[12] But the fact that the main agents of Korean civil society were mainly driven by *minjung* ideology does not imply that the common people themselves played the most significant role in "resurrecting, reactivating, and re-mobilizing" Korean civil society,[13] even though it is true that their broad participation in the June Uprising was critically instrumental in pressuring the ruling regime to initiate democratic reform. What is more important in the present context is what kind of moral discourse was present, motivating the main protagonists of Korean civil society to organize their political confrontations with the state with a view to the interests of the common people, rather than their own.

In this regard, Namhee Lee's attention to "a discourse of moral privilege" provides an important clue, which she understands as "a practice that was embedded in the traditional role of intellectuals, a long tradition of providing social criticism" (Lee 2007, pp. 152–3).[14] At the heart of Lee's observation is that the Korean tradition of social criticism is historically rooted in the Confucian legacy of

---

[10] For a helpful survey of this debate, see Shin (2000).

[11] For the characterization of Korean civil society in the 1970s and 1980s in terms of counterpublic space, see Lee (2007). Though not using this specific concept, the following studies subscribe to a similar observation: (Koo 1993a; Park 2005; Lee 1993).

[12] Alternatively but similarly, Koo (1993b, p. 131) understands *minjung* in terms of "a broad alliance of 'alienated classes', people alienated from power and from the distribution of the fruits of economic growth."

[13] For a description of Korea's democratizing civil society as "resurrected, reactivated, and re-mobilized", see Kim (2000, p. 174).

[14] It is worth noting that several scholars interested in modernizing Confucianism draw attention to the Confucian tradition of social criticism as one of the vital resources upon which to build a Confucian democracy. (See Ackerly 2005; Angle 2012; Kim 2014).

remonstrance to the ruler, expected of "students at the National Academy and the public schools, soon to be future officials." As Lee puts it, the key to social criticism was "the Confucian concept of knowledge, which was instrumental for political power and prestige and which dictated that knowledge should be employed not only to enhance one's own status and position in society but also to maintain the proper and stable order of society, 'rectifying it if gone astray and restoring it if in disarray'" (Lee 2007, p. 153). Lee's central claim is that like their Confucian predecessors the Korean *minjung* activists possessed "a sense of [moral] entitlement and aspiration for political power as the elites of the society" and this cultural-moral elitism enabled them to fight for the right way (*dao* 道)—for them democracy—often at the expense of their private interest (also see Tu 2006, pp. 220–2).

Like most social scientists, however, Namhee Lee, notwithstanding her acknowledgment of a notable connection between Confucian moral discourse and Korean civil society, does not actively explore a Confucian dimension of Korean (democratic) politics, as though traditional culture is marginal to politics, civic activism in particular, or Confucianism is no longer relevant in post-democratic Korean politics. Not surprisingly, Korean social scientists are reluctant to characterize Korean civil society during the transitional and consolidating periods as a *Confucian civil society*, a civil society whose ideal of civility and its mode of political engagement is deeply (but not exclusively) saturated with Confucian values, ideals, norms, and ethics. But if a moral discourse that presents intellectuals and students as representing "the conscience of the whole society" is an integral element of Confucianism and this self-imposed moral privilege gives rise to a distinctively confrontational mode of civil politics, it is difficult to understand why we cannot call this sort of civil society a Confucian civil society, distinguishing it from a Western-style civil society, in which individual rights, value pluralism, social diversity, and economic interests are central.

In conceptualizing a distinctively Chinese form of civil society, therefore, Thomas Metzger pays close attention to "the moral awareness of the scholarly elite, who defined themselves as super-citizens [struggling with the] disjunction between the completely practicable ideal order and the actual bad condition of society in the present." Central to this conception of civil society is "the utopian, top-down view of progress as based on the moral dynamism of super-citizens able to influence a corrigible state [which has] never [been] replaced by an un-utopian, bottom-up view of progress as based on the efforts of ordinary free citizens fallibly pursuing their economic interests and organized in a practical way to monitor an incorrigible state" (Metzger 2001, p. 224). As is apparent, there is an undeniably strong resonance between Lee's description of Korean civil society during the democratizing period and the Chinese-Confucian ideal of civil society advanced by Metzger.

This observation finally leads us to revisit one of the most controversial arguments on the origin of Korean civil society. In his study on the indigenous development of Korean civil society, Hein Cho traces its historical origin back to the moral and spiritual authority, distinct from political authority, of the Confucian scholar-officials who were equipped with the ritually sanctioned right to remonstrate with the king. Cho pays special attention to the equivalent right exercised by the "backwoods literati (k. *sarim* 士林)" who, withdrawn from the political center, immersed themselves in Confucian studies and moral self-cultivation[15] but wielded tremendous moral authority over local communities in which they resided. Echoing Lee's notion of the scholarly privilege of offering social criticism, Cho claims that "critical communication, the main medium used by officials to assert the autonomy of their bureaucracy relative to the kingship, was also used by backwoods literati to assert the autonomy of their civil society relative to the bureaucracy" (Cho 1997, p. 32).

It is far from my intention to resolve the controversy on the historical origin of Korean civil society generated by Cho's provocative argument. In the present context, it is unimportant whether or not the moral privilege enjoyed by local Confucian scholars can be reasonably identified as "civil society",

---

[15] The appearance of the backwoods literati was one of the distinctive social phenomena during the late Chosŏn Korea since the eighteenth-century. On the backwoods literati and their emergence as a political force, see Wu (1999).

as it is understood in the Western liberal context. What is important here is the fact that there was a much stronger tradition of social criticism in premodern Korea than in China where the backwoods literati did not emerge as a key political force checking or competing with the government at the center, and this tradition of moral and political criticism *from society* enabled the Confucian scholars to enjoy not only moral but also (relative) political autonomy in relation to the state. This gives a new element to the idea of Confucian civil society whose concept is currently under construction. While our earlier notion of Confucian civil society, informed largely by the Chinese experience, emphasizes the Confucian intellectuals' epistemic optimism and their moral authority of providing social criticism as super-citizens, the Korean experience adds here an important *liberal* element by highlighting moral and political autonomy held by the Confucian intellectuals *within* society, practically distinguished from formal state institutions.[16]

When an important dimension of Korean civil society is captured from the conceptual framework of Confucian civil society marked by moral elitism (or super-citizenship), epistemic optimism, moral and political autonomy, social criticism, and confrontational engagement with the state,[17] then a more persuasive explanation for the cultural character of the state-society relation during the democratizing and consolidating periods can be available. This neither implies the Confucian origin of Korean civil society nor denies the influence of other philosophical traditions on its formation and operation. When we say that Korean civil society is a kind of Confucian civil society, it points to the observation that the distinctive cultural aspect of Korean civil society can be best captured with reference to the idea of Confucian civil society as constructed here. As such, in this paper Confucian civil society refers not so much to a historical reality but to a conceptual framework that can shed new light on the cultural and deeply ethical nature of Korean civil society that has been socially active in contemporary Korea. Is this framework still relevant in post-democratic Korea, especially in illuminating the driving force of the Candlelight Revolution? I now turn to this question.

3. Candlelight Revolution: Dis/Continuity with Old Democratization Movement

Even if it is agreed that the ethical dimension of Korean civil society during the democratizing and consolidating periods can be captured in terms of a Confucian civil society as defined above, it may nevertheless be forcefully opposed that it is far-fetched to suppose any meaningful connection between the candlelight protest and Confucianism. One may even claim that in post-democratic Korea the nature of civil society has undergone a dramatic change. In the course of democratic consolidation in the 1990s, the argument goes, Korean civil society, whose main locomotive thus far had been the *minjung* movement, was transformed into what Korean social scientists call the "citizens' movement" (*simin undong*), a new and more everyday form of social movement initiated by citizens themselves who, being internally diverse in their beliefs, values, economic interests, and political orientations, are organized into numerous voluntary groups, organizations, and associations, pursuing not so much revolutionary political goals with radical political means but pragmatic social goals in the service of their sectional or pluralist interests using moderate means. For many Korean social scientists, the

---

[16] On this broad conception of "liberal" with reference to the Confucian tradition, see De Bary (1983).

[17] Several scholars have explored the Confucian concept of civil society but their focus has generally been on the unique mode of civility through which individuals in society are related to one another, thereby forming a fiduciary society, a society that valorizes trust and harmony over conflict and litigation. See for instance Madsen (2002) and Tan (2003). Though I believe that this is a useful way to reconstruct Confucian civil society, I cannot help feeling that it tends to downplay the creative political tension between Confucian civil society and the state in which the former can boldly confront the latter in the name of the Way in the context of pre-democratic or democratizing East Asia. Of course, this does not mean that the fundamentally antagonistic state and society relation, which is at the heart of the classical liberal notion of civil society, should be an essential component of Confucian civil society. As Tan (2003, p. 206) rightly notes, Confucian civil society's critical, even confrontational, engagement with the state denotes civil society's independence, not its stark opposition to the state. After all, Confucian civil society is not constructed by a social contract among rights-bearing individuals in the state of nature. Nonetheless, I believe that a constructive tension between the state and civil society is the defining characteristic of Korean Confucian civil society.

citizens' movement signifies the true advent of "civil society" in its authentic liberal-pluralist sense (Cho and Kim 2007; Shin 2006).

It is understandable why Korean scholars are fascinated by and eagerly welcome the emergence of the citizens' movement. First, it offers a powerful explanation for the successful consolidation of a new democratic system in Korea, which is sharply contrasted with the greater struggles endured by its Eastern and Central European counterparts that experienced regime transitions roughly around the same time. Many political scientists agree that democratic consolidation was critically hindered in some of the key Eastern and Central European countries because, among other things, they failed to transform their grandiose, nation-wide ethical civil society into a liberal pluralist civil society, composed of citizens freely organizing themselves into various interest groups or associations.[18] In marked contrast, the emergence of the citizens' movement in post-democratic Korea signifies the successful transformation of ethical civil society into a pluralist civil society and the reconstruction of the counterpublic space into an indefinite number of citizen organizations mediating between individuals and the state.

Second and relatedly, the citizens' movement signals a radical disjuncture with the previous democratic movement that I have associated with Confucian civil society with regard to the key agents: While the *minjung* movement was led by super-citizens who acted on behalf of ordinary citizens often at the sacrifice of their own well-being,[19] the citizens' movement is organized through mutual consent among citizens who shared common interests, concerns, and goals. Driven by a monolithic ethical, political, and national cause, the *minjung* movement rarely allowed internal diversity, often identifying it as a dangerous sign of dissonance and fissure within the pro-democracy camp, and relied heavily on few intellectual elites comprehensively dedicated to the common good. The citizens' movement radically differs from the *minjung* movement in that it is an expression of social pluralism and allows, in principle, no internal hierarchy among citizens—hence no valorization of super-citizens. In theory, it is motivated by the citizens' own everyday interests arising from their ordinary life and is constitutionally protected as based on the right to freedom of association and assembly. Therefore, unlike the *minjung* movement that aims to create an alternative public sphere parallel to and countervailing the state with a superior moral authority, the citizens' movement operates within the given constitutional structure, thus without generating a counterpublic.[20] As many Korean social scientists believe, the citizens' movement is an indispensable incubator of participatory and/or deliberative politics, commonly regarded as the backbone of democracy.

When the citizen's movement is radically differentiated from the previous *minjung* movement and it is viewed as constituting a more authentic form of civil society, a trouble arises when assessing the Candlelight Revolution as a civil society movement. As widely observed, the candlelight protest initially demanding Park's voluntary resignation and later her formal impeachment was initiated by a number of unorganized ordinary citizens gathering at central Seoul in order to express their deep frustration with the president's alleged crimes and utter incompetence in governance as evidenced by Choi's illegal intervention in key public affairs. In a series of public protests which, as it turned out, took place for twenty consecutive Saturdays across the whole county, citizens came from different social, political, and religious backgrounds and formed under no conspicuous organizational leadership a

---

[18] As some leading political scientists put it, "[e]thical civil society represents 'truth', but political society [read: civil society] in a consolidated democracy normally represents 'interest'. In political society the actor is only seldom the 'nation', but more routinely 'group'. 'Internal differences' and 'conflict' are no longer to be collectively suppressed, but organizationally represented in political society" (Linz and Stepan 1996, p. 272).

[19] This is not to say that there were no other participants than the educated elites involved in the *minjung* movement. My point is that the main engine for social reform that the *minjung* movement aspired to achieve came largely from social elites equipped with a self-imposed mission for political transformation. It is an interesting question, though, whether this moral elitism sat comfortably with the *minjung* activists' avowed vision for social egalitarianism.

[20] In Jang-Jip Choi's language, in order for the citizens' movement to truly contribute to democratic consolidation, it should be a form of civil society movement freed from the zeal for mass mobilization and institutionalized into stable party politics (Choi 2009, p. 83).

broad and bottom-up coalition of civic activism that transcended narrow sectarian interests, while fully concentrated on Park's misconduct and the "accumulated evils" that in their view had long bedeviled Korean society, of which the Choi Soon-sil scandal was the most revealing symptom. Was the candlelight protest a typical form of the citizens' movement that emerged during the consolidating stage?

There are two main reasons to believe that the Candlelight Revolution was the culmination of the citizens' movement. First, it was not guided by a radical political agenda, aimed at total social change or emancipation. Rather, it was motivated to achieve a specific political goal, that is, removal of the president from office, and a variety of nonviolent and civil forms of protest were exercised, such as visual arts, pop and traditional music, poetry and other literary writings, and, of course, public speeches and collective singing, making the public protest a semblance of a "civic festival" of the kind Jean-Jacques Rousseau valorized as an epitome of participatory democracy. Second, though initially prompted by civic rage, citizens did not express their anger violently or rise up against the president simply for the sake of bringing her down. What was remarkable about the candlelight protest was that citizens were able to sublimate their collective rage by means of democratic constitutional procedures by pressuring the political society to formally make an impeachment prosecution and the constitutional court to uphold the motion presented by the political society. In short, the candlelight protest was conducted strictly in accordance with democratic civility and the principle of constitutionalism.

That being said, however, there are equally good reasons to reject affiliating the Candlelight Revolution with a conventional form of a pluralist civil society whose institutionalization social scientists argue is essential for democratic consolidation. First of all, the citizen activism that evolved into the Candlelight Revolution does not seem to conform to the general feature of the citizens' movement that is in principle to be motivated by sectional interests. According to Jang-Jip Choi, the success of Korea's democratic consolidation critically hinges on the prospect that the so-called "politics of square", at the core of which lie mass mobilization and emotional outburst, can be successfully transformed into stable party politics undergirded by a pluralist civil society of calm reason and civility (Choi 2009, pp. 83–92). From the perspective of mainstream political science, therefore, the Candlelight Revolution is an anomaly rather than the norm in the course of liberal democratic consolidation. It is strongly reminiscent of "the politics of square" that propelled Korean civil society in the past, except that it was citizens themselves, not super-citizens, who played a central role. After all, the political society initially showed reluctance to join civil society, not to mention to impeach the president, when the Choi scandal was first brought to public attention and citizens began to protest in the streets. It was only after the bottom-up pressure from civil society that the political society joined the candlelight protest.

Second, Korean civil society during the candlelight protest remained consistently "ethical". As we have noted earlier, ethical civil society is qualitatively different from a liberal pluralist civil society as commonly understood in social sciences in that it is organized not so much around (sectional) interest but around shared norms and values that underpin collective self-consciousness which in turn includes and promotes "an attitude of self-reflexivity".[21] As historically demonstrated by Poland's Solidarity Movement and Czechoslovakia's Velvet Revolution, ethical civil society, nationally mobilized in its typical form, thus representing itself as politics of square, tends to transcend internal disagreement and difference without dismissing the pivotal importance of the plurality of values, ideas, opinions, and interests in a civil life, in search of a common higher moral goal, be it communal solidarity or a life of truth against the petrified (communist) bureaucratic regime. Though the proximate cause of the revitalization of the politics of square during the candlelight protest was certainly the desire to

---

[21] According to Keane (1998, p. 51), "Civil societies promote an attitude of self-reflexivity, by which I mean the shared understanding among socially interacting and socially interconnected subjects that their world never stands still, that it is a puzzling product of their own making, and that as subjects of inquiry into the meaning of life they are an intrinsic part of the object of their enquiries."

remove the incumbent president, what galvanized Korean civil society throughout the whole process was citizens' collective search for an authentic democracy, a democracy that is fair and just and one that truly represents equal citizens' collective self-determination, as was implicit in their slogan "Is this a country"?

If the Korean civil society of candlelight protest is similar to an old form of Korean civil society both in its modality and in ethical nature, and yet simultaneously distanced from it in terms of the key agents and its institutional position within the entire constitutional system, how should we make sense of it? However we answer this question, it does seem inaccurate to understand the citizens' movement as having nothing to do with the previous democratization movement. In this regard, Dong-Choon Kim's following statement is worth special attention.

> [W]hile distancing itself from previous movements in terms of objective and approach, the citizens' movement is closely connected to the political opposition that existed during the military dictatorship. The start of the Korean citizens' movement can be traced back to the democratization movement that strived to reform Seoul-based national politics. . . . These 'comprehensive' citizens' movement organizations [that were established in the 1990s such as Citizens' Coalition for Economic Justice and People's Solidarity for Participatory Democracy] implicitly set as their goal macro-structural changes in Korean society, believing that their mission was the monitor of Seoul-based national politics (Kim 2006, pp. 103–4)[22].

Kim's statement leads us to a more puzzling question: If there is a meaningful continuity between the citizens' movement and the old democratic movement and, by extension, between the candlelight protest and the ethical civil society of the past, what does this mean for Confucianism in today's Korean politics? Does Confucianism still culturally underscore Korean civil society? Or, more moderately, does the idea of Confucian civil society still remain a useful concept in capturing a significant cultural dimension of Korean civil society?

4. Two Kinds of Confucian Civil Society

At first glance, the civil society of the candlelight protest appears to have nothing to do with Confucianism. It was not led by super-citizens armed with superior moral knowledge and moral authority over both the state and the common people, and furthermore, none of its participants reportedly drew on Confucianism as the source of their political activism. If the gist of Confucian civil society lies in the moral hierarchy between super-citizens as active political agents and ordinary citizens, the beneficiaries of the former's selfless devotion to the common good, thus reproducing a modern version of rule *for* the people, it indeed seems difficult to associate Confucianism with the candlelight protest that was fundamentally egalitarian and inclusive.

Indeed, the inegalitarian nature of Confucianism poses a serious challenge to any endeavor to make it relevant to today's democratic Korea. Despite its long history and intra-traditional diversity, Confucianism never developed from within the idea of political equality and remained un-democratic until some modern reformers began to explore its democratic transformations. Traditionally, its political ideal was a rule *for* the people in which the ruler assisted by Confucian scholar-bureaucrats devotes himself to the well-being of the people who have no institutional access to political participation, and as long as the ruler fulfills this "service" well, which was believed to have been mandated by Heaven, the highest moral authority in the cosmos, he enjoys full political legitimacy without being held accountable by the people.[23]

However, it is presumptuous to conclude that the inegalitarian nature of Confucianism makes it categorically impossible to be create a civil society consistent with the Confucian tradition. As it is

---

[22] Elsewhere I discuss how organizations such CCEJ and PSPD (the latter in particular) have been continuing to keep the nature of Korean civil society ethical. See Kim (2008).

[23] Therefore, Chan (2014) captures the Confucian conception of political authority in terms of the service conception.

now clear, for Confucian scholar-bureaucrats, "assisting" (*xiang* 相) the ruler did not mean absolute obedience. For them, the fact that the ruler had the Heaven-given mandate to serve the well-being of the people implied that he was under a significant normative constraint, though without being legally checked, and, as versed in Confucian classics and immersed in a life-long process of moral self-cultivation themselves, the scholar-bureaucrats considered it their self-imposed (or Heaven-given) responsibility to keep the ruler on the right track (*dao*) of governance. This seminal idea of "Confucian constitutionalism" (Kim 2011) was further developed and refined during the Neo-Confucian stage when Confucian political theory was given a complex metaphysical foundation. Now, the universe was seen to be penetrated by universal moral principles (*li* 理) that interconnect the natural world with the normative world and politics with ethics, integrating "all under Heaven" into a seamless whole that is internally coherent and harmonious.[24]

In Neo-Confucianism, by which the founding of the Chosŏn dynasty (1392–1910) in Korea was profoundly influenced (Deuchler 1992) and which still, though partially, influences the Korean conception of the good life (personal, familial, and political) (Park and Shin 2006; Bae and Park 2013), the Confucian scholar-bureaucrats acquired a special access to Heaven (or Heavenly Principle) via their virtue and scholarship and enjoyed the exalted moral authority as the successors of the lineage of the Way (*dao tung* 道統), which gave them moral power by which to counterbalance the ruler's political power predicated on his hereditary right. As Wood (1995, p. 16) puts it, their "fundamental concern was to form a view of authority that would constitute a basis for civil order and national unity but would also contain within it an acknowledgment of the moral purpose of human social life, serving indirectly to restrain the arbitrary exercise of imperial power and prevent government from degenerating into tyranny." More importantly, as Neo-Confucianism understands what is "public" (*gong* 公) fundamentally in ethical terms, associating it with whatever represents Heavenly Principle or the Way, scholars in society, who were not formally involved in the government, could claim with equal force their *public* status as the successors of the lineage of the Way and present themselves as the unflinching moral and political critics of the ruler.[25]

The account of Confucian civil society inspired by this Neo-Confucian political ethos has several underlying assumptions: (1) the purpose of the state is to serve the well-being of the people; (2) when the state fails to protect or actively encroaches upon people's well-being (both economic and moral), thereby departing radically from the Way, those who are committed to the Way ought to strive to rectify the state; (3) civil society refers to the public sphere created by Confucian intellectuals who are committed to the Way and it exists in parallel with the state with an aim to put it back on the right track of what traditional Confucians call "the benevolent government" (*renzheng* 仁政); and finally (4) the key agents of Confucian civil society are those who are dedicated to the public good, even at the sacrifice of their private interest, hence morally superior to the laypeople preoccupied with their own well-being, and they carry on the public role played by their Neo-Confucian predecessors outside the formal governmental structure. We can call this version of Confucian civil society that is directly predicated on the core premises of Neo-Confucianism *Confucian meritocratic civil society*. Metzger's idea of Chinese civil society fits this model perfectly.

Korea's democratizing civil society propelled by the *minjung* ideology also fits well the model of Confucian meritocratic civil society. One irony with the *minjung* ideology is that while presenting the common people (*min* or *minjung*) as its central concern and aiming to elevate them as a political force with its own distinct voice, in reality it relies heavily on a small number of dedicated political activists who act and speak on behalf of the uneducated mass who made up the majority of the Korean people in the 1970s and 1980s, when only a select few were privileged enough to receive higher education. Like Neo-Confucian scholars and scholar-bureaucrats, especially those who were most conscious of

---

[24] For a helpful discussion on Neo-Confucian metaphysics, see Angle and Tiwald (2017, pp. 29–36).
[25] For the complex meaning of *gong* in Neo-Confucian Korea during the Chosŏn dynasty, see Lee (2003).

their public role as the guardians of the Public Way (*gong dao* 公道), but without drawing explicitly from the Confucian political discourse, the political activists of democratizing Korean civil society regarded themselves as the champions of right principles, which they associated with democracy, and fought against what they deemed to be an autocracy or (*p'okchŏng* 폭정), a government that is diametrically opposed to the ideal of a benevolent government.

It is important to note that there is always a certain moral distance presupposed between political activists and ordinary citizens in a Confucian meritocratic civil society, and this makes it difficult to present the civil society in question as an egalitarian public space of the citizens themselves. As Namhee Lee shows, when Korean civil society was most militant during the heydays of Korean democratization, it was always the civil society *of* select intellectuals and student activists called undongkwŏn, though it was certainly *for* the common people. The rare occasions in which the undongkwŏn was joined by the common people in the streets were when some members of the undongkwŏn, most commonly university students, were brutally treated or killed by the repressive state. To many ordinary Koreans, the suffering or death of young students fighting against a despotic government were reminiscent of the "Confucian martyrs" during the Chosŏn dynasty, typically often young and upright Confucian scholar-bureaucrats who were executed by the autocrat for their open and bold political criticism. For example, though the origins of the June Uprising of 1987 are complicated, its most proximate cause was undoubtedly the deaths of two university students, Park Chong-ch'ŏl, a Seoul National University student who was tortured to death by the police, and Lee Han-yŏl, a student at Yonsei University who was killed by the riot police during an anti-government protest. Their innocent deaths were portrayed in the progressive news media as well as in the public discourse as "democratic martyrs", encouraging tens and thousands of ordinary Koreans to take to the streets, who would otherwise be reluctant to venture into political activism.

Seen in this way, Confucian meritocratic civil society would be effective in initiating civic activism. But it seems to be quite limited in functioning as a civil society once the regime has been democratized, upon which what is at stake, we are told by liberals, is no longer mobilizing the people and creating a counterpublic, but rather accommodating the plurality of interests, values, and faiths in an orderly fashion under the constitutional structure governed by the democratic principle of equality. But is there an ineluctable reason that a civil society that can accommodate the plurality of interests, values, and faiths in an orderly and egalitarian fashion must be a liberal pluralist civil society? Notice that by nature, liberal pluralist civil society is socially conservative in the sense that its primary concern is to create a space where personal and associational interests, rights, and freedoms can be best protected or exercised within the constitutional boundary (Cahoone 2002), not so much to create a counterpublic space which aims to challenge the very (quasi-)constitutional limit authorized by a non-democracy. It also generates an intermediary social sphere where private individuals, otherwise atomistic, can be inculcated in the virtue of civility, reconnected with others, and reborn as social beings who are in a symbiotic relationship with the community (Glendon and Blankehorn 1995). In the course of liberal pluralization of civil society, however, the initial political energy of civil society often gets lost, along with its enthusiasm to assert the people's collective self-government as well as its power to redesign the direction of the polity according to the general will. Given that liberal pluralism supports a form of civil society that is purportedly congruent with liberal constitutionalism designed to constrain the assertion of popular sovereignty as best shown in its valorization of judicial review as the most effective instrument of counter-majoritarianism (Macedo 2001), it is hardly surprising that liberal pluralist civil society is critically at odds with the politics of square of the kind Confucian meritocratic civil society promotes. It may provide social capital that can fight against atomistic individualism and social anomie but it is doubtful that it can offer itself as a powerful political bulwark for public freedom and civic activism.

In my view, the civil society of the Candlelight Revolution represented a novel mode of civil society that strikes a complex middle ground between the *minjung* movement and the new citizen's movement, between civic-political activism and social pluralism, and between Confucian meritocratic civil society and liberal civil society. While being the culmination of the citizens' movement that had emerged in the post-democratic context as a new mode of organizing and expressing the power of democratic citizens, the candlelight protest went far beyond merely forging social capital that helps bridge various social differences and bring them under one civil society to which everyone belongs equally as citizens, when it evolved *within* the existing democratic constitutional structure into a political revolution in which the citizens themselves were empowered as super-citizens. In participating in the public protest, citizens were transformed into active political agents who reclaim their sovereign status, hijacked by the president's "betrayal of public trust,"[26] and demand fundamental reform of the Korean polity that in their judgment should begin with removal of a bad ruler.

We can call this alternative mode of civil society a *Confucian democratic civil society*, at the core of which is a strong ethico-political nature supplemented by its great respect for constitutional politics. On the one hand, like Confucian meritocratic civil society, Confucian democratic civil society is deeply inspired by the Korean Neo-Confucian tradition of social criticism, the moral and political autonomy of those who are committed to the people's well-being, and political activism motivated by such moral commitment. On the other hand, however, Confucian democratic civil society is neither led by select super-citizens nor does it aim to create a counterpublic space outside a normal constitutional politics. Though retaining civic enthusiasm to keep the government on the right track, informed in part (but importantly) by the traditional Confucian conception of the good government, Confucian democratic civil society parts company with its meritocratic counterpart by pursuing this ethical ideal within the existing democratic constitutional structure, even when it strives for reform. It is a civil society that is particularly suited for a traditionally Confucian society that has undergone democratic transformation—or simply, suited for a *Confucian democracy*, a democracy whose underlying principles, public institutions, and social practices, which are all of the Western provenance, are in constant negotiation with the existing Confucian societal culture that still informs the habits of the heart of the local people.[27]

The idea of Confucian democratic civil society provides a useful theoretical framework to make sense of the cultural dimension of the Candlelight Revolution, which is difficult to capture from the perspective of liberal pluralist civil society. Our next question, then, is precisely how Confucian the Candlelight Revolution was in terms of its motivation and moral discourse.

5. Lighting Candles for Our Country's Right Name

Like other similar mega public protests that took place in Korea, the Candlelight Revolution initially began as a series of public remonstrations by ordinary citizens, joined by university professors and public intellectuals issuing a Declaration of the Current Situation (*siguksŏnŏn* 시국선언), against the president who, according to the KCC, is supposed to be "the symbolic existence personifying the rule of law and the observance of law toward the entire public."[28] However, KCC's understanding of the president only partially captures what is commonly expected of the president in Korea. For the Korean people, the president is not merely the head of the state who has a legal and democratic procedural mandate to carry out his or her public duties—most important of which is to protect citizens' constitutional rights—in accordance with the constitution and other statutory laws, only grave violations of which can remove him or her from office. This formal definition of the president focuses purely on the office's legal and democratic authority within the liberal democratic constitutional structure but falls far short of addressing the normative ideal of moral leadership expected of the nation's highest political leader.

---

26 This is the expression that the Korean Constitutional Court employed when it described the gravity of Park's wrongdoing as being sufficient to warrant her impeachment (KCCR, 2016Hŏn-na1).
27 I discuss how this type of democracy can be formed and valued in East Asia in Kim (2014, 2016).
28 The KCC provided this understanding of the president in the Korean constitutional structure when it adjudicated President Roh Mu-hyun's impeachment in 2004 (KCCR, 2004Hŏn-Na1).

No doubt, it was the Choi scandal and the president's legal violations involved in it that prompted Koreans to organize public protests. But was the president's violation of the law the only reason for the revitalization of mass civic activism? What made the Korean people so convinced that the president's illegal misconduct was "grave" enough to warrant her impeachment? In answering these questions, it is highly suggestive that it was the president herself who helped transform what had begun as public remonstrations into an all-encompassing political movement, calling not only for impeaching the president but also for a total change of the Korean polity, when she made a public statement (a third one to be precise) on 29 November 2016. In this statement intended to be a public apology, Park refused to step down, denying her complicity in the Choi scandal, while only apologizing for her failure to manage well the people around her, and defending her illegal support for the foundations run by Choi as resulting from her selfless concern with the public good. The public uproar that followed was not simply due to the fact that the president had violated the law, which should be the sole concern of the constitutional court in deliberating her impeachment in light of liberal constitutionalism, but, more importantly, her utter failure to live up to the normative ideal of the nation's highest political leader widely held among the Korean people. What then does this normative ideal consist of?

In the face of staggering civic pressure to impeach the president, the National Assembly of Korea finally passed the impeachment motion on 9 December 2016 on the ground of the president's "extensive and serious violations of the Constitution and the law." More specifically, the motion contained eight main accusations under two rubrics—first, violation of the constitution and second, violation of the statutory laws. Under the first rubric, the president was accused of violations of (a) popular sovereignty and other duties to uphold the Constitution; (b) the constitutional principle of equality and the president's right to appoint or dismiss public officials; (c) the presidential duty to uphold free market order and the right to private property; (d) the right to freedom of speech; and (e) protection of the right to life. Under the second rubric, the charges consisted of (f) abuse of power, (g) extortion, and (h) leakage of confidential documents. What is interesting is that except for (a) and (e), none of these formal charges, which directly concern citizens' basic rights, liberties, opportunities or what John Rawls calls "constitutional essentials", was at the center of the public discourse that invigorated civil society, even though citizens were strongly convinced that the president had committed all of these wrongs, and thus was legally culpable. Since (a) concerns an abstract principle governing the basic duties of the president in any constitutional democracy and it is expected to be invoked in the constitutional adjudication of a presidential impeachment, what is truly remarkable about the Candlelight Revolution is why (e) was so important for the Korean public and, as will be discussed shortly, how it had anything to do with the normative ideal of the nation's highest political leader.

Though the National Assembly included the violation of the duty to protect citizens' right to life as one of the reasons for impeaching the president, it is hard to deny that inclusion of this charge in the impeachment motion was largely due to enormous popular pressure and had nothing to do with the Choi scandal. Unlike other charges, violation of the duty to protect citizens' right to life was brought up based on a widely held popular observation that the president had failed to respond effectively to "the Sewol incident" that had occurred two years earlier, which caused the deaths of more than three hundred people, mostly secondary school students on a field trip, who were on a ferry named "Sewol". When this tragedy occurred, the president did not appear publicly for as long as seven hours, did not give any proper orders for rescuing the people on a sinking ship, and when she finally showed up, she appeared clueless about what had been going on, making the majority of Koreans watching the whole incident on live broadcast dumbfounded, then enraged (also see Kim 2017, pp. 7–10).

For the members of the National Assembly who were under staggering pressure to channel the citizens' civic anger and rage into the process of impeachment, "violation of the constitutional duty to protect citizens' right to life" was the best language available to them because apparently it was the only legitimate language that Korea's liberal-democratic constitutional system could make sense of and would legally recognize. From the standpoint of ordinary Koreans, however, what was at issue was not necessarily the right to life, typically referenced in cases of death penalty, terminal illness, or abortion, but rather the most basic well-being of citizens, namely, their physical survival. Many Koreans found the president completely irresponsible when she disappeared for unknown reasons at the moment she was desperately needed and they also found her insincere when she offered neither an explanation for her disappearance nor an apology for her failure to fulfill her duty as both legally stipulated and public-culturally expected. As the citizens watched the president take no responsibility for the deaths of the people who could have survived if she had taken proper action during the short window, as well as show no genuine sense of empathy toward the victims' families when she refused to meet them despite their repeated requests, the people realized that the president was critically lacking something important, something that they would normally expect from the nation's highest political leader, but that which the Korean constitution does not specify or formally require. This "something" that the president was critically devoid of was the virtue of sincerity and an empathetic heart. However, at the time of the Sewol incident, the Korean public did not know how to process their frustration with the president in a constitutionally acceptable manner but merely remonstrated with her in the open space of civil society, because there was no constitutional resource available on the basis of which to formally express the public's blame for her insincerity, irresponsibility, and lack of an empathetic heart, or all put together, her fatal failure to exercise a benevolent government.

For the Korean public, the Choi sandal only confirmed their deep suspicion that the president lacks the core virtues that they believe are essential for good political leadership. Now, on top of her putative legal crimes, when she once again shirked her responsibility for the Choi scandal and instead rationalized her misconduct and legal violations as unintended outcomes of a selfless commitment to the public good, Korean citizens, though initially willing to give her an opportunity to keep face by letting her step down, finally gave up all hope on her as a political leader and decided to put her out of office via impeachment by pressuring the legislature.

Two points are important to note here. First, as the KCC rightly noted later, though with some ambiguity, it was not so much the president's legal violations as such but her "betrayal of the trust of the people" that drove the people to the streets, initially as a sign of remonstration, then as that of protest and contention. The KCC noted that the purpose of impeachment was to deprive the president of the (institutionally conferred) trust of the people (via democratic election). From the perspective of democratic legitimacy, the KCC concluded, "there are grounds for impeachment when the President is found to have betrayed the trust of the people by committing crimes that are serious enough to warrant removal of him or her from office during his or her tenure" (KCCR, 2016Hŏn-na1, p. 18). However, if the president's legal violation itself implies her forfeiture of the trust of the people, why should there be an additional "test of gravity", according to which impeachment of the president is justified only if the crime is grave enough to ensure that the expected public interest incurring from removal of her from office clearly overrides the public cost that would follow? That is, if the president's legal violation alone satisfies the betrayal of public trust condition, how can the gravity condition be met?

While the democratic procedural interpretation of "the betrayal of the trust of the people" was supposed to generate this legal conundrum and it was indeed the very problem with which the KCC later struggled,[29] for Korean citizens the problem was not as complicated as this legal judgment. For those who were participating in the public protest, the president betrayed not only democratic trust with her crimes, but *additionally*, the traditional Confucian notion of trust between the ruler and the ruled, according to which the ruler serves the well-being of the people while the people reciprocate the ruler's care with voluntary cooperation and compliance.[30] From the standpoint of

---

[29] I discuss this issue extensively in Kim (). As I argue in the cited paper, it is quite clear that Korean constitutional justices (at least several of them) were influenced, albeit implicitly, by the Confucian moral ideals of good government and good leadership, strongly resonating with Korean Confucian democratic civil society.

[30] On this point, Chan (2014, p. 40) writes, "A personal quality essential to authority is trustworthiness. Confucians think that ultimately the effectiveness of political power rests on the level of trust the people have in their ruler. A government must have the people's cooperation and compliance in order to accomplish its tasks."

civil society, the gravity condition was clearly met when the president was found to have violated this second requirement of public trust, although this moral and purely normative binding is only tacitly acknowledged in Korean politics and therefore has no (direct) legal foundation in the Korean Constitution—hence the court's trouble in adjudicating the gravity condition.

Second, the fact that the president's response to the victims of the Sewol incident and their families was one of the most important factors that galvanized the Korean civil society during the Candlelight Revolution shows that Koreans held a normative ideal of democratic political leadership, which cannot be fully satisfied by its liberal ideal that holds rational accountability as its central concern. When it was later disclosed to the public that the president was at her private residence during her regular working hours as more than three hundred people drowned and that she never showed an interest in meeting the victims' families, their repeated requests and public support for them notwithstanding, it was clear that the president was far from the traditional ideal of the virtuous ruler who cares for and is capable of empathizing with the people.

Though this empathetic dimension of political leadership is less emphasized in liberal constitutionalism, it is the central feature of Confucian leadership as strongly vindicated in the ideal of benevolent government. While the Confucian benevolent government does not rest on the naive belief that a virtuous ruler always produces a good government, its driving force certainly comes from the ruler's care and responsibility for the people, even when the problem at hand (the most serious of which is suffering of the people) is not directly caused by his own misrule.[31] When Koreans were raising candles and demanding the president's resignation and eventually her impeachment, they might not have actually believed that she had proactively violated the citizens' right to life. As it turned out, the KCC did not uphold this charge when brought by the National Assembly. What is clear though is that in the eyes of the Koreans the president did not possess the right moral character expected of the nation's highest political leader. When it was repeatedly proven that she not only lacked core virtues for good leadership such as benevolence, sincerity, trustworthiness, responsibility, and compassion, but rather had gone actively against the ideal of good government by being callous to the suffering of the people and entrusting the government to a friend who was totally unqualified and had no interest in the public good, many ordinary Koreans finally came to the conclusion that she was unsuited for this post and should be removed immediately.

In the end, for the Korean people, the president failed to live up to the "right name" of her office, the Confucian litmus test for good government, as much as she failed in democratic legitimacy. It should be reminded that when asked what he would do first if entrusted with the government, Confucius replied that he would "rectify the names" (*zheng ming* 正名) before anything else because "if names are rectified, things will be successfully accomplished" (*Analects* 13.3).[32] More specifically, in advancing the rectification of the names as the method of Confucian statecraft, Confucius articulates its content as nothing less than "letting the ruler be a ruler, the minister be a minister, the father be a father, and the son be a son" (*Analects* 12.11, my translation). Accordingly, bad government arises when members of society do not conduct themselves according to the normative ideal of the social positions that they hold. Though, ideally, good government can be attained when all members of society fulfill their social roles faithfully in accordance with what is morally intended by the titles of such roles, it begins with the ruler's ability to rectify (*zheng* 正) himself and put himself on the right track of the Way. Hence, Confucius's famous statement, "To govern (*zheng* 政) is to correct (*zheng* 正). If you [the ruler] set an example by being correct, who would dare to remain incorrect?" (*Analects* 12.7) According to Confucius, self-rectification is not merely to follow the conventional social roles blindly (Roetz 1993). It involves critical self-reflection and a rigorous process of self-discipline that enables one to overcome one's untutored private desires and follow the social patterns expressive of the Way (thus

---

[31] On the Confucian non-causal conception of political responsibility, see Kim (2010).
[32] Unless noted otherwise, throughout this paper the English translations of the *Lunyu* 論語 are adapted from Confucius (1979).

not any social norms), the faithful practice of which would lead him or her to acquire the virtue of benevolence (*ren* 仁) (*Analects* 12.1), the Confucian moral virtue par excellence, and thus enabling a benevolent government.

Seen in this way, the greatest wrong that the president committed was that she did not act like the nation's highest political leader and she actively violated norms associated with her moral and political role *as culturally understood*, which is more than just following the public duties attached to the office of the president as stipulated by the constitution, although she did fail in this as well. Otherwise stated, the president's legal violation, which was to be the only concern of the KCC in adjudicating her impeachment, was one important reason for collective civic activism, but the Candlelight Revolution was about much more. It was about the failure of a new democracy in living up to its right name. In its right name, Korean democracy ought to have operated on the Way in which (West-originated) democratic principles and traditional Confucian values are dialectically intertwined, it ought to have had a national leader equipped with character traits necessary for good government, and ultimately, it ought to have developed a political system that not only ensures protection of liberal rights but also helps realize citizens' collective self-government in light of their shared conception of the good life that is at once liberal and Confucian.

For Koreans, the Choi scandal and the president's failed leadership symbolized the fatal failure of the promise of *this* democracy ("Confucian democracy" as I called it earlier) and this realization inevitably brought them to seek something far more fundamental than the impeachment of the sitting president—a democracy of its right name. As such, what had originally began as public remonstration with the president underwent a radical self-transformation when the people participating in it finally turned their attention to the question of what it means to live in a democracy. Participants of the June Uprising of 1987, preoccupied with removing the evils of a repressive government and bringing about a procedural democracy that can protect basic rights, could not think deeply about this ontological meaning of democracy as a way of life. The participants of the 2016–2017 candlelight protest, however, gave democratic life a new political significance by affiliating the impeachment of the president who violated both law and traditional norms of good government with a more fundamental question about the nature of their democratic life and constitutional system. For them it had to be an event that would signal a radical departure from "accumulated evils" of the existing mode of democracy (or pseudo-democracy) and make the Korean polity start anew in light of its democratic promise. Therefore, it must go beyond mere political protest and evolve into a "revolution" in which bad old practices are replaced by reformed institutions and practices. Finally, the candlelight protest grew to become a political revolution when ordinary people brought down the ruler with their own power and in their own name for the first time in Korean history, yet in accordance with constitutional procedure and the democratic duty of civility.

6. Conclusions

That the Candlelight Revolution was strongly motivated by moral concerns closely affiliated with Korea's traditional Confucian political ideal and culture does not necessarily mean that Confucianism was its only motivating force. Nor does it imply that all Confucian motivations that have been identified in this paper were directly relevant to the problem at hand. For instance, and as noted already, given the only tangential relation between the Sewol incident and the Cho scandal, it is arguable whether Korean civil society was rightly motivated in launching a mass public protest against the president when their political action was in part propelled by their frustration with the way in which she had responded to the Sewol incident. Again, this was a critical point for the justices in the KCC in adjudicating the impeachment, and, to be sure, their first task was to disentangle the legal questions surrounding this profoundly political case from all other moral claims and political contentions arising from civil society, although it is another matter whether KCC indeed handled the case consistently from its professed apolitical stance. The point that I am trying to make in this paper is that the Korean civil society of the Candlelight Revolution can be called a Confucian democratic civil society not least because of its remarkable distance from liberal pluralistic civil society but also because of the saliently Confucian content of the moral discourse that motivated it.

In Korean political studies, Confucian civil society is one of the most underdeveloped and underappreciated concepts. Furthermore, a meritocratic version of Confucian civil society, which is more popular among the Chinese advocates of civil society, does reveal its critical limitations in the democratic context that defines Korean politics after democratization, where public equality has become an inviolable social norm. Confucian democratic civil society provides a useful theoretical concept that can help us to not only philosophically reconstruct a normatively attractive and socially practicable vision of civil society in a society that is politically democratic and culturally Confucian, but also to understand as well as evaluate the social practice of civic activism that is taking place in East Asian societies of the Confucian heritage from a more culturally nuanced perspective. It is hoped that our cultural analysis of Korea's Candlelight Revolution demonstrates the conceptual utility of Confucian democratic civil society in the evaluative-empirical study of civil society in East Asia.

Funding: This work was supported by the Ministry of Education of the Republic of Korea and the National Research Foundation of Korea (NRF-2017S1A3A2065772).

Conflicts of Interest: The author declares no conflicts of interest.

References

Ackerly, Brooke A. 2005. Is Liberalism the Only Way toward Democracy? Confucianism and Democracy. *Political Theory* 33: 547–76. [CrossRef]

Angle, Stephen C. 2012. *Contemporary Confucian Political Philosophy: Toward Progressive Confucianism*. Cambridge: Polity.

Angle, Stephen C., and Justin Tiwald. 2017. *Neo-Confucianism: A Philosophical Introduction*. Cambridge: Polity.

Bae, Mun-jo, and Se-jeong Park. 2013. Taehakseng-ŭi hyo-e taehan insikkwa kachokgach'igwan-e yŏnghyang-ŭl ich'inŭn pyŏnin [Consciousness of Filial Piety and Family Values in College Students]. *Journal of the Korean Contents Association* 13: 275–85. [CrossRef]

Cahoone, Lawrence E. 2002. *Civil Society: The Conservative Meaning of Liberal Politics*. Malden: Blackwell.

Chan, Joseph. 2014. *Confucian Perfectionism: A Political Philosophy for Modern Times*. Princeton: Princeton University Press.

Cho, Hein. 1997. The Historical Origin of Civil Society in Korea. *Korea Journal* 37: 24–41.

Cho, Tae-yŏp, and Ch'ŏl-kyu Kim. 2007. *Han'guk Siminsahoe-ŭi Kujo-wa Tonghak [The Structure and Dynamic of Korean Civil Society]*. Seoul: Jimmundang.

Choi, Jang-Jip. 2009. *Minjung-esŏ Simin-ŭro [From People to Citizens]*. Seoul: Tolbegae.

Cohen, Jean L., and Andrew Arato. 1994. *Civil Society and Political Theory*. Cambridge: The MIT Press.

Confucius. 1979. *The Analects*. Translated by D. C. Lau. New York: Penguin.

De Bary, William Theodore. 1983. *The Liberal Tradition in China*. New York: Columbia University Press.

Deuchler, Martina. 1992. *The Confucian Transformation of Korea: A Study of Society and Ideology*. Cambridge: Council on East Asian Studies, Harvard University.

Diamond, Larry. 1999. *Developing Democracy: Toward Consolidation*. Baltimore: Johns Hopkins University Press.

Doucette, Jamie. 2017. The Occult of Personality: Korea's Candlelight Protests and the Impeachment of Park Geun-hye. *Journal of Asian Studies* 76: 851–60. [CrossRef]

Galston, William A. 2002. *Liberal Pluralism: The Implications of Value Pluralism for Political Theory and Practice*. Cambridge: Cambridge University Press.

Glendon, Mary A., and David Blankehorn, eds. 1995. *Seedbeds of Virtue: Sources of Competence, Character, and Citizenship in American Society*. Lanham: Madison Book.

Howard, Marc M. 2003. *The Weakness of Civil Society in Post-Communist Europe*. Cambridge: Cambridge University Press.

Keane, John. 1998. *Civil Society: Old Images, New Visions*. Stanford: Stanford University Press.

Kim, Dong-Choon. 2006. Growth and Crisis of the Korean Citizens' Movement. *Korea Journal* 46: 99–128.

Kim, Nan. 2017. Candlelight and the Yellow Ribbon: Catalyzing Re-Democratization in South Korea. *Asia-Pacific Journal: Japan Focus* 15: 1–17.

Kim, Sŏng-chae. 2018. Orak k'ŏmyunikeishyŏn: Ch'oppulhyŏkmyŏng, punno-esŏ yuhŭi-ro [The Communication of Entertainment: The "Candlelight Revolution", from Anger to Amusement]. *Hyŏndae yurŏpch'ŏrak yŏn'gu* 50: 167–205.

Kim, Sungmoon. 2008. Transcendental Collectivism and Participatory Politics in Democratized Korea. *Critical Review of International Social and Political Philosophy* 11: 57–77. [CrossRef]

Kim, Sungmoon. 2010. The Secret of Confucian *Wuwei* Statecraft: Mencius's Political Theory of Responsibility. *Asian Philosophy* 20: 27–42. [CrossRef]

Kim, Sungmoon. 2011. Confucian Constitutionalism: Mencius and Xunzi on Virtue, Ritual, and Royal Transmission. *Review of Politics* 73: 371–99. [CrossRef]

Kim, Sungmoon. 2014. *Confucian Democracy in East Asia: Theory and Practice*. New York: Cambridge University Press.

Kim, Sungmoon. 2016. *Public Reason Confucianism: Democratic Perfectionism and Constitutionalism in East Asia*. New York: Cambridge University Press.

Kim, Sungmoon. Forthcoming. From Remonstrance to Impeachment: ˙A Curious Case of "Confucian Constitutionalism" in South Korea. *Law and Social Inquiry*.

Kim, Sunhyuk. 2000. *The Politics of Democratization in Korea: The Role of Civil Society*. Pittsburg: University of Pittsburg Press.

Kim, Sunhyuk. 2004. South Korea: Confrontational Legacy and Democratic Contributions. In *Civil Society and Political Change in Asia: Expanding and Contracting Democratic Space*. Edited by Muthiah Alagappa. Stanford: Stanford University Press, pp. 138–63.

Kim, Yong-ki, and Dong-hee Lee. 2017. Daet'ongnyŏng t'anhaek ch'otppulchipoe-ŭi kyoyukchŏk ŭimi [The Educational Implications of Candlelight Vigil Protests for President Impeachment]. *Hang'uk K'ontenchŭhakhoe Nonmunchip* 17: 311–18.

Koo, Hagen. 1993a. Strong State and Contentious Society. In *State and Society in Contemporary Korea*. Edited by Hagen Koo. Ithaca: Cornell University Press, pp. 231–49.

Koo, Hagen. 1993b. The State, *Minjung*, and the Working Class in South Korea. In *State and Society in Contemporary Korea*. Edited by Hagen Koo. Ithaca: Cornell University Press, pp. 131–62.

Kymlicka, Will. 1995. *Multicultural Citizenship*. Oxford: Oxford University Press.

Lee, Junghoon. 2015. Confucianism and the Meaning of Liberalism in the Contemporary Korean Legal System. In *Confucianism, Law, and Democracy in Contemporary Korea*. Edited by Sungmoon Kim. London: Rowman and Littlefield International, pp. 149–71.

Lee, Namehee. 2007. *The Making of Minjung: Democracy and the Politics of Representation in South Korea*. Ithaca: Cornell University Press.

Lee, Seung-Hwan. 2003. The Concept of *Gong* in Traditional Korea and Its Modern Transformations. *Korea Journal* 43: 137–63.

Lee, Su-Hoon. 1993. Transitional Politics of Korea, 1987–1992: Activation of Civil Society. *Pacific Affairs* 66/3: 351–67. [CrossRef]

Linz, Juan J., and Alfred Stepan. 1996. *The Problem of Democratic Transition and Consolidation*. Baltimore: Johns Hopkins University Press.

Macedo, Stephen. 2001. The Constitution, Civic Virtue, and Civil Society: Social Capital as Substantive Morality. *Fordham Law Review* 69: 1573–93.

Madsen, Richard. 2002. Confucian Conceptions of Civil Society. In *Alternative Conceptions of Civil Society*. Edited by Simone Chambers and Will Kymlicka. Princeton: Princeton University Press, pp. 190–204.

Metzger, Thomas A. 2001. The Western Conception of Civil Society in the Context of Chinese History. In *Civil Society: History and Possibilities*. Edited by Sudipta Kaviraj and Sunil Khilnani. Cambridge: Cambridge University Press, pp. 204–31.

Park, Chong-Min, and Doh Chull Shin. 2006. Do Asian Values Deter Popular Support for Democracy in South Korea? *Asian Survey* 46: 341–61. [CrossRef]

Park, Mi. 2005. Organizing Dissent against Authoritarianism: The South Korean Student Movement in the 1980s. *Korea Journal* 45: 261–89.

Rawls, John. 1993. *Political Liberalism*. New York: Columbia University Press.

Roetz, Heiner. 1993. *Confucian Ethics of the Axial Age*. Albany: State University of New York Press.

Rosenblum, Nancy L. 1998. *Membership and Morals: The Personal Uses of Pluralism in America*. Princeton: Princeton University Press.

Shils, Edward. 1997. *The Virtue of Civility*. Edited by Steven Grosby. Indianapolis: Liberty Fund.

Shin, Jong-Hwa. 2000. The Limits of Civil Society: Observations on the Korean Debate. *European Journal of Social Theory* 3: 249–70.

Shin, Kwang-Yeong. 2006. The Citizens' Movement in Korea. *Korea Journal* 46: 5–34.

Son, Ho-ch'ŏl. 2017. *Ch'oppulhyŏkmyŏng-kwa 2017nyŏn ch'eje [The Candlelight Revolution and the 2017 System]*. Seoul: Sogang University Press.

Swidler, Ann. 2000. Cultural Power and Social Movements. In *Culture and Politics: A Reader*. Edited by Lane Crothers and Charles Lockhart. New York: St. Martine's Press, pp. 269–83.

Tan, Sor-hoon. 2003. Can There Be a Confucian Civil Society? In *The Moral Circle and the Self: Chinese and Western Approaches*. Edited by Kim-Chong Chong, Sor-hoon Tan and C. L. Ten. Chicago: Open Court, pp. 193–218.

Tu, Wei-ming. 2006. *Munmyŏngdŭl-ŭi Taehwa [A Dialogue among Civilizations]*. Translated by T'ae-sŏng Kim. Seoul: Hyumŏnisŭtŭ.

Wedeen, Lisa. 2002. Conceptualizing Culture: Possibilities for Political Science. *American Political Science Review* 96: 713–28. [CrossRef]

Wood, Alan T. 1995. *Limits to Autocracy: From Sung Neo-Confucianism to a Doctrine of Political Rights*. Honolunu: University of Hawaii Press.

Wu, In-su. 1999. *Chosŏnhugi Sallimseryŏk Yŏn'gu [A Study on the Backwoods Literati as Political Forces in the late Chosŏn Period]*. Seoul: Ilchogak.

Article

Ritualization of Affection and Respect: Two Principles of Confucian Ritual

Jaesang Jung

Department of Oriental Science, Wonkwang Digital University, Seoul 07448, Korea; jung.jaesang@gmail.com

Received: 14 February 2019; Accepted: 21 March 2019; Published: 26 March 2019

Abstract: Confucian rituals have constituted the foundation of religious practice in the traditional societies of East Asia. Paying attention to the Confucian ritual, this article explores the way Confucianism constructs its symbolic system based on people's natural feelings, particularly in the case of three-year mourning. It intends to show how the two feelings of "affection for the family" (*chinchin/qinqin*, 親親) and "respect for the honorable" (*chonjon/zunzun*, 尊尊) are ritualized in Confucian rites, and to illuminate the religious and social dimensions of Confucianism in premodern Korea by analyzing a seventeenth-century controversy over royal mourning from the perspective of these two principles.

Keywords: religiousness of confucianism; korean confucianism; affection (*chinchin/qinqin*); respect (*chonjon/zunzun*); three-year mourning; controversy on mourning attire; Chosŏn Dynasty; Song Siyŏl; Hŏ Mok; Yun Hyu

---

1. Introduction

Confucianism has played a central role in establishing the foundation of East Asian civilization, covering not only China but also neighboring regions, such as Korea, Japan, Vietnam, and the Ryukyu Kingdom (Okinawa), functioning as the dominant norm in various fields, including philosophy, ethics, law, politics, and religion. The starting point, or the basis, of social norms of Confucianism is natural human feelings. Emotions such as joy, anger, grief, and delight are regarded as natural tendencies, which should be positively expressed and at the same time properly controlled. The Confucian ritual is a way of guiding and cultivating those human feelings, through which Confucianism pursues the realization of the ideal man, society, and state.

There might be various ways of approaching the meaning and role of Confucianism in Korea, but here I focus on the ritual aspect, particularly the ritualization of natural feelings. I focus on Confucian ritual and investigate the way it constructs its symbolic system based on people's natural feelings, particularly in the case of the three-year mourning ritual. I delve into how Confucian scholars ritualize the two fundamental feelings of "affection for the family" (*chinchin/qinqin*, 親親) and "respect for the honorable" (*chonjon/zunzun*, 尊尊). To present a showcase, I will analyze the controversy over royal mourning in the seventeenth-century Chosŏn dynasty from the perspective of the two competing principles of 'affection' and 'respect', a case that illuminates the religious and social dimension of Confucianism in pre-modern Korea.

2. Ritualization of Natural Feelings

Confucianism has played the encompassing role of giving meaning to and regulating everyday life in pre-modern East Asia. Rites of passage especially, which commemorate one's birth, the transition from childhood to adulthood, marriage, and death, have been fundamentally based on Confucian rituals. In this section, I want to overview the general Confucian understanding of the relationship between the Confucian rituals and natural feelings.

An illustrative example to show that Confucian ritual is designed and based on 'human natural feeling' is the three-year mourning ritual, which is for expressing grief over the death of one's parent. It is a lengthy ritual lasting precisely twenty-five months. During the mourning period, one must retire from official social activities and live ascetically in a hut near the grave, giving offerings to the dead every morning and evening.

Twenty-five months is quite a long time in fact. Considering that the average lifespan in ancient China was much shorter than today, to impose twenty-five months' mourning could be a harsh demand. However, Confucianism emphasizes that this period of mourning and ascetic life are not arbitrarily chosen but rather designed and guided by natural feelings. It seems that there were voices of dissent over this harsh ritual. A disciple of Confucius, Zai Wo 宰我, whose name is Yu 予, objected to it, saying that three years is too long, and one year is enough. At that time, Confucius answered as follows:

The Master said, "If you were, after a year, to eat good rice, and wear embroidered clothes, would you feel at ease?"

"I should," replied Wo.

The Master said, "If you can feel at ease, do it. But a superior man, during the whole period of mourning, does not enjoy pleasant food which he may eat, nor derive pleasure from music which he may hear. He also does not feel at ease, if he is comfortably lodged. Therefore, he does not do what you propose. But now you feel at ease and may do it."

Zai Wo then went out, and the Master said, "This shows Yu's want of virtue. It is not till a child is three years old that it is allowed to leave the arms of its parents. And the three years' mourning is universally observed throughout the empire. Yu must have also received the three years' love from his parents!". (*Analects* 17.21) (Confucius 1960)

According to Confucius, the three-year mourning is based on the feeling of grief at the death of a parent, when people usually cannot feel at ease even at home, taste delicious food, or delight in wearing good clothes. The mourning rite ritualizes such emotions, and sets the period as the time for natural recovery from the shock of a family member's death. But the psychological state and the duration of grief can be different from person to person. On this matter, the problem of the extent that the ritual outlasts the emotion occurs.

Zai Wo suggested that one year is enough for mourning a deceased parent. One year means a cycle of four seasons, following which political, economic, and religious ceremonies were held in the agricultural society of ancient China. A year represents a completed time unit unfolding the birth, growth, decline, and death of life. Zai's opinion was probably based on this concept of time. Although Confucius answered Zai, "if you can feel at ease, do it," he was being sarcastic and critical toward Zai's opinion. Given that he maintained the period of mourning following the natural feeling, Confucius might not have had a choice but to answer in such a positive way whatever his intention may have been.

How could the period of mourning be legitimized by a natural feeling? As to the meaning of the mourning ritual, besides the aspect of grief, Confucius also explained it as a return for the parent's love. Every human grows up relying exclusively on their parents' care until the age of twenty-five months—that is what the Chinese count as being three years old and is when one acquires the basic physical and linguistic ability to survive. Grounded in this parent-child relationship in the first phase of human life, Confucius claims that the meaning of the mourning lies in gratitude for one's parents' nursing and caring. It appears that Confucius is explaining its meaning in two distinct ways—grief and gratitude—nevertheless, the two are indivisible if we take into consideration that one's grief for the dead is often intensified with the memory of love. Indeed, Confucius' argument is consistent in that he associates the period of three-year mourning with 'natural feelings.' Confucius claims that one ought to feel what many people do feel. "Feelings" occur naturally. In addition, "what people ought to feel" belongs to a moral dimension because it accompanies a certain amount of learning and obligation. There might be continuity and discontinuity between the two. This is the point on which Daoist thinkers criticize Confucianism for its arbitrariness and anti-naturalism. However, Confucian thinkers tried to set up 'natural feeling' by defending the homogeneity or continuity between what one does feel and what one ought to feel, and use this principle as a foundation to conceptualize moral sentiment and construct rituals.[1]

Another important argument legitimatizing the mourning period is found in the thought of Xunzi 荀子, a Confucian of the second century BCE. Just like Confucius, Xunzi agreed that the three-year mourning is based on natural sentiments (*qing* 情), but he pointed out moreover that some artificial sophistication is imposed on the setting of the mourning period.

Firstly, drawing on the fact that the birds and other animals have their own ways to express their grief over a loss, Xunzi explained that human feeling when faced with the death of one's parents has no limit. The three-year mourning is a ritual to ornament (*xiushi* 脩飾) the feeling in order to achieve "a good form and a proper order." Since the extent and the duration of grief can vary depending on the person, some will forget their grief in just one day, and some will suffer the pain of loss throughout their life. Even though grief may be the expression of natural feelings, if it is too weak or too intense, it might cause conflicts with other people's feelings and social chaos at the end. To prevent those conflicts and chaos, Xunzi said, "the former kings and sages accordingly established a middle way and fixed a proper measure for it," and made the three-year mourning ritual (Xunzi 2014, pp. 213–14). The function of the mourning ritual is to guide one to express one's feeling of grief in a proper way. It strengthens a feeling that is too weak, such as 'the grief of one day,' and cuts off excessively intense feeling, such as 'lifetime grief.'

Xunzi also made it clear that the period of mourning was artificially fixed. As seen previously, Zai Wo argued that one year is enough to mourn for parents. In the same way, Xunzi also said the standard period of the mourning is one year in principle, according to a cycle of four seasons. Nonetheless, the reason for taking three years is "to add loftiness" (*jialong* 加隆) (Xunzi 2014, p. 214)[2]. According to Xunzi, grief can naturally die down in one year, but the mourning period for parents was fixed as more than double that because of an artificial factor, which is that the parents have an 'exalted position (*long* 隆)' compared to other blood relatives. Xunzi put it, "The lord occupies the most exalted position in the state, and the father occupies the most exalted position in the family. When the most exalted position is held by one person alone, there will be order, but if held by two people, there will be chaos" (Xunzi 2014, pp. 143–44). In human society, both the lord and the father have the 'exalted position and power.' However, those are not naturally endowed but institutionally formulated in comparison to love or grief for family.[3] The fact that the death of the lord also demands a three-year mourning reveals that there is an artificial factor playing as the principle of the mourning ritual, alongside natural feelings for blood relations.

---

[1] Among the Confucian thinkers, it was Mengzi (孟子, 372–289 BCE) or Mencius who claimed that there is a close relationship between feeling and ritual. Although we cannot find any specific statement about mourning in *Mencius*, he tried to justify ritual on the basis of natural feelings in a more explicit way by saying that the feeling of reverence (*gongjing zhi xin* 恭敬之心) and modesty (*cirang zhi xin* 辭讓之心) is the beginning of ritual propriety (*li zhi duan* 禮之端) (Mencius 6A.6; 2A.6) (Mencius 1970).

[2] An almost identical statement about the three-year mourning is included in the *Liji* 禮記 [*Record of Rites*], in the chapter "Questions about the Mourning for Three Years" (*Sannian wen* 三年問). See (Liji 1968, p. 393; Liji 2000, juan 58, pp. 1818–19).

[3] In Confucianism, the power and privilege of monarch or father were conceived as arbitrary/artificial things, but they are also regarded as natural constraints at the same time. For example, Xunzi suggested a perspective that emphasizes the arbitrariness/artificiality of a ritual and ruling system, but he still used the analogies of a natural model to connect ritual and class system with natural order when he said, "However, just as there is Heaven and Earth, there is a difference between above and below. . . . As for the fact that two nobles cannot serve each other, and two base men cannot employ each other, this is the Heavenly order of things" (Xunzi 2014, p. 69). Thus, "naturalness" and "artificiality" in this paper are relative terms that are not completely separable.

3. The Principles of Affection and Respect

As seen in the previous section, we can identify in the explanations of Confucius and Xunzi about the period of mourning for three years two factors at work in Confucian rituals, namely 'naturalness' and 'artificiality.' The terms in Confucian texts corresponding to this 'naturalness' and 'artificiality' are, respectively, '*qinqin* 親親' (affection) and '*zunzun* 尊尊' (respect). These two factors are operative not only in the three-year mourning, but also in deciding other periods of mourning and the types of mourning garments. In this chapter, I will delve into how they are working in particular cases.[4]

First of all, it is worthwhile to review the meaning of the terms. '*Qinqin*' literally means "to give affection to those closest" (normally, family), which is working as the principle to decide the period and style of mourning according to the distance or intimacy in kinship. '*Zunzun*' literally means "to show respect to those respectable," which decides the period of mourning according to the hierarchical order or social class. In other words, the principle of 'affection' emphasizes natural aspects like kinship or blood relation; that of 'respect' considers artificial aspects such as social status and authority. However, the principle of 'respect' covers not only the relationship between the sovereign and the subject among social status but also the superior and the subordinate inside one's household.[5] These two principles are sometimes applied alone, and sometimes interwoven to decide the period and style of mourning.

There are six kinds of Confucian mourning periods: three years, one year, nine months, seven months, five months, and three months. The different mourning clothes are divided into five, known as the 'Five Garments' (*wufu* 五服), which are ranked by the emotional weight of grief: 'unhemmed sackcloth' (*zhancui* 斬衰), 'hemmed sackcloth' (*zicui* 齊衰), 'greater processed cloth' (*dagong* 大功), 'lesser processed cloth' (*xiaogong* 小功), and 'fine hemp' (*sima* 緦麻). Among the five, the 'unhemmed sackcloth' is the heaviest, and the 'fine hemp' is the lightest. 'Heaviness' and 'lightness' here refer to the degree of emotional weight, due to the closeness of blood for the relation.

Literally, '*zhan* 斬' means "to cut," and '*cui* 衰' designates "humble clothes for mourning." Thus, in the context of the mourning ritual, '*zhancui*' designates the unhemmed garment made of rough cut fabric like sackcloth. For example, the death of the closest family member, such as a parent, does not afford a psychological state for hemming the cloth, so the son wears the 'unhemmed sackcloth' to represent the intensity and depth of his grief. The next grade of mourning, '*zicui* 齊衰' (hemmed sackcloth) designates 'to hem the edges of sackcloth to be even (*zi* 齊),' which implies that the psychological severity of the situation is slighter and it allows one to add hemming. In this way, the mental weights that the mourning clothes represent are symbolized by the degree of artificial processing of fabric, its roughness or fineness, and sewing or hemming.

The six periods and the five styles are combined to provide the diverse patterns of mourning for different occasions: unhemmed sackcloth for three years, hemmed sackcloth for three years, hemmed sackcloth with a staff for a year (*zicui zhangji* 齊衰杖期), hemmed sackcloth without a staff for a year (*zicui bu zhangji* 齊衰不杖期), hemmed sackcloth for three months, greater processed cloth for nine months, lesser processed cloth for five months, and fine hemp for three months, etc. The term '*ji* 期' means one cycle of the four seasons, or a year. The use of a staff (*zhang* 杖) has two meanings. Firstly, it designates the chief mourner; secondly, it represents that the mourner's state is such as to be unable to stand up without the staff due to great sorrow. The staff has variants depending on the rank of mourning. In case of the unhemmed sackcloth, a raw bamboo stick is used; the hemmed sackcloth is

---

[4] The *Record of Rites* or *Liji* 禮記 specifies six principles to decide the mourning garments in the "Great Treatise" (*dazhuan* 大傳) chapter. These are: affection (*qinqin* 親親), respect (*zunzun* 尊尊), names (*ming* 名), living in the parental home or outside the home (*chulu* 出入), age (*changyou* 長幼), and affinity and external relationship (*congfu* 從服) (Liji 1968, p. 393; Liji 2000, juan 34, p. 1172). The main and higher principles are the first two, and the rest are subordinate to those two.

[5] The two principles of "affection" and "respect" are explained by analogies with mother and father, or water and fire. "The mother is close/affectionate but not revered; the father is revered but not close/affectionate. [It is similar to the relationship of] water and people; water receives affection but not reverence; fire receives reverence but not affection." (Liji 1968, p. 341; Liji 2000, juan 54, p. 1732). 'Fire' implies the relationship of respect which requires that one keep a distance, and on the other hand, 'water' is a good metaphor for the relationship of affection.

worn with a staff made from the paulownia tree. The closer the kinship and the higher the status of the deceased, the longer the mourning period, and the closer the mourning clothes and accessories are to natural objects, omitting artificial processing.

"Mourning Attire"(*Sangfu* 喪服) in the *Ceremonies and Rites* (*Yili* 儀禮) is an essential manual for the Confucian mourning garments. It describes the periods and the attires I have just mentioned, illustrating the ornaments and objects, as well as their ritual meanings (Yili 2000, juan 28–34, pp. 621–758). In particular, it clarifies what kind of attire and period should be followed, according to the relationship between the deceased and the mourner. Since those explanations are too detailed and specific to discuss in full on this occasion, here I want to focus on the four types of mourning pattern, and summarize the typical cases for wearing these clothes. This will illustrate how the two principles of affection and respect work together in the ritualization of mourning.

(1)   The Case of Unhemmed Sackcloth for Three Years (*zhancui sannian* 斬衰三年)

    ①   For one's father
    ②   For one's lord
    ③   Father wears this for his eldest son
    ④   An adopted son of the head of the family wears this for his adoptive father[6]
    ⑤   Wife wears this for her husband
    ⑥   A divorced daughter, who returns to her parental home, wears this for her father

(2)   The Case of Hemmed Sackcloth for Three Years (*zicui sannian* 齊衰三年)

    ①   If father has passed away, the children wear this for their mother
    ②   Mother wears this for her eldest son

(3)   The Case of Hemmed Sackcloth with the Staff for a Year (*zicui zhangji* 齊衰杖期)

    ①   If the father is alive, (children wear this) for mother
    ②   (Husband wears this) for his wife

(4)   The Case of Even Sackcloth without the Staff for a Year (*zicui buzhangji* 齊衰不杖期)

    ①   For one's grandfather and grandmother
    ②   For one's other sons [beyond the eldest son]
    ③   For one's eldest grandson
    ④   An adopted son wears this for his biological parents
    ⑤   A married daughter wears this for her natal parents and for her natal brother who became her natal father's successor
    ⑥   A woman wears this for the lord of her husband
    ⑦   For the parents, wife, eldest son, and grandparents of the lord
    ⑧   A daughter-in-law wears this for her parents-in-law

The preceding examples show how the ranks of mourning are decided by the principles of 'affection' and 'respect.' In cases of mourning for kin, the length and style primarily depend on the principle of 'affection,' which is a natural feeling of bonding among family members. The degree of the feeling makes the material and style of attire different. The period of mourning takes into account the time required for 'natural recovery from the emotional shock' of a family member's death.

---

[6]   I follow the interpretation of Lei Cizong 雷次宗 (386–448 CE) on this part, as recorded in the commentary of Jia Gongyan 賈公彥 (fl. 7th ctry. CE) (Jia 2000, juan 29, p. 642).

The expected recovery time was estimated variously, depending on the closeness of the kin relationship. For example, it was set as three years for one's parents and one year for one's grandparents; the father with a deceased eldest son spends three years in mourning, while the grandfather with a deceased eldest grandson spends a year in mourning. All of these indicate the 'affection,' that is, the intimacy, among kin relations.

The basic rule of mourning for family members is 'affection,' but the principle of 'respect' is also considered. For example, the periods of mourning for parents are all three years, but the kinds of attire differ, so the son wears unhemmed sackcloth for his father and hemmed sackcloth for his mother. It is also noteworthy that the three-year mourning for the mother is only practiced when the father has passed away previously, and otherwise it is shortened to one-year mourning. What is the reason for this? As for 'affection,' the relationship between mother and son is no less intimate than that of father and son. It can be more intimate if pregnancy and childbirth are considered. Nevertheless, if the mourning for one's mother is graded lower, some factor other than 'affection' is decisive. That is consideration of 'respect' for one's father.

In the "Mourning Attire" chapter, it is said that "the father is the most respected [position in the family]" (Yili 2000, juan 11, p. 639). In the patriarchal family model, the 'most respected' position should not be held by two people, but rather only one, and the father is taken as the authoritative figure in the house, just the same as the lord is in the state. In this way of thinking, the mourning for one's mother is downgraded due to the highest status of one's father. In this case, an artificial determination of the 'most respected' position may restrict the son's grief over the loss of his mother. How does the Confucian mourning ritual deal with this problem? If the mother passed away while the father is still alive, the son should take off his mourning attire (hemmed sackcloth with a staff) after a year, but he can maintain *xinsang* 心喪, 'inner mourning' for his mother for the remainder of the three years.[7] And the father is allowed to remarry three years after his wife's death, so as to accommodate the son's will to complete the inner mourning (Yili 2000, juan 11, p. 658). All of these situations are resolutions that reconcile one's 'affection' for one's mother with 'respect' for one's father.

Every son wears the unhemmed sackcloth for three years to mourn his father. However, in the case of paternal mourning for one's sons, the mourning attire for the eldest son differs from the other sons. For the eldest son, the father wears the unhemmed sackcloth for three years; for the other sons, he wears the hemmed sackcloth without the staff for one year. In these cases, another factor is also intervening. The only reason for wearing the unhemmed sackcloth for the eldest son is respect for the heir to the household. The "Mourning Attire" chapter explains, "[This is because the eldest son is] the legitimate body connected with the ancestors, and he will convey the weight [of responsibility of the heir]" (Jia 2000, p. 640). This principle of inheritance, the so-called patriarchal family system (*zongfa* 宗法) has great importance in Confucianism, which aims to prevent disputes over inheritance by imposing consistent principles on the succession of heirs, and ensures a unified kinship order. Unlike for the other sons, the three-year mourning for the eldest son indicates that he inherits a particular authority. In other words, the mourning ritual is a kind of declaration that the principle of inheritance is inviolable and carried through even after the death of the prospective inheritor.

There may be cases where the head of a family is not able to produce a son and adopts one from a brother or a paternal relative in order to continue the family. If so, what kind of mourning should the adopted son undertake, when his adoptive father or his biological father die? For the adoptive father, he should wear the unhemmed sackcloth for three years; for his birth father, the hemmed sackcloth without the staff for a year. In this case, the mourning ritual is not characterized by the 'affection' but by the 'respect' derived from the position of the heir of the household. Because the father is the

---

[7]   In 674, the Empress Wu Zetian 武則天 (624–705) proclaimed three-year wearing of the hemmed sackcloth for one's mother, regardless of whether one's father had died. After several disputes, it became a regulation in the *Kaiyuan Ritual Manual of The Great Tang* (*Da-Tang kaiyuan li* 大唐開元禮), published in 732 (Jiutangshu 1975, vol. 27, pp. 1023–31). After the Tang, it was common to wear the hemmed sackcloth in three-year mourning for one's mother. See (Nishikawa 2012).

highest and there cannot officially be two fathers, the adopted son is not allowed to undertake the three-year mourning for his original father, but rather he needs to adjust his feeling of 'affection' in a downgraded form.

When a daughter gets married and leaves her parental home, another artificial rearrangement of the familial hierarchy can be found as in the case of the adopted son. A married daughter wears the one-year morning of hemmed sackcloth for her natal parents. If she gets divorced and returns to her parental home, she wears the unhemmed sackcloth for three years for her father. Marriage is purely an artificial relationship, however, in which the husband is set in the higher status and the wife in the lower. In contrast to the wife wearing the unhemmed sackcloth for three years for her husband, a husband wears the hemmed sackcloth for his wife, according to the principle of the 'respect' due to the patriarch.

For the lord, one must wear the unhemmed sackcloth for three years. It is the same as the case of mourning one's father. However, unlike how the latter occurs due to a blood relationship, the former is based on the political and hierarchical relationship, governed by the principle of 'respect.' Although a wife has no direct relationship with the lord, she wears a mourning garment following her husband. In this case, she wears the garment of the next lower level (i.e., the hemmed sackcloth), in order to express her respect for the husband.

4. The Controversy over Mourning Attire in Seventeenth-Century Chosŏn

A particular controversy over mourning attire is one of the representative debates in the history of Chosŏn thought. Modern scholars often refer to it as the *yesong* 禮訟 or 'Dispute on Ritual.' The dispute was about more than just theoretical differences and it expanded into a political conflict. In this regard, most studies have analyzed the dispute in the context of the political history of 'factional competition' (*tangjaeng* 黨爭). The main contention of such studies is that the discrepancy in opinions of the seventeenth-century scholars about mourning was due to the schools and factions to which they belonged. Of course, it is noteworthy that those who participated in the dispute each belonged to some faction and had some political stance. But even so, it is too simplistic and schematizing to characterize the controversy as only the conflict of factions.[8] In this section, I want to approach the controversy from a liturgical perspective concerned with the principles of 'affection' and 'respect.'

As seen in the previous section, the mourning attire for the one who has blood ties to the deceased is basically determined according to the principle of 'affection,' and on top of that, the length of the mourning period and the kind of attire are adjusted by considering the aspect of 'respect.' On the other hand, when it comes to the lord–servant relationship, the principle of 'respect' is dominant. That being so, in the case of those who have a kinship with the lord, which principle should they follow in mourning for the lord? The royal family occupies a unique position that differentiates them from an ordinary household in that the family relationship overlaps with the lord-servant relationship. In short, the problem of whether the lord's kin should wear mourning attire according to their family relations or their socio-political relation to the lord can occur. This was the core issue underlying the seventeenth-century Chosŏn controversy over the mourning ritual.

In 1659, the seventeenth King of Chosŏn dynasty, Hyojong 孝宗 (r. 1649–1659) died. He was the second son of the sixteenth King, Injo 仁祖 (r. 1623–1649). His death brought on a heated dispute over the length and style of mourning to be undertaken by Hyojong's stepmother, the Dowager Queen Cho (*Cho-taebi* 趙大妃). It was concerned with how the mother should represent her family relationship to her stepson liturgically as well as her hierarchical relationship to the lord. The scholar-officers' various

---

[8]   Since the late 1990s, several studies appeared that pointed out the limitations of previous studies centered on the history of politics and clarified the philosophical and ritual meaning of the controversy. These new studies paid attention to the concepts of 'affection' and 'respect' and discussed it from the perspective of Confucian Studies of Classics (*jingxue* 經學) (Lee 1996a, 1996b; Chang 1998; Rhee 2014). These approaches provide an important perspective on understanding the cultural implications of Confucianism in Chosŏn period.

proposals for her mourning attire can be summarized by three positions: she should wear the hemmed sackcloth for one year, she should wear the hemmed sackcloth for three years, and she should wear the unhemmed sackcloth for three years. The arguments for each claim are as follows.

Firstly, Song Siyŏl 宋時烈 (1607–1689), the leader of the 'Westerners' (*Sŏin* 西人), who succeeded the Yulgok 栗谷 school, suggested that the Dowager Queen Cho wear the hemmed sackcloth for one year. Song argued that it is proper for her to wear the "*kibok/jifu* 期服," i.e., the one-year mourning attire, because Hyojong was the second son and not the first-born son. In the case of a first-born son's death, his mother should wear the three-year mourning attire, just as what "the father wears for the eldest son" as prescribed in the *Ceremonies and Rites*. On the other hand, in the case of a second son, like Hyojong, the one-year mourning attire (the hemmed sackcloth without a staff) must be applied following the prescription for how to mourn "for the other sons [beyond the eldest son]." Before Hyojong succeeded to the throne, Injo's firstborn son, the Crown Prince Sohyŏn 昭顯 (1612–1645) had died earlier. Injo had worn the three-year hemmed sackcloth attire for him. Since the eldest and first-born son had already mourned for three years with hemmed sackcloth attire, Song believed that the Dowager Queen should wear the mourning attire appropriate for the second son, not for the eldest son (Song 1993, pp. 112, 473–76).

In the case where a father had already mourned for his first-born and eldest son by wearing the unhemmed sackcloth, if he were to wear it again for the next eldest son who became the new heir and thus treat him the same as the firstborn son, Song believes, it would offend against the principle of "not wearing the unhemmed sackcloth twice (*buricham/bu er zhan* 不貳斬)" (Yili 2000, vol. 30, p. 668). In addition, if a father were to undertake the three-year mourning for every heir—such as in the case of consecutive deaths of many sons—and names each next-eldest son as 'the eldest son' (*changja/zhangzi* 長子) one after another, Song argued, it would not only confuse 'the legitimate line of descendants' (*chŏkt'ong/ditong* 嫡統), but also lead to excessive use of the unhemmed sackcloth. Therefore, he claimed that only the legitimate first-born son is eligible to be mourned with the unhemmed sackcloth; any other son merits only mourning with the one-year hemmed sackcloth, even if he is the successor to the throne (Song 1993, pp. 108, 207). In sum, Song's claim was based on a general perspective that did not distinguish between King's family and ordinary families. Eventually, it was criticized in that it failed to takes the peculiarity of the royal family into consideration.

Secondly, the suggestion that the Dowager Queen should wear the hemmed sackcloth for three years was maintained by Hŏ Mok 許穆 (1596–1682), who belonged to the 'Southerner' (*Namin* 南人) faction that succeeded the Toegye 退溪 school. Hŏ argued against Song as follows: although Hyojong was the second son, because he had ascended the throne and continued the royal line, he should be regarded as 'the eldest son.' Therefore, the King's mother should wear the hemmed sackcloth for three years for him. Specifically rejecting Song's concepts of "the legitimate son" and "the eldest son," Hŏ argued that 'the legitimate son' (*chŏkcha/dizi* 嫡子) designates every son of one's legal first wife (*chŏkch'ŏ/diqi* 嫡妻). According to his interpretation, every son of the first wife can become 'the eldest son,' on the ground of Jia Gongyan's commentary, which states, "If the first son is dead, the second eldest son born of one's legal wife is chosen to be established [as the heir] and called 'the eldest son (*changja/zhangzi* 長子)'" (Jia 2000, p. 640). Thus, his conclusion is that since Hyojong was the legitimate second son who succeeded the heir, the Dowager Queen Cho must wear the hemmed sackcloth for three years, on the grounds that is what "the mother wears for the eldest son" according to the "Mourning Attire" chapter (Hŏ 1992, pp. 456–57).

Hŏ also reputed the principle of "not wearing the unhemmed sackcloth twice" on which Song's argument was based. According to Hŏ, that regulation corresponds to those cases where a married daughter or an adopted son downgrades their mourning for their biological parents from the three-year to the one-year practice, but it does not apply to a case where the father wears the three-year mourning attire for his 'eldest son' who succeeded the heir. The reason for the father's practicing the three-year mourning for his eldest son is to give greater importance to the succession of the heir than to the blood ties between father and son. Therefore, it would not be erroneous for the father to undertake the three-year mourning several times (Hŏ 1992, pp. 459–61).

Thirdly, it was Yun Hyu 尹鑴 (1617–1680), who also belonged to the 'Southerners,' who advocated that the Dowager Queen should wear the unhemmed sackcloth for three years. He applied to her case the regulation of what is demanded by the "Mourning Attire" chapter when mourning "for the lord." He backed up his claim by appealing to three Confucian ritual books, the *Ceremonies and Rites*, *the Rites of Zhou* (*Zhouli* 周禮), and the *Explanation of the Record of Rites* (*Liji shu* 禮記疏). Firstly, he based his claim on the statement in the "Mourning Attire" chapter of the *Ceremonies and Rites* as just noted, and secondly, he found evidence concerning mourning for the monarch in the *Rites of Zhou*, which states that, "generally, the mourning [attire] for the Heavenly King is unhemmed sackcloth" (Zhouli 2000, juan 21, p. 654). Finally, he found support in the commentary of Kong Yingda 孔穎達 (574–648) on the *Record of Rites*, which reads, "generally, the five kinds of relatives[9] of a feudal lord wear the unhemmed sackcloth [in mourning for him]. Because the body of a feudal lord should be respected, they cannot wear any lighter attire designated for their original kinship relation [to him]" (Kong 2000, p. 1154).

On the ground of these protocols, Yun maintained that "wherever the heir to the throne is, that is certainly where the legitimate line belongs" (Yun 1994, pp. 398–402; Yun 1974, pp. 1045–51). This was a criticism against Song's approach that differentiates the first-born son from the second, even when the latter is the King who succeeded to the throne. At the same time, this remark also targeted Hŏ, who thought that the three-year mourning is not permitted for the sons of concubines, even when one of them was the heir to the household, for they are not 'legitimate sons.'[10] Yun claimed that even in the case where a son of a concubine became King, his relatives should wear the three-year attire in mourning. Yun's stance makes clear that royal rituals cannot be the same as the rituals of ordinary families. In other words, if the principle of 'affection' is foremost in the ritual of ordinary families, the principle of 'respect' is predominant in the rituals of the royal family, where succession to the throne is most important.

These are the main points of the three scholars' claims. Each claim can be illuminated further when viewed from the perspective of 'affection' and 'respect.' Song's argument that the Dowager Queen should wear the one-year mourning attire for Hyojong considers only whether or not Hyojong is the first-born son. It disregards his being the successor of the royal family. Of course, the fact that Song placed great emphasis on 'the first-born son' is because he attached importance to succession in the family. However, his argument has the following problems. In a case where the successor in the family was one of younger sons, if the one-year attire is practiced, then the ritual reveals only that this son was not 'the firstborn son,' but fails to represent his being the successor in the family. As a result, it neglects the principle of 'respect' which emphasizes succession. The standard suggested by Song made no exception for the royal family. Thus, it values only biological relations as determined by the natural birth order and fails to take the political status of the King into account. Indeed, this is a quite sensitive matter that could provoke dispute over the legitimacy of the succession. Song faced criticism and blame that he has downplayed the kingship.

The claims of Hŏ and Yun that the Dowager Queen Cho should wear the three-year mourning attire are intended to highlight the status of the king who succeeded as the heir of the royal family.

---

[9] The five kinds of relatives (*wuzhu* 五屬) designate the kin relation who wear 'Five Garments' (*wufu* 五服). The extent to whom the 'Five Garments' are applied covers vertically from the paternal great-great-grandfather (*gaozu* 高祖) down to the great-great-grandson (*xuansun* 玄孫), and horizontally includes the collateral families as well as those of the direct line.

[10] As seen in the previous section of this paper, the "Mourning Attire" chapter explains the reason that father wears the unhemmed sackcloth for three years in mourning for the eldest son by saying that "[the eldest son is] the legitimate body connected with the ancestors, and he will convey the weight [of responsibility of the heir]." Song thought that the "legitimate body (*chŏngche/zhengti* 正體)" designates literally the legitimate son born of the first wife, and in case of a younger son (次子), he is not eligible to be mourned with the unhemhed sackcloth despite his succeeding as heir. Hŏ thought that every son of the first wife is the "legitimate body," but denied that status to the sons of concubines, who have "the body [connected to ancestors] but illegitimate." Yun admitted the differentiation between the eldest and the younger sons, the legitimate and the illegitimate sons, but he argued that in the case where one of them succeeded as heir and became King, his status goes beyond the standard of mourning for 'the legitimate body' and instead the attire for mourning him should be the three-year unhemmed sackcloth, as is demanded for "the most respected (*chijon/zhizun* 至尊)."

However, the difference between Hŏ and Yun should be noted. Hŏ argued that the Dowager Queen Cho should wear the hemmed sackcloth, which is supposed to be worn by the mother when mourning for the eldest son who was the heir. Through such a ritual, Hŏ aimed to highlight the status of the King as based primarily on the ground of blood relationships. However, his suggestion was also based on a general perspective that did not distinguish between an ordinary family and the royal family. Although Hŏ criticized Song for failing to display Hyojong's position as a sovereign, he was likewise unable to offer any approach that considered the particularity of the royal family. This is evident in what he said about the mourning for an illegitimate son, namely: "If an illegitimate son is established as the successor [of a family], he is referred to as the body [connected to ancestors] but illegitimate, and not eligible to be mourned for three years. This is because he is the son of a concubine" (Hŏ 1992, p. 457). Eventually, this view arrives at the same conclusion, even in the case of the monarch who is the son of a concubine but succeeds to the throne.

Yun has a firm stance that no matter who succeeds to the throne, regardless of whether he is the eldest or a younger son, a legitimate or an illegitimate son, all his relatives should wear the unhemmed sackcloth for three years, just like every servant of the monarch, so as to show respect for the King, the most exalted station. His viewpoint was that the mourning of the royal family should not be the same as that of ordinary families. While Hŏ's view adds the principle of 'respect' to the base of 'affection,' Yun's view was based on the principle of 'respect' from the beginning and absolutized the position of the monarch.

However, a problem with Yun's argument is that the "Mourning Attire" chapter has no prescription for the mourning of the royal family. That chapter of the *Ceremonies and Rites*, as a matter of fact, provided rituals for the learned class (*shi* 士), and not for the monarch. Because of that, Yun drew his evidence related to mourning for the king from the *Rites of Zhou*. Nevertheless, Yun's claim still has a problem. If the Dowager Queen wears the unhemmed sackcloth only in virtue of her hierarchical relationship to the King, the lord–servant relationship is emphasized in the ritual more than the mother–son relationship, resulting in treating his mother like his servant. Because of this, Yun's theory provoked enormous antipathy and suffered severe criticism, being blamed as 'a theory that regards [the King's] mother as a servant' (*sinmo-sŏl* 臣母説). The cause of the resentment is rooted in the Confucian ethic in which even the King must lower his head in front of his mother and fulfill his duty of filial piety, an unbreakable norm. Notably, Song attacked Yun's thought as anti-Confucian. Portraying himself as a defender of Confucianism, he accused Yun of being a heretic in his interpretation of Classics. In this way, the controversy over the mourning ritual became overheated and expanded as a political struggle, involving many schools and factions.

The conflict among schools or political interests might underlie the seventeenth-century controversy on mourning attire. However, we should not overlook what made the struggle so bitter and fierce was that the mourning ritual is directly linked to the core values of Confucianism, as well as the problem of legitimacy of political power. In terms of schools or factions, Song belonged to the 'Westerners' who succeeded the Yulgok school, while Hŏ and Yun belonged to the 'Southerners' who succeeded the Toegye school. As the former defended the one-year mourning attire, and the latter defended the three-year mourning attire, the controversy may seem to be a battle between the two academic groups on the surface. However, as we have seen above, in terms of the principles of 'affection' and 'respect,' Song and Hŏ adopted the same stance that prioritizes the principle of 'affection' to the blood relationship; on the contrary, Yun belonged to a different group that gives priority to the principle of 'respect' for the political position of the monarch.

All three claims have scriptural bases, including the authoritative exegeses of the Confucian ritual books of ancient China, which were considered as canonical scriptures. Although those liturgical texts give information about the principles of 'affection' and 'respect,' the texts themselves permit various and even contradictory interpretations, due to their imperfections, inconsistencies, or contradictions. If one tries to practice the mourning ritual in situations for which those scriptures give no clear and unambiguous prescription, it is unavoidable to either prioritize or harmonize those two principles.

5. Concluding Remarks

Confucianism articulated a way to live and the value of living in accordance with human nature, aiming to realize such a life through practicing *li* 禮, that is 'ritual' or 'propriety,' in every behavior. The mourning ritual was designed to allow the living to properly express sadness and grief for the dead. As we have seen above, the period of the mourning and the type of attire were determined by the two principles of 'affection' and 'respect,' and the mourning ritual played a role in maintaining the primogenital order by ritualizing the practice of 'affection among blood relationship' and 'respect for the eldest and the lord.' The primogenital order has been the basis of the traditional Chinese family, society, and state system, and the ritual of mourning has been particularly emphasized among the various rituals of Confucianism.

The Chosŏn Dynasty was founded on the national ideology of Neo-Confucianism, called the "Studies of Nature and Principle (*Sŏngnihak* 性理學)." Chosŏn can be called a liturgical state in the sense that all institutional systems were designed with great concern that Confucian ethics and moral sentiments should be emphasized and realized through various ritual codes. Through careful exploration of the controversy over mourning attire in seventeenth-century Chosŏn, we can see that all debaters were trying to find a ritual which they could best manifest 'affection' and 'respect.' For them, the crucial question was how to embody both principles in the rituals for the royal family, where the family relationship and the lord–servant relationship overlapped each other.

It is especially noteworthy that many scholars of Chosŏn at that time denounced Yun's opinion for treating the King's mother as his servant. Although Yun had no such intention and his evidence was all drawn from the Confucian Classics, he was blamed for denying or ignoring the feeling of affection between mother and son and the required filial piety toward one's mother. For most Confucian scholars, those sentiments had absolute priority over the respect that the mother of the King should show to her son.

The following is another example of prioritizing the relationship of 'affection' between parents and children over that of 'respect' between the lord and the servant: when a parent of a bureaucrat died, the bureaucrat should resign from the post and return to his hometown for the three-year mourning ritual. If we take such an atmosphere during the Chosŏn period into account, we can understand why the reaction against Yun was not just an academic criticism but also an emotional rejection. Emotion and the value of affection were regarded as the basis of humanity and morality, and this kind of ethos appears throughout the history of Confucianism, and in the case of the Chosŏn Dynasty, it had been internalized even more intensely through rituals.

The existence of a vast amount of studies and commentaries on the *Family Rituals of Master Zhu* (*Zhuzi jiali* 朱子家禮)[11] shows how much Chosŏn Confucians endeavored to ritualize everyday life.[12] Future study should give further consideration to the ritualization of human feeling in Confucianism. It will lead to a new understanding of its influence on East Asian culture.

Funding: This research was supported by the Wonkwang Digital University for Academic Research Grant (2018).

Acknowledgments: I want to thank Eric Hutton for offering precious comments and helpful corrections and suggestions. This paper also has been much improved from the feedback of anonymous reviewers and Sungho Lee.

---

[11] The *Family Rituals of Master Zhu* was written by the famous Confucian Zhu Xi (朱熹, 1130–1200) in the Southern Song dynasty. It is also called the *Family Rituals of Wen Gong* (文公家禮). It was indispensable for family rituals not only in China but also in Chosŏn, and consists of manuals for the capping ritual (*guanli* 冠禮), wedding ritual (*hunli* 婚禮), mourning ritual (*sangli* 喪禮), and sacrificial ritual [for ancestors] (*jili* 祭禮). An English translation is available: see (Ebrey 1991).

[12] More than 450 kinds of commentaries, studies, and manuals concerning the *Family Rituals of Master Zhu* were published during the Chosŏn from the sixteenth to the early twentieth century. Such a large volume of publications indicates that, beyond academic interest, detailed manuals were in high demand for practicing family rituals in everyday life. It shows a particular characteristic of Chosŏn Confucianism, in comparison with that of the contemporary Ming-Qing dynasties. For a complete list of commentaries and studies of the *Family Rituals of Master Zhu* published in the Chosŏn period, see (Chang 2013a, 2013b).

Conflicts of Interest: The author declares no conflict of interest.

References

Chang, Dongwoo. 1998. A Study on Ta-San (茶山)'s Lihsueh (禮學): Laying Stress on the Comparative Study of Ili 儀禮 "Sangfu 喪服" and Sanglyesachon 喪禮四箋 "Sanggipyol 喪期別". Ph.D. thesis, Yonsei University, Seoul, Korea. (In Korean)

Chang, Dongwoo. 2013a. Studies of the Family Rituals of Master Zhu in the Chosŏn Period. Translated by Byeon Yeong-ho, Jung Jae-sang. *The Tsuru University Review* 78: 45–68. (In Japanese)

Chang, Dongwoo. 2013b. Studies of the *Family Rituals of Master Zhu* in the Chosŏn Period. *Tae-dong Yearly Review of Classics* 31: 209–55. (In Korean)

Confucius. 1960. *Confucian Analects, The Chinese Classics*. Translated by James Legge. Hong Kong: Hong Kong University Press, vol. 1.

Ebrey, Patricia Buckley. 1991. *Chu Hsi's "Family Rituals": A Twelfth-Century Chinese Manual for the Performance of Cappings, Weddings, Funerals, and Ancestral Rites*. Princeton: Princeton University Press.

Hŏ, Mok. 1992. *Kiŏn* 記言 *[Record of Sayings]*. Edited by Minjok Munhwa Chujin Wiwŏnhŏe. HMC *Han'guk Munjip Ch'onggan [Korean Literary Collections in Classical Chinese]*. Seoul: Kyŏngin Munhwasa, vol. 98.

Jia, Gongyan. 2000. *Yili Yishu* 儀禮義疏 *[Explanation on Meanings of the* Ceremonies and Rites*]*. In *Shisanjing zhushu* 十三經注疏 *[Commentaries and Explanations on the Thirteen Classics]*. Edited by Shisanjing zhushu zhengli weiyuanhui 十三經注疏整理委員會. Beijing: Beijingdaxue Chubanshe.

Jiutangshu 舊唐書 *[Old Book of Tang]*. 1975. Beijing: Zhonghua shuju.

Kong, Yingda. 2000. *Liji Zhengyi* 禮記正義 *[Orthodox Meaning of the* Book of Rites*]*. In *Shisanjing zhushu* 十三經注疏 *[Commentaries and Explanations on the Thirteen Classics]*. Edited by Shisanjing zhushu zhengli weiyuanhui 十三經注疏整理委員會. Beijing: Beijingdaxue Chubanshe.

Lee, Bongkyoo. 1996a. Rethinking of Philosophical Analysis on the Dispute on Ritual 禮訟의 哲學的 分析에 대한 再檢討. *Daedong Munhwa Yeongu* 31: 151–77. (In Korean)

Lee, Bongkyoo. 1996b. Philosophical Analysis of Chŏng Yak-yong on the Dispute on Ritual in the 17th Century 17세기 예송 (禮訟) 에 대한 정약용의 철학적 분석. *Gongja Hak* 2: 223–53. (In Korean)

Liji 禮記 [Record of Rites]. 1968. In *Sacred Books of the East*. Translated by James Legge. Delhi: Motial Banarsidass, vol. 28.

Liji 禮記 [Record of Rites]. 2000. In *Shisanjing Zhushu* 十三經注疏 *[Commentaries and Explanations on the Thirteen Classics]*. Edited by Shisanjing zhushu zhengli weiyuanhui 十三經注疏整理委員會. Beijing: Beijingdaxue Chubanshe.

Mencius. 1970. *Mencius*. Translated by Din Cheuk Lau. London: Penguin Books.

Nishikawa, Yukihiro. 2012. The Empress Wu Zetian and the Grace of Mother 則天武后と母の恩. *Chugoku Kenkyu Shukan* 中國研究集刊 *[Bulletin of Chinese Studies]* 54: 16–35. (In Japanese)

Rhee, Won-taek. 2014. The Controversy about the Confucian Funerary Rituals in the 17th C. Choson Dynasty. *The Tsuru University Review* 79: 163–76. (In Japanese)

Song, Siyŏl. 1993. *Songja Taejŏn* 宋子大全 *[The Completed Works of Master Song]*. HMC. Seoul: Kyŏngin Munhwasa, vols. 108–16.

Xunzi. 2014. *Xunzi: The Complete Text*. Translated by Eric L. Hutton. Princeton: Princeton University Press.

Yili 儀禮 [Ceremonies and Rites]. 2000. In *Shisanjing zhushu* 十三經注疏 *[Commentaries and Explanations on the Thirteen Classics]*. Edited by Shisanjing zhushu zhengli weiyuanhui 十三經注疏整理委員會. Beijing: Beijingdaxue Chubanshe.

Yun, Hyu. 1974. *Paekho ChŏnSŏ* 白湖全書 *[The Completed Works of Paekho]*. Daegu: Kyungpook University Press, vol. 2.

Yun, Hyu. 1994. *Paekho Sŏnsaeng Munjip* 白湖先生文集 *[The Collected Works of Master Paekho]*. HMC. Seoul: Kyŏngin Munhwasa, vol. 123.

Zhouli 周禮 [Rites of Zhou]. 2000. In *Shisanjing zhushu* 十三經注疏 *[Commentaries and Explanations on the Thirteen Classics]*. Edited by Shisanjing zhushu zhengli weiyuanhui 十三經注疏整理委員會. Beijing: Beijingdaxue Chubanshe.

Article

Confucian Democracy and a Pluralistic *Li-Ki* Metaphysics

Hyo-Dong Lee

The Theological School, Drew University, 36 Madison Ave., Madison, NJ 07940, USA; hlee5@drew.edu

Received: 6 October 2018; Accepted: 22 October 2018; Published: 23 October 2018

Abstract: This essay explores the possible constructive role of a Confucian metaphysics in the pluralistic Confucian-democratic context of South Korea. In his recent landmark study, Sungmoon Kim has argued that South Korean democracy is sustained by a public culture of civility that is grounded in Confucian habits and mores and yet is pluralistic in ethos. I appreciatively interrogate Kim's thesis in order to advance a claim that a comprehensive Confucian doctrine such as Confucian metaphysics can contribute significantly to the flourishing of Confucian democratic public culture, provided that it affirm a pluralistic ontology. I contend that the tradition of Korean Neo-Confucian *li-ki* metaphysics, particularly one found in the works of Nongmun Im Seong-ju, offers rich resources for a pluralistic ontology despite its history of ethical monism. By putting Nongmun's thought in conversation with some of the contemporary critiques of the Schmittian (mis-)appropriation of the notion of popular sovereignty, I outline a pluralized version of the Rousseauian general will—a kind of critically affectionate solidarity of diverse groups of people—that is Confucian in character. My claim is that such a critically affectionate solidarity finds its grounds in and draws its nourishment from a pluralistic Confucian ontology.

Keywords: Korean Neo-Confucianism; *li-ki* metaphysics; Confucian democracy; popular sovereignty; pluralism; public culture

1. Introduction

Given the spate of political drama that has unfolded in South Korea in the last few years, it is probably safe to assume that the nation has become a flourishing democracy, not only in a formal, procedural sense of the term but also in a substantive manner, encompassing the political, economic, and cultural dimensions of South Korean society. The Candlelight Revolution—the months-long nonviolent street protests of millions of citizens against then-President Park Geun-hye's corruption and abuse of power—led to the first impeachment and removal from office of a sitting president in the spring of 2017. The new election that immediately followed ushered in a more progressive government that has implemented various liberalizing policies aimed at strengthening civil rights protections, freedom of the press, and labor rights, among others. At the same time, it has waged a campaign to root out the corrupt and authoritarian elements in the government that had undermined and subverted the rule of law. The Candlelight Revolution has also revitalized the civic sphere, with civic organizations and trade unions freshly empowered to counter the entrenched alliance among politicians, high-ranking government officials, and the giant family-controlled business conglomerates (*chaebeols*). The voices representing the human rights of oppressed and marginalized people—foremost among them feminist and LGBTQI—are increasingly asserting themselves in the public square and the media landscape, most prominently igniting a #MeToo movement directed against prominent politicians, business leaders, intellectuals and more.

This kind of momentous historical development, of course, does not spring out of nowhere. A prominent feature of South Korean society is that it is, to this day, deeply Confucian. Up until 1910,

Korea was ruled for five centuries by one of the most Confucian dynasties of all times. Long before the end of Joseon dynasty in the early twentieth century, Confucian habits and mores, centered around the ritual of ancestor veneration and the familial ethical code of filiality, had filtered down from top to bottom, infiltrating all levels of society and all aspects of daily life (Deuchler 1992). It is true that the great social upheavals of the twentieth century—the experience of the nearly half-century-long Japanese colonial rule, the division of Korean peninsula into two Koreas and the devastating Korean War, the rapid process of modernization that has profoundly transformed post-war South Korea into an industrial, urban society—have interrupted and destroyed so much that was tradition. Nonetheless, the Confucian habits and mores have persisted, having been profoundly entrenched in the psyche of the people and in the ways they relate to one another on a daily basis.

Many studies have been conducted in the last decade or so on what role, if any, Confucianism has played in the successful democratization of South Korea and the establishment of constitutionalism in the nation.[1] It is however beyond the scope of this essay to investigate the possible historical causal relations between the Korean Confucian tradition and the democratic transformation of South Korea. In this essay I will take the reality of vibrant pluralistic democracy in South Korea as a context within which I examine a much-debated political-philosophical problem concerning the relationship between Confucianism and democracy, namely the question of the possibility of a *Confucian* democracy.[2] More specifically, I will explore possible contributions that Confucianism as a *comprehensive doctrine* could make for the flourishing of a pluralistic democracy.[3] For that purpose, I will center my discussion on the tradition of so-called Neo-Confucian "moral metaphysics" (Tu 1982, p. 10)[4] and ask what role it may play in developing a robust theory of Confucian democracy.

2. Confucian Democracy and "Religious" Confucianism

In his recent landmark study, *Confucian Democracy in East Asia*, Sungmoon Kim envisions a democracy with characteristics indigenous to East Asia. The kind of democracy he envisions is one sustained and animated by a public culture grounded in Confucian habits and mores, befitting the social context of South Korea where Confucianism governed almost every aspect of life just a century ago and still does in a much more attenuated, yet deeply lingering sense. The Confucian habits and mores that Kim proposes are qualitatively different from those of a traditional Confucian society, which was a "ritual-constituted gemeinschaft that aims at an organic whole" (Kim 2014, p. 14). Rather, they are core components of a more loosely circumscribed Confucian public culture shared by the citizens of a democratic civil society who subscribe to different comprehensive moral doctrines (p. 10).

In articulating those habits and mores, Kim highlights the familial moral sentiments traditionally at the heart of the Confucian ethical and ritualistic tradition, namely filial affection (親 *qīn*) in the parent–child relation, the most primordial of all relations in Confucian thought (p. 145). In the dominant, Mencian strain of Confucian tradition, filial affection is thought to reflect in the most primordial sense the heart of empathy (惻隱之心 *cèyǐnzhīxīn*), which is endowed by Heaven in all of us and which grows into the virtue of humanity or benevolence (仁 *ren*) in and through ethical and ritual practices within the context of the so-called Five Relations (五倫 *wulun*). Hence, the parent–child relation serves as the model for the rest of the Five Relations, and in so doing makes the familial the paradigm for the public and the political (145–47).

According to Kim, in the Mencian perspective people's moral-political self-cultivation starts out from their practice of filial affection in the familial context, whose characteristic ethico-ritual form is filiality (孝悌 *xiaoti*), and their extension (推 *tui*) of it beyond the familial context (p. 141). This is how

---

[1]   See, among others, (Shin 2012; Kim 2015).
[2]   For an excellent survey of the debate, see (Angle 2012).
[3]   I borrow the phrase "comprehensive doctrine" from (Kim 2014, p. 144).
[4]   The phrase "moral metaphysics" was coined by Mou Zhongsan to highlight the Neo-Confucian attempts to provide a metaphysical basis of human existence as moral agents.

people come to cultivate various manifestations of the virtue of humanity, such as trustworthiness (信 *xin*), social harmony (和 *he*), respect of the elderly (敬老 *jinglao*), and respectful deference (辭讓 *cirang*), among others (p. 90). The Mencian political tradition confers the Mandate of Heaven to rule upon the virtuous and sage ruler because the sage ruler is the one who has acquired these virtues of humanity in a consummate fashion. He has nurtured the Heaven-endowed humanity (*ren*) in him to perfection and has thereby become the genuine human being who is able to extend the familial moral-sentiment in him analogically to encompass even strangers as if they were quasi-family members. As the supreme embodiment of the filial affection, the king, as the Son of Heaven and the Father to all his subjects, rules by extending that affection in the form of benevolence (*ren*) toward people and love (愛 *ai*) toward all living things (146–47).[5] In so doing, the monarch, as consummate exemplar-teacher, is able to nurture the moral cultivation of his subjects, not least by implementing public policies designed to provide favorable material conditions for their moral development. Here lies the essence of Confucian virtue politics (德治 *dezhi*) realized through a benevolent government (仁政 *renzheng*) (75–76).

In the contemporary East Asian context, Kim argues, it is however important to realize that "the capacity to envisage strangers as if they were (quasi-)family members does not necessarily have to rely on the foundational metaphysical account of human nature and particular moral virtues affiliated with it" (p. 147). In other words, the familial moral sentiments can be decoupled from the Mencian metaphysical account of filial affection as rooted in the Heaven-endowed virtue of humanity. The public virtues, mores, and habits which the familial moral sentiments nurture can be unmoored from the cosmological-metaphysical understanding of the familial as the political best exemplified in the idea of the Mandate of Heaven to rule given to the virtuous ruler.

Kim's reasons for this move lie in the fact such cosmological-metaphysical accounts are comprehensive moral doctrines. Central to a pluralist democracy today is the sound moral-political judgments of its citizens, not the kind of full-blown moral ideal of sagehood and the concomitant programs of moral cultivation found in the classical Confucian cosmological-metaphysical accounts of the familial as political, especially when the latter's exaltation of moral equality—that anyone can become a sage—is intertwined with an unquestioning acceptance of political inequality (p. 144). Going further, Kim distinguishes Confucian *public* culture, which he advocates, from Confucian culture in an ethically monistic sense, a case of which is Cheng-Zhu Neo-Confucianism that had exercised a socio-political and cultural monopoly in Korea for centuries. Korean Cheng-Zhu Neo-Confucianism allowed no room for ethical pluralism by instituting a patriarchal social hierarchy undergirded by clan law (宗法 *zongbeop zongfa*) and family rituals (家禮 *garye jiali*) (p. 283). As "religious Confucianism"—and a monistic/patriarchal one to boot—such a Confucian culture should not constitute the core of Confucian *public* culture, although citizens may hold it as their private value system (that is, as "private Confucianism") (p. 284). In summary, comprehensive moral doctrines are something of an overkill when it comes to the task of constituting a democratic public culture, and are to be sidelined when their ethical monism collides with the value pluralism at the heart of a pluralistic democracy.

Today, Kim observes, the Confucian virtues, both familial and political because they are based on the capacity to regard strangers as if they were quasi-family members, are "widely cherished as public virtues and socially available through the continued ritual practices" in traditionally Confucian societies in East Asia (p. 90). What renders East Asian societies Confucian today is not their citizens' adherence to comprehensive Confucian moral doctrines but the distinctively Confucian character of their public mores and habits in the sense mentioned above, which is predicated on "the social

---

5   Kim notes that the will of the people—their contentment or discontent—was always understood to express vicariously the Mandate of Heaven, leading to the demand that the ruler translate his moral accountability to Heaven into his political responsibility for the well-being of the people (p. 193). This is the meaning of the time-honored Confucian political thesis of "people-centrism" (民本 *minben*) (p. 158). The Confucian literati, the ruling class, "saw themselves not merely as king's servants but Heaven servants, *public servants* (公僕 *gongpu*)", sharing with the ruler moral accountability to Heaven (p. 194).

semiotics of Confucian rituals" still widely practiced (p. 90). How, then, do these public mores and habits give rise to the public culture of a thriving pluralistic democracy?

Because it is rooted in, and nurtured and sustained by various ethical and ritual expressions of filial affection, Kim claims that such a Confucian public culture is characterized by civility. At the same time, this public culture consists in a kind of public reason animated by "critical affection" (p. 132) or "critical familial affection" (p. 137), which prevents civility from degenerating into docility. A family is often filled with psychological tension and moral disagreements because of the "affective resentment" present in one's love of one's family members, enabling the family members to love the virtues of one another while hating the injustices (p. 149). This is why familial moral sentiments consist in *critical* affection, which, when extended to the public, forms the core of Confucian public reason, empowering the citizens of a pluralistic democratic society to regard one another as members of a quasi-family even when vehemently and passionately disagreeing with one another (p. 150).[6] Critical affection forms the heart of the ethos indispensable to a well-functioning Confucian pluralistic democracy.

Relating this notion of Confucian public culture of civility to the specific context of South Korea, Kim suggests that a concrete example of the familial moral sentiments in the South Korean context is found in *jeong*, the sense of closeness and mutual affection which Koreans feel as they reason with one another, as if they were all members of one big family. Since *jeong* enables Koreans to regard the Korean nation as one extended family, it nurtures in them a sense of ethical responsibility toward one another, which Kim calls "*uri* (we)-responsibility", which allows them to maintain a bond of "critical affection" even when disagreeing with one another across deep differences as strangers to one another. This, as "a uniquely Korean-Confucian mode of general will" (p. 222), is the key to a public culture of civility in the South Korean context—the kind of public reason and culture that has sustained and continues to sustain the drive toward a pluralist democracy in South Korea.

Kim's thesis is a provocative one with profound implications for assessing the role that the deeply embedded Confucian heritage in East Asia has to play in the growth and maturing of democratic institutions and cultures across the East Asian nations. His key argument—that in order to accommodate the value pluralism of a democratic public culture, the Confucian public virtues nurtured by the familial moral sentiments must be decoupled from the Confucian moral cosmology and metaphysics in which those virtues have traditionally been embedded—represents a significant breakthrough in so assessing the role of Confucian heritage in today's East Asia. This is especially the case in the context of the current debates around the notion of Confucian democracy, since Kim's thesis is an important corrective, in my view, to the similar attempts made by the contemporary advocates of Confucian meritocracy and "perfectionism", such as Daniel Bell, Tongdong Bai, Jiang Qing, and Joseph Chan, to divorce the ideal of moral-political meritocracy from the cosmology and metaphysics underlying traditional Confucian virtue politics (Bell 2006; Bai 2012; Qing 2013; Chan 2014). The principal difference between Kim and the Confucian meritocrats/perfectionists lies in the fact that, due to their retention of Confucian conceptions of (objectively) good life, the latter end up providing inadequate explanations of how they can avoid ethical monism when their non-comprehensive doctrines of political meritocracy/perfectionism are all about publicly promoting moral-political cultivation of citizens guided precisely by those substantive conceptions of good life.[7] Given the limited scope of this essay, however, I will not discuss further the disagreements between the said advocates of Confucian meritocracy and the Confucian democrats like Kim.[8]

---

[6] This is precisely why Kim calls Confucian public reason a *bridging capital* that "bonds citizens horizontally across their deep differences" rather than a *bonding capital* that "cements the existing social fabric of moral community" (p. 148).

[7] Of the Confucian meritocrats/perfectionists, Joseph Chan comes closest to addressing seriously the issue of value pluralism in modern constitutional democracy, while Jiang Qing explicitly foregrounds his desire to rehabilitate the traditional Confucian ideal of virtue politics to the extent of appealing to the transcendent, sacred legitimacy of "heaven".

[8] Among the ranks of Confucian democrats are Deweyan communitarians like Roger Ames, David Hall, and Sor-hoon Tan. See (Ames and Hall 1999; Tan 2004).

I would like, rather, to raise a question that Kim does not explicitly pursue in his work: what would then be the role of Confucianism as a comprehensive moral doctrine or ethical system in a Confucian public culture? Kim names such a Confucianism "religious Confucianism" or "private Confucianism" and relegates it to the status of a private value system held by individual citizens or associations, with little if any role to play in constituting the core of Confucian public culture. However, if, as Kim argues, Confucian public values and practices such as "filial and fraternal love and responsibility, respect of elders, moral criticism and rectification of government, and social harmony" (p. 284) have made a critical contribution to the democratization of South Korea and still underpin its Confucian public culture, then one is driven to ask: what gave birth to those values and practices, and nurtured them through the centuries? The answer is pretty straightforward: it is Confucianism as a comprehensive moral doctrine, and, more specifically, in the case of Korea, ethically monistic and socially patriarchal Cheng-Zhu Neo-Confucianism. It is therefore apropos to ask if Confucian public culture could sustain itself as Confucian without the gestating womb and the nourishing breastmilk of Confucianism as a comprehensive ethical system. While it may be necessary to distinguish clearly Confucian public culture from "religious" or "private" Confucianism" and not to allow the latter to be legally established at the core of the former, it does seem beneficial for the health of a pluralistic Confucian democracy to consider the public—that is, political—role of Confucianism as a comprehensive doctrine or worldview.

In the context of the United States, we find analogues of "religious" Confucianism having a public, political role to play. Given its history, one could persuasively argue that the public mores and habits of the citizens of the United States are still Christian in an attenuated sense of the term, despite the "wall of separation" between church and state erected by the First Amendment to the Constitution. Precisely due to the loosely Christian character of the public culture of the United States, Christianity as a comprehensive doctrine and ethical system wields in this land a considerable influence on public discourse. Its influence, however, is a double-edged sword. The enduring political power of right-wing, fundamentalist—and even theocratic—Christian evangelicalism, as prominently displayed in the election of President Donald Trump, is an exemplary case unveiling the danger posed by a comprehensive doctrine when a significant part of the public culture traces its roots to and is still very much nurtured and animated by that doctrine.[9] At the same time, Martin Luther King Jr. and progressive black churches are a shining testament to the salutary effects that a form of Christianity as a comprehensive doctrine can have on the maturing of a pluralistic democratic civil society.

In assessing the public role of Confucianism as a comprehensive doctrine, then, the key point at issue is what kind. A comprehensive doctrine seems by definition to boast a totalizing horizon that engulfs all differences. Nevertheless, encompassing does not necessarily or always mean nullifying. There may be a comprehensive doctrine or ethical system that offers a space for myriad differences to blossom within its horizon without subsuming them all under a single authoritative orthodoxy. Such a doctrine or system would nurture the kind of public culture that "relaxes what counts as an assault upon the sacred", as William Connolly has suggested (Connolly 2005, p. 147). Within the context of South Korea, a good candidate for such a "pluralistically" comprehensive moral doctrine would have to be found within the orbits of Cheng-Zhu Neo-Confucianism, given the dominant—almost exclusive—role it has played in shaping the Confucian character of the nation's public culture.

3. Neo-Confucian Moral Metaphysics: Monism or Pluralism?

It is beyond doubt that Cheng-Zhu Neo-Confucianism tended to be ethically monistic, historically speaking, as Sungmoon Kim has argued. There may be various reasons for its being so, but my suspicion is that its ethically monistic tendency may have something to do at least partly with its intellectual heritage, namely, Neo-Confucian moral metaphysics, especially its focus on the ordering,

---

9   For a trenchant analysis of the political power and influence of the right-wing conservative evangelical Christianity in the United States, see (Connolly 2008).

unifying, and harmonizing power of pattern (理*li*). According to Neo-Confucian metaphysics, everything consists in a union of pattern (理 *li*) and psychophysical energy (氣 *qi*). Psychophysical energy is the vital energy of the universe that constitutes everything—visible and invisible, with form and without form, living and non-living, material and ideal, and body and mind.[10] Pattern, on the other hand, refers to the metaphysical structure of reality that is logically, ontologically, and normatively prior to psychophysical energy, yet is always found "embodied" in the latter and dependent on it for creative dynamism.[11] Pattern and psychophysical energy are intertwined in the following manner. Pattern in its state of sheer—structuring—potentiality is one, simple, indeterminate, and abstract. When "activated" by psychophysical energy, however, this one Heavenly Pattern (天理 *tianli*) issues forth into myriad concrete patterns that structure the "ten thousand things" (萬物 *wanwu*) of the world. This is the crucial point made by Zhu Xi, the "systematizer" of Cheng-Zhu Neo Confucianism, when he says, famously, "Pattern unites, [whereas] psychophysical energy differentiates (理同氣異 *litong qiyi*)" (Zhu 2000b, vol. 5, p. 2075)[12] in relation to another well-known statement by one of his predecessors, Cheng Yi, "Pattern is one, but its manifestations are many (理一而分殊 *liyi er fenshu*)" (Cheng 1981a, vol. 2, p. 609).

This ontological account of one and many raises a critical question: if difference and multiplicity are introduced into pattern only insofar as pattern is activated by psychophysical energy, then does that not signal an unarticulated premise that pattern is originarily and ultimately one, and only derivatively and penultimately many? Insofar as pattern is the metaphysical ultimate with logical, ontological, and normative priority over psychophysical energy, an undercurrent of ontological asymmetry between one and many is unmistakable. One can detect this undercurrent in the celebrated and much-discussed saying of Cheng Yi on pattern: "Empty and tranquil, and without any sign, and yet all figures are luxuriantly present [沖漠無朕, 萬象森然已具 *chongmo wuzhen, wanxiang senran yiju*] ... It is like a tree one hundred feet high. From the root to the branches and leaves, there is one thread running through all ... Actually there is only one track." (Cheng 1981b, vol. 1, p. 153).[13] In illustrating the relationship between pattern as the simple, indeterminate and quiescent One ("empty and tranquil, and without any sign") and the myriad configurations of individual patterns found in it ("all figures are luxuriantly present"), Cheng Yi employs a historically influential arboretic metaphor in which the branches and leaves all derive from and depend on the single root system and trunk.[14]

This ontologically asymmetrical rendition of the relationship between one and many is accompanied in Cheng-Zhu Neo-Confucian metaphysics by a propensity to devalue psychophysical energy not merely as the source of difference but also of evil. The unavoidable excesses and deficiencies in psychophysical energy's differentiating movements, it claims, inevitably give rise to individual configurations of psychophysical energy that are opaque, impure, turbid, indolent, and therefore less open and communicative. Zhu Xi locates the source of evil, which is understood as selfishness, in these non-resonating and uncommunicative configurations of psychophysical energy. When human beings are born with these kinds of psychophysical configuration, they more often than not obstruct the full realization of the virtue of humanity as empathy in them, namely, the essence of

---

[10] "Psychophysical energy" is a slight modification of Daniel K. Gardner's translation of *qi* into "psychophysical stuff" (Gardner 1990, p. 49 n. 52). A more precise translation would be "psycho-bio-physical energy".

[11] I follow A. C. Graham's translation of *li* as "pattern" (Graham 1986, p. 421). In its interpretation by Zhu Xi, the duality of pattern and psychophysical energy comes to resemble the Western distinction between the metaphysical and the physical, as can be seen from the following well-known remark: "Pattern is the Way above physical form (形而上之道) and the root from which all things are born. Psychophysical energy, by contrast, is the vessel with physical form (形而下之器) and the instrument by which all things are produced" (Zhu 2000c, vol. 6, p. 2798).

[12] The sentence also appears quoted in *Zhuzi yulei*: "If we discuss it from the perspective of the single origin of the myriad thing-events, pattern unites, while psychophysical energy differentiates" (Zhu 1986, vol. 1, p. 57). See also "What makes them similar is their pattern; what makes them different is their psychophysical energy" (Zhu 1986, vol. 1, p. 59).

[13] I am using Wing-tsit Chan's translation of this saying with one modification, substituting "all figures" for "all things" (Chan 1963, p. 555).

[14] This is in contrast to the famed "rhizomatic" metaphor employed by Deleuze and Guattari to underscore the ontological ultimacy of multiplicity (Deleuze and Guattari 1987).

the Heaven-endowed human nature that is their individual pattern (*li*) (Ching 2000, pp. 98–101).[15] It is a common Neo-Confucian observation that the vast majority of people are born with such non-resonating, uncommunicative and therefore involuted configurations of psychophysical energy (98–101). When this observation is coupled with the assignment of ontological penultimacy to the multiplicity of individual patterns, all derived from concrete determinations of the one indeterminate and abstract Heavenly Pattern by the morally ambiguous differentiating dynamic of psychophysical energy, the offspring is the Neo-Confucian *de facto*—if not *de jure*—devaluation of the moral agency of the vast majority of people.

This anti-egalitarian tendency shows itself in the Cheng-Zhu Neo-Confucian opposition of "Heavenly Pattern" (天理 *tianli*), which is "public" (公 *gong*), to "human desire" (人欲 *renyu*), which is "private" (私 *si*), and its social patriarchalism in which the ruling class of cultured male gentry, who are versed in the classics and thus trained in the way of the sages to exercise public leadership, stand as "superior persons" (君子 *junzi*) over women, the working mass of commoners, and foreign "barbarians" as "inferior persons" (小人 *xiaoren*) (Zhu 2000a, vol. 4, p. 1746). The ruling elites impose their own parochial patterns—their ritual ways (*dao*)—upon the ruled subjects with the claim of representing Heavenly Pattern allegedly discovered by the ancient sages and preserved in the classics.[16] The way of the ruling elites enjoys unrivaled hegemony over any other ways of the oppressed multitude and does not suffer a competitor, since it stands for the "objectively settled" and "unchanging" universal pattern of the revered founding figures of human culture in whose name the elites rule and from whose legacy they derive the legitimacy of their rule as the guardians of the sagely learning (Angle 2009, pp. 35–36).[17] In this sense, the ethical monism and social patriarchalism of Cheng-Zhu Neo-Confucianism prove to be the two sides of the same coin.

Hence, Cheng-Zhu Neo-Confucian metaphysics in its traditional form is a poor candidate to serve as an inspiration for a pluralistically comprehensive moral doctrine that could sustain and nurture the Confucian public culture of a pluralistic democracy. Nevertheless, there are strains of Neo-Confucian thought, both in and outside the hegemonic Cheng-Zhu school, that reject the ontologically asymmetrical rendition of the one-many relation, i.e., ones that do not devalue the spontaneous movements of psychophysical energy in order unduly to valorize the unifying and harmonizing power of pattern. Let me hint at two possible sources, both from Korean Neo-Confucianism, for envisioning a pluralistically comprehensive moral doctrine. Hwadam Seo Gyeong-deok (花潭 徐敬德 1489–1546), for one, famously argued that at the ultimate ground of the world lies the One Psychophysical Energy (一氣 *ilgi*), also called "the Great Void" (太虛 *taeheo*), not pattern. The Great Void is in a state of utter clarity, stillness, oneness, purity, and emptiness (湛一虛 *damil cheongheo*) (Seo 2004, pp. 190, 202)[18] yet its spontaneously differentiating and structuring movements give rise to the myriad things of the world (p. 192).

A similar yet more sophisticated understanding of psychophysical energy as the creative ground of the cosmos is put forward by Nongmun Im Seong-ju (鹿門 任聖周 1711–1788). The core thesis of Nongmun's Neo-Confucian metaphysics, that "pattern and psychophysical energy are equally actual

---

[15] Zhu Xi states, "Human nature is always good, yet there are some who are good from the time of their births, and there are those who are evil from the time of their births. This is due to the differences in their physical endowment . . . The goal of learning is to transform the physical endowment, although such transformation is very difficult" (Zhu 1986, vol. 1, p. 69).

[16] Dai Zhen, a Qing Dynasty Neo-Confucian, criticized the Song and Ming Neo-Confucians for claiming the authority of the Heavenly Pattern to justify their own parochial interests and desires: "Of those who regard pattern as something obtained from Heaven and endowed in the heart-mind, there is none who does not replace it with their personal opinions" (Dai 1995, vol. 6, p. 155).

[17] For the Cheng-Zhu Neo-Confucians, Heavenly Pattern—which Angle translates as "universal coherence" (Angle 2009, p. 36)—is objectively settled (定 *ding*) and unchanging (常 *chang*), having been discovered by the early sages who had deep insights into the human nature.

[18] Following Zhang Zai, Hwadam calls the One Psychophysical Energy also "the Great Void" (太虛 *taeheo/taixu*). (Seo 2004, p. 200). Hwadam understands 一氣 (*ilgi*) as the ultimate creative ground of the cosmos, in contrast to the dominant usage of the term within the Confucian and Daoist traditions.

[理氣同實 *ligi dongsil*]," claims that principle and psychophysical energy completely correspond to each other in all respects, in all their modes of being and operation (Son 2004, p. 443; Hong 2003, p. 97).[19] Metaphysical *li* and physical *ki* (*qi*) are, in other words, two distinct yet intertwined, mutually irreducible, and co-extensive aspects of the ultimate reality, i.e., what he calls "one transparently all-encompassing and overflowingly large thing-event [一箇虛圓盛大底物事 *ilgae heowon seongdae jeo mulsa*]" which is no other than the dynamic substance-in-process of all that is and becomes (Im 2001e, 19.1a/p. 383).[20] The two are different characterizations of the same ultimate reality, psychophysical energy being its characterization from the perspective of the world simply being the way it is, while pattern is the characterization of the ultimate reality from the perspective of the reason why the world is or must be the way it is (Im 2001d, 5.5b/p. 91).[21] The two characterizations together give expression to the ultimate reality's visible and spontaneous movement of creative harmonization that constitutes the world on the one hand and its invisible function of rationally grounding and normatively governing the same world on the other. The ontological and cosmic creativity manifest in the universe, i.e., the ubiquitous phenomenon of the so-called "life-giving intention" (生意 *saeng-ui/sheng yi*) frequently extolled by the Neo-Confucians, is a joint manifestation of pattern and psychophysical energy.[22]

Nongmun's thesis of the co-extensive and equal actuality of pattern and psychophysical energy implies that the ultimate reality is both the principle of unity and harmony on the one hand, and the principle of differentiation and delimitation on the other. In other words, he introduces difference and multiplicity directly into the heart of the "one transparently all-encompassing and overflowingly large thing-event" that is both pattern and psychophysical energy. His innovative rendition of the concept of "the original substance of psychophysical energy" (氣之本體 *ki ji bonche*) (Im 2001e, 19.24b/p. 394), which is all-pervasively present in the very process of its concrete delimitation into myriad individual configurations of psychophysical energy, underpins his key claim that "psychophysical energy is one, but its manifestations are many (氣一分殊 *gi-il bunsu*)" (Im 2001e, 19.4a/p. 384). By thus making psychophysical energy both the principle of unity *and* differentiation, he not only overturns the Cheng-Zhu Neo-Confucian devaluation of psychophysical energy but also locates in it the source of the creativity and fecundity observed in the cosmos.[23]

In line with his ontologically symmetrical rendition of both the *li-ki* relation and the one-many relation, Nongmun veers away from the Cheng-Zhu Neo-Confucian distinction between the Heaven-endowed original nature of things (本然之性 *benran zhi xing*), which is traditionally regarded as pattern in abstraction from psychophysical energy, and the so-called physical nature (氣質之性 *qizhi zhi xing*), i.e., the individually unique natures of concretely existing things determined and delimited by their specific psychophysical endowments. He rejects the distinction between the two on the ground that the individually unique natures retain their original impulse toward unity and harmony—the telltale sign of the efficacious presence of the original nature—in the form of their shared life-giving intention (Im 2001c, 3.5a/p. 44; cf. Choe 2009, pp. 354–56). In the case of humans whose individually unique natures are determined primarily by the respective psychophysical constitution of their heart-minds (心 *sim*), his disavowal of the distinction between the original nature and the physical nature leads him simply to label human nature the original nature (Im 2001d, 5.19a–b/p. 98). In fact, he insists on the original goodness of the concrete human heart-minds to such an extent that he draws up the following corollary to his main thesis: "The heart-mind and the nature are equally actual

---

[19] Nongmun's thought amounts to a parallel and "dipolar" construction of the pattern-psychophysical energy relation.

[20] For citations from Im Seong-ju's *Nongmunjip*, I give the book number and the page number in the traditional format, and then (after a slash) the page number in the modern pagination, as its "modern" edition is in fact a facsimile of the traditional format.

[21] Nongmun states, "Its being so refers to psychophysical energy, while its reason for being so corresponds to pattern [其然者 氣也; 所以然者理也]".

[22] The notion of "life-giving intention" was championed by Cheng Hao and Zhu Xi. Nongmun himself acknowledges the influence of Cheng Hao and Zhu Xi on his notion of "life-giving intention" (Im 2001e, 19.10b–11a/pp. 387–88).

[23] Nongmun regards the phenomenon of "life-giving intention" as a principal evidence for the creatively harmonizing power of psychophysical energy (Im 2001e, 19.3a/p. 384, 19.6b/p. 385, 19.28a/p. 396).

(心性同實 *simseong dongsil*)" (Im 2001a, 9.37a/p. 191; Im 2001b, 6.12b/p. 112).[24] The end-product of his renovation of Cheng-Zhu Neo-Confucian metaphysics is a robust defense of the inherent moral subjectivity and agency of all human beings—the Mencian heritage—whose political implications are still much to be drawn out and explored.

4. Toward a Pluralistically Comprehensive Doctrine of Confucian Democracy

Nongmun was, of course, neither a pluralist nor an advocate of democracy. He remained within the orbit of ethically monistic and socially patriarchal Korean Cheng-Zhu Confucianism and did not develop the possible, ethically and politically liberating, implications of his thought. Nonetheless, if differences and multiplicity are at the heart of ultimate reality as he suggested, then this may provide us with an occasion to reconsider the moral and political significance of a Confucian metaphysics for a pluralistic democracy. In a Confucian metaphysics inspired by Nongmun, the plurality and differences that characterize our embodied existence could no longer be viewed as secondary and derivative qualities co-emergent with our individual birth from our supposedly singular, unitary origin and ground of being. This implies that, for such a pluralistically comprehensive Confucian doctrine, the existence within a pluralistic democracy of different values and groups of people, named along various markers of identity and difference (gender, race, ethnicity, sexuality, religion, etc.), would reflect the nature of reality as such. Pluralism, including political pluralism, would be an intrinsic feature of the landscape within its allegedly totalizing horizon. Furthermore, by giving the nod to the idea of popular sovereignty as capable of underpinning the constitution of a body politic made up precisely of diverse groups of people beholden to different value systems, such a Confucian metaphysics would reject the much-debated conception of popular sovereignty as unitary.[25]

For much of the history of the modern nation-states, popular sovereignty was understood and exercised on the model of absolute monarchy, by opposing the unity of the sovereign to the multiplicity of the multitude.[26] Hobbes, one of the early theorists of the modern sovereign state, famously described the hypothetical social contract through which human beings, desperate to overcome the state of nature fraught with a "war of every man against every man" (Hobbes 1958, p. 256), voluntarily surrendered their individual sovereignty, i.e., their natural right to govern and to defend themselves, to a single sovereign power—either a monarch or an assembly—in order to constitute a commonwealth that promised protection and security (335–40). Although the sovereign was, for Rousseau, the law-giving "general will" of the people forming one nation instead of the will of the monarch, its sovereignty was, nevertheless, indivisible (Rousseau 1993, pp. 200–2). Furthermore, for popular, democratic sovereignty to work, the multitude, who were no more than a rabble, must be molded into a people with a unitary will, which required the state with legitimate political authority to subject the chaotic bodies of the multitude.[27]

This unitary view of popular sovereignty finds one of its most sinister contemporary renditions in Carl Schmitt, who defines the essence of the political as consisting in a friend-enemy distinction, publically conceived, and the existential struggle of the people to survive against external and internal

---

[24] Nongmun's main theses, "Pattern and psychophysical energy are equally actual [理氣同實 *i gi dong sil*]" and "The heart-mind and the nature completely correspond [to each other] [心性一致 *sim seong il chi*] were originally coined by his teacher, Yi gan, to refer primarily to the human heart-mind in its un-activated state in which the original substance of psychophysical energy fully resonates with the original human nature's mandate of empathy and harmony. Nongmun applied this insight to what might be called ultimate reality, expanding the notion of *i gi dong sil* to cover the ground and depth of the entire cosmos (Choe 2009, p. 352).

[25] In affirming the notion of popular sovereignty, the pluralistically comprehensive Confucian metaphysics which I am suggesting in this essay sides with Confucian democrats like Sor-hoon Tan and Sungmoon Kim over against the advocates of Confucian meritocracy, such as Joseph Chan and Jiang Qing.

[26] For the following discussion of popular sovereignty, I am indebted to Clayton Crocket (Crocket 2011, pp. 45–49).

[27] Rousseau describes how the "multitude" (p. 194) becomes united in one sovereign body politic though social contract, and claims that when the sovereign democratic state is dissolved, democracy, the rule of the citizens, degenerates into *ochlocracy*, the rule of the (chaotic) multitude (p. 259).

threats (Schmitt 2007, pp. 26–27). The political entity, i.e., the state, decides on the friend-enemy distinction, separating out the "public enemies" from the body politic internally and defending itself from other states externally (pp. 29–30). The state's sovereignty lies precisely in its power to create the friend-enemy grouping and, in so doing, to produce itself as a political community beyond mere societal or associational groupings (p. 39). The citizens of a democratic state, the *demos*, exercise popular sovereignty insofar as they purge themselves of hostile, alien elements within and stand united in opposition to enemies without.

A pluralistic Confucian metaphysics would not be able to accommodate the unitary conception of popular sovereignty, let alone Schimtt's extreme version of it. It would refuse to conceive the people's autonomous capacity to rule themselves as predicated on a production of "them"—i.e., the politically externalized remainder that Giorgio Agamben memorably calls *homo sacer* (Agamben 1998). In face of the political storm and the media war stirred up in South Korea recently by the arrival of Yemeni refugees in the southernmost island of Jeju, it would repudiate any notion of a homogeneous and unitary *demos* that can come into being only by erecting border walls, both visible and invisible, beyond which immigrants, refugees, and undesirable minorities are to be cast out. In response to the heated confrontations between LGBTQI-pride marchers and violent counter-demonstrators in the city of Incheon, it would support the notion of popular sovereignty as the freedom of self-governance enjoyed by a body of people bound together even across deep differences by critically affectionate solidarity, which Sungmoon Kim insightfully captures with his notion of Confucian public reason based on critical affection (*jeong*) and *uri*-responsibility. The *Confucian* character of such a pluralistic metaphysics lies precisely in this—that it underwrites the idea of a body politic, which is capable of peaceably holding together diverse groups of people beholden to different value systems, on the basis of the humane heart of empathy claimed to be in all of us, whose many names are *ren*, *jeong*, critical familial affection, critically affectionate solidarity, and so on. The *democratic* character of such a Confucian metaphysics comes to the fore when it rejects the elitism of traditional Confucian virtue politics, viz., when it declines to prioritize the objectively settled and unchanging universal pattern of benevolent sociopolitical organization, allegedly discovered by the ancient sages and entrusted to the care of the enlightened *junzi*, as the most unsullied articulation—patterning (*li*)—of the humane heart of empathy.

Precisely how, then, does such a pluralistically comprehensive Confucian doctrine appeal to the humane heart of empathy in order to provide support to the idea of a Confucian democratic polity? Here, the all-encompassing metaphysical horizon of the pluralistic Confucian doctrine serves to anchor, ontologically, the pivotal moral-political notion of critically affectionate solidarity. Its affirmation of the ontological ultimacy of both one and many, both unity and diversity, in a universe as lush and bountiful as ours would enable us to surmise, if not to know for certain, that the differences at the heart of reality are held together peaceably by something analogous to the humane heart of mutual empathy, so that myriad patterns (*li*) and harmonies—a cosmos—could be born. In other words, despite the chaotic percolation of *différance* that all-pervasively characterizes the ontological depth of our being (to borrow Derrida's celebrated term for the unending non-teleological processes of elemental mutual differentiation at the core of any seemingly stable essential unity), what prevents reality from collapsing into a state of perpetual conflict and barren chaos is no other than something like mutual affection that brings together the differences to ground—that is, to "pattern"—a meaningful and valuable cosmos. It is precisely in this sense that the two prominent examples of mutual empathy and affection, namely the cardinal Confucian virtue of *ren* and the Korean *jeong*, are manifestations in the human sphere of the cosmic and metacosmic "life-giving intention," i.e., the boundlessly generous creativity at the root of things. Notwithstanding the Daoist rejoinder, that "heaven and earth are not humane (天地不

仁 *tiandi buren*)"[28] the pluralistic Confucian metaphysics would insist on the affective—empathetic and therefore humane—constitution of the world's *suoyiran* (所以然), i.e., the reason for there being a world.

Such a Confucian doctrine of the affective grounding of a pluralistic cosmos would enable us to claim that the peaceable co-flourishing of different values and diverse groups of people in a world as vital and fecund as ours—all its discord and conflicts notwithstanding—reflects the deepest undercurrent of reality pulsing with mutual empathy and affection. The pluralistic Confucian metaphysics of the kind I have suggested would allow us to venture a thesis, that our freedom to live and thrive, each of us in our own distinct way, will not inevitably jeopardize the bonds of critical affection that sustains a pluralistic Confucian democracy, and that, even without the learned elites' paradigmatic ethico-political patterning (*li*) of our mutual empathy, we can in our freedom traverse our differences to forge patterns (*li*) of peaceable co-flourishing. Such a Confucian metaphysics would offer a "religious" basis for the trust we put in the strength and resilience of Confucian public culture to hold our fractious democratic commonwealth together. It would even be able to provide a metacosmic rationale for believing in the power of Confucian public culture to bridge our disparate and contentious ways with what Kwok Pui-lan and Joerg Rieger call "deep solidarity"—the solidarity of those who have compassion for one another on account of their shared suffering, i.e., their common experience of oppression, exploitation, and marginalization, even with all their differences in terms of gender, race, ethnicity, class, sexuality, religion, and so on (Rieger and Kwok 2012, p. 28). Confucianism as a comprehensive doctrine, when so reimagined, could even be said to be indispensable for the well-being of a pluralistic democratic commonwealth in East Asia, given the power to tug at the body and mind, which the Confucian discourses still wield widely in East Asian nations, especially in South Korea, despite more than a century of intellectual marginalization and neglect.

Funding: This research received no external funding.

Conflicts of Interest: The author declares no conflict of interest.

References

Agamben, Giorgio. 1998. *Homo Sacer: Sovereign Power and Bare Life*. Translated by Daniel Heller-Roazen. Stanford: Stanford University Press.

Ames, Roger T., and David L. Hall. 1999. *The Democracy of the Dead: Dewey, Confucius, and the Hope for Democracy in China*. Chicago: Open Court.

Angle, Stephen C. 2009. *Sagehood: The Contemporary Significance of Neo-Confucian Philosophy*. New York: Oxford University Press.

Angle, Stephen C. 2012. *Contemporary Confucian Political Philosophy: Toward Progressive Confucianism*. Cambridge and Malden: Polity Press.

Bai, Tongdong. 2012. *China: The Political Philosophy of the Middle Kingdom*. London and New York: Zed Books.

Bell, Daniel A. 2006. *Beyond Liberal Democracy: Political Thinking for an East Asian Context*. Princeton and Oxford: Princeton University Press.

Chan, Wing-Tsit, trans. 1963. *A Source Book in Chinese Philosophy*. Princeton: Princeton University Press.

Chan, Joseph Chan. 2014. *Confucian Perfectionism: A Political Philosophy for Modern Times*. Princeton and Oxford: Princeton University Press.

Cheng, Yi. 1981a. Da Yang Shi Lun Xi Ming Shu [Reply to Yang Shih's letter on the Western Inscription]. In *Er Cheng Ji [Collected Works of Cheng Brothers]*. Edited by Xiaoyu Wang. Beijing: Zhonghua Shuju, vol. 2.

Cheng, Yi. 1981b. Yichuan xiansheng yuyi [First sayings of teacher Yichuan]. In *Er Cheng Ji [Collected Works of Cheng Brothers]*. Edited by Xiaoyu Wang. Beijing: Zhonghua Shuju, vol. 1.

---

[28] Daodejing 5.1. Of course, the famous Daoist saying does not imply that heaven and earth—nature—are not fecund. It merely rejects any attempt to subsume that cosmic fecundity and creativity under what the Daodejing regards as human artifice responsible for the creation of human values, institutions and ways of life.

Ching, Julia. 2000. *Religious Thought of Chu Hsi.* Oxford: Oxford University Press.

Choe, Yeong-Jin. 2009. 18~19 segi joseon seongnihak ui simhakhwa gyeong-hyang e daehan gochal [An examination of the tendency toward the Learning of the Heart-Mind from the 18- to 19th-century Korean Neo-Confucianism]. *Han-Guk Minjok Munhwa* 33: 339–68.

Connolly, William E. 2005. *Pluralism.* Durham and London: Duke University Press.

Connolly, William E. 2008. *Capitalism and Christianity, American Style.* Durham: Duke University Press.

Crocket, Clayton. 2011. *Radical Political Theology: Religion and Politics after Liberalism.* New York: Columbia University Press.

Dai, Zhen. 1995. Mengzi ziyi shu zheng [An evidential commentary on the meanings of terms in Mencius]. In *Dai Zhen Quanshu [Complete Works of Dai Zhen].* Edited by Zhang Dainian. Hebei: Huangshan Shushe, vol. 6.

Deleuze, Gilles, and Felix Guattari. 1987. *A Thousand Plateaus: Capitalism and Schizophrenia.* Translated by Brian Massumi. Minneapolis and London: University of Minnesota Press.

Deuchler, Martina. 1992. *The Confucian Transformation of Korea: A Study of Society and Ideology.* Cambridge: Council on East Asian Studies.

Gardner, Daniel K., trans. 1990. *Learning to Be a Sage: Selections from the Conversations of Master Chu, Arranged Topically.* Edited by Xi Zhu. Berkeley: University of California Press.

Graham, Angus C. 1986. The Ch'eng-Chu theory of human nature. In *Studies in Chinese Philosophy and Philosophical Literature.* Singapore: Institute of East Asian Philosophies.

Hobbes, Thomas. 1958. *Hobbes: Selections.* Edited by Frederick J. E. Woodbridge. New York: Charles Scribner's Sons.

Hong, Jeong-Geun. 2003. Im Seong-ju wa Na Heum-sun hakseol ui daebijeok gochal [A comparative examination of the theories of Im Seong-ju and Na Heum-sun]. *Yugyo Sasang Yeongu* 18: 87–116.

Im, Seong-Ju. 2001a. Dap Gwon Saeng-gyeong [Reply to Gwon Saeng-gyeong]. In *Nongmunjip [Collected Works of Nongmun].* Edited by Minjok Munhwa Chujinhoe. Seoul: Gyeongin Munhwasa.

Im, Seong-Ju. 2001b. Dap Kim Baek-go [Reply to Kim Baek-go]. In *Nongmunjip [Collected Works of Nongmun].* Edited by Minjok Munhwa Chujinhoe. Seoul: Gyeongin Munhwasa.

Im, Seong-Ju. 2001c. Dap Song Yeok-cheon [Reply to Song Yeok-cheon]. In *Nongmunjip [Collected Works of Nongmun].* Edited by Minjok Munhwa Chujinhoe. Seoul: Gyeongin Munhwasa.

Im, Seong-Ju. 2001d. Dap Yi Baeng-nul [Reply to Yi Baeng-nul]. In *Nongmunjip [Collected Works of Nongmun].* Edited by Minjok Munhwa Chujinhoe. Seoul: Gyeongin Munhwasa.

Im, Seong-Ju. 2001e. Nongryeo japji [Miscellaneous writings from the Deer Hut]. In *Nongmunjip [Collected Works of Nongmun].* Edited by Minjok Munhwa Chujinhoe. Seoul: Gyeongin Munhwasa.

Kim, Sungmoon. 2014. *Confucian Democracy in East Asia: Theory and Practice.* New York: Cambridge University Press.

Kim, Sungmoon, ed. 2015. *Confucianism, Law, and Democracy in Contemporary Korea.* London and Lanham: Rowman & Littlefield International.

Qing, Jiang. 2013. *A Confucian Constitutional Order: How China's Ancient Past Can Shape Its Political Future.* Edited by Daniel A. Bell and Ruiping Fan. Translated by Edmund Ryden. Princeton and Oxford: Princeton University Press.

Rieger, Joerg, and Pui-Lan Kwok. 2012. *Occupy Religion: Theology of the Multitude.* Lanham and Plymouth: Rowman & Littlefield.

Rousseau, Jean-Jacques. 1993. *The Social Contract and Discourses.* Translated by George Douglas Howard Cole. London: J. M. Dent; Rutland: Charles E. Tuttle.

Schmitt, Carl. 2007. *The Concept of the Political.* Edited and Translated by George Schwab. Chicago and London: The University of Chicago Press.

Seo, Gyeong-Deok. 2004. *Gugyeok Hwadamjip [Collected Works of Hwdam, Translated].* Translated by Hwang Gwang-Uk. Seoul: Simsan Munhwa.

Shin, Doh Chull. 2012. *Confucianism and Democratization in East Asia.* New York: Cambridge University Press.

Son, Heung-Cheol. 2004. *Nongmun Im Seong-Ju Ui Sarm Gwa Cheorak [A Study on Nongmun Im Seong-Ju's Life and His Philosophy].* Seoul: Jisik saneopsa.

Tan, Sor-Hoon. 2004. *Confucian Democracy: A Deweyan Reconstruction.* Albany: State University of New York Press.

Tu, Wei-Ming. 1982. T'oegye's creative interpretation of Chu Hsi's philosophy of principle. *Korea Journal* 22: 4–15.

Zhu, Xi. 1986. *Zhuzi Yulei [Conversations of Master Zhu, Arranged Topically].* Edited by Li Jingde and Wang Xingxian. Beijing: Zhonghua Shuju, vol. 1.

Zhu, Xi. 2000a. Da He Shujing [Reply to He Shujing]. In *Zhuzi Wenji [Collected Literary Works of Master Zhu]*. Edited by Chen Junmin. Taibei: Defu Wenjiao Jijinhui, vol. 4.

Zhu, Xi. 2000b. Da Huang Shangbo [Response to Huang Shangbo]. In *Zhuzi Wenji [Collected Literary Works of Master Zhu]*. Edited by Chen Junmin. Taibei: Defu Wenjiao Jijinhui, vol. 5.

Zhu, Xi. 2000c. Da Huang Daofu [Response to Huang Daofu]. In *Zhuzi Wenji [Collected Literary Works of Master Zhu]*. Edited by Chen Junmin. Taibei: Defu Wenjiao Jijinhui, vol. 6.

Article

"Korea National Prayer Breakfast" and Protestant Leaders' Prophetic Consciousness during the Period of Military Dictatorship (1962–1987)

Yohan Yoo * and Minah Kim

Department of Religious Studies, Seoul National University, Seoul 08826, Korea; kyu486@snu.ac.kr
* Correspondence: yohanyoo@snu.ac.kr

Received: 17 September 2018; Accepted: 5 October 2018; Published: 10 October 2018

Abstract: This paper illuminates the prophetic consciousness of Korean Protestant leaders by examining the "Korea National Prayer Breakfast" (*Gukgajochangidohoe*, 국가조찬기도회) that they hosted, particularly during the military regimes. In explaining the motivation for and intention of this special religious event in the political arena, most scholars have emphasized the Protestant leaders' political ambition and their agendas to get the government support and expand their power in Korean society. However, we should take heed of the leaders' religious aspirations to make the country righteous in God's sight. They attempted to have a good influence on the inner circle of the military dictatorship, which some Christians regarded as an evil force. Though they preached to and prayed for the military regimes, their sermons were often unpleasant and challenging to the presidents and their associates. The Protestant leaders wanted to play the role of John the Baptist rebuking Herod Antipas rather than the compliant chief priests and scribes serving Herod the Great.

Keywords: Korean religion; Korean Protestants; *Gukgajochangidohoe* (Korean National Prayer Breakfast); prophetic consciousness

1. Introduction: A New Perspective on the Korea National Prayer Breakfast

The Korea National Prayer Breakfast (*Gukgajochangidohoe*, 국가조찬기도회) was first hosted and organized in 1966 by prominent pastors of Korean Protestant churches. Since then, leading authorities in Korean Protestantism, along with many Korean political leaders who are Christian or sympathetic to the Christian faith, have gathered together every year to pray for the country. This annual meeting began in Korea influenced by the U.S. Presidential Prayer Breakfast, the name of which was changed to the National Prayer Breakfast in 1970. Rev. Joongon Kim (1925–2009), who had founded Korea Campus Crusade for Christ (K.C.C.C) in 1958 and served as its president since then until 2003, was one of the first organizers of the meeting. He was personally acquainted with Rev. Clifton Robinson and Rev. Richard Halverson of the Fellowship Foundation, or "the family," who organized the U.S. Presidential Prayer Breakfast and Senate-House prayer breakfast meetings. Kim was invited to participate in the joint Senate-House prayer breakfast meetings in 1963 and 1964. Subsequently, Robinson and Halverson were invited to Korea in 1964 and encouraged Kim to take the lead in organizing a National Assembly Prayer Breakfast in Korea. Kim accepted this suggestion and held the National Assembly Prayer Breakfast meeting with about twenty Protestant members of the National Assembly on 27 February 1965. The next year, Kim and many other Korean Protestant leaders cooperated for preparing and hosting the Korea Presidential Prayer Breakfast. But President Chunghee Park (in office 1961–1979), who was not a Christian, did not participate that year. Park, however, along with more than five hundred well-known figures, did attend the next Presidential Prayer Breakfast that was convened on 8 May 1968. Since then, this meeting became an annual event that was in principle carried out in May every year. The title of the meeting was changed to Korea National Prayer Breakfast in 1976.[1] It is remarkable that the National Prayer Breakfast could successfully take hold in Korea, which in 1971 had a Christian population of only 12.2% (9.8% Protestant and 2.4% Catholic).[2]

Most scholars of modern Korean history or Korean church history who examine this meeting label it as pro-government. They assert that Korean Protestant churches received significant benefits from the government and that it is a conspicuous example of the mutual back-scratching relations between the government and the church during the period of military dictatorship, which began from the military coup of Chunghee Park in 1961 and were continued by the military insurgencies of Doohwan Chun (in office 1981–1988) on 12 December 1979 and 17 May 1980. However, we will demonstrate that Korean Protestant leaders planned and held the meeting in their wish for contributing to making the country prosperous and righteous from a Protestant Christian perspective. In other words, some Protestant leaders had the prophetic objective to exert a good influence on the inner circle of the military dictatorship, which many Christians in those days regarded as an evil force. We are not denying that the Protestant leaders received benefit through their close relations with the government and to expand influence and numbers of the Protestant church. However, we would like to emphasize that their religious motivation also should be considered.

In Judeo-Christian traditions, prophets often played the role of social critics and their teachings have been regarded as "attempts to denounce injustices practiced against the weak and powerless" (Sheppard and Herbrechtsmeier 1987, pp. 7425–26). Some Christian leaders in the period of the military dictatorship warned about the unrighteousness of the ruling regimes on the basis of this prophetic consciousness, sometimes campaigning against the government. In this article, we will illuminate the reflection and determination of the Protestant leaders who hosted the prayer meetings by articulating their prophetic messages which are seen in sermons delivered in the Korea National Prayer Breakfast meetings and their proceedings, and in contemporary news articles covering them.

As mentioned above, many scholars criticize the Protestant leaders for standing by brutal military dictatorships (Lee 2004, p. 277; Yoon 2016, pp. 51–54; Kown 2015, pp. 194–96; Chang 2006, pp. 114–19; Han 2004, pp. 29–31). The "Prayer Breakfast for the Future of the Country and the Nation," (국가와 민족의 장래를 위한 조찬기도회) which was broadcast live across the country in August 1980, is often regarded as the most notorious example of Korean Protestant support for the dictatorship. In this meeting, Rev. Kyungchik Han (1902–2000) prayed that Chun might become "the great leader whom God gave to our nation, just like Moses who saved the Israel from Egypt" and blessed Chun and the other new military cliques in the name of God. As this meeting was held right after the military junta had brutally crushed the Gwangju Democratization Movement, a civil uprising against the military on 18 May, some scholars say that Han's blessing was an implicit sanction of the violent repression. They assert that the blessing of one of the most prominent Protestant pastors of that time signified no less than the support of the whole Korean Protestant church for the military (Kim 2007, p. 75; Kim 2011, p. 84). However, as we will demonstrate in Section 3, we should pay attention to the pastors' aspiration to pray for a country in deep crisis, though it is true that the military used the endorsement of the Protestant leaders for political propaganda (Kim 2009, pp. 327–33; Chun 2014, pp. 40, 42;

---

[1] Though President Park was not a Christian and did not have a specific religion, he showed respect to Korean Protestant leaders by attending the Korea Presidential Prayer Breakfast. He attended the Korea Presidential Prayer Breakfast from 1968 to 1974. The 1975 meeting did not convene because of the unstable political situation affected by anti-government protest movements. Park again attended the meeting in 1976 when the title of the event changed to the Korea National Prayer Breakfast. From 1977 to 1979, the year when Park was murdered by one of his right-hand men, the director of the Korean Central Intelligence Agency, the chairman of the National Assembly or the prime minister attended and acted for the president. Though President Chun participated in the special prayer breakfast meeting held in 1980, which was before he became the president, and the 1981 National Prayer Breakfast, he neither attended nor sent the prime minister instead from 1982 to 1987 (Choi 2002, pp. 49–50; Han 2004, p. 28; Chang 2006, pp. 114–15).

[2] According to the 1971 census, 9.8% of the Korean population was Protestant and 2.4% was Catholic, among a total population of 32,882,704. The census shows that Buddhists were 21.7% and those without religion were 45.4% (Korea Research Institute for Religion and Society 1993, p. 174). For reference, according to the most recent census in 2015, Protestants were 19.7%, Catholics 7.9%, Buddhists 15.5%, those without religion 56.1%, and others 0.8%.

Yoon 2016, pp. 56–57). Han's blessing was a part of a process of exhorting the military and delivering to it religious and ethical messages, rather than justifying it.

Another common criticism is that the Korea National Prayer Breakfast helped the Korean Protestant church receive exclusive benefits from the military government during the 1970s and 80s that other religions could not enjoy (Choi 2002, pp. 75–77; Chang 2006, pp. 122–25; Yoon 2016, pp. 49–51). This criticism is often supported by the fact that the government granted valuable lands in Seoul to K.C.C.C, the founder and president of which, Joongon Kim, was one of the organizers of the early prayer meetings. Besides this, some critics point out that the military allowed the Protestant church to hold massive revival services in public areas of Seoul and other major cities. They argue that permission for these massive rallies is evidence of the government's exceptional support for the Protestant circle, as the freedom of press, publication, assembly and association had been strictly restricted since the October Restoration in 1972, a self-coup through which president Chunghee Park reconfirmed his dictatorial powers (Chang 2006, p. 123; Chun 2014, p. 40). It would be worthwhile to mention two super-massive revival rallies that were held during this period.[3] First, on 3 June 1973, about 1.1 million people attended an evangelistic rally at which Billy Graham preached. Han was the main organizer of the evangelistic rally, which was held at the Yeouido Plaza. This rally is famous as "Graham's largest ever Crusade" (Billy Graham Evangelistic Association 2018). Second, Joongon Kim organized the "Explo '74," revival services that were held at the Yeouido Plaza from the 13th to 18th of August, 1974. It is said that some 6.5 million participants attended over the six days (Chang 2006, p. 123). However, the military governments of the period pursued a policy of treating Buddhism, Catholicism, and Protestantism, the so called three major religions of Korea, where Catholicism and Protestantism are often regarded as different religions (see Shin 1998). Though Catholics and Buddhists did not seek to hold massive public services or to secure new strongholds in Seoul other than temple or church sites, they also received remarkable benefits from the government. When the government began to designate religious facilities as cultural heritage and subsidize them in 1970s, the main beneficiaries were Catholics and Buddhists, not Protestants (Kim 2016, p. 302). In addition, Buddhist military chaplains were authorized in 1968 and Buddha's Birthday became a national holiday in 1975. President Chun and the New Military offered unwavering support to the visit of Pope John Paul II in 1984 and allowed the Catholic Church to hold a special mass at Yeouido Plaza in which about 600,000 Catholics participated (*The Kyunghyang Sinmun*, 6 May 1984). In short, it is not at all clear that the benefits that the Korean Protestant church received thanks to the National Prayer Breakfast were significantly greater than those of the other major religious traditions.

This overemphasis on the benefits that the Protestant church allegedly enjoyed by cooperating the dictatorship is based on the one-sided idea that religion is passively affected by the socio-political realm. According to this view, religion maintains its authority and sphere of power by reacting to and adapting itself to social influences. However, by paying attention to the particular religious aspirations of the early organizers of the National Prayer Breakfast to have God's will be done on earth or, more concretely, to make Korea into a righteous and just country, we will confirm that religion also can exercise influence on other areas in a society and cause its changes. Peter L. Berger points out that the relationship between religion and society is dialectical, suggesting that religious ideas often lead to changes in the social structure and that religion has the potency to act back upon its infrastructure in specific historical situations (Berger 1967, p. 128). Likewise, Andrew Greeley emphasizes that "religion is an important predictor variable in the modern world" (Greeley 1995, p. 28). He reminds that Max Weber and Émile Durkheim, two pioneers of sociology, demonstrated strong influences of religion over other elements in a society. Then, Greeley asserts that even in our "modernized,

---

[3] Those who first organized and hosted the Korea National Prayer Breakfast were evangelical Protestant pastors, though they tried to include non-evangelical Christians also in the Prayer Breakfast meetings. It was American and Canadian evangelical missionaries who exerted critical influence on the beginning of the Korean Protestant churches in the late 19th century. Since then, the evangelical Protestants have been the mainstream in Korean Protestantism.

urbanized, rationalized, Western world," religion still has considerable influence on human attitudes and behaviors in the social, political, and economic sphere (Greeley 1995, pp. 29–30). This article will contribute to overcome the limitations of precedent researches that stress the passivity of religion, by articulating that religious motives of the Protestant leaders for exerting positive effect on the country were an important factor in hosting the Korean National Prayer Breakfast.

In the second section, we will examine the characteristics of faith and theology of the Protestant leaders who took the lead of the meeting. Special attention will be paid to their theological views on society and country, which were obviously reflected in the meeting, because these views are helpful in understanding the goal that the leaders wanted to attain through the prayer meeting. The third section analyzes the prophetic consciousness of the Protestant leaders that was revealed in the prayer meeting. We will scrutinize their religious anguish and aspiration that are seen in their sermons, prayers, speeches, and writings.

2. Theological Views of the First Organizers

Joongon Kim, Kyungchik Han, and Sinmyeong Kang (1909–1985) are often considered as the Protestant leaders who played the most important role in planning and organizing early National Prayer Breakfast meetings (Chun 2014, pp. 37–38; Yoon 2016, p. 52; see Appendix A, Table A1). By investigating their theological perspective, in which they all emphasized the responsibility of Protestant Christians for the society and country, we will be able to understand better the messages they wanted to deliver to the rulers and the vision of the country's future they tried to suggest through the National Prayer Breakfast.

Joongon Kim, who first introduced prayer breakfast meetings in Korea, gave sermons or led prayers at the Prayer Breakfast meetings in 1966 and for five consecutive years from 1969 to 1973. In Kim's theology, the most important work for Korean Protestant Christians to do for their homeland was evangelizing Korean people. He did not separate loving the country from spreading the gospel to people. That was the reason he emphasized "national evangelization" so strongly. He officially announced the launching of the "national evangelization movement" at midnight on New Year's Day, 1971 on the Christian Broadcasting System, saying poetically and ardently, "let us invite the season of Christ into this country by imprinting the bloodstained Christ upon the mind of every Korean person" (Kim 2005a). By "national evangelization," Kim meant the endeavor to make Korea a country where "Jehovah becomes our nation's God, Jesus becomes our Lord, and the Old and New Testaments become the standard of our nation's faith and deeds." He hoped that "Korea will become the second Israel, the only non-Western Protestant country" (Kim 2005a). To fulfill this purpose, he did not hesitate to be actively engaged in missionary work within the socio-political realm. In order to make Korea a real Protestant country, he promoted the "Total Religionization Movement in the Military Services," (전군신 자화 운동) in which he used the term of "religionization" in the sense of evangelization (see Kim 2006), in addition to engaging in overseas missions, and founding the Korea National Prayer Breakfast.

Kyungchik Han played the key role in the Prayer Breakfast meetings of 1970, 1971, 1974, 1980, 1984, and 1987, preaching, leading prayers, and giving benedictions. He was very influential not only in the Protestant circle but also in society at large, which is to be seen at the Prayer Breakfast in August 1980, where he prayed while laying hands on military dictator Chun, who was a Buddhist. Han thought that the church should have a positive influence on politics. On the one hand, he put a great deal of value on national security and emphasized anti-communism. According to Han, the Protestant church should be actively involved in politics when it came to national security, even if the church could be politically exploited. But at the same time, he also placed emphasis on the church helping the socially weak. At first glance, his sermon focused on personal salvation and changed lives of individual Christians who were saved. However, he went further and stressed that the church, the congregation of the saved individuals, had the responsibility of evangelizing the secular world. He even believed that the democratization of Korea could be realized by the obedience of Christians and the church to God (Kim 2011, p. 168). In concrete, he believed that Christians should have good fellowship with the socially weak and provide services for them in obedience to God. He said that the church should establish a theology for the poor and neglected and that it had the mission of helping and caring about them. He also argued that Christians should practice their faith by siding with laborers and peasants.

> If we see Christianity through the glasses of social thought, it sympathizes more with laborers and peasants than with capitalists. (. . .) Christianity has had the mission of giving good news to the poor and releasing the oppressed. (Han 2009 [originally from the sermon in 1947], vol. 1, p. 91)

In this passage, Han, who was an anti-communist, so strongly emphasized social justice that he even seemed to be sympathetic to communist propaganda. Furthermore, he advocated building up a democratic nation both on the basis of the Protestant ethic and evangelicalism of the Korean people. From the early period of his ministry, he insisted that the Korean Protestants should make Korea "a country where ideals of a Protestant state, especially liberty, equality, and fraternity, were achieved on a foundation of righteousness" (Han 2009). Just like Joongon Kim, Han also believed that a new Republic of Korea could be built only through the evangelization of the nation because the virtues necessary for a democratic state, such as freedom, equality, and ethics, came from the Protestant faith. According to Han,

> Evangelization of the nation is the greatest patriotic movement. (...) Let's make the spiritual root of our democratic state strong by evangelizing our nation. The ideals of human dignity, liberty, and equality came from the Bible. When all of our people come to believe in the Lord, the democratic state will be firmly established. In addition, national evangelization will make our ethical foundation solid. Only a person with complete ethics can enjoy complete liberty. Evangelization will make the whole nation new. Real social purification, social stability, and national consensus will be necessarily achieved through national evangelization. (Han 2009 [originally from the sermon in 1980], vol. 16, p. 199)

In reality, Han was not exactly right in that not all democratic states are Protestant. But it is obvious that Han tried to argue for the inseparable relation between democracy and Protestantism by saying "those who do not understand Protestantism do not understand democracy" (Han 2009). His assertion is that not only in Korea but also in any other countries in the world, building a democratic nation was impossible without Protestantism (Han 2009).

It was an important theological view of Kim and Han that national evangelization was necessary for making Korea a just and moral democratic country in which liberty and equality were guaranteed. They strived to persuade politicians to embrace their conviction that national evangelization was needed to make Korea a better country. We will examine this view in more detail in the next section.

Rev. Sinmyeong Kang, another leading figure in organizing early Prayer Breakfast meetings, began to attend from 1966. He gave the benediction in 1969 and 1976, led a prayer in 1973, and preached in 1978. While he did not explicitly state national evangelization in sermons, he was the Protestant leader who articulated the prophetic mission of the church more clearly than any other figures of the time (Kim 2009, pp. 261–63). In order to fulfill the mission, according to him, Korean Protestants should not limit the gospel within the church but contribute to society by active involvement in public concerns. He thought Protestantism had the capability of changing a value system of a society. Through this capability, the Protestant church should contribute to social reform as well as personal salvation. In this respect, it is said that this world and the world to come are not separated in his theology (Kim 2009, p. 288).

On the basis of this theological view, Kang tried to be actively engaged in socio-political issues. He agreed with President Park on anti-communist policies, the pro-American stance, and the ideal of nation building. But he clearly opposed the dictatorship and the corruption of the Park regime, which he thought "interfere[d] with the cultivation of personal and social ethics and the formation of democratic citizens" (Kim 2009, p. 286). In 1963, he directly criticized the Park regime, which was trying to prolong the military administration, by announcing a public statement demanding President Park's fulfillment of his promise to transfer power to a civilian government in the name of the National Council of Churches in Korea (The National Council of Churches in Korea 1974, pp. 296–97). Since then, he kept openly declaring opposition to Park's unilateral rule and anti-democratic policies: The conclusion of the Treaty on Basic Relations between the Republic of Korea and Japan, despite the strong public protests, in 1965; the constitutional amendment called *Samseon Gaeheon* that allowed the incumbent president to run for a third reelection in 1969; the October Restoration in 1972; the harsh crackdown on *Mincheonghangnyeon* (National League of Democratic Youth and Students) in 1974 (Kim 2009, p. 314). Kang persistently called up Park's anti-democratic consciousness and the corruption of his regime, even in the prayer he led at his funeral in 1979 (Kim 2009, pp. 311, 320).

Kim, Han, and Kang shared the theological view that the Protestant church should contribute to society. Kim thought that the Protestant church should help Korea become one of the developed nations. Han regarded caring about and aiding the socially marginalized as the mission of Protestants. Kang asserted that Protestantism could bring about positive changes in Korean society. While these pastors argued for the church's active involvement in society, they all gave the first priority to the gospel by emphasizing that it should be based on "the gospel of Jesus" (Kang 1960, p. 42; Han 2009; Kim 2009, pp. 369–70). Kim and Han believed that the Protestant church would be able to contribute to Korea through national evangelization. Kang's definition of social justice was the realization of the God's will in this world. This theology was expressed at Korea National Prayer Breakfast meetings as prophetic voices delivered to military regimes.

Another common belief of these three pastors was that Christianity, especially Protestantism, was necessary for enhancing morality and establishing a democratic state. For all three, their experience in the United States was critical in the formation of this belief. All three had studied in the US: Kim attended Fuller Theological Seminary, while Han and Kang studied at Princeton Theological Seminary. It was with the influence of his own experience in the States that Kim preached as follows in the sermon delivered at the National Prayer Breakfast in 1969:

> Let us consider the basically Christian countries of the United States and Europe. Modern democracy sprang from these countries in which the majority of the common people had a basic Christian outlook. Even modern science flowered in these countries. (. . .) The German spirit of science and art was rooted in the religious spirit. (Kim 2006 [originally from the sermon in 1969], p. 77)

Kim and other first organizers of the Prayer Breakfast thought that Korea should follow the example of the United States and Europe, which to them were advanced countries whose foundations were laid on Christian principles. On the basis of this belief and experience, they put forth the argument that Korea could be renewed through being evangelized and they tried to persuade the non-Christian participants to convert in the Korea National Prayer Breakfast.

We should be careful lest we conclude that they attempted to win the favor of the dictators for this evangelization, though it is true that the Protestant leaders stressed the importance of evangelizing the country so strongly. They were not too Protestant-centric, considering that they tried to avoid exclusive Protestant collectivism in the Prayer Breakfast by inviting Catholic leaders, which was successful in 1969 and 1970 when Bishop Ginam Noh and Cardinal Suhwan Kim read the Bible in order. More importantly, they did not endeavor to make the meeting palatable to the military dictators. The organizers did not prevent those who were unfriendly towards the government from participating actively in the event. Various denominations with different political stances played parts in the meetings of this period and pastors from the Presbyterian Church in the Republic Korea (PROK), which is said to be the most liberal and progressive denomination in Korea, also took roles to preach, lead prayers, or give benedictions.[4] Rev. Jaejun Kim, who was one of the founders of PROK and a democratic activist (Christian Institute for the Study of Justice and Development 1983, p. 10), delivered the benediction at the Prayer Breakfast in 1968, which was the first meeting that President Park attended. Ilhyeong Jeong, chairman of the preparatory committee of the Prayer Breakfast from 1968 to 1972, was a National Assembly member of the opposition party. He was very critical of Park's dictatorship and finally lost his seat in 1976 due to his open opposition to the October Restoration regime (Chun 2014, pp. 37–38). By hosting the National Prayer Breakfast, the prophetic objective to make the country better and more righteous in God's sight was a crucial part of their motivation.

3. National Prayer Breakfast Organizers' Prophetic Consciousness

The early organizers of the National Prayer Breakfast exhorted the rulers including the presidents to repent of their wrongdoings and to cultivate moral virtues, such as humility, mercy and integrity. They also suggested a concrete future vision for Korea, namely, making it a democratic nation on the basis of the spirit of Protestantism. In a situation where the country should overcome political turmoil, economic backwardness, and moral laxity, the pastors tried to give sermons and prayers, which were motivated by their religious aspiration for the country. Their prophetic sense of vocation for leading Korea in crisis to the right way is confirmed in their messages carried in Prayer Breakfast meetings. We should not neglect their genuine religious motivation though some of them may have wanted to expand influence and numbers of the Protestant church by supporting the military governments and winning their favor.

The focus of most sermons was on the restoration of general morality, which they thought was necessary to make Korea a just and orderly country. The Protestant leaders during the period of the military dictatorship thought that not only the general public but also those in power should repent and be changed. They pointed out that a person of higher social standing should have greater moral responsibility. Joongon Kim called on the participants of the meeting to resolve on a moral revolution because "the moral resolution of a person in the position of leading ten thousand people will influence ten thousand and that of a person leading ten million people will influence ten million" (Kim 2005a). While messages for the general public were spread in the church or massive revival rallies, exhortations for those in power to be morally awakened were given in the National Prayer Breakfast. It was in this context that the preachers blessed the presidents by quoting biblical figures. Though they mentioned very often Israelite leaders from the Old Testament such as Moses, Joshua, David, and Solomon, they neither used expressions of flattering Park and Chun nor identified the dictators with these great persons. Pastors did not say that the presidents were like heroes in the Bible, but they encouraged the presidents to become like the heroes who had the virtues of gentleness, integrity, faith, wisdom, and humility (Kim 2005a).

The main message of Han's sermon preached at the "Prayer Breakfast for the Future of the Country and the Nation" in August 1980, which was mentioned in the first section, was that the rulers should enact justice, love kindness, and act humbly. Though Han might seem to have accepted Chun's dictatorship for the simple reason that he hosted the meeting, he emphasized the importance of Christian virtues such as mercy, justice, kindness, and humility. This sermon, which was based on Micah 6:6–8, ended with Han's exhortation that Chun and other members of the National Security Emergency Measure Committee should be blessed by having these virtues (Han 2009). It is true that Han blessed Chun when he prayed. But he never stated that Chun was the legitimate leader of the country in his sermon unlike some scholars' critiques (Kim 2007, p. 75; Kim 2011, p. 84).

---

4   These different political stances of the participants in prayer breakfast meetings are not found during the period of President Myungbak Lee (2008–2013) and President Geunhye Park (2013–2017), who were supported by a few conservative Protestant pastors on their presidential election campaigns. Some criticize that a few influential Protestant leaders maintained and showed off a cozy relationship with the presidents by hosting the National Prayer Breakfast while the presidents tried to bring around the Korean Protestant circle through the meetings (*The Christian Newspaper*, 12 February 2018).

The early organizers also often argued that the whole country should fight against corruption. In the sermon delivered at the meeting held in 1970, Joongon Kim seemingly credited the coup in 1961, which was carried out by Park, saying that he had been deeply moved to see corruption lessen in Korea after the coup (Kim 2006). However, he was actually stressing an urgent need of eradicating corruption rather than supporting the coup itself. The next part of the sermon clearly shows that his focus was on anti-corruption. He quotes the dying words of Dr. Frank W. Schofield, a widely respected missionary in Korea, who came from Canada and died a month before the meeting. "From his death-bed he [Schofield] said that the only hope for Korea is to rid herself of injustice, corruption and divisions. This is a painful rebuke for us" (Kim 2005a). Then he asserted that the government, the political leaders, and the whole nation must repent to God for the prevailing social evils. He went further and said,

> This dishonesty is a deadly disease for our nation. We cannot continue to live like this. Something needs to be done urgently. Of course, these things don't just happen overnight. They are the accumulation of a long history of social evils. Because of these shameful practices which have divided our country we have often been subject to foreign powers. Let us not forget the days spent under Japanese and Communist domination. We had no freedom and no security for life or property. We must not bequeath these evils to our children. (Kim 2006 [originally from the sermon in 1970], pp. 99–100)

In this part, we can see that his focus was not on the legitimation of Park's regime but on the reprimand for corruption and immorality of Korea. In other words, Kim was pointing out that the coup failed to change the moral integrity of Korea though the military ostensibly sought to it.

In the 1978 meeting, Sinmyeong Kang preached that Christians be spiritual and moral guides of the nation. He emphasized the responsibility of Christians for eradicating social illegality, corruption, and irregularities. Relating the story of the Prophet Ezekiel, he preached as follows:

> It was the responsibility of prophets who were called as the watchmen of the Israelite people to receive the words of God, with which they treated both the good and the evil in place of God. They exhorted the evil to listen to the words of God, to turn from the evil way, to come back to God and be saved, and to get life. They also forewarned the good and righteous to listen to the words of God, to keep living the good and righteous lives, and to be careful not to betray the words of God in spite of temptations and seductions. (…) We Korean Christians are also the watchmen of this nation. We should accomplish our mission as watchmen in every area in which we are involved. We should encourage righteousness while we reprimand and warn of sins and injustice to set the sinners on the right track. (Kang 1987 [originally from the sermon in 1978], vol. 1, pp. 169–79)

In this sermon, Kang articulated that Protestant Christians should have the prophetic mission, just like the Israelite prophets, to be watchmen of the nation. He also said that Christians should play the role of "the conscience and spiritual anchor of the nation." By this message, he encouraged Christian politicians to take the responsibility of prophets. At once, he was urging non-Christian rulers to turn from injustice and sins and to make every effort to conduct their offices in a good and righteous way.

There were other pastors who preached at the Prayer Breakfast that it was right in God's sight to obey God rather than those in power. At the Prayer Breakfast meeting held in 1977, Rev. Jingyeong Cheong said, "We should stand in awe of the unseen God who looks deep into us and sees the other side of history in depth. Fear God, not visible power" (Han 2004, p. 30). He made it clear that obeying God's will should not be equated with obeying those in power. In 1981, Rev. Seonhui Gwak urged the rulers to become wise persons which would be possible when they were willing to hear the voice of people, that of conscience, and that of God (Han 2004, p. 30). We can see that Protestant leaders gave the presidents and their associates in power the message that they also should fear God and that they should not delude themselves by thinking of their power as absolute.

Morality was the most important standard of judgement even when the Protestant leaders raised their voices outside the church or prayer meetings against a government policy. For instance, in July 1965, 215 Protestant leaders announced the statement of opposing the conclusion of the Treaty on Basic Relations between the Republic of Korea and Japan, which was signed one month before. The rally against the treaty was held in the Youngnak Presbyterian Church, of which senior pastor was Han (Kim 2005b, pp. 69, 107; Chang 2006, pp. 112–13). The statement, signed by several influential Protestant leaders including Han, Kang, and Jaejun Kim, first emphasizes a general morality, followed by leveling strong objections to the offering of humiliating diplomatic relations.

> We Christians protest all forms of dictatorship, all injustice, illegality, and corruption. We denounce subordination or servility to foul and low foreign powers in economics, culture, morality, politics and any other area. And we promise to contribute to the construction of the history of our nation by following the lead of the Holy Spirit, prayer, and services. (Kim 2009, 315–16)

As we have seen, Protestant leaders consistently suggested a kind of moral crusade. Protestant leaders thought that moral virtues included in the gospel could be useful in overcoming conflicts and confrontations between political ideologies. By proclaiming this message to those in power at the Korea National Prayer Breakfast, the pastors exhorted them to repent of their wrongdoings and to cultivate their character. It would be impossible for them to admonish and reprimand the rulers without their senses of prophetic mission, considering the military government became suspicious of anyone who made minor criticism and often regarded them as dissidents or even communists. Their efforts have not been fully appreciated for the reason that they did not develop a protest movement against the military. But it cannot be denied that they tried to set the stage for facing the military regimes, pointing out their problems, and suggesting the direction the country should follow.

It is true that the Protestant leaders sometimes proclaimed the utmost importance of Christianity, especially Protestantism, and tried to evangelize those in power including the presidents. However, their point in talking about the significance of Protestantism at the Prayer Breakfast meetings was that it was needed for completing the moral crusade and making the country anew. As mentioned above, they did not just attempt to propagate Protestantism by building good relationships with the government, considering that they often said offensive words to the dictators and had some opponents of the government play roles in the meetings. Rather, they were proclaiming what they believed was necessary for the country on the basis of their faith and theology. They believed that only God's Justice and love could make Korea become a rich, strong, secure, democratic, and culturally developed country, in which all people would enjoy liberty and equality. Then, according to Kang, Korea would become "the kingdom of God established on the earth," a righteous and moral country based on the Protestant faith (Kang 1961, p. 37; Kim 2009, pp. 282–83). At the meeting held in 1969, Joongon Kim preached as following.

> Our task for today is threefold: modernization, democratization, and national prosperity. In order to achieve these goals we must have the spirit of the New Frontier, courage, and power for living. In order to better our country, we must look to every possible source. (...) Especially for now, we should redevelop the vitality of faith. (...) Protestant faith is the never-failing source of vital energy that is necessary for the political, economic, and spiritual revival. (Kim 2006 [originally from the sermon in 1969], p. 72)

Kim and other early organizers believed that the economic development and the establishment of democracy would be impossible in Korea without the Protestant faith. According to them, a great many Koreans should become Protestants if Korea would become powerful and prosperous like the advanced countries of the West. In the sermon preached at the meeting in 1971, Han argued that a thorough understanding of the fundamental ideals of democracy, the moral dignity of people, respect for law and order were basic elements of a democratic country and asserted that all these elements originated from Protestantism. It was the Protestant faith, he also said, that supported law, education, liberty, and morality, all of which were necessities for a democratic country (Han 2009). Then, he encouraged Park and other participants to become Christians.

> Honorable Mr. President Park and all the participants here who have not had faith yet. Please receive the Lord now, in order to save your souls that are more valuable than earth and heaven, and to establish our homeland that you love more than your lives on an eternal spiritual foundation. (Han 2009 [originally from the sermon in 1971], vol. 12, p. 380)

Han was arguing that Christianity was needed not only for personal salvation but also for nation building. The basis on which he urged the non-Christian dictator president to have Christian faith was also the belief that it could help establish the country firmly. Though Han and other Protestant leaders tried to evangelize the rulers by delivering sermons to them at the Prayer Breakfast, they often said words offensive to the military regimes and even invited to the pulpit Jaejun Kim and Ilhyeong Jung who were outspokenly critical of the government.

4. Conclusions: John the Baptist Facing Herod Antipas

In this article, we have illuminated prophetic missions of Korean Protestant leaders through examining the Korea National Prayer Breakfast held during the period of military dictatorship. It was not our purpose to deny that political calculations were a factor also. We have emphasized that Protestant leaders' religious aspiration also should be considered. They ventured into the corridors of power and urged the rulers to become leaders of a righteous and just country by having higher moral standards and Christian faith. The first organizers of the meeting tried to help restore the morality of those in power in order to make the country just and clean-handed. They believed that they could influence the country to become prosperous, strong, and just by making the rulers have Christian faith. They exhorted the presidents and their associates to change for the purpose of having Korea become like "the kingdom of God," a country in which the love and justice of God reigned.

It is true that the prophetic consciousness of the Protestant leaders was obviously related to their ideal of evangelizing the country. This is one of the important characteristics of Korean Protestantism that is not seen in Western cultures where Christianity has been so prevalent. Be reminded that Protestantism has been one of three major religions of Korea and that its adherents constituted less than 10 percent of the population. However, it is also clear that the leaders aimed at changing their poor, unjust, and underdeveloped homeland into a better country. The prophetic mission of the Protestant leaders during the period of the military dictatorship was shouting for the country to become righteous and just in God's sight. This sense of mission was revealed in the Korea National Prayer Breakfast in which they proclaimed that Korea should become a prosperous and also democratic country where all people would enjoy liberty and equality. They sometimes urged all the participants, including the presidents, to become Christians. But it was because they believed that Christian countries of the West were the model for Korea to copy and so Christianity was necessary for Korea to become an advanced democratic country. Their aspiration to build the kingdom of God on earth was an important motivation for their organizing and hosting the Korea National Prayer Breakfast.

Jaejun Kim said that Protestants had the mission of prophets who should proclaim the righteousness of God in this world with strong historical awareness. According to him, Protestants, just like prophets, should not hesitate to speak forthrightly to politicians and rulers.

> To see the historical situation is to face up to and criticize the present in terms of God's will. That is a warning. Then [the prophet] should prophesy the future under the present situation. It is a proclamation of the judgment that the country would collapse unless it turns from its sins of the present. (Kim 1973, p. 63)

In the Bible, we can find many models of this notion of the prophet Kim suggested, such as Elijah who chided the evil ways of King Ahab, Amos who sharply criticized the social corruption and religious laxity in Judah, and John the Baptist who squarely rebuked the wrongdoings of Herod Antipas the tetrarch. Like them, Korean Protestant leaders warned of moral laxity and corruption of the rulers and boldly exhorted them to have Christian faith to establish Korea as a country which was founded on the justice and love of God. Though many scholars have criticized that the Protestant leaders played the role of the compliant chief priests and scribes serving Herod the Great, they actually tried to play the role of John the Baptist rebuking Herod Antipas.

Author Contributions: Writing-original draft: Y.Y., M.K. Investigation: M.K. Supervision and writing-review & editing: Y.Y.

Conflicts of Interest: The authors declare no conflict of interest.

Appendix A

Table A1. Persons who took on roles at the Korea National Prayer Breakfast, 1968–1987. (Choi 2002, pp. 51–52; Kim 2009, pp. 327–38; Yoon 2016, pp. 53–54).

	8 March 1966	1 May 1968	1 May 1969	1 May 1970	1 May 1971
Moderator		Insik Yun (N.A.M.)	Insik Yun (N.A.M.)	Samsang Kim (N.A.M.)	Joongon Kim (Pastor)
Opening Address	Hyeonsuk Park (N.A.M.)	Ilhyeong Jeong (N.A.M.)	Ilhyeong Jeong (N.A.M.)	Ilhyeong Jeong (N.A.M.)	Hyeonsuk Park (N.A.M.)
Opening Prayer		Seokgyu Kim (Pastor)	Daeseon Park (Yonsei U.P.)	Kyungchik Han (Pastor)	Changdeok Yun (Pastor)
Scripture Reading (O.T.)	Youngsam Kim (N.A.M.)	Hyeonsuk Park (N.A.M.)	Ginam Noh (Bishop)	Suhwan Kim (Cardinal)	Jongpil Kim (N.A.M.)
Scripture Reading (N.T.)	Jongpil Kim (N.A.M.)	Yeong-gwan Kim (Admiral)	Gyewon Kim (General)	Myeongsin Chae (Lieutenant General)	Insik Yun (N.A.M.)
Prayer for President	Hwal-lan Kim (Doctor)	Li-in Baek (Professor)	Okgil Kim (Ewha Womans U.P.)	Haeyeong Lee (Pastor)	Sangdeok Song (Pastor)
Sermon	Joongon Kim (Pastor)	Hwansin Lee (Pastor)	Joongon Kim (Pastor)	Joongon Kim (Pastor)	Kyungchik Han (Pastor)
Benediction		Jaejun Kim (Pastor)	Sinmyeong Kang (Pastor)	Hyeonseol Hong (Pastor)	Hyeongyong Park (Pastor)
Venue	Chosun Hotel	Walkerhill Hotel	Sejong Hotel	Chosun Hotel	Tower Hotel
President's Attendance	No	Yes	Yes	Yes	Yes
President			Chunghee Park		
	1 May 1972	1 May 1973	1 May 1974	1 May 1976	1 May 1977
Moderator	Insik Yun (N.A.M.)	Insik Yun (N.A.M.)	Insik Yun (N.A.M.)	Namjung Yun (Pastor)	Beomjun Lee (N.A.M.)
Opening Address	Ilhyeong Jeong (N.A.M.)	Hyeonsuk Park (N.A.M.)	Hyeonsuk Park (N.A.M.)	Insik Yun (N.A.M.)	Insik Yun (N.A.M.)
Opening Prayer	Hyeonsuk Park (N.A.M.)	Giseon Jo (Pastor)	Hwang-gyeong Ko (Doctor)	Indeuk Kim (Elder)	Jojun Park (Pastor)
Scripture Reading (O.T.)	Shin Kim (Minister)	Junhwan Jang (N.A.M.)	Ilhyeong Jeong (N.A.M.)	Dohwan Shin (N.A.M.)	Yundeok Kim (N.A.M.)

Table A1. *Cont.*

Scripture Reading (N.T.)	Jongpil Kim (N.A.M.)	Byeonghwa Kim (Prosecutor)		Huigyeong Jeong (Educator)	Yeongtae Shin
Prayer for President	Joongon Kim (Pastor)	Sinmyeong Kang (Pastor)	Kyungchik Han (Pastor)	Changwon Park (Elder)	Gyeong-gyu Jang (Pastor)
Sermon	Daeseon Park (Yonsei U.P.)	Joongon Kim (Pastor)	Sang-geun Kim (Pastor)	Sang-geun Yu (Elder)	Jin-gyeong Cheong (Pastor)
Benediction	Jinhyeon Noh (Pastor)	Myeongsun Bae (Pastor)	Gyu-o Jeong (Pastor)	Sinmyeong Kang (Pastor)	Yunseon Park (Pastor)
Venue	Chosun Hotel	Chosun Hotel	Chosun Hotel	Chosun Hotel	Chosun Hotel
President's Attendance	No (The First Lady)	Yes	Yes	Yes	No (Prime Minister)
President			Chunghee Park		
	1 May 1978	**1 May 1979**	**1 May 1980**	**8 August 1980**	**14 May 1981**
Moderator	Beomjun Lee (N.A.M.)	Uryang Byeon (N.A.M.)	Byeonghak Jeong (Pastor)	Manpil Moon (Pastor)	Taeseop Lee (N.A.M.)
Opening Address	Insik Yun (N.A.M.)	Insik Yun (N.A.M.)	Insik Yun (N.A.M.)		Hojun Yu (Pastor)
Opening Prayer	Ikjun Kim (N.A.M.)	Dongjin Choi (Pastor)	Wonsang Ji (Pastor)	Hyangrok Jo (Pastor), Jigil Kim (Pastor), Indeuk Kim (Elder)	Yeongsu Lee (Pastor)
Scripture Reading (O.T.)	Je-eon Ryu (Minister)	Yundeok Kim (N.A.M.)	Bongho Kim (N.A.M.)		Seokho Nah (N.A.M.)
Scripture Reading (N.T.)	Sangnyeon Kim (N.A.M.)	Sangnyeon Kim (N.A.M.)	Hongseok Oh (N.A.M.)		Hongseok Oh (N.A.M.)
Prayer for President	Seong-eun Kim (Minister)	Seok-yong Oh (Pastor)	Gwanseon Kim (Chief of Chaplains)	Jin-gyeong Cheong (Pastor)	Bongseong Lee (Pastor)
Sermon	Sinmyeong Kang (Pastor)	Haedeuk Kim (S.A.C.)	Giwon Han (Pastor)	Kyungchik Han (Pastor)	Seonhui Gwak (Pastor)
Benediction	Huibo Kim (Pastor)	Myeongwon Park (Pastor)	Chang-in Kim (Pastor)	Seongchil Jang (Pastor)	Ju-o Kim (Pastor)
Venue	Chosun Hotel	Chosun Hotel	Silla Hotel	Lotte Hotel	Silla Hotel
President's Attendance	No (Chairman of the N.A.)	No (Prime Minister)	No (Prime Minister)	No (Doohwan Chun Chairman of N.S.E.M.C.)	Yes
President		Chunghee Park		Kyuhah Choi	Doohwan Chun
	4 May 1982	**3 May 1983**	**29 May 1984**	**1 May 1985**	**14 May 1986**
Moderator	Jeongsu Park (N.A.M.)	Hyeonja Kim (N.A.M.)	Gyeongsuk Lee (N.A.M.)	Se-eung Oh (N.A.M.)	Okseon Kim (N.A.M.)
Opening Address	Jin-u Lee (N.A.M.)	Jin-u Lee (N.A.M.)	Jin-u Lee (N.A.M.)	Seokho Nah (N.A.M.)	Seokho Nah (N.A.M.)
Opening Prayer	Gyeongrae Kim (Elder)	Hanbin Lee (Former Minister)	Jungwan Eun (Pastor)	Yeongsi Hwang (Comptroller General)	Sejik Park (Minister)

Table A1. *Cont.*

Scripture Reading (O.T.)	Byeonghyeon Ko (N.A.M.)	Jaeho Kim (N.A.M.)	Taesu Kim (N.A.M.)	Nakdo Choi (N.A.M.)	Seongsik Kim (N.A.M.)
Scripture Reading (N.T.)	Byeongbong Jo (N.A.M.)	Seongpyo Hong (N.A.M.)	Ujun Hong (N.A.M.)	Yeongjeong Kim (N.A.M.)	Yangsun Han (N.A.M.)
Prayer for President	Daesun Lee (N.A.M.)	Chang-gi Yu (Chief of Chaplains)	Sichae Jeong (N.A.M.)	Jungseo Kim (Supreme Court Justice)	Taeseop Choi (Elder)
Sermon	Ok Im (Pastor)	Hyangrok Jo (Pastor)	Hun Choi (Pastor)	Janghwan Kim (Pastor)	Jongseong Lee (Pastor)
Benediction	Seongwon Choi (Pastor)	Yonghwan Choi (Pastor)	Kyungchik Han (Pastor)	Changwon Choi (Chief of Chaplains)	Jigil Kim (Pastor)
Venue	Silla Hotel	Silla Hotel	Silla Hotel	Hyatt Regency	Silla Hotel
President's Attendance	No	No	No	No	No
President	Doohwan Chun				

	1 May 1987
Moderator	Daesun Lee (Minister)
Opening Address	Seokho Nah (N.A.M.)
Opening Prayer	Gitae Kim (Chief of Chaplains)
Scripture Reading (O.T.)	Cheolgyun Shin (N.A.M.)
Scripture Reading (N.T.)	Hyeong-gwang Kim (N.A.M.)
Prayer for President	Sang-geun Yu (Elder)
Sermon	Kyungchik Han (Pastor)
Benediction	Jungseop An (Pastor)
Venue	63 Building
President's Attendance	No
President	Doohwan Chun

Abbreviations: N.A. (National Assembly); N.A.M. (National Assembly Member); N.S.E.M.C. (National Security Emergency Measure Committee); N.T. (New Testament); O.T. (Old Testament); S.A.C. (Salvation Army Commander); U.P. (University President).

References

Berger, Peter. 1967. *The Sacred Canopy: Elements of a Sociological Theory of Religion.* New York: Anchor Books, ISBN 0385073054.

Billy Graham Evangelistic Association. 2018. Seoul, South Korea: A Look Back at Billy Graham's Largest Ever Crusade. *Billy Graham Evangelistic Association.* Available online: https://billygraham.org/story/seoul-south-korea-a-look-back-at-billy-grahams-largest-ever-crusade/ (accessed on 26 July 2018).

Chang, Kyushik. 2006. Church and State during the Military Regime: Alliance of Church and State and the Overcoming of the Past. *Christianity and History in Korea* 24: 103–37.

Choi, Taekjin. 2002. The Study of Korean Reformed Church's Political Ideology and Conservatism. Master's thesis, Sogang University, Seoul, Korea. Available online: http://www.riss.kr.libproxy.snu.ac.kr/link?id=T9163330 (accessed on 30 April 2018).

Chun, Myungsoo. 2014. A Study on Political Participation in Religion: A Critical Approach to Correlation of Religion and Political Development in Korea. *Discourse 201* 17/3: 31/56. Available online: http://www.riss. kr.libproxy.snu.ac.kr/link?id=A100096150 (accessed on 1 May 2018).

Christian Institute for the Study of Justice and Development. 1983. *1970Nyeondae Minjuhwa Undong-gwa Gidokgyo (Democratization Movement and Christianity in 1970s)*. Seoul: Christian Institute for the Study of Justice and Development.

Greeley, Andrew. 1995. The Persistence of Religion. *Cross Currents* 45/1: 24–41. Available online: http:// onlinelibrary.wiley.com.libproxy.snu.ac.kr/journal/10.1111/(ISSN)1939-3881 (accessed on 2 May 2018).

Han, Gyumu. 2004. Gukgajochangidohoe, Mueoseul Namgyeotneonga? (What Did the Korea National Prayer Breakfast Leave?). *Christianity Thought* 541: 26–35.

Han, Kyungchik. 2009. *Han Kyungchik Moksa Seolgyojeonjip (The Complete Collection of Rev. Kyungchik Han's Sermons)*. Seoul: The Rev. Kyungchik Han Memorial Foundation, vol. 1–18, ISBN 978-89-96790-0-2.

Kang, Sinmyeong. 1960. Naui Jeung-in (My Witnesses). *Christianity Thought* 30: 42–43. Available online: http://www.dbpia.co.kr/Journal/ArticleDetail/NODE00000570 (accessed on 13 August 2018).

Kang, Sinmyeong. 1961. Apeuro Simnyeonganui Naui Gyehoek (My Plans for Ten Years from Now). *Christianity Thought* 41: 34–37. Available online: http://www.dbpia.co.kr/Issue/VOIS00001281 (accessed on 9 August 2018).

Kang, Sinmyeong. 1987. *Kang, Sinmyeong Sinangjeojakjip (The Collected Works of Rev. Sinmyeong Kang)*. Seoul: Gidokyomunsa, vol. 1–2.

Kim, Jaejun. 1973. Hanguk Gyohoeui Ye-eonjajeok Samyeong: Ye-eonja uisigeul Jungsimeuro (The Prophetic Mission of Korean Churches: Focusing on the Prophetic Consciousness). *Christianity Thought* 178: 62–70. Available online: http://www.dbpia.co.kr.libproxy.snu.ac.kr/Journal/ArticleDetail/ NODE00142411 (accessed on 25 May 2018).

Kim, Joongon. 2005a. *C.C.C.wa Minjokbogeumhwa Undong (C.C.C. and National Evangelization Movement)*. Seoul: Sun, ISBN 89-389-0164-5.

Kim, Kiseon. 2005b. *Hanilhoedam Bandaeundong (The Movement against the Korean-Japanese Conference)*. Seoul: Korea Democracy Foundation, ISBN 89-91057-15-2 44910.

Kim, Joongon. 2006. *Dr. Kim's Messages at the National Breakfast Prayer Meeting*. Seoul: Sun Publication, ISBN 8938901963 03230.

Kim, Jibang. 2007. *Poli-Church*. Seoul: Gyoyangin, ISBN 9788991799288.

Kim, Myeonggu. 2009. *Kang, Sinmyeong Moksa: Gyohoewa Minjogeul Wihan Han Arui Mirari Doe-eo (Rev. Sinmyeong Kang: Being a Kernel of Wheat for the Korean Churches and People)*. Gwangju: Seoul Jangsin University Publication, ISBN 9788996236807 03230.

Kim, Yohan. 2011. Hanguk Gaesingyo Bosugyoheoui Jeongchijeok Hangtae-e Deahan Bipanjeok Gochal: Constantinianism-waui Gwalryeounseong-eul Jungsimeuro (The Critical Research on Political Attitude and Behavior of the Conservative Protestant Churches in Korea: Focusing on Relevance to Constantinianism). Master's thesis, Yonsei University, Seoul, Korea. Available online: http://www.riss.kr.libproxy.snu.ac.kr/ link?id=T12578943 (accessed on 30 April 2018).

Kim, Seonpil. 2016. A Study on the Formation and Transformation of Structure of Domination in Korean Catholic Church: Sociological Review for the Renewal of Korean Church. Ph.D. thesis, Jeju National University, Jeju, Korea. Available online: http://www.riss.kr/link?id=T14037575 (accessed on 25 July 2018).

Korea Research Institute for Religion and Society. 1993. *The Yearbook of Korean Religions*. Seoul: Korea Halimwon, vol. 1, ISBN 8985448013.

Kown, Hyeokryul. 2015. Nugureul Wihan Gukgajochangidoheo-inga? (For Whom is Korea National Prayer Breakfast?). *Christian Thought* 674: 192–97.

Lee, Suin. 2004. Political actions of Protestant Conservatives: A Sociological Study. *Economy and Society* 64: 265–99.

The National Council of Churches in Korea. 1974. Gong-gaegeonui Seohan (An Open Recommendation to the Government). In *Gidokgyo Yeongam (The Yearbook of Korean Protestantism)*. Seoul: The National Council of Churches in Korea.

Sheppard, Gerald T., and William E. Herbrechtsmeier. 1987. Prophecy. In *The Encyclopedia of Religion*, 2nd ed. Edited by Lindsay Jones. Detroit: Macmillan Reference USA, vol. 11, pp. 7423–29. ISBN 0-02-865980-5.

Shin, Gwangcheol. 1998. *Cheonjugyowa Gaesingyo: Mannamgwa Galdeung-ui Yeoksa (Catholicism and Protestantism: A History of Encounters and Conflicts)*. Seoul: The Institute of the History of Christianity in Korea, ISBN 8985628143.

Yoon, Kyungro. 2016. Seventy Years after National Division: Cases and Nature of Korean Christianity's Adhesion to Power. *Christianity and History in Korea* 44: 27–65. Available online: http://www.riss.kr.libproxy.snu.ac. kr/link?id=A101826409 (accessed on 30 April 2018).

Article

A Critical Evaluation of Religious Education in Korea

Chae Young Kim

Department of Religious Studies, Sogang University, Seoul 04107, Korea; chaekim@sogang.ac.kr;
Tel.: +82-2-705-8361

Received: 29 September 2018; Accepted: 15 November 2018; Published: 18 November 2018

Abstract: This essay will discuss the general orientation of Korean religious education and some of the problematic issues that are related to its position within the current Korean educational systems. It will focus especially on four critical aspects pertaining to religious education as found today in the Republic of Korea (we will not consider the situation of religious education in North Korea because it is so difficult to get accurate information). The first section will begin to identify the contemporary 'communicational dilemma' of religious education in Korea and its roots in the lack of a proper understanding of religious education from a non-confessional academic perspective. The second section will place the problem in the context of Korean religious demography as it pertains to the necessity of religious education and the conventional image of religious education within schools. The third section will enumerate a number of critical issues and analyze their impact on the direction of religious education policy since the establishment of the government's equalization educational policy in 1969. The fourth section will critically examine a number of constitutional issues as they bear on the question of where compulsion exists in current religious education.

Keywords: religious education; equalization policy; confessional perspective; non-confessional perspective; religion and state; religion and constitution; religion and human rights; teaching rights of religion

1. The Communicational Dilemma of Korean Religious Education

In Korea, full-fledged modern religious education (RE) programs, as we find these in Europe and North America, have yet to be fully developed, despite the fact that Koreans have been teaching about religions in schools for quite a long time. The problem is rooted in a misunderstanding of the concept of religious education in Korean society, which can be seen in how institutional changes have been mandated by the Korean government since 1969, with the implementation of a policy that has been known as the equalization education policy of 1969.

Initially, the concept and application of RE began in mission schools as well as other schools that have a religious foundation. Because of the misunderstanding of the term 'religious education' and its popular understanding that is linked with mission or religiously oriented schools, Korean public schools have not willingly initiated RE curriculum. Many stakeholders in schools and also many scholars in the pedagogical field have confused the present orientation of current RE with a "membership" kind of education that belongs to the mission or the beliefs of a particular religion. This confessional model of RE continues to be apparent not only in Buddhist and Christian mission schools but also in some schools that belong to New Religious Movements. In each case, the format or mode of implementation has been framed to strengthen and to communicate the beliefs and practices of a particular religious identity. This interpretation of RE is problematic and it betrays the fundamental value of religious freedom in the Korean constitution. For people in general, it suggests a biased image with respect to RE. Moreover, this image has served to simplify and to reduce the complex dynamic meaning that is found in the Korean constitution as it touches on the separation of religion and state. The situation of a flight from a proper, non-confessional understanding of RE has been misused by various political interest groups to propagate themselves or criticize rival groups with different religious/non-religious backgrounds.

Currently, most Korean RE can be categorized as fitting into either of these two situations—"to teach to understand and to teach to be religious in a particular way" (Hazra 2009, p. 143; Jackson 1997; Kim 2016, pp. 1–15; Park 2002, pp. 57–58). The more that RE is turned into an issue in public schools, the more that most of the religiously founded schools try to defend the merits of their own "religious" framework, seeking to strengthen it. On the other hand, public schools try to avoid an exploration of the concept. Today, this unwillingness of investigation, and, especially, of communication is to be regarded as the chief obstacle that works against the development of RE in all schools. If there is to be a breakthrough in a way that does not ignore the Korean government's educational policy on RE, it would seem that the best, perhaps only viable alternative would be to seek a policy based on a proper understanding of the term, "religious education" in which the diversity and value of religion as a global phenomenon can be can be explored and promoted.

In particular, this essay embraces the vision of Ninian Smart (1927–2001) that was developed through his work and his engagement with the practice of RE in the UK (Smart 1968, pp. 1–12), a development that can be traced back to the psychology of religion movement (Jordan 1986, pp. 287–88) that was initiated earlier by William James (1842–1910) and his former student, Granville Stanley Hall (1844–1924). According to Smart, a proper RE in general should fulfill both functions: to provide students with understanding about their own traditions and/or the dominant religions that play an important role in the construction and identification of their culture and community; and also to equip them with the knowledge of religion and other religions; both should be carried out free from assumption and in a comparative manner (Smart 1968, p. 106; Smart and Horder 1975, pp. 7–10; Smart and Wiebe 1986, pp. 227–29). This model is very meaningful for the development of Korean RE and it needs to be implemented creatively within the pluralistic context of religions in Korea. It requires the Korean educational system and educators to move beyond a confessional practice of RE to communicate and collaborate with one another.

With that in mind, this essay will then attempt to contextualize this goal in relation to the specific problematic issues regarding RE in the contemporary Korean educational system. The next section will deal with the situation of Korean religious demography as it pertains to the necessity of RE and the conventional image of RE within the schools. The third section will try to list and speak about a number of critical issues and the kind of impact that they have on the direction of RE policy since the establishment of the government's equalization educational policy in 1969. The fourth section will critically examine a number of constitutional issues as they relate to the question of where compulsion exists in current RE. My discussion does not cover the situation of RE in North Korea because it is beyond my expertise and outside the boundaries of verifiable data.

2. Religious Demography and Religious Education Image in Korea

Officially in 2005, the Korean National Statistical Office issued the most recent population census (Korea Gallop Research Institute 2015; Choi 2011), which was the most reliable source for determining the dimensions of the Korean religious population. Unfortunately, the census does not capture the diversity of religious understandings operational within Korea. The language of the census, like the understanding of RE, is based on 'membership' within a particular religious community—not religious understanding itself. According to this census, the South Korean population stands at about forty seven millions and about twenty five million (53%) of the population practice their own religious tradition. More specifically, in the population, the biggest groups consisted of (1) the Buddhists comprising 22.8% (10,726,463 members), (2) the Protestants, 18.3% (8,616,438), (3) the Catholics 10.9% (5,146,147), and finally (4) the Confucians 0.2% (104,575). The population numbers for various New Religious Movements were not identified as clearly active members in this census. The followers of Shamanism and Confucianism were also not actively identified.

Generally we could claim, on the basis of the census, half of the Korean religious population is Buddhist and the other half, Christian (the Protestants and the Catholics being lumped together). In addition, we can see that, in the total Korean population, half of the population can be regarded as officially religious, the other half, non-religious. This point, once recognized, can easily lead one to conclude that the Korean religious situation is such that it is balanced with respect to the rate of religious and non-religious and that, within the religious population, the Buddhist and Christian population rate is also well balanced.

As a consequence of these conditions, religious voices from Buddhism and Christianity are always attentively concerned and dominate conversations with respect to what could be happening in politics, media, education, and in other public life domains. Especially during general elections, despite what could exist as personal religious preferences among politicians, most candidates try explicitly to distance themselves from an unbalanced view of religious matters. It is very rare that any of them would try to attend to the role or the place of religious minorities and listen to their voices. Public media evinces no serious concern for them either. However, when problematic situations emerge with respect to the being of religious minorities, the media engage in extensive coverage that often assumes a prosecutorial tone, as shown by their treatment of the ferry boat disaster of 2014. The disaster was related to a new religious movement: the Salvation Sect (구원파), which is a Christian sectarian group (Tak 2009, pp. 88–91; Tak 2011, pp. 52–57).

A "middling" point of view that is conditioned by the specifics of Buddhist/Christian demography is continuously maintained in order to emphasize the current balance argument, as it exists in the current Korean demographic religious situation. Certainly, externally, this seems to be quite proper with respect to how we should understand the current Korean religious demographic situation. Hence, most scholars in religious studies assume that the Korean religious demographic situation is quite unique and exceptional as a consequence of the demographic balance (Kim 2017, pp. 277–79). In addition, they argue that this highly unusual balance has played a key role in helping to avoid religious conflicts or wars within the Korean peninsula. This presumed balance is generally accepted not only within public spheres (as for instance, in political policy and the daily media), but it is also accepted within these two religious circles. This religious rivalry is found in many aspects of Korean society. It is an unfortunate consequence of the official "external" religious census that inaccurately captured the distribution and diversity of actual "internal" religious membership of the different religions that exist within Korea (Jung 2001, pp. 3–42).

However, apart from this type of external focus which has emerged as a kind of habitual response over time, another interpretation or another sense of reality can be alluded to. By shifting our focus and attention to the "being" that exists as an internal form of religious consciousness among Korean people, the meaning and the value of the religious census can then begin to appear in a different light. By moving in an inward direction and by attending to the question of religious consciousness, a space can be cleared or room can be created for another point of view that can include the ancient traditions of Shamanism and Confucianism and, from there, determine how they can function within the traditions of Buddhism and Christianity and, at the same time, also live and function in a way that can be appreciated by persons who claim to have no religious affiliation. We can perhaps move from the concept of religion as belonging to a particular faith community to a concept of religion as a particular sensibility and consciousness that transcends current language and unfortunately eludes census counters.

This issue has been discussed and argued by two creative scholars of religion. According to Yu Dong-Sik, the undercurrent within Korean religions, including Korean Christianity, is rooted in Shamanism (Ryu 1985, pp. 321–50; Ryu 1987, pp. 399–413). In contrast, but along a similar argument, Kil Hee-Sung speaks about an undercurrent that comes not from Shamanism, but from Confucianism. His claim is that the different religions, now expressed in Korea, are all formed within a Confucian framework (Kil 2015, pp. 1–24). He thinks and believes that contemporary Korean Buddhism, contemporary Korean Christianity, contemporary Shamanism, and the diverse New

Religious Movements all function within the imprint of Confucianism. For him, Confucianism is key if we are to move toward a deeper understanding of contemporary Korean religions. Although both men stress different points of departure, both agree that the population census does not reflect the true reality of Korean religions—as they really and truly exist and as they are lived today. In other words, their arguments imply that the census is not able to identify the complexity of different variables that function as hidden operators or movers within the life of Korean Buddhism and Christianity.

If we follow Yu's and Kil's perspectives, then the Korean religious demographic situation can be understood differently. To confirm their arguments in a telling fashion, a further exploration and analysis of religious consciousness, not just religious affiliation, based on empirical data, should be conducted. This is something that has not been fully tried. Most especially, a different kind of measurement process is needed in order to more accurately assess the demographic situation of Shamanism and Confucianism (unlike what we have for Buddhism and Christianity). Very few Koreans identify themselves as adherents and participants of Shamanism and Confucianism. Hence, the registered numbers in the population census are far fewer than the actual population practicing shamanism and various New Religious Movements.

Unfortunately, the Korean government's census-generated blind spot helps to cause a situation in which political calculations and decisions are made by an incomplete understanding of the Koreans' religious consciousness based primarily on the dynamic of only two traditions, Christianity and Buddhism. A broader perspective is absent: a perspective beyond what the data of the Korean religious census can offer. Perhaps, within the current academic community, questions can be raised about how informative and valuable it is to assume that half of the population is religious while the other half is non-religious.

Have we missed something qualitative? Are these assumptions the basis for a policy of avoiding issues that pertain to the question of RE in Korea's schools, private and public? In failing to rethink how RE can be conceived to exist in a new manner within the public schools, do we not perpetuate a more challenging problem than any issue which deals with the question of RE in private schools with their historical religious affiliations?

In this sense, then, it is necessary to take a look at what has been the general image of RE in Korean history. Irrespective of different population percentages in the census and any emphasis that can be given to the role of Shamanism and Confucianism for an in-depth understanding of the Korean demographic religious situation, it cannot be denied that Korean religions, within their context, have independently created means and institutions for the purpose of effecting and implementing each their own brand of RE (Seymour 2005, pp. 337–39). They have been distinctively concentrating on forming a religious clergy, and they have also engaged in the work of evangelization within their schools. As Shamanism, Buddhism, Confucianism, Christianity (Roman Catholicism and Protestantism), and also the New Religious Movements have spread throughout the Korean peninsula, they have created diverse educational institutions for these two purposes.

When compared with Christianity and New Religious Movements, the practice of RE in Shamanism, Buddhism, and Confucianism has had a long history in Korea. Especially within Buddhism, diverse educational institutions for the training of clergy and schools connected to temples have existed since the fourth century. Confucianism has also intensively focused on traditional RE in the context of *seowon* (서원) and *seodang* (서당) during the Joseon Dynasty (1392–1910) (Choi 2011), covering over 500 years since 14th century, prior to the colonization of Korea under Japanese Imperial rule that lasted for 36 years (from 1909 through to 1945). Prior to the current modernization, most of the educational framework that existed in Korea was largely based on the dominance of Confucianism within Korea. Yet, the Confucian based traditional schools were not transformed into modernized Confucian schools. Instead, they were replaced by modern public government schools. Instantly, they ceased to survive within the new ethos of the modern educational system.

Compared with the Buddhist and Confucian religious traditions and respectively their schools, the Shamans did not bequeath much in terms of educational literature for the training of clergy nor for the works of their mission, since their types of thinking and training were transmitted orally through the relations that existed between shamans and their disciples (Yoon 1999, pp. 81–96). As with Shamanism in other parts of the world, the RE of clergy candidates who were to become shamans would not be done on the basis of written documents but by means of oral instruction and training under the personal guidance of individual shamans. A few years ago, as a counter to this past tradition, the existing Shamanist association in Korea attempted to establish a modernized official department of RE for the training of their clergy and a process of accreditation for RE teachers in the context of university life, but this attempt did not succeed, leaving the Shamanists without any schools.

Although Christianity and the New Religious Movements in Korea have not had a long history in Korea as compared to what has existed for Buddhism, Confucianism, and Shamanism, they have also established their own institutions of RE. Relatively speaking, the Catholics have had a small number of official seminaries; the Protestants, many denominational seminaries (Seymour 2005, pp. 337–39). They have also many elementary-secondary schools that have been founded according to their varying mission statements and have introduced RE course within their curriculum. In the case of the New Religious Movements, some NRMs have had their own RE institutions while others have not. Some NRMs offer instruction in other places. Some Buddhist related NRMs (as, for instance, Won Buddhism) offer further training within the context of Buddhist studies, as these exist within Buddhist founded universities. Without being identified, many clergy who had belonged to the Unification Church, in the early years, were trained within liberal protestant theological seminaries. Korean NRMs have also established a few elementary-secondary schools in order to teach their form of RE within the context of the school curriculum (Kim 2017, p. 289).

Currently, the modern elementary-secondary schools that have been founded through the mission statements of various religious bodies comprise one-fifth of all schools in Korea. Among them, the percentage of the Protestant schools exists as more than 50% (Kim 2016, pp. 1–15). They number more than 250 schools. Next come the Catholic schools with almost 65 schools. The third largest belongs to the Buddhist schools with more than 22 schools. Among the schools belonging to various New Religious Movements, the Won Buddhists have 22 schools and the Eastern Learning (천도교) one school. Others, such as the Unification Church and Daesoon Thought, have also a few schools. The distinctively dominant numbers belong to the Christian elementary-secondary schools, especially here, the Protestant schools. This distinctive feature is also to be found among the numbers of kindergartens and higher educational institutes as these exist among universities, colleges, and seminaries. The highest percentage belongs to the Protestant churches and their institutes.

Even though the numbers of private schools that have been founded by religious foundations as compared to the total number of schools in Korea appears to be very high, the orientation of RE still remains within a traditional and confessional framework: it is concerned with transmitting a specific religious world view. The style of RE is to teach to be religious in a particular way according to the mission statement. At best, it only fulfills one out of the two fundamental functions of RE mentioned at the end of the previous section. No attempt is made to try and go beyond the "religious" education of a particular religious world view although, if we look at this pattern, we find that it does not seem to differ too much from a common pattern that exists across religious differences in terms of demography and the number of religious schools. However, given the large number of Christian schools, whenever problematic questions about RE emerge, criticisms appear to be more frequently directed toward these schools although the other religious schools are not exceptional in their status. They too are confronted by the same challenges.

In this sense, a non-confessional model of RE, emerged from a foundation that is based on religious studies, has yet to be solidly established. Unlike the kind of general tendency that we find among the public schools, private schools neither question nor reject fundamental assumptions about the necessity of RE. A consensus prevails across private religious schools that secularism constitutes the principal threat to religious consciousness within Korea. However, their definitions of religion remain so tightly enshrouded within the precepts of their confession that they have not been successful in inculcating a sense of what a religious consciousness might actually consist of and what it might aspire to do.

3. The Emerging New Ethos of Religious Education after the Implementation of the Equalization Educational Policy

As can be seen, in their individual histories, Korean religions have all established RE institutes for the training of their clergy and related religious schools for the education of children and youth. However, a different situation exists if we attend to the modern schools that, later, were established by newly arriving Christian missionaries. Given the influence of these new Christian mission schools, almost all modern schools that were later founded by Korean religious foundations have offered their own form of RE in an independent way within the context of offering a general curriculum. Most teachers are not officially trained as RE teachers, although they have functioned as clergy within the context of their religious institutions. Almost all teachers have been clergy despite the religious differences that have existed among the different schools as one finds these in Korea.

In the confessional type of RE which is currently provided, little thought or concern has been given to the meaning of RE within a context of religious and cultural pluralism. Students are not encouraged to reflect in a critical way on diverse religious questions and concerns in a global context. The sole focus appears to be given to a form of upbringing and nurturing that is determined by one's religious worldview. In the Christian schools and in the Buddhist dharma schools, most classes in RE are centered on the study of, respectively, the Christian and Buddhist scriptures and so do the New Religious Movement schools. The situation of the public schools is not as different as one might have expected. Although the RE classes that are offered in Korean public schools are given a special independent status within the regular curriculum, the format of this education does not differ from the traditional RE that has been given to students in Buddhist and Confucian schools, prior to the establishment of modern schools by the later Christian missionaries (Jung 2001, pp. 3–42). Both traditional and modern forms of RE do not go beyond an education within one's own religious worldview and the kind of confessional transmission that is then given and passed on to students. In other words, the format of modern RE has not changed over the years. It continues to exist as an extension of traditional RE as this has been given within Korea.

This image of RE is deeply embedded within the consciousness of contemporary Koreans. It is a parochial understanding about the nature of RE. Nourishing this parochial sense of things constitutes a major challenge to the organization of education within Korean schools today. The challenge that presents itself around the understanding of RE is the most serious of all problems that are currently facing Korean educators. A fundamental transformation of traditional RE is now urgently needed within a religiously diverse educational environment.

Policy makers and stakeholders from different backgrounds in Korean schools have been aware of the changing educational context. Increasingly aware of Korea's participation in a global world, many are willingly seeking new ways of operating within schools today. In this sense, the curriculum of RE is not to be regarded as an exception. In fact, exemptions have usually been granted (no change or interference in current practices) because of a respectful ethos that exists for the foundational principles of many schools. When compared to the kind of innovation that exists with regard to the curriculum of other subjects, RE continues to focus on the teaching of one's own particular religious worldview. This fact and focus of RE has been accepted. It is understood and practiced broadly within the organization and structure of schools in Korea.

However, this understanding and practice of RE cannot be maintained. It inhibits transdisciplinary academic inquiry concerning the understanding of religion, and it retards the growth of Korean students into global citizens. Along with this criticism of current practices of RE affecting school curriculum and style of pedagogy in the classroom, another seemingly unrelated development in government policy demands an urgent response from Korean educators and scholars of religion.

The Korean government since 1969 in Korean middle schools, and similarly since 1974 in Korean high schools initiated some major educational reforms in order to reduce the intense pressure that is experienced by students as they prepared for the competitive administration of school entrance examinations (Yoon 1999, pp. 81–96). Despite some critical problems, these educational reforms has served to reduce the fever of competition that has plagued the taking of entrance examinations for admission to schools and colleges in Korea. At the moment, things have settled down to some extent—students feel less pressure and competition. However, another set of problems and conflicts have unexpectedly arisen and they are surprisingly linked with the questions of RE. Not only are these new problems linked with the insufficient understandings and current practices of RE, they also show that the communicational dilemma concerning the term 'religious education' can only be resolved if we embrace another understanding and practice of RE in Korean schools.

When these policies were being implemented in the early stages, most religion education teachers managed their classes according to the ways that they have always known. The new situation that was emerging was not fully understood. Now, most students do not come to a school because they have chosen it, but because they are being sent to it according to their place of residence and the location of nearby schools. However, in most cases, teachers and other persons who have had a vested interest in the well-being of their schools were not equipped to effect changes in the offering of RE classes within this newly changing context.

In the pre-policy era, students lived and worked freely within a relatively homogeneous religious background as their context for maintaining a distinct religious culture at a given school. However, after the activation of new government policy, most schools have been faced with difficulties. This new situation is because students come now from diverse religious backgrounds. The Christian mission schools are being especially challenged, since Buddhist and other non-Christian religious students tend to be uncomfortable in RE classes where the goal and style of teaching is not inter-religious understanding but understanding within a particular religious framework/membership. Buddhist mission schools have been challenged in a similar way. Christian students and other non-Buddhist religious students tend to be uncomfortable participating in RE classes that are conducted by Buddhists. In the old days, most students and parents had not been troubled by such things. To some extent, they seemed to accept the spirit of foundation which had existed with respect to the being of the school of their choice. They were part of a seemingly homogeneous community grounded in a particular religious framework and common language.

Hence, today, most schools have found that they cannot implement a policy that stipulates that RE should not be taught in a regular class, but only as an extracurricular activity. In addition, they cannot abide by a policy that would forbid the use of long established resources as these are especially found in the use of sacred scriptures that belong to a given religious tradition. Forcefully, many schools began to challenge the unilateral imposition of government policy, and, eventually, their criticisms were accepted through the enactment of the 4th national curriculum standard (in 1981–1987) (Cha 2006, pp. 443–59). Two critical issues with respect to the curriculum could only be resolved at an institutional level: (1) RE is seen to exist as one of the elective regular subjects that belong to the school curricular; (2) resource materials belonging to a given religious tradition are recognized as qualified educational material, similar to the being of books that belong to other subjects that are taught within the school curriculum.

Within this situation, for the first time, the Korean Association for the History of Religions (KAHR, known as the Korean Association for Religious Studies (KARS) since 2014) became involved. The association began to address issues and themes that pertained to RE, persuasively suggesting a conceptual reorientation to schools and the Korean Ministry of Education. Especially, during the 1985 spring annual conference of the KAHR, two key scholars, Yoon Yi-hum and Jung Jin-hong, tackled a number of issues from the perspective of a religious studies viewpoint (Yoon 1986; Jung 1986). Both emphasized that RE should not be limited to the focus on religious conversion and evangelization. Instead, they suggested that the field of religious studies/education ought to seek to move toward a deeper understanding of history, humanity, culture, and cosmos. Each scholar attempted to speak about the direction and the future of RE within the context of the 4th national curriculum standard.

In the 5th national curriculum standard (1987–1992), the conceptual RE-orientation of religious education in terms of the academic study of religion was further embodied and put into effect. An institutional strategy was provided to schools in terms of (1) officially recognizing a RE text book that was to be published for each religious body and (2) requiring a licensing for RE teachers. Each school, if it wished, could use a textbook that was published by its sponsoring religious body if reviewed and approved by the Minister of Education.

At the time that this new policy began to be implemented, most of the RE teachers had only received their training (mostly clerical) from their own religious seminaries (Cusack 2017, pp. 530–31). They had not been originally trained as RE teachers by a department of religious studies nor by any department of education in university or college. They were actually clergy functioning as RE teachers within schools designed for young people. Neither had their training included exposure and learning about other religions. Hence, they were not properly trained how to teach other religions to their students and they were not in accordance with the revised guidelines outlined in the new RE curriculum. In addition, they lacked experience in using textbooks of academic study of religion. Up until that time, they had only used materials that worked with specific scriptural texts or catechisms that were designed for use in the mission field.

To address this, for the first time in 1990, an intensive course for the training and licensing of unlicensed teachers in RE was provided during the school vacation periods. Participants took subjects in religious studies and pedagogy in a program that was created by the School of Teachers College, which, in turn, belonged to Seoul National University. Through this program, 90 unlicensed teachers successfully obtained their teaching certificates in RE (Korean Ministry of Education 2001, p. 128). Every five years, since then, the Ministry of Education continues to provide the same course of studies for new participants.

Beginning in 1995, this training and licensing course of studies has been run through a collaboration between the aforementioned Teachers College and the University's Department of Religious Studies. Subjects of Religious Studies have received a greater emphasis than subjects associated with educational pedagogy and teaching. At the same time also, a number of scholars within Religious Studies have strongly urged that more support should be given to the value of RE in a manner that transcends any particular confessional concerns. The advocates of religious studies have sought to clearly distinguish between the confessional teaching for membership in a particular religious community and the value of a non-confessional perspective. This distinction is crucial in order to emphasize the latter perspective as the fitting and proper orientation of RE to be applied within Korean schools. This emphasis was then strengthened by the promulgation and implementation of the 6th national curriculum standard (1992–1997) (Kim 2016, pp. 1–15).

However, in the 7th national curriculum standard (2000–2004), the curriculum guide for RE began to come under some critical scrutiny (Jung 2001, pp. 3–42). It was questioned not only by students and their parents but also by teachers. Both groups were not satisfied with how classes in RE were being conducted. Except for those students that belonged to the same religion as that which was professed by their respective schools, many students and their parents were not happy with the style of teaching the compulsory RE. Rather than aligning with the non-confessional approach emphasized by the 6th national curriculum standard, this style of teaching RE was still concentrating only on the beliefs of a particular religion, and depending on the religious foundation of the particular school attended. Teachers and schools were also not satisfied with the new government policy. They thought that it was too intrusive. They complained about not being allowed to freely teach their own religions. They began to ask questions, in a critical way, about the foundational purposes of their schools.

Both sides could not find any solution for the proper understanding and administration of RE within the new situation of schools in the wake of the government's curriculum policy. RE teachers defended themselves on the basis of the charters of foundation that had been drawn up in the establishment of their respective schools. Publicly, some students and their parents began to complain about how RE was being conducted. They also began to protest against having RE with the help and support of their respective religious and political interest groups. This protest, from students and parents, revealed a new ethos that was emerging further demanding and encouraging revisions in how RE was to be understood, conceived, and implemented. However, these concerns and complains were not discussed in a fully public manner. Nothing was said outside of school boundaries. Eventually, after some discomfort, students and parents would withdraw their complaints out of respect for their teachers and schools, which is an inherent cultural norm in Korea.

However, in 2004, this restraint proved untenable after a student, Kang Eui-Suk, engaged in a public form of demonstration that opposed the kind of RE that was being given at his school (Kim 2008, pp. 305–22). Mr. Kang was then serving as president of the student body at his school, the Daekwang High School. The school had a Christian foundation. He rejected the RE that was given to him and because of his publicly voiced criticism, he was expelled from his school. In the train of events which followed, he launched a civil suit against his school, seeking damages. He received strong support from the Korean Institute of Religious Freedom, an NGO with a Buddhist orientation. Eventually a favorable ruling was issued in his favor from the Korean Supreme Court in 2010 (Kim 2008, pp. 305–22). This was a stunning event in the history of modern Korean education. It was a first for a student to successfully rebel against the educational authority of his school. The impact rattled against traditional assumptions and values both with regard to the nature of school RE instruction and the kind of respect that should be ascribed to the operation of schools and other possible centers of learning.

Prior to the 2010 Supreme Court ruling of Mr. Kang's case, several more civil lawsuits had been launched (Kim 2008, pp. 305–22). In 2005, Mr. Oh Byeung-Heun and in 2007, Mr. Lee Dong-Gyu launched civil lawsuits against their schools. Simultaneously, in 2007, a research professor who was based in a Christian university was dismissed because, allegedly, he had bowed to an image during his visit to a Buddhist temple. In addition, the administration of President Lee Myung-bak (2008–2013) was criticized for its alleged Christian favoritism and for the exclusion of many Buddhists from high office in the government administration. Buddhist oriented NGO groups and other groups began to denounce the Lee government policy on religious matters. They also actively supported Mr. Kang's civil suit and also the civil suit that was launched by the aforementioned professor in 2007.

Since then, thus, whenever religious issues have emerged in the public sphere, the proportional rate of balance as this pertains to Christians and Buddhists is regarded as a more important variable in the employing of officials than the alleged ability of a potential public servant in government. In addition, the Lee government was immediately forced to inaugurate and administer a new program within the Ministry of Culture, Sports, and Tourism, whose object was to prevent any discrimination on religious grounds among all Korean public servants, teachers in public schools included. The program continues to function up to the present.

In this situation, the 7th national curriculum standard revision committee of the Department of Education could not resist rethinking how RE was to be done in Korean public schools. When compared to other things, formerly, questions about the RE curriculum had not been a major concern. Much freedom had been given to individual schools. However, this was no longer possible. RE was emerging as a key question in regards to curriculum revisions (Ryu 2013, pp. 1–34). Accordingly, this committee began to invite scholars in the field of religious studies in order to involve them in the revision of guidelines governing the conduct of RE.

In 2007, the revision committee of the 7th national curriculum standard issued new revised guidelines for RE, focusing on its fundamental orientation and content (Ryu 2013, pp. 1–34). In drawing up this new policy, it can be concluded with some certainty that not all suggestions were accepted as these could have come from scholars in religious studies who belonged to this committee. At the same time, also, the concerns that came from school teachers and administrators could not be ignored or disregarded. The result thus was a decision to give more discretion to Korean public schools in conducting RE. Alternative subjects and courses were to be provided to students who did not want to receive any formal religious instruction. Students could also freely move to other schools within their residential district if they wanted to attend schools that belonged to their religion of preference. In this context, several scholars from the field of religious studies and RE spoke about the direction of RE in a manner that ranged from the "extreme" perspective of religious studies toward a more moral character type of education that might prove viable within the context of Korean public schools.

4. Unresolved Constitutional Issues in the Revised Curriculum of Religious Education

After the issue and proclamation of the 7th national curriculum standard revision in 2007, itself being shaped by the activation of a mandatory equalization educational policy, the guidelines of the curriculum revision had to be immediately applied not only to all public schools but also to almost all private schools that existed in Korea. As with the previous national curriculum standards that had been issued in earlier years, the most recent curriculum revision guidelines could not avoid two core problems for legal and constitutional reasons. In seeking for some form of educational consensus that all could possibly agree on, in the end, no such agreements could be reached. This impasse was because of the influence of a number of political considerations: issues and concerns that0 surfaced when questions about educational matters arose.

A first problem that plagues this educational policy is that the new policy takes away from the autonomy of private schools. Private schools can no longer apply their own criteria in selecting students for acceptance into their schools. Now, without having to pass any entrance examination, students are to be accepted if they reside within the local school district. Academic aptitudes and performances were no longer to be the governing criteria. As a result, legal problems have been created because most private schools do not dare to challenge the government policy, particularly if they need to receive large government subsidies in order to remain in operation. The government is in a stronger position to dictate policy with them. Most private schools find that they are required unwillingly to follow the direction of current government policy. So, as a further result of this, almost all Korean private schools have begun to look like public schools, avoiding a mission style of RE. They can no longer insist on their proper autonomy or on any increases in autonomy that they believe that they should have.

A second problem is the issue of students' and parents' rights to choose their respective schools. According to the Constitutional Court of Korea, parents have educational rights with respect to their children as a consequence of natural law (Constitutional Court of Korea 1995, 91 Hun-Ma 204). The rights of parents prevail over the rights of teachers. Yet, the government's equalization policy refrains from seriously considering this aspect. In the early period of policy implementation, many parents were not worried about their rights given the traditional respect that existed for the work and status of teachers. They accepted the teaching rights of teachers before thinking about other things with respect to the good administration of the schools that were being attended by their children. However, at the present time, this right of parents has become a dominant consideration, even if it functions in a more or less almost invisible way when there is no severe conflict between parents and government officials.

These two problems also affect the question of RE, more explicitly and directly so, than with any other curriculum subject. Three issues can be indicated. Above all, in this revision of the curriculum, the freedom of RE rights in schools is being ignored largely as a consequence of the government's mandated equalization educational policy where, legally and constitutionally, RE rights are being annulled as these touch on the founding spirits of many Korean schools. If RE classes cannot be administered in a manner that meets the requirements of a school's foundation, it would seem to be the case that about a fifth of existing schools should not continue to remain in existence. On the other hand, if this problem is approached in a manner that is a bit more realistic or more pragmatic, possibly an accommodation can be reached. As we have noted, where extreme views prevail about the need to give RE, many private schools are faced with the problem of survival if they must receive large government subsidies and also pay for the salaries of RE teachers.

Secondly, students and parents should have the right of religious freedom. But, this freedom is clashing with the current practice of RE in schools. The fundamental reason for this clash is the abolishment of the right to choose which school should be the object of one's educational choice. Fortunately, in recent times, when RE in schools becomes problematic, then one could evade this problem simply by changing schools or by taking alternative course as a substitute for RE classes.

In relation to RE, other issues have also flared up. Compulsory participation in chapel services has become an issue. How can students deal with the issue of eligibility if certain offices of the student body demands the participation? How can one cope with religious tests that require a subscription to specific doctrines? Especially, since the case of Mr. Kang, these issues have come together in a way which has created a complex legal and constitutional situation for how religion is to be handled within the context of Korean schools. Some groups who champion the freedom of students with respect to choice of religion have rejected any type of obligatory RE and religious activities. In opposition and contrast, the other group defends traditional custom and practice, emphasizing the legitimacy of religious instruction as this is drawn from the mission statements of religiously founded schools. Both groups have engaged in extensive legal and constitutional arguments. The first group tends to be supported mainly by Buddhist and other religious groups; the second group, by Christian groups.

In addition, after Mr. Kang's successful lawsuit of 2007 that had won strong support from a Buddhist oriented NGO, the newly emerging critical perspective on religious matters has been strengthening and growing in schools and beyond. No longer can the Christian schools operate freely in the conduct of their RE classes and in other religious activities. This reduces their rights to freedom in religious matters. As was mentioned above, the pro-Christian government of President Myung-baek Lee had come under criticism. The subsequent administration of President Geun-hye Park showed a marked improvement with regard to its general policy on religious matters, although there was no change with regard to the treatment of RE in Christian schools. The policy of the current Jae-in Moon administration does not noticeably differ. The current political situation is continuously pushing the Christian schools toward a kind of truncation, as this affects religious matters.

In these years, amid these controversies, Mr. Kang's case—a public lawsuit for human rights and religious freedom that was vindicated by decisions that came from the Korean Supreme Court—has been mistakenly viewed as a civil lawsuit that had been launched by him, personally seeking revenge for his expulsion from his school. In general, traditionally, it had been believed that RE and other religious activities were "taboo" subjects and this attitude cast a wide shadow, influencing public sectors, as these could be found in universities, social welfare organizations, and kindergartens—anything founded by religious organizations. However, unlike the kind of case which has existed with respect to the administration of Korean secondary schools, parental and student choice was not an issue with respect to these other organizations. Yet, during the time of the Lee administration, related issues, including the Christian use of public spaces, has given rise to lawsuits that have been supported by the same NGO that had supported Mr. Kang's successful lawsuit. This group in conjunction with other likeminded groups had been accusing the Lee government of Christian favoritism. So, in the wake of these criticisms, in order to defuse criticism and confrontation, the Ministry of Culture, Sports and Tourism has been establishing prevention programs that are directed against religious discrimination among public servants, including teachers in government funded public schools (see the Website of Ministry of Culture, Sports and Tourism for the prevention of religious discrimination). These programs continue to be in effect under the present government administration.

Currently, under the present government, the level and harshness of criticism from NGO groups that had been critical of the former government's Christian favoritism has lessened as a consequence of what appears to be a more just policy about the place of religious matters in the public sector. However, at this time, Christian groups are beginning to raise their voices against a form of Buddhist favoritism that is being shown through the granting of subsidies that are devoted to Buddhist projects of one kind or another: the renovation of historic Buddhist temples, the sponsorship of temple stay programs, and aid offered to Buddhist studies and research. At the same time, they have begun to criticize how RE is being dealt with in the 7th national curriculum standard revision. In their criticisms, their focus is not with RE *per se*, but with the illegality of the equalization educational policy. To publicize their concerns, in 2014, they organized a powerful new organization: the National Association for Christian Education (see their homepage at www.nace.or.kr).

Thirdly, the issue of school choice rights is related to the practice of assigning students to public schools. Public schools are failing to open new RE classes although they employ professional teachers who are trained in a teachers college or by a religious studies department. According to currently available statistics, no single public school is organizing new RE classes. In this situation, thus, some students would prefer to take a RE class of their own choosing within their schools, but they cannot because of the equalization educational policy that is currently in effect. Strictly speaking, in their defense, public school authorities emphasize the constitutional separation of religion and state as the key reason to explain why they should not create new RE classes.

This defense is not without a measure of merit if students go to schools according to their personal choice. But, if this is not the case, public schools should open new classes that could offer RE to all comers. However, this omission continues to exist as a kind of blind spot in current RE. The omission grows in urgency to the degree that public educators tend to ignore any form of RE that is centered on a specific religion. This attitude expresses a kind of parochial secularism that has been emerging in public schools. So, we have an issue that is especially problematic for the implementation of RE in Korea, a problem that cannot be easily resolved by referring to a constitutional article that comes to us under the present ruling of the equalization educational policy.

5. Conclusions

As is to be seen, the present situation of RE is such that it is caught between two perspectives: a confessional perspective that only focuses on teaching a particular religious world view and passing on their judgments (despite subtle differences between different traditions/schools); and, a non-confessional perspective that tries to provide a comparative understanding of religion and religions. Amid that situation also arose a type of barren and dangerous secularist response that tends to ignore RE and a school's foundational spirit all together.

With the challenges that have been emerging against the first perspective, without plan or premonition, the second has been invited to participate in the theoretical and practical development of RE in Korean schools, especially since the issue of the 4th national curriculum standard (1981–1987). More currently, the non-confessional perspective is emerging as a curriculum that transcends the parochial religious perspective (belief in one's own religion). With its foundation in religious studies, this perspective also transcends a parochial secular perspective that rejects any place for RE in the public sector. However, in the process of implementation, the non-confessional perspective does not sufficiently meet the requirements that belong to the understanding and style of RE in private religious schools. Unfortunately, the Christian schools reject the strict application of a non-confessional perspective, preferring to ignore a flexible possibility that can exist to some extent for the confessional perspective within some schools. As a consequence of Mr. Kang's successful lawsuit, the Christian schools (which comprise more than 50% of schools with a religious foundation) tend to fight for the validity and the acceptance of their perspective, and, more so than before, they voice their criticisms. They explicitly argue that the non-confessional perspective is incompatible with their perspective, because it leaves no space for the possible involvement of a confessional perspective (an unfortunate regrettable consequence that has arisen from all the legal and political criticism that has been levied against the operation of Korean schools).

Hence, to reverse this tendency in the Christian schools, the non-confessional perspective needs to be openly discussed with the Christian schools and also with other schools. Relatively

Religions **2018**, *9*, 369

speaking, the non-Christian schools seem to think that the non-confessional perspective supports their perspective against that which exists as the (Christian) confessional perspective. However, this also points to a major misunderstanding of the non-confessional perspective. In fact, the perspectives that are found in the non-Christian founded schools are not free from the same kind of problems that exist in the Christian schools. Each works with a particular religious perspective and, at the same time, each school needs to transcend their confessional perspectives in order to facilitate an understanding of other religions. A non-confessional, as in the suggestion of Ninian Smart, encourages both types of understanding with an emphasis on a neutralist and assumption-free position. Of course, a neutral and balance approach like that is difficult to be achieved, since it requires a really secular or pluralist social context (Barnes 2000, p. 320).

Indeed, it is impossible to apply the strict non-confessional perspective to all religious schools in the current Korean context. As mentioned above, among all schools, more than 20% are religiously founded and their roles are essential in the structure and order of Korean education. They contribute to the quality of education in Korean society as if they exist also as public schools. Yet, they cannot administer any kind of free RE in a manner that ignores the different students that attend their schools and the different parent groups that exist. In this situation, thus, the religiously founded schools and the policy makers for RE should ask for mutual concessions, so that both sides can think about the form of a proper RE within a religiously diverse school context. If schools would like to teach and to communicate their religious identity for their students, they should be allowed to do so with the proviso that other students could take alternative classes. This type of policy should be extended to the students of public schools who would also want to have a RE class of their own.

In relation to other religious activities as these exist in terms of religious ceremonies and chapel services, schools should obtain the assent of students and parents and ask them if they would be willing to respect of the spirit of a school's foundation before they would begin to attend a given school. However, if schools do not want to compromise on these matters and if they want to adhere to the compulsory nature of their RE and other religious matters, they should not receive any governmental subsidies. In order to fund the salaries of RE teachers with the governmental subsidy, they should not insist of the demands and needs of their confessional perspective. With respect, however, to the existence of independent schools, the Ministry of Education should not interfere with their policies and this includes not interfering with their RE policies. Their full autonomy should be respected.

Funding: "This research received no external funding."

Conflicts of Interest: "The author declares no conflicts of interest."

References

Barnes, L. Philip. 2000. Ninian Smart and the Phenomenological Approach to Religious Education. *Religion* 30: 315–32. [CrossRef]

Cha, Mihi. 2006. 4cha Gyoyukgwajunggi (1982–89) Jungdeung Kooksagwa Gyoyookgwajungŭi Sungkyuk. 4차 교육과정 기(1982~89) 중등 국사과 교육과정의 성격 (Content Direction of National History Education at the Middle and High School in the National Curriculum Period). *Gyogwagyoyookhak Youngu* 교과교육학연구 10: 443–59.

Choi, Hyunjong. 2011. *Hankookchongyo Ingubeodonge Gwahan Yeongu* 한국종교 인구 변동에 관한 연구 (A Study on Religious Population Change in Korea). Bucheon: Seoul Theological University Press.

Constitutional Court of Korea. 1995. *Korean Constitutional Report*; Constitutional Court of Korea.

Cusack, Christine L. 2017. The Empirical Science of Religious Education. *Journal of Contemporary Religion* 32: 530–31. [CrossRef]

Hazra, Orla O'Reilly. 2009. Evoking the Spirit to Practice Religiously: Somatic and Narrative Ways of Knowing for Transformative Learning in a Living Tradition. Ph.D. Thesis, Fordham University, Bronx, NY, USA.

Jackson, Robert. 1997. *Religious Education: An Interpretive Approach*. London: Hodder & Stoughton.

Jordan, Louis Henry. 1986. *Comparative Religion*. Georgia: Atlanta, Scholars Press. First published 1905.

Jung, Jinhong. 1986. "Gonggyoyookgwa Chongyogyoyook" 공교육과 종교교육 (Public Education and Religious Education). *Chongyo Yeongu* 종교연구 2: 21–37.

Jung, Jinhong. 2001. "Je 7cha Gyoyookgwajunggwa Chongyogyook" 제7차 교육과정과 종교교육 (The 7th Curriculum Revision and Teaching Religion). *Chongychogyoyookhakyeongu* 종교교육학연구 13: 3–42.

Kil, Heesung. 2015. "Chongyo Dawonsidaeŭi Sinhak" 종교 다원시대의 신학 (Christian Theology in the Age of Religious Plurality). *Chongyo Yeongu* 종교연구 75: 1–24.

Kim, Yoohwan. 2008. "Cho, jungdenghakgyo Chongyogyoyookŭi Moonjaejumgwa Haegyulbangan" 초, 중등학교 종교교육의 문제점과 해결방향 (Problems and Policy Directions of Religious Education in Elementary and Secondary Schools - The Meaning and Prospect of Mr. Kang Case). *Gongbuphak Yeongu* 공법학연구 9: 305–22.

Kim, Jongseo. 2016. "Chongyogyoyookŭi Jeongaewa Insunggyoyookzuk Haŭi" 종교교육의 전개와 '인성교육'적 함의 (The Development of Religious Education and Its Implications for 'Education of Humanism'.). *Moonhakgwa Chongyo* 문학과 종교 21: 1–15.

Kim, Chae Young. 2017. Religious Studies as a Modern Academic Discipline in Korea. *Religion* 47: 277–92. [CrossRef]

Korea Gallop Research Institute. 2015. *Religions of Koreans 1984–2014*. 한국인의 종교, 1984–2014. Korea Gallop Research Institute.

Korean Ministry of Education. 2001. *Commentary on High School Curriculum—Liberal Arts*; Seoul: Korean Ministry of Education.

Park, Bum-Suk. 2002. "Chongyosung Hamyangui Gyoyookhakjuk Eumi" 종교성 함양의 교육학적 의미 (Educational Significance of Cultivating Religiosity). *Religious Education Research* 14: 57–69.

Ryu, Dongsik. 1985. "Hankookgidokgyo (1885–1985)ui Tachongyoe Daehan Ihae" 한국기독교(1885–1985)의 타종교에 대한 이해 (Understanding of other religions in Korean Christianity (1885–1985)). *Yonseinonchong* 연세논총 21: 321–50.

Ryu, Dongsik. 1987. "Hankookinui Youngsungwa Chongyomunhwa" 한국인의 영성과 종교문화 (Korean Spirituality and Religious Culture). *Dongbanghakji* 동방학지 56: 399–413.

Ryu, Sungmin. 2013. "Gongrimhakgyoaesui Chongyoe Gyoeyook" 공립학교에서의종교교육 (Religious Education in Public Schools). *Research on Religious Culture* 20: 1–34.

Seymour, Jack L. 2005. Religious Education and the Future of Religious Education. *Religious education* 100: 337–39. [CrossRef]

Smart, Ninian. 1968. *Secular Education and the Logic of Religion*. London: Faber and Faber.

Smart, Ninian, and Donald Horder, eds. 1975. *New Movement in Religious Education*. London: Temple Smith.

Smart, Ninian, and Donald Wiebe, eds. 1986. *Concept & Empathy: Essays in the Study of Religion*. London: Macmillan Press.

Tak, Jlil. 2009. "Guwonpa" 구원파 (Salvation Group). *Saegajung*: 88–91.

Tak, Jlil. 2011. "Gyoyookuero Mannanuen Mokhwe: Idanae Daehan Bareun Ihae" 교육으로 만나는 목회: 이단에 대한 바른 이해 (Pastoral Meeting with Education: Understanding Heresy). *Gyoyookgyohwe* 교육교회 400: 52–57.

Yoon, Ihum. 1986. "Dachongyomoonhwasokeseoŭi Chongyogyoyook" 다종교문화속에서의 종교교육 (Religious education in religious pluralism). *Chongyo Yeongu* 종교연구 2: 3–10.

Yoon, Ihum. 1999. "Shamanismgwa Hankookmoonhwasa" 샤머니즘과 한국문화사 (Shamanism and Korean Culture History). *Shamanism Yeongu* 샤머니즘 연구 1: 81–96.

Article

Some Contemporary Dilemmas of Korean Buddhism: A Critical Review of the Jogye Order's 2018 Periodic Report

Kyungrae Kim, Eunyoung Kim, Wangmo Seo and Cheonghwan Park *

Department of Buddhist Studies, Dongguk University 30, Pildong-ro 1gil, Jung-gu, Seoul 04620, Korea; wizkyung@naver.com (K.K.); 820131kimey@daum.net (E.K.); jeongdo@dongguk.edu (W.S.)
* Correspondence: avadana@gmail.com

Received: 12 February 2019; Accepted: 26 March 2019; Published: 28 March 2019

Abstract: According to the Jogye Order's 2018 periodic report, the average age of monks is increasing and the number of monks is decreasing. In order to offer solutions to these problems, the report presents and analyzes by dividing those themes into six sub-topics, namely: decrease of births; decrease of postulants; aging of postulants; rapidly changing educational environment; teaching aptitude of educators; education budget. The report lists a variety of information derived from the raw data and offers suggestions regarding these six topics. However, the report has several failings, as the research misunderstands the data at times, and their report does not present proper interpretations and concrete solutions. The final suggestions that the report proposes to increase the number of monks seem to be misguided and ineffective. This article critically scrutinizes the Jogye Order's latest report to identify and correct some data misinterpretations and offer new insights that the authors believe would help our leaders come up with better solutions.

Keywords: the Jogye Order; decreased number of monks; aging monks; education for monks; educational innovation

---

1. Introduction

Buddhist monks are suffering negative public perceptions in modern Korean society. As the media continues to report the moral corruption and sectarianism of the Jogye Order (조계종), the main Buddhist sect in Korea,[1] the public simply does not regard Buddhist ordination as a decision to be respected.

For example, a few years ago, a video clip of monks in the Jogye Order gambling while drinking and smoking at a hotel was released on the news.[2] More recently, the violence and sex scandals of the Jogye Order monks were reported by a famous television program.[3] Regardless of the veracity of these reports and accusations, the religious authority and public respect of the Jogye Order have been seriously damaged. Another example would be Hyun Gak (현각), a Harvard-educated American who became a famous monk of the Jogye Order and was highly respected by the public in the late 1990s. Through the media in 2016, he announced that he would no longer follow the Jogye Order, even though he would maintain his life as a Buddhist monk. When leaving Korea, he strongly criticized the

---

1 In general, the Jogye Order represents Korean Buddhism. With the liberation of Korea in 1945, a movement to restore genuine Korean Buddhism took place, and consequently the Jogye Order was established in 1962. The title was named after the Jogye mountain in China which was a hot spot of the Chinese Chan tradition. Although there are 146 Buddhist sects in modern Korean society, the Jogye Order is the biggest (Ko 2018, pp. 98–107).
2 https://www.youtube.com/watch?v=THrfsZaXXnQ.
3 https://www.youtube.com/watch?v=4wb6j-qvP1c.

anachronism of Korean Buddhism. His criticism of Korean Buddhism was in fact directed toward the Jogye Order (Kim 2016; Lee 2016, available online).

Indeed, the news above caused quite a stir and the public strongly condemned the outdated perspectives and corruption of the monks of the Jogye Order. Since the Jogye Order has been neither determined nor effective in coping with these scandals, the criticism toward the monks of the Jogye Order still remains strong. Subsequently, the public begins to view the Buddhist ordination more negatively.

To address this negative perception of the Jogye Order by society at large and facilitate comprehensive discussions to improve the Order's educational system in line with the decreasing number of monks, the periodic seminar titled 'A Study for the Improvement of Sangha Education of the Jogye Order' (조계종 승가교육 개선방안; hereafter 'the seminar' or 'the report') was held on 12 July 2018, at the International Conference Hall of the Korean Buddhist History and Culture Museum (한국불교역사문화기념관 국제회의장). This seminar was hosted by the Education Committee (대한불교 조계종 교육원), the division responsible for the education of the Jogye Order monks.

The Jogye Order publishes an annual report <Statistics of the Jogye Order>. However, the statistics have not been released to the public since 2008. The report discussed in this article reveals specific changes in the number of monks. Of course, there have been reports on the decreasing number of monks before. However, the report examined in this article is meaningful and valuable in that it is an official report published directly by the Education Committee of the Jogye Order in charge of teaching monks.

The main theme of the seminar report was about how to encourage more people to be ordained. This theme is discussed by the following six divided sub-topics: (1) decrease of births, (2) decrease of postulants, (3) aging of postulants, (4) rapidly changing educational environment, (5) teaching aptitude of educators, and (6) education budget. The first three topics discuss the membership crisis of the Jogye Order. There has been a considerable reduction in the number of the ordained, and the average age of postulants is increasing. It has subsequently led to a depletion of monks entering the priesthood and providing dharma preaching in the field. The remaining topics focus on discussing the educational crisis of the Jogye Order. This problem originates from the outdated educational system of the Jogye Order. Given that the contemporary educational system of Korean society is changing rapidly, the Jogye Order has failed to catch up with this trend. Finally, the report concludes with several suggestions for the improvement of Buddhist education for monks.

While some of the contents of the report are noteworthy, many other discussions are less persuasive. The report offers various data and figures, but it is unclear how they are closely related to the main topics. In addition, it is difficult to grasp the intended objectives of the report because its description and organization are vague and incoherent.

In this article, we will critically examine the validity of the analysis and the resolution of the latest Jogye Order report. For the facts and points that we identify as problematic as we analyze the report, we will try to offer more accurate interpretations and share solutions that we think would be more viable. Given that the periodic seminars of the Jogye Order have never been open to the public, the reports of the seminars have not been examined critically so far. Therefore, various discussions in this article will offer a unique opportunity to highlight and critically analyze the challenging situation of the Jogye Order particularly in the field of education.

This paper is bound to be very limited because it is not intended to provide solutions. Nevertheless, our critical analysis of the report will reveal the fact that the Jogye Order does not have a clear understanding of the fundamental problems of its educational crisis. We also hope that our critical review will help the community of the Jogye Order revisit the crisis in recruiting postulants so that it can come up with better solutions.

2. Summary of the Report

For our discussion, we will begin by summarizing the Jogye Order's latest report. The report announces that the decreased number of monks is an inevitable consequence of the decrease in the national birth rate. It states that the decreased number of births from the mid to late 1980s, along with the modern trend of ignoring religion, is decreasing the number of monks. In the past decade, the number of Buddhist ordinations has decreased significantly. In 1999, there were a total of 532, with 306 males and 226 females. However, in 2015, that figure was more than halved to 130 males and 74 females. There were 104 males and 53 females in 2016, and 94 males and 57 females in 2017. At this rate, the annual postulant rate will reach zero by 2025. This decreased number of the ordained has led to a decline in enrollment at the Monastic Seminary (강원, *Kangwŏn*), which means that no one will be admitted to the Monastic Seminary in the next few years.

In fact, the problem of the decreased number of monks is not something new (Jackson 2018; Lew 2004; Lew 2016, pp. 361–86; Park 2016, pp. 323–59). This is due to a combination of multiple factors such as the low birth rate, aging, and indifference toward religion. The Jogye Order has prepared several self-rescue measures to recruit more postulants. For example, the Jogye Order founded the "Special Committee for Improving the Ordination System (출가활성화추진 특별위원회)" in 2016 to encourage ordination. The Jogye Order planned to provide educational and health benefits to those who received ordination, and it even planned to provide full tuition fees for bachelor's degrees. Although these measures have only had very limited success, they show how seriously the Jogye Order is considering the problem of the decreased number of monks.

After serious consideration, the report concludes that the basic educational institutions should be reorganized, which is summarized as below:

- Reduce Monastic Seminary (강원, *Kangwŏn*) from fourteen institutions to six: four for male, two for female.
- Let Joong-Ang Sangha University (중앙승가대학교) be the only basic education institution (reduced from four institutions to one).
- Integrate Joong-Ang Sangha University into Dongguk University (동국대학교).
- Convert the Elementary Seon Meditative Institute (선원, *Seonwŏn*) into a two-year educational institution to foster future monk leaders.

However, the panelists who attended the seminar remained negative on the proposed reform of the Jogye Order. To sum up, the objections were as follows: Firstly, the Order's suggestions cannot lead to a fundamental solution. Rather, the goal is to revive the traditional Buddhist education of the Monastic Seminary, which mainly focuses on Buddhist texts such as the *Chimungyeonghun* (치문경훈) and develop the seminaries into basic educational institutions. Dongguk University and Joong-Ang Sangha University should remain as separate institutions offering Buddhist studies. Secondly, a unified educational system is not always the best solution. There is a risk that the traditional Buddhist education will be impoverished by the institutional integration. Thirdly, it is very unreasonable to reduce the amount of education that monks receive. This possibly poses a risk of undermining the very foundation of the Monastic Seminary.

Indeed, at the seminar, most of the participants admitted that the educational system for monks should be modernized in line with contemporary educational trends. However, the majority of participants opposed the reorganization of basic education institutions in the same way that the report suggested. This means that there are conflicting views within the Jogye Order. In other words, there is a consensus of the membership crisis within the Jogye Order. However, there is no unified view of how to solve it.

In the following sections, we will critically review the findings of the report and discuss some problems.

3. Analysis and Critique

3.1. Membership Crisis

According to the report (p. 12), compared to the 1990s, the number of postulants has decreased by a third. In the 1990s, the annual number of newly ordained averaged around 500, but that decreased to 151 in 2017 (See Table 1).

Table 1. Decreasing Number of Postulants.

Year	1993	1999	2003	2008	2013	2017
Postulants	510	532	373	286	236	151

The Jogye Order's report categorizes the reasons why this happened as follows: (1) decrease of births, (2) decrease of postulants and (3) aging of postulants. However, as we shall see, the report's analysis is too superficial.

Firstly, the report (pp. 10–14) claims that this decline is in line with Korean population trends, such as the decreased birth rate and aging population that began in the mid to late 1980s. The report argues that the decreased number of children born has led to the decline and aging of the entire monkhood. In order to support this assumption, the report compares the number of births and postulants for the last 20 years (pp. 10–11).

First of all, the age distribution of postulants mentioned in the report is flawed (See Table 2):

Table 2. Age Distribution of Postulants in the Report.

Year	1996	1998	2000	2002	2003	2010	2013	2014	2015	2016		2017	
Semester	2nd	1st	1st	1st	1st	1st	1st	1st	1st	1st	2nd	1st	2nd
10s	8	3	3	2	2	5	5	5	5	4	5	6	4
20s	50	49	36	26	21	23	20	17	19	21	18	25	17
30s	36	38	46	46	39	31	33	35	25	24	29	24	10
40s	6	10	14	26	38	41	42	43	51	51	48	30	35

The report lists the age distribution of postulants from 1996 to 2017. However, there is no data for 1997, 1999, 2001, 2004–2009 and 2011–2012. In addition, the ordination ceremony, which is held twice a year, is not clearly described in the data. This missing information in the report above fails to reveal exactly what it is trying to propose.

It is true that the problem of a low birth rate and an aging population are problems of the Korean society as a whole. However, this cannot be the decisive reason for the decrease in numbers and the aging of monks. If that were the case, the number of priests in all religions in Korea should have decreased. However, statistics show otherwise.

For example, according to <Statistics of the Catholic Church in Korea 2017 (한국 천주교회 통계 2017)>, the number of priests in parishes over the past decade has alternated between growth and decline (Catholic Bishops' Conference of Korea 2018, pp. 13–15). In 2017, however, it jumped 33.9 percent and this growing trend has continued into 2018 and 2019, producing the largest number of new priests since 2009. This is in stark contrast to the Jogye Order, which has seen a sharp decline in recent years. Therefore, this implies that the first data and its subsequent analysis presented in the report are misguided or, at least, require a more detailed interpretation.

Secondly, the report (p. 12) provides annual figures for the number of postulants from 1993 to 2017 in order to analyze the decreased number of monks. According to these figures, the number of postulants has significantly declined since 1999 (See Table 3).

Table 3. Number of Postulants from 1993 to 2017.

Year	1993	1995	1999	2002	2003	2006	2008	2013	2015	2016	2017
Number	510	448	532	406	373	334	286	236	204	157	151

Although the data set itself is informative, the report fails to address some significant problems, particularly the gender gap. Despite the greater decline of female postulants being found in the data set, the report does not recognize these gender differences. According to statistics, there were approximately half as many female postulants in 2017 (94 male vs. 57 female). However, in 1993, the difference between genders was insignificant (282 male vs. 228 female). As time goes by, the number of female postulants has decreased more rapidly when measured with that of male postulants. However, the Jogye Order has yet to recognize this sharp decline in female postulants (See Table 4).

Table 4. Gender Ratio of Postulants.

Year	1993	1999	2003	2008	2013	2017
Male	282	306	216	168	163	94
Female	228	226	157	118	73	57

Korean Buddhism has the longest history of the nun (*Bhikhuni*) tradition among East Asian Buddhist countries. Since the 6th century CE, the tradition of nuns has continued to modern society.[4]

Nevertheless, there has been an institutional contradiction in the status of nuns and their role restrictions in the Jogye Order. Given that the authority of the Jogye Order is concentrated on just a few male monks, nuns are currently demanding more of a voice within the organization. In actual fact, nuns handle a lot of important day-to-day work; however, they do not receive the recognition they deserve.[5] If the number of postulants and monks continues to decrease and the power of the Jogye Order remains concentrated on only a few male monks, then these criticisms will continue to grow in the future. Consequently, it is more likely that the number of the nuns will continue to decline within the Jogye Order. This is a significant factor directly related to the decrease in the number of monks in Korea.

In order to prevent the decrease of female ordinations, gender discriminative elements should be removed in the Jogye Order's systems and laws. It is also necessary to develop a short- and long-term plan to prevent the decline of nuns and expand their roles. For example, it will be helpful to scrutinize the cases that show the active role of the nuns in the field. A good example would be the activities of the world-renowned Taiwanese *Fo Guang Shan* Monastery (佛光山寺, https://www.fgs.org.tw/en), or closer to home, Korean *Hanmaum Seonwon* (한마음선원, http://www.hanmaum.org/eng) which is leading overseas missionary work.[6] *Fo Guang Shan* Monastery led by nuns has propagated Buddhist teachings in the U.S. and even in Africa. In addition, their social activities play an important role in Taiwanese society, helping to support the poor. *Hanmaum Seonwon* runs temples without gender discrimination, and actively supports social and cultural education projects and overseas activities. These organizations provide useful templates that the Jogye Order could model itself after to help increase its number of monks and improve gender equality.[7]

Furthermore, the report does not exactly address why postulants for monkhood give up during the process of receiving the ordination. The report simply concludes that the main reason for the recruitment crisis is that the Buddhist monkhood is not as attractive a vocation as in the past. It then suggests the

---

4   The oldest record for the existence of the nuns traces back to the Silla Dynasty (Ha 2018, pp. 118–24; Kim 2010, pp. 175–86).
5   For more details on this discussion, see (Cho 2011; Park 2010, pp. 109–30; Park 2011).
6   For general information for Hanmaum Seonwon, see (Park 2017).
7   For a comprehensive discussion on 'Women in Monasticism,' see (Crosby 2014, pp. 218–37).

improvement of the temple educational centers. However, this is a serious misunderstanding of the underlying problems. As is well known, the temple educational centers are institutions for those who have already been ordained, not for monkhood candidates. This misunderstanding conveys that the Jogye Order does not clearly distinguish between monkhood postulants and monks who have already been ordained. It seems that the Jogye Order is not deeply concerned about recruiting postulants.

The declined retention rate implies that there is a fundamental problem with the initial education of monks. We believe that a better understanding of the gender, age, and educational level of the dropouts and some correlations of these factors would help us figure out the cause of the problem. In other words, a careful study of the common reasons for the withdrawal is demanded. If the Jogye Order has a clear understanding of and effectively addresses the main cause of the drop-out, we can hope that the retention rate will get back to the level of the 1990s.[8]

Thirdly, the average age of monks is increasing. According to the report (pp. 21–23), monks are getting older, and the average age of postulants is also increasing as well. In order to solve this problem, the report suggests shortening the basic educational period for monks.

This idea comes from the notion that four years of basic education for monks is too long, especially for middle-aged postulants since they are already highly educated. For this assumption, the report (p. 21) suggests the data showing that educated postulants have increased in recent years. There is, however, no sufficient evidence to prove the assumption that all middle-aged postulants are and will be highly educated. If this were the case, the relevant data should have been presented in the report.

Furthermore, assuming a postulant's education level based on their academic credentials in other fields is misguided, for they are nevertheless laymen in the monkhood. Even if the aged postulants were highly educated in other fields, this does not guarantee that they are ready to become sincere monks. In sum, it is a fact that secular education does not guarantee that a postulant is of good character for monkhood.

3.2. Educational Innovation: The Solution for the Membership Crisis

After discussing the membership crisis, the report points to the Jogye Order's educational system as the reason for the decreasing number of monks. The report (pp. 24–33) discusses this with three sub-topics as follows: (1) rapidly changing educational environment, (2) teaching aptitude of educators and (3) education budget.

Firstly, given that the educational environment is changing rapidly, the report proposes that the current Buddhist educational curriculum should be changed to reflect contemporary educational trends. The report (p. 24) summarizes the trends in four keywords, namely, Massive (no restriction on the number of students), Open (open to all), Online (based on the Internet), and Course (based on a curriculum).

These concerns and discussions in the report about educational environments are very relevant. Educational innovation corresponding to a fast-changing contemporary society is an important issue and not just limited to Buddhism. The problem is, however, the report's (or the Jogye Order's) ambiguous attitude toward contemporary trends. Given that the report discusses this topic with four pages (pp. 24–27), it takes three and half pages to discuss the characteristics of general public education that are unrelated to Buddhist education for monks. Consequently, it is then ambiguous what the report is trying to discuss. (Actually, this is also true for the discussions of the following topics.)

There are four basic education institutions in the Jogye Order, namely, Joong-Ang Sangha University (중앙승가대학교), Monastic Seminary (강원, *Kangwŏn*), Elementary Seon Meditative Institute (선원, *Seonwŏn*) and Dongguk University (동국대학교). These educational institutions aim to teach

---

[8]   For improvement suggestions on this topic, see (Han 2012).

the character and skills of monkhood.[9] These institutions are, however, mixed with temple-oriented education such as the Monastic Seminary and the Elementary Seon Meditative Institute, and public academic education such as provided by Joon-Ang Sangha University and Dongguk University. Many monks and Buddhist scholars have made various suggestions such as merging, separating, reorganizing and unifying the monastic and academic institutions.[10] The Jogye Order, however, has not taken these suggestions seriously, rather it has just repeatedly mentioned that the number of monks is decreasing and that the educational system needs to be changed. The 2018 report is representative of their approach.

Secondly, the report emphasizes that educators should improve their teaching methods in line with contemporary educational trends. Subsequently, the report highlights the duties of the educators, such as "education," "research," "service," "administration," and a method of teaching to satisfy the needs of students.

These duties for educators listed in the report, however, correspond to general university students who are not involved in the education of monks. The report mentions three references here, namely, 'An Effective Teaching in University,' an article written by Seungil Na who is a professor of Seoul National University, the Basic Education Act of the Constitution and 'The Prospects and Tasks of Educational Reforms' published by the Korean Educational Development Institute. Having taken us through these quoted references, the report then draws the following extraordinary conclusion: "The professors at Monastic Seminary have improved their professionalism a lot, but their expertise is still insufficient. They should make efforts to improve their ability (p. 31)."

The discussions found in the report are not easily understandable. The discussions about educators for the monkhood would be vague without an agreement on what and how to teach. If the Jogye Order wants to improve the current educational system for monks, first of all, the direction and goals of their improvement should be clearly set. It should be based on researching previous educational studies.[11] Once the direction of these improvements has been established, the ability and responsibilities of educators should be specifically required to align with this direction. Nevertheless, the report overlooks the peculiarity of monastic education, and unhelpfully lists the duties of an educator without a definite plan.[12]

Thirdly, the report (pp. 32–33) mentions financial support for educational improvement. Although the report does not disclose it, it is necessary to first look at the entire budget of the Jogye Order and the budget allocated to the Education Committee.

According to the Buddhist Broadcasting System (BBS),[13] the Central Committee of the Jogye Order, which was held on the 13 November, 2018, announced its budget for 2019. The budgets over the past four years were as follows: 47.9 billion won in 2015, 53.3 billion won in 2016, 70 billion won in 2017, and 82.7 billion won in 2018, and the budget for 2019 is about 100.45 billion won, which has increased by 17.7 billion won compared to that of 2018. From that total, 18.5 billion won will be spent for regional missionary work and to buy religious land. The project to rebuild the Jogye Temple, the main temple of the Jogye Order, will be set aside 11.6 billion won. The Education Committee has been allocated 3.9 billion won (excluded Sangha Education Fund).

The report (p. 33) informs that it is impossible to continue providing more budget support to basic educational institutions since the Jogye Order spends money on a variety of fields. Nevertheless, as seen above, the educational budget is only less than 4% of the total budget in 2019. Inevitably,

---

9. For more details on Buddhist basic education and monastic education, see (Pŏpsŏng 1995; Sŏngbon 2008; Sŏran 1995; Educational Institute of Jogye Order 2009a, 2009b, 2009c; Hyŏnŭng 1994, pp. 110–29).
10. (Chihwan 1992, pp. 277–307; Chongbŏm 1997; Changik 2010, pp. 109–28; Kwŏn 2005; Ko 2011, pp. 201–35; Youm (Ven. Ja-Hyun) 2018, pp. 111–45).
11. (Cho 2002, pp. 264–85; Chŏng 1999; Hyŏnung 1995; Kaksa 2003; Kaplan 2015; Kim 2013, pp. 313–40; Kim 2010, pp. 189–214; Kim 2016, pp. 168–78; Lee 2012, pp. 65–84; Mugwan 1995; Mun 2012).
12. Kim (2017, pp. 77–98) is useful to understand the training system for the Buddhist educator.
13. http://news.bbsi.co.kr/news/articleView.html?idxno=908497.

this will make all educational sectors demand more financial support. It implies that there might be a problem with financial support for the monk's educational innovation.

The report (p. 32) introduces the data regarding the budget of the Jogye Order as below (See Tables 5 and 6):

Table 5. Total Budget of Education Committee 2011~2017 (included Sangha Education Fund).

Year	2011	2012	2013	2014	2015	2016	2017
Thousand Won	5,079,731	6,295,424	6,404,017	6,778,756	6,663,818	6,607,344	6,427,409
(USD)[14]	(4,511,306)	(5,590,962)	(5,687,404)	(6,020,209)	(5,918,133)	(5,867,978)	(5,708,178)

Table 6. Education Committee's Financial Support for Basic Education.

Year	1995	1997	2001	2003	2004	2006	2010	2015	2010	2017
Thousand Won	1,245,205	1,634,481	2,298,709	2,369,000	2,825,800	3,015,626	3,603,325	3,433,981	3,436,780	3,491,620
(USD)	(1,105,865)	(1,451,581)	(2,041,482)	(2,103,907)	(2,509,591)	(2,678,175)	(3,200,111)	(3,049,716)	(3,052,202)	(3,100,905)

Given that there are fourteen Monastic Seminaries, the financial support that the Educational Committee provides to the Monastic Seminaries are as follows (See Table 7):

Table 7. Financial Support for the Monastic Seminary.

Year	2012	2013	2014	2015	2016	2017
Thousand Won	434,586	525,100	616,287	620,300	556,800	607,020
(USD)	(385,955)	(466,341)	(547,324)	(550,888)	(494,493)	(539,094)

As seen above, despite the considerable discussions of educational innovation by the Jogye Order, the actual budget allocation for the Monastic Seminary is less than 1 percent of the total budget of the Jogye Order in 2017. Furthermore, the Education Committee wants to integrate them into a more general academic institution. What the Education Committee wants is for the Monastic Seminary to provide a graduate level education. By contrast, the Monastic Seminaries want to maintain their traditional educational system. They disagree with either unifying the fourteen seminaries or reforming them into modern academic institutions. In order to reform the monk's education, the different views of the Education Committee and the Monastic Seminary must be reconciled first. The report, however, avoids direct comment on these issues.

Of course, the increased financial support will be of great help to reform the monk's educational system. However, if the report had really considered such financial support, there should have been specific plans, such as using at least part of the Jogye Order's budget for a monk's education. Furthermore, there should also be discussions about how the budget allocation of the Education Committee, namely, 3.9 billion will be used and specifically in what areas additional funding is needed in 2019. Long-term financial investments should be continued only after a proper educational environment has been established.

4. Conclusions

This article has critically examined the Jogye Order's latest report regarding the decreased number of monks, and their idea that educational innovation is the solution. The report itself contains much good raw data. As seen above, however, there are various problems in the explication of that data, which can be summarized as below.

---

[14] Exchange rate in 8 February 2019.

Firstly, the report says that the number of postulants has decreased due to the decrease in the general population. However, given that the number of Catholic priests is on the rise, this claim needs to be reviewed. Without more persuasive analysis of the data, an effective solution will prove to be elusive. Secondly, the report is indifferent to gender discrimination in the course of analyzing the number of monks. In the Jogye Order, nuns are not given satisfactory positions compared to their abilities. To increase the number of postulants, the welfare of nuns should be improved. Thirdly, the report does not make a clear distinction between applicants and those who are already ordained. The solutions to the decrease in the number of monks have been more focused on the monks rather than on the postulants. An effective system for postulants should be established. These new members of the monkhood will lead the Jogye Order in the near future. During their apprenticeship, a postulant should be given religious motivation through professional counseling and education. Fourthly, the report argues that the period of basic education should be shortened as a solution to the decreasing number of monks. However, the aging of monks and monk's education are irrelevant; furthermore, there is a fundamental difference between general education and Buddhist education. The report argues for an educational revolution but, in actual fact, it is just focused on increasing numbers. Fifthly, the report argues for educational innovation in response to contemporary social trends. However, the report does not accurately recognize the mix of Buddhist monastic and general academic education. As a result, the solution presented to make educational improvement is not effective either. Sixthly, the report emphasizes the ability and duty of educators to teach monks. But it only lists the duties of the general educator, without establishing a clear plan for educational innovation. Lastly, the report emphasizes financial support for educational innovation. However, there is no explanation as to exactly what the financial support is needed for. Their request for financial support without a particular purpose for it is nothing more than a vague fiscal theory.

To make things worse, these reflections and analyses are without critical review. Despite many previous in-depth discussions, the Jogye Order has failed to examine and react upon them. In a way, the problems above may have been caused by a lack of continuous debate. Since the previously proposed opinions have not been reviewed, it is difficult to come up with new perspectives or ideas. Rather, only the same inappropriate interpretations and ineffective solutions are repeated.

In fact, the decreasing number of monks is a phenomenon occurring in all contemporary Buddhist countries. However, the Jogye Order in Korea has quite a different reason for it. Different from other Buddhist countries, as briefly mentioned in the introduction, it is the moral laxity of the Jogye Order, which has been exposed through the media by a series of scandalous behaviors of the monks. Therefore, one of the essential causes for the decreasing number of postulants and monks is possibly due to the bad image of Korean monks.

Nevertheless, the report never comments on the scandals within the Jogye Order while discussing their membership crisis. It seems that the report is trying to find the reason for the decreased number of monks elsewhere, while intentionally ignoring the most fundamental issues. Consequently, the analysis and solutions of the report are only a limited and theoretical discussion.

Although the Jogye Order has been and is the epitome of Korean Buddhism, it has caused numerous problems. Nevertheless, as seen above, the Jogye Order is not fully aware of its problems and is consistent with a formal and complacent attitude. It is a serious problem that even the chief leader and main officials in charge of the Jogye Order hold this view. The monks, who are currently in office, should reflect on themselves and try to build an ethical and sacred Buddhist community. More important than improving various systems is the religious maturity of the monks who make up the Jogye Order. In order for the Jogye Order to become a true representative of Korean Buddhism, it needs to continue to reflect on itself and embrace external criticism. If this does not occur, the status of the Jogye Order will become very uncertain in Korean society.

Author Contributions: Writing—Original draft preparation, K.K.; writing—Review and editing, E.K. and W.S.; supervision, C.P.

Funding: This research received no external funding.

Conflicts of Interest: The authors declare no conflict of interest.

References

Catholic Bishops' Conference of Korea. 2018. *Statistics of the Catholic Church in Korea 2017*. Seoul: CCK.

Changik. 2010. The Issue of Contemporary Buddhist Apprentice Education. *Chonggyo kyoyukhak yŏn'gu* 32: 109–28. (In Korean).

Chihwan. 1992. Postulant Education Programs for Nurturing Desirable Practitioners. *Sŏnu toryang* 2: 277–307. (In Korean).

Cho, Pyŏng-hwal. 2002. The past and present of sangha education in the world. In *Sŭngga kyoyuk*. Edited by Educational Institute of Jogye Order. Seoul: Jogye Order of Korean Buddhism, pp. 264–85. (In Korean)

Cho, Eunsu. 2011. Female Buddhist practice in Korea: A Historical Account. In *Korean Buddhist Nuns and Laywomen: Hidden Histories, Enduring Vitality*. Edited by Eun-su Cho. Albany: State University of New York Press.

Chŏng, Yŏng-hoe. 1999. *Research of Religious Educational Movements in the Age of Civilization*. Seoul: Hyean Press. (In Korean)

Chongbŏm. 1997. The Educational System and Reform Objectives of Monastic Seminaries. In *A Comprehensive Survey of Monastic Seminaries*. Edited by Educational Institute of Jogye Order. Seoul: Jogye Order of Korean Buddhism. (In Korean)

Crosby, Kate. 2014. *Theravada Buddhism Continuity, Diversity, and Identity*. Chickester: Wiley Blackwell.

Educational Institute of Jogye Order, ed. 2009a. *The History and Culture of Jogye Order of Korean Buddhism's Chan Communities*. Seoul: Jogye Order of Korean Buddhism. (In Korean)

Educational Institute of Jogye Order, ed. 2009b. *The History and Culture of Nun Seminaries*. Seoul: Jogye Order of Korean Buddhism. (In Korean)

Educational Institute of Jogye Order, ed. 2009c. *The Histories and Cultures of Sangha Universities*. Seoul: Jogye Order of Korean Buddhism. (In Korean)

Ha, Choon-Sang. 2018. *Korean Bhikkhunī*. Seoul: International Cultural Foundation.

Han, Tae-Sik (Ven. Bo-kwang). 2012. Current State of Entering the Buddhist Priesthood in Korean Buddhist Jogye Order and Improvement Suggestion for Entering the Buddhist Priesthood System. *Maha Bodhi Thought* 17: 209–43. (In Korean).

Hyŏnŭng. 1994. The Order's Laws and Constitution and Sangha Education. *Sŏnu toryang* 6: 110–29. (In Korean).

Hyŏnung. 1995. The Present Problems of Jogye Order of Korean Buddhism's Sangha Education. In *Sŭngga kyoyuk 1*. Edited by Educational Institute of Jogye Order. Seoul: Jogye Order of Korean Buddhism. (In Korean)

Jackson, Ben. 2018. Karma Back! Buddhist Ad Campaign Tries to Reverse Falling Numbers. *Korea Exposé*. Available online: https://www.koreaexpose.com/buddhist-south-korea-declining-jogye/ (accessed on 30 June 2018). (In Korean).

Kaksa, ed. 2003. *Sangha Education and Korean Buddhism*. Taegu: Chŏn'guk kangwŏn yŏnhap pulgyo haksul taehoe chunbi wiwŏnhoe. (In Korean)

Kaplan, Uri. 2015. Transforming Orthodoxies: Buddhist Curriculums and Educational Institutions in Contemporary South Korea. Ph.D. dissertation, Religion Duke University, Durham, NC, USA.

Kim, Chŏng-ja. 2010. Research Regarding the Educational System and Practice of Unmunsa's Monastic Students. *Tongbuka munhwa yŏn'gu* 24: 189–214. (In Korean).

Kim, Youngmi. 2010. The Beginning and Development of the Korean Bhikkhuni Sangha: The position in the Period of the Three Kingdoms and Koryo. In *The History and Current Status of the Korean Bhikkhuni*. Kimpo: Korean Bhikkhuni Institute. (In Korean)

Kim, Chi-hyŏn. 2013. Research Regarding the Standard Curriculum of Jogye Order of Korean Buddhism's Basic Education Institutions. *Han'guk Pulgyohak* 65: 313–40. (In Korean).

Kim, Eunyoung. 2016. A Study on the Religious Education in Buddhist Secondary Schools: Focusing on the Influence of the National Curriculum on the Buddhist Religious Education. Ph.D. dissertation, Dongguk University, Seoul, Korea. (In Korean).

Kim, Hyung-eun. 2016. Foreign Monk Denounces Jogye Order. *Korea Joogang Daily*. Available online: http://koreajoongangdaily.joins.com/news/article/article.aspx?aid=3021984 (accessed on 1 August 2016).

Kim, Eunyoung. 2017. A Study on the Teacher Training System of "Subject of Religion" and Its Transition: Focused on Secondary Schools Established by Buddhism. *Korean Journal of Religious Education* 55: 77–98. (In Korean).

Ko, Pyŏng-ch'ŏl. 2011. The Special characteristics and prospects of the Korean Buddhist Jogye Order's Education. *Chonggyo yŏn'gu* 62: 201–35. (In Korean).

Ko, Pyŏng-ch'ŏl. 2018. *The Present Situation of Religions in Korea*. Sejong: Ministry of Culture, Sports and Tourism. (In Korean)

Kwŏn, O-min. 2005. Doctrinal and Religious Learning: Re-thinking the Buddhist Seminary Curriculum. Paper presented at the 42nd Korean National Buddhist Scholarship Conference, Jogye Temple, Seoul, Korea, April 29. (In Korean).

Lee, Jong-su. 2012. Monastic Education and Educational Ideology in Late Choson Buddhism. *Journal of Korean Religions* 3: 65–84. [CrossRef]

Lee, Jae-hoon. 2016. American Monk to Leave South Korea, Saying Foreigners Just "Decoration". *Hankyore*. Available online: http://english.hani.co.kr/arti/english_edition/e_entertainment/755201.html (accessed on 4 August 2016).

Lew, Seung-mu. 2004. What Will Be Done about the Reduction of Sangha? *Buddhist Review*. Available online: http://www.budreview.com/news/articleView.html?idxno=338 (accessed on 4 August 2016). (In Korean).

Lew, Seung-mu. 2016. The Reduction of Newcomers of Korean Sangha and the Reform of Status and Role of Its Own Members. *Journal of Dharma Dissemination Studies* 10: 361–86. (In Korean).

Mugwan. 1995. The Development and the Objectives of the Education System at Regional Sangha Universities. In *Sŭngga kyoyuk 1*. Edited by Educational Institute of Jogye Order. Seoul: Jogye Order of Korean Buddhism. (In Korean)

Mun, Sun hoe (Ven. Toehyu). 2012. A Historical Study on Monastic Education in Modern Korean Buddhism. Ph.D. dissertation, Joong-Ang Sangha University, Gimpo-si, Korea. (In Korean).

Park, Jin Y., ed. 2010. *Makers of Modern Korean Buddhism*. Albany: University of New York Press.

Park, Pori. 2011. The Establishment of Buddhist Nunneries in Contemporary Korea. In *Korean Buddhist Nuns and Laywomen: Hidden Histories, Enduring Vitality*. Edited by Eun-su Cho. Albany: University of New York Press.

Park, Su-ho. 2016. Internal and External Causes for Reducing Buddhist Renunciate and Countermeasures. *Journal of Dharma Dissemination Studies* 10: 323–59. (In Korean).

Park, Pori. 2017. Uplifting Spiritual Cultivation for Lay People: Bhiksunī Master Daehaeng (1927–2012) of the Hanmaum Seonwon (One Mind Son Center) in South Korea. *Contemporary Buddhism* 18: 419–36. [CrossRef]

Pŏpsŏng. 1995. About the Systematization of Basic Sangha Education. In *Sŭngga kyoyuk 1*. Edited by Educational Institute of Jogye Order. Seoul: Jogye Order of Korean Buddhism. (In Korean)

Sŏngbon. 2008. Selection of Unified Curriculums for Basic Education Facilities and the Problems with Sangha Education. In *Sŭngga kyoyuk 7*. Edited by Educational Institute of Jogye Order. Seoul: Jogye Order of Korean Buddhism. (In Korean)

Sŏran. 1995. Research on the Development of Korean Buddhist Sangha Education. In *Sŭngga kyoyuk 1*. Edited by Educational Institute of Jogye Order. Seoul: Jogye Order of Korean Buddhism. (In Korean)

Youm (Ven. Ja-Hyun), Jung-Seop. 2018. Problems of Korean Buddhism in the Fourth Industrial Age and Future Alternatives. *Seon Studies* 50: 111–45. (In Korean).

MDPI

St. Alban-Anlage 66

4052 Basel

Switzerland

Tel. +41 61 683 77 34

Fax +41 61 302 89 18

www.mdpi.com

Religions Editorial Office

E-mail: religions@mdpi.com

www.mdpi.com/journal/religions

www.ingramcontent.com/pod-product-compliance
Lightning Source LLC
Chambersburg PA
CBHW041139120626
46547CB00020B/3042